Newman in the Story of Philosophy

Newman in the Story of Philosophy

The Philosophical Legacy of Saint John Henry Newman

D. J. Pratt Morris-Chapman

◆PICKWICK *Publications* • Eugene, Oregon

NEWMAN IN THE STORY OF PHILOSOPHY
The Philosophical Legacy of Saint John Henry Newman

Copyright © 2021 D. J. Pratt Morris-Chapman. All rights reserved. Except for brief quotations in critical publications or reviews, no part of this book may be reproduced in any manner without prior written permission from the publisher. Write: Permissions, Wipf and Stock Publishers, 199 W. 8th Ave., Suite 3, Eugene, OR 97401.

Pickwick Publications
An Imprint of Wipf and Stock Publishers
199 W. 8th Ave., Suite 3
Eugene, OR 97401

www.wipfandstock.com

PAPERBACK ISBN: 978-1-7252-8316-9
HARDCOVER ISBN: 978-1-7252-8317-6
EBOOK ISBN: 978-1-7252-8318-3

Cataloguing-in-Publication data:

Names: Pratt Morris-Chapman, D., author.

Title: Newman in the story of philosophy : the philosophical legacy of Saint John Henry Newman / D. J. Pratt Morris-Chapman.

Description: Eugene, OR: Pickwick Publications, 2021 | Includes bibliographical references.

Identifiers: ISBN 978-1-7252-8316-9 (paperback) | ISBN 978-1-7252-8317-6 (hardcover) | ISBN 978-1-7252-8318-3 (ebook)

Subjects: LCSH: Newman, John Henry, 1801–1890 | Catholic Church and philosophy | Christianity—Philosophy | Theology, Doctrinal—History—19th century | Philosophical theology | Knowledge, Theory of (Religion) | Faith and reason—Christianity

Classification: BX4705.N5 P738 2021 (print) | BX4705.N5 (ebook)

I am grateful for permission to reuse the following material here: parts of chapter 2 have appeared in "The Philosophical Legacy of John Henry Newman: A Neglected Chapter in Newman Research" in *New Blackfriars* 98.1078 (2017) 722–50; and as "'H Newman' and Ludwig Wittgenstein: Re-evaluating the History of John Henry Newman's Philosophical Reception" in *New Blackfriars* 101.1096 (2020) 716–25. Part of chapter 5 appeared in "Newman and the 'Problem of the Criterion' Revisited" in *Newman Studies Journal* 13.1 (2016) 55–67. Part of chapter 6 appeared in "Canon Criterion and Circularity: An Analysis of the Epistemology of Canonical Theism" in *HTS Theological Studies* 74.1 (2018) 1–9.

This work is dedicated to my doctoral supervisor
Dr Mervyn Davies (1940–2014) and to my mentor
and father in the faith
Revd A William Wathes (1926–2014).

Table of Contents

Acknowledgments ix
Abbreviations x

1. Introduction: Newman and the Story of Philosophy 1
2. The Underestimation of Newman's Philosophical Reception 14
3. Newman Considered in Relationship
   to Epistemological Particularism 59
4. Antecedents of Particularism in Newman's Work 101
5. The Grammar of Assent and the Development
   of Epistemological Particularism 144
6. The Justification of Religious Belief in Abraham and Newman 190
7. Conclusion: Reconsidering Newman's Philosophical Legacy 241

Bibliography 245

Acknowledgments

I WISH TO ACKNOWLEDGE the following: Paul Shepherd, "the human means of divine faith in me" and to whom "I almost owe my soul." He taught me to follow "truth wherever it led."

Tim Woodford, who taught me to pursue "Holiness rather than peace." Revd Peter Grimwood who "planted deep in my mind that fundamental truth of religion." Prof Carolyn Muessig, for being a "gentle and encouraging instructor" and for helping me to find my voice. Prof Oliver Crisp, who "emphatically, opened my mind, and taught me to think and to use my reason." Prof William Abraham and Ian White, who "opened upon me a large field of thought." Revd Sandy Williams, who "led me to have freer views." Bishop Jonathan Pye, who showed me that "material phenomena are both the types and the instruments of real things unseen." Revd Norman Wallwork, whose "opinions arrested and influenced me." Baba and Mama C. K. Chiza, Richard M Smith, Dr N. and K. Rooms, Vernon Bayliss, Steve Berrill, Revd Alan Burgess, Revd Harry Jones, Revd David Haywood, Sister Barbara Crocket, Prof D. Pailin, Dr W. Allen, Dr H. Mellor, Dr M. Atkins, Dr P. Phillips, Dr G. Watt, Revd Tim Bradshaw, Revd John Simms, Dr C. and C. Stebler, Dr Aboseh, Dr Ensor, Dr J. Muyo, Dr R. Epiengome, Dr L. Epiemembong, Dr D. Mbengu, Dr Mike Brealey, Revd Roly Sims, Revd Jeff Hall, Catherine Feeney, Brenda Stephenson, Bernhard Gruber, Muriel Pilkington, John Beale, Allen Wakefield, Kathleen Maltas, Revd Lisa Quarmby, President M. Mannochio, Dr T. Macquiban, Archbishop I. Ernest, Fr Warren, Fr T. Currer, Fr G Whelan, Fr R. McCulloch, Dr P. McCenhill and, Revd M. Laferty. Special thanks to Ryan and Sylvia Kelley, the Good Revd Peter, Dr Linda, and, Sue Bates. The Most Revd Titus and Anna Pratt. Anna, Ed, Sofia and, Dominic Hill. Last but not least, I thank my family: Ray, Norma, Grace, Kwame, John, Anna, and, Ewuradwowa Morris-Chapman.

Abbreviations

Apo	John H. Newman, *Apologia Pro Vita Sua Being a History of His Religious Opinions.* London: Longmans, Green, 1908.
Ari	John H. Newman, *The Arians of the Fourth Century.* London: Longmans, Green, 1908.
AW	John H. Newman, *Autobiographical Writings.* London: Sheed and Ward, 1956.
DA	John H. Newman, *Discussions and Arguments on Various Subjects.* London: Longmans, Green, 1907.
Dev	John H. Newman, *An Essay on the Development of Christian Doctrine.* London: Longmans, Green, 1909.
Diff 1–2	John H. Newman, *Certain Difficulties Felt by Anglicans in Catholic Teaching.* 2 vols. London: Longmans, Green, 1900–1901.
EM	*Encyclopaedia Metropolitana.* 30 vols. Edited by E. Smedley et al. London: Rivington, 1817–45.
Ess 1–2	John H. Newman, *Essays Critical and Historical.* 2 vols. London: Longmans, Green, 1907.
GA	John H. Newman, *An Essay in aid of a Grammar of Assent.* London: Longmans, Green, 1903.
HS 1–3	John H. Newman, *Historical Sketches.* 3 vols. London: Longmans, Green, 1906–9.
Idea	John H. Newman, *The Idea of a University Defined and Illustrated.* London: Longmans, Green, 1907.

LD 1–32	*Letters and Diaries of John Henry Newman.* 32 vols. Edited by C. S. Dessain et al. Oxford: Clarendon, 1961–2010.
Mir	John H. Newman, *Two Essays on Biblical and Ecclesiastical Miracles.* London: Longmans, Green, 1907.
Mix	John H. Newman, *Discourses Addressed to Mixed Congregations.* London: Longmans, Green, 1906.
OCP	*The Oxford Companion to Philosophy.* Edited by T. Honderich. Oxford: Oxford University Press, 1995.
OS	John H. Newman, *Sermons Preached on Various Occasions.* London: Longmans, Green, 1908.
PN 1–2	Edward Sillem, ed. *Philosophical Notebook of John Henry Newman.* 2 vols. New York: Humanities, 1969–70.
Prepos	John H. Newman, *Lectures on the Present Position of Catholics in England.* London: Longmans, Green, 1908.
PS 1–8	John H. Newman, *Parochial and Plain Sermons.* 8 vols. London: Longmans, Green, 1907–9.
TP 1	Derek Holmes, ed. *The Theological Papers of John Henry Newman on Faith and Certainty.* Oxford: Clarendon, 1976.
TP 2	Derek Holmes, ed. *The Theological Papers of John Henry Newman on Biblical Inspiration and on Infallibility.* Oxford: Clarendon, 1979.
US	John H. Newman, *Fifteen Sermons Preached before the University of Oxford.* London: Longmans, Green, 1909.
VM 1–2	John H. Newman, *The Via Media of the Anglican Church.* 2 vols. London: Longmans, Green, 1901.

1

Introduction

AS A SIGNIFICANT CHRISTIAN thinker, John Henry Newman (1801–90) has never lacked commentators. However, while he has now become a saint,[1] Newman scholars lament that his "canonization" as a philosopher remains far off. For example, in *Newman's Approach to Knowledge* (2007) Richardson argues that his "recognition as a philosopher is long overdue."[2] In an article on "Newman and Wittgenstein" (1997) Cyril Barrett, a Roman Catholic philosopher, contends that until comparatively recently it has been deemed eccentric to regard Newman as a philosopher.[3] In *Newman and Gadamer* (1996) the Oxford-trained philosopher of religion Thomas Carr argues that Newman is "rarely acknowledged as a genuine philosopher."[4] In *The Achievement of Newman* (1991) Ian Ker argues that he "has been too long ignored by philosophers."[5] Two other philosophers who worked in Oxford, Antony Kenny and Basil Mitchell, contend that Newman's contribution has been overlooked by philosophers for over a hundred years (1990).[6] Thus, although commentators frequently make parallels between Newman and professional philosophers, the general

---

1. Saint John Henry was canonized on October 13, 2019.
2. Richardson, *Newman's Approach to Knowledge*, xxi.
3. Barrett, "Newman and Wittgenstein on the Rationality of Belief," 89–99.
4. Carr, *Newman and Gadamer*, 12.
5. Ker, *The Achievement of Newman*, 72.
6. Mitchell, "Newman as a Philosopher," 241.

view within the Newman literature is that his writings have only recently become of interest to professional philosophers.[7]

A paradigmatic example of this view is Fergus Kerr's article, "In an Isolated and, Philosophically, Uninfluential Way" (2000), which centres unduly upon his relation with Oxford philosophy.[8] Kerr states that Newman, "the greatest thinker Oxford produced in the nineteenth century," has been "ignored" by philosophers.[9] He complains that "there would be no need to study Newman for the philosophy of religion paper" in Oxford[10] and questions what it is about Newman that disqualifies him from "being respected as an interesting philosopher by Oxford-trained philosophers."[11] Kerr's analysis does draw attention to the fact that there is no entry devoted to Newman in *The Oxford Companion to Philosophy* (1995), *The Blackwell Companion to Philosophy* (1996), or *A Companion to the Philosophy of Religion* (1997).[12] While his omission is curious, Newman's absence from these particular philosophical manuals does not in itself justify the contention that he has been ignored by philosophers; in Oxford or elsewhere.[13] While Newman may not have featured prominently in the discipline of philosophy an omission from some philosophical textbooks does not equate to an elimination from the philosophical canon.

Were Kerr's thesis correct, that Newman has been an isolated figure in Oxford, then it is conceivable that other commentators based in Oxford, such as Carr, Mitchell, and Kenny, might also believe that Newman has been ignored by professional philosophers generally. Nevertheless, if these particular commentators examine Newman's work from a philosophical perspective, appropriating his ideas for constructive philosophical purposes, then Newman has not been ignored by philosophers in Oxford. This is especially true for the case of Mitchell who was Professor

---

7. Kerr, "Newman and Oxford Philosophy," 155–79.
8. Kerr, "Newman and Oxford Philosophy," 179.
9. Kerr, "Newman and Oxford Philosophy," 158.
10. Kerr, "Newman and Oxford Philosophy," 160.
11. Kerr, "Newman and Oxford Philosophy," 163.

12. Quinn and Taliaferro, *Philosophy of Religion*; Bunnin and Tsui-James, *Blackwell Companion to Philosophy*; Honderich, *Oxford Companion to Philosophy*. Since Kerr's protest Newman has received a small entry in the *Concise Routledge Encyclopaedia of Philosophy*. Ker, "John Henry Newman," 627.

13. Newman does not have an entry in the following: Shand, *Central Works of Philosophy*; Scruton, *Short History of Modern Philosophy*.

of Philosophy of the Christian Religion at Oxford and is influenced considerably by Newman's account of the rationality of religious belief.[14] Kenny, also based in Oxford, devotes a chapter to Newman in his *History of Philosophy* (2007).[15] In view of the above, it is strange that these philosophers do not feel Newman has been given sufficient philosophical recognition.

This book will not argue that Newman has played a major role in the history of philosophy. When compared with figures like John Locke (1632–1704) or Ludwig Wittgenstein (1889–1951) it is clear that Newman was not a towering figure in the philosophical landscape. However, while he does not have a prominent place in the canon, Newman commentators overstate their case when they say he has been ignored. While Newman's philosophical legacy may not be equal to figures like David Hume (1711–76), an expansive list of references indicates that Newman has been cited in relation to a number of important discussions within the discipline of philosophy. Over the last two centuries there have been many American, European, and even Oxford philosophers who have taken considerable interest in Newman. This indicates that, while he is not present in every philosophical textbook, Newman does have a place in the story of philosophy. Despite this, Kenny contends that "the only philosopher until recently to place Newman in the top rank" was Henry Price (1889–1984).[16] Unfortunately, this gloomy assessment of Newman's philosophical reception has been a dominant theme within Newman scholarship.[17] Price's tenure at Oxford (1935–59), as Chair of Logic, during the 1930s, offers a case in point. During this time, the American Roman Catholic philosopher and Newman commentator James Francis Cronin expressed deep concern in his *Theory of Knowledge* (1935) at the

---

14. Mitchell, *The Justification of Religious Belief*, 51.

15. Kenny, *New History of Western Philosophy*, 100.

16. In his Gifford lectures (1969) Price discusses Newman's rejection of the evidentialist ethic of belief and states that the positive doctrine that Newman's chapter on unconditional assent supports raises issues that are of considerable significance for understanding the nature of belief and the role it plays in everyday life. Nevertheless, he also laments that Newman has been left out of the literature discussing the empiricist tradition. Price, *Belief*, 133.

17. Kenny, "Newman as a Philosopher of Religion," 100. An exception to this trend is the work of Frederick Aquino, who has demonstrated that "the Grammar of Assent has been read and connected with contemporary problems and issues in philosophy (principally within the analytic tradition)." For further discussion see Aquino and King, *Receptions*, 54–55.

lack of recognition given to Newman by philosophers; Cronin feared Newman's writings had fallen into "oblivion."[18] The very fact that during this period Price occupied a prestigious philosophical position suggests that these negative assessments of Newman's philosophical legacy are exaggerated. For instance, in that decade Newman's contribution to philosophy was examined in detail by Martin D'Arcy's (1888–1978) *The Nature of Belief* (1931),[19] Jean Guitton's *La Philosophie de Newman* (1933),[20] and fifteen pages were devoted to Newman's philosophy in Rudolf Metz's *A Hundred Years of British Philosophy* (1935).[21] While he may not have featured prominently, proper attendance to the philosophical reception of John Henry Newman illustrates that during his lifetime, right up until the present, his writings have been discussed by philosophers.[22]

Throughout the twentieth century, even in "Oxford,"[23] philosophers have engaged with Newman. For example, the Oxford philosopher F. C. S. Schiller (1864–1937) emphasizes the importance of Newman's work for the development of pragmatism in his *Studies in Humanism* (1907).[24] The Oxford philosopher (1936–52), and president of India (1962–67),

---

18. Cronin, *Theory of Knowledge*, ix.

19. Although critical of Newman's separation of proof and assent D'Arcy gives Newman's *Grammar of Assent* substantial treatment. For further discussion, see D'Arcy, *Nature of Belief*.

20. Guitton examines Newman's philosophy of history comparing it with that of Hegel and Darwin. For further discussion, see Guitton, *La Philosophie de Newman*.

21. Metz, *A Hundred Years of British Philosophy*, 185–200.

22. Even a selective list of nineteenth- and twentieth-century philosophers who read and discuss Newman is a long one: Rogers, "Puseyism," 501–62; Martineau, "Personal Influences on Our Present Theology," 464–65; M'Cosh, *Method of the Divine Government*, 510; Graham, *Idealism*, ix–x; Martineau, *A History of the Thirty Years' Peace*, 4:270; Jevons, *Logic*, 449–51; Sidgwick, *Miscellaneous Essays*, 358–59; Hodgson, *The Metaphysic of Experience*, III, 354; Caldecott, *Philosophy of Religion in England*, 258–72; Turner, *History of Philosophy*, 642; Fraser, *Biographia Philosophica*, 78, 264; Seth, *English Philosophers*, 331; Rogers, "Belief and the Criterion of Truth," 393–94; Sorley, *A History of English Philosophy*, 265–66; Ryan, *An Introduction to Philosophy*, 239; Randall, *Readings in Philosophy*, 111–34; Hick, *Faith and Knowledge*, 86–105; Costello, *A Philosophy of the Real*, 6; Skinner, *Contingencies of Reinforcement*, 279; Garver. "What Violence Is," 247; Rorty, "Keeping Philosophy Pure," 21; Parfit, *Reasons and Persons*, 49; Mackie, *The Miracle of Theism*, 103–6; Pailin, *Groundwork of Philosophy of Religion*, 73; Phillips, *Faith after Foundationalism*, 84–86; Kenny, *Brief History of Western Philosophy*, 309–12; Van Inwagen, *Ontology*, 15; Swinburne, *Revelation*, 188–95.

23. Those who have taught, studied and worked in Oxford.

24. Schiller, *Studies in Humanism*, 351–53.

Sarvepalli Radhakrishnan (1888–1975) discusses Newman's conception of religion in *The Reign of Religion in Contemporary Philosophy* (1920).[25] Moreover, his discussion of original sin in his work *Religion in a Changing World* (1967)[26] cites Newman, as does his (posthumous) publication on *The Idealist View of Life* (1981).[27] The "Oxford-trained" moral philosopher and former tutor in philosophy at Oxford (1968–98) Jonathan Glover (1941–) mentions Newman in his discussion of conscience in *Responsibility* (1970)[28] and examines Newman's conception of sin in *Utilitarianism and Its Critics* (1990).[29] The Oxford Philosopher John R. Lucas (1929–) refers to Newman in his work *Freedom and Grace* (1976)[30] and in his Durham Lectures *Butler's Philosophy of Religion Vindicated* (1978).[31] In his work *Moral Luck* (1981), the Oxford philosopher—and White's Professor of Moral Philosophy from 1990 to 1996—Bernard Williams (1929–2003) appropriates Newman's distinction between notional and real assent (from Newman's *Grammar of Assent*) in his discussion of relativism.[32] J. L. Mackie, Reader in Philosophy at Oxford University, compares Newman's discussion of how conscience offers evidence for the existence of God with Kant's contention that moral consciousness presupposes the existence of God.[33] Brian Davies, a Roman Catholic philosopher based in Oxford, compares Newman's understanding of morality with Kant in that both writers, he argues, consider there to be a relationship between morality and religion. In this regard, he argues that Newman, like Kant, views morality as being dependent upon the existence of God.[34] Though critical, Richard Swinburne discusses Newman in his work *Revelation: From Metaphor to Analogy* (2007).[35] Most significantly, the "Oxford-trained" philosopher of religion William J.

---

25. Radhakrishnan, *The Reign of Religion in Contemporary Philosophy*, 21.
26. Radhakrishnan, *Religion in a Changing World*, 91.
27. Radhakrishnan, *The Idealist View of Life*, 141.
28. Glover, *Responsibility*, 89.
29. Glover states that: "Cardinal Newman made such a claim about pain and sin. He believed that both of these were bad, but that no amount of pain could be as bad as the least amount of sin." Glover, *Utilitarianism and Its Critics*, 148–50.
30. Lucas, *Freedom and Grace*, 2.
31. Lucas, *Butler's Philosophy of Religion Vindicated*, 2.
32. Williams, *Moral Luck*, 138.
33. Mackie, *The Miracle of Theism*, 106, 110.
34. Davies, *An Introduction to the Philosophy of Religion*, 168–70.
35. Swinburne, *Revelation*, 188–95.

Abraham (1947–) acknowledges that his conception of the epistemology of religious belief is constructively operating out of the epistemological framework implicit within the writings of John Henry Newman.[36]

What is most striking about Abraham's acknowledgement of Newman is that he is not only influenced by him, but he directly links his exposure to Newman's writings to his time at Oxford under his doctoral "supervisor, Basil Mitchell . . . [who] opened up a line to the brilliant insights of John Henry Newman."[37] This indicates that it is precisely during his time in Oxford, under Mitchell's influence, that Abraham was inspired by Newman's philosophical insights. Here is one of Mitchell's own doctoral students, an "Oxford-trained" philosopher of religion, stating that the influence of Newman came to him during his time at Oxford through the philosopher, and Newman commentator, Basil Mitchell. Abraham presents a patent example that exposes the way in which Newman commentators miss the mark in terms of evaluating his philosophical reception. Using Abraham as an example, this work will demonstrate that Newman has received far more philosophical attention than Kerr, Kenny, Mitchell, and others envisage.

Re-evaluating Newman's Philosophical Reception

The expression "philosophical reception" may be interpreted in a variety of ways.[38] This book begins by surveying Newman's *general* reception by philosophers, during his life and up to the present. It then explores the *particular* way in which Newman's work has been, and can be, constructively engaged and appropriated by a specific group of philosophers. Therefore, it offers first a *general* survey of the way in which a variety of philosophers have read and referred to Newman; in diverse ways and with various levels of interest. It then provides a detailed examination of Newman's relationship to the development of one *particular* philosophical position.

In its general examination of the philosophical reception given to Newman's works during his lifetime the study is forced to widen the scope of enquiry away from professional philosophers. As will be discussed in chapter 2, the contracted nature of professional (English) philosophy at

---

36. Abraham, *Logic of Renewal*, 166.
37. Abraham, "The Emergence of Canonical Theism," 145.
38. Aquino and King, *Receptions*, 2, 54–55.

the beginning of the nineteenth century entails an examination of the way in which a wide range of academics who wrote upon philosophical themes attend to Newman's work.[39] However, in its survey of Newman's philosophical reception, during the twentieth and twenty-first centuries, the focus is upon examining professional philosophers from a number of the different branches of this subject. The way Newman is associated with a variety of different philosophical positions and movements, with which twentieth-century philosophers affiliated, is also explored.

The scope then moves away from surveying Newman's general philosophical reception in order to explore the significance of William Abraham's admission that his particularist approach to the philosophy of religion, in *Crossing the Threshold of Divine Revelation* (2006), is shaped by Newman's work. Though Abraham uses the particularist approach to epistemology in order to examine theological claims, this epistemological theory was first developed by the philosopher Roderick Chisholm. Thus, in order to fully appreciate the implications of Abraham's acknowledgement to Newman, this book will explore whether Newman's ideas are of importance to Abraham's work and whether Newman's writing is relevant to that of other particularist writers. Therefore, it will examine why Newman's work is of interest to particularist writers like Abraham. A number of possibilities will be looked at here. Does Newman anticipate some of the tendencies that are characteristic of this position? Does he engage with any of the background sources used by these writers in formulating their epistemological proposals? For this reason, it is important here to emphasize the historical nature of this research. Examining Newman's work in relation to these particularist writers entails both an exploration of his reception by key proponents of this approach, such as Roderick Chisholm, and an investigation into whether Newman has connections with the key sources that Chisholm acknowledges as having influenced this epistemological theory. Likewise, examining the significance of Newman's ideas for particularist approaches to the epistemology of theology necessitates a detailed investigation into the reception given to Newman's work by philosophers of religion like W. J. Abraham, whose work offers a paradigm of how the particularist approach to epistemology can be applied to Christian belief.

Hence, this study involves assessing whether or not Newman's writing is relevant to two branches of philosophy. The first of these being

---

39. Quinton, "English Philosophy," 234.

epistemology, or the branch of philosophy that deals with questions relating to the nature, possibility, and scope of knowledge.[40] Second, examining Newman's work in relation to particularist approaches to the epistemology of theology involves exploring whether or not Newman has shaped a contemporary approach to the philosophy of religion, that branch of philosophy that deals with the meaning and justification of religious claims.[41]

Before closing this topic it is important to state why this philosophical position, epistemological particularism, as opposed to say pragmatism, warrants our focus here. Newman's reception by particularist writers represents an example of his philosophical reception that, hitherto, has been largely overlooked. While there is an abundance of literature comparing Newman with, for example, pragmatist writers, there are only a handful of articles comparing Newman with epistemological particularist writers.[42] However, what is interesting about these tentative comparisons is that they suggest that Newman's thought has the potential to shed light on this approach to epistemology.[43] Moreover, William J. Abraham's contribution to the philosophy of religion spans thirty years.[44] The invitation for him to supply the seminal article for the first edition of the *Journal for Analytic Theology* (2013), a journal in which the analytic approach to philosophy is used to examine theological themes,[45] reinforces Vidu's description of Abraham as a "well-established voice" at the forefront of the philosophy of religion.[46] Thus, if it is the case that Newman shapes

---

40. Hamlyn, "History of Epistemology," 242.

41. Swinburne, "Problems of the Philosophy of Religion," 763.

42. Ford's comparison is little more than a remark in his review of a philosophical work by William J. Abraham. For further discussion, see Ford, Review of *Crossing the Threshold of Divine Revelation*, 184.

43. Jay Newman, in particular, indicates that J. H. Newman's conception of reason has the potential to enhance Chisholm's theory. Jay Newman, "Epistemic Inference," 327–39.

44. His work includes: Abraham, "Some Trends in Recent Philosophy of Religion," 93–103; Abraham, *Introduction to the Philosophy of Religion*; Abraham, "Cumulative Case Arguments," 17–38; Abraham, "Epistemological Significance of the Inner Witness of the Holy Spirit," 434–50; Abraham, "Faraway Fields Are Green," 162–72; Abraham, "Scripture and Revelation," 584–90; Abraham, "The Epistemology of Conversion," 175–94; Abraham, "Loyal Opposition and the Epistemology of Conscience," 135–47; Abraham, "Systematic Theology as Analytic Theology," 54–69.

45. Abraham, "Turning Philosophical Water into Theological Wine," 1–16.

46. Vidu, Review of *Crossing The Threshold of Divine Revelation*, 134–35.

Abraham's proposal, it indicates that Newman's work is of contemporary relevance to this area of philosophy.

In summary, by examining these different aspects of Newman's philosophical reception, *general* and *particular*, the book offers a historical investigation and re-evaluation of the claims of Newman having a feeble philosophical legacy.

Sources of the Study

In its examination of Newman's writings, Newman scholarship has tended to focus upon the Longmans Green edition of his works as being the standard text.[47] To take one prominent example, *The Newman's Studies Journal* has requested that submissions use this edition "unless there is a cogent reason for using another edition."[48] Though it is immensely helpful for Newman scholarship to have this common reference point, there are a number of problems with the assumption that this later edition supersedes the original texts. First of all, Newman made some drastic changes to some of his works in this later edition of his writings.[49] If one only attends to the Longmans Green edition of his works one can easily miss these textual variations. Moreover, the primacy given to this later edition of Newman's publications has the potential to divorce commentators from the original context in which this "occasional writer" initially composed his work.[50] The historical nature of this study demands an analysis of both the original publication of Newman's writings, since it is discussing his philosophical reception by his contemporaries, and the later edition of his works. That is to say, in assessing how Newman's works were received by his nineteenth-century contemporaries it is important to engage with the same texts that the reviewers engaged with.[51] That

---

47. Newman, *Collected Works*.

48. Goetz, 'submission Guidelines,' line 190. .

49. For example, the Longmans Green edition of Newman's original *Discourses on the Scope and Nature* (1852) does not even contain the discourse on "General Knowledge Viewed as One Philosophy."

50. As Ker explains, nearly all Newman's published writings were "occasional," that is to say, they were written for a particular occasion, often of a controversial nature. Ker, *The Achievement of Newman*, 54.

51. The first editions of these works become particularly important when one considers that the reception of Newman's work on the continent relied upon them. For example, while the 1845 *Essay on Development* was translated into German, the

said, we will not fail to attend to later editions. The amendments present in the Longmans Green edition are Newman's personal redactions of his earlier works. It is likely that these revisions can enable the clarification of obscure passages present in earlier editions. Therefore, we will make use of both the original and later editions of Newman's writings. For clarity the standard abbreviations used for Newman's works (such as G.A. for the *Grammar of Assent*) will only be used for references to the Longmans Green edition.[52] Original publications will be cited normally.[53]

In our analysis of the way in which Newman's works have been received by philosophers, we will engage with a wide variety of Newman's writings. A detailed examination of Newman's *Grammar of Assent* is provided because it is this work that receives the most sustained attention by particularist writers. Newman's published correspondence, as well as his unpublished papers, also serve as a guide where these offer clarification for the analysis of Newman's work. In examining Newman's unpublished writings, it is important to stress the importance of his handwritten notations in his personal copies of philosophical works in the Birmingham Oratory. In its examination of the sources common to Newman and Chisholm, this book attempts wherever possible to reference the edition of philosophical works that Newman himself consulted and annotated.[54]

Other texts important for this study are works by the particularist writers Chisholm and Abraham. With regard to the former, we will discuss some of Chisholm's writings upon epistemology. The most important of these for the present enquiry is his work on *The Problem of the Criterion*, for it is here that Chisholm first coins the phrase epistemological particularism. Other works by Chisholm are also mentioned—especially where they refer to Newman. Texts relevant in this regard include his work on *Perceiving* (1957), his *Theory of Knowledge* (1973), and his essay on "Epistemic Principles" (1981). With regard to Abraham's writings, his own acknowledgement stresses Newman's influence upon his religious

---

1878 revision was not. For further discussion, see Becker, "Newman's Influence in Germany" 176.

52. These are listed on page x.

53. For example: Newman, *Grammar*, 40 [*GA*, 42]. This reference to the original publication of the *Grammar* is followed by an abbreviated reference "*GA*," [in brackets]. Where such abbreviations are used they refer generally to the posthumous Longmans Green edition. When citing the original edition of Newman's publications the Longmans edition will also be given (wherever possible) so as to facilitate comparisons between earlier and later editions.

54. Newman's books are as he left them in his room at the Birmingham Oratory.

epistemology, *Crossing the Threshold of Divine Revelation* (2006).[55] We offer a detailed examination of this text essential to our present enquiry.[56] Nevertheless, Abraham's contention that "all of my own work in theology" is undergirded by philosophical themes indicates that if the full extent of Newman's importance to this writer is to be realized, his works should be consulted liberally.[57]

Throughout, an attempt will be made to situate the discussion within Newman scholarship generally by referring to a wide range of Newman commentators. Unfortunately there are only a small number of articles that make reference to Newman's similarities with particularist writers.[58] However, while scarcely anything has been written concerning Newman and Abraham,[59] two Newman commentators stand out for their serious engagement with both the similarities and differences in Newman and Chisholm. In particular, the philosopher and Newman scholar Jay Newman (1948–2007) indicates a number of parallels.[60] Likewise, Marty Maddox offers a detailed comparison of the positions held by Chisholm and Newman; identifying a number of similarities and differences.[61] These commentators will be discussed in further detail in chapters 3 and 5.

Before closing this section it is important to stress that a survey of Newman's general philosophical reception requires us to consult a wide variety of philosophical literature. Philosophical textbooks, such as the *Oxford Companion of Philosophy*, will serve as a guide for determining the parameters of philosophical discourse during the historical periods to be examined.[62]

---

55. Abraham, *Logic of Renewal*, 166.

56. Abraham, *Crossing*; Abraham, *Logic of Renewal*, 166.

57. Abraham, "Response to Marc Cortez," 28.

58. Commentators who compare Newman and Chisholm include: Collins, "Newman, Foundationalism and Teaching Philosophy," 147–48; McCarthy, "Newman, Foundationalism, and the Ethics of Belief," 74–75; Grimm, "Cardinal Newman, Reformed Epistemologist?" 504.

59. To my knowledge, apart from Ford's review of Abraham's *Crossing the Threshold* (2006), which briefly notes Abraham's similarity with Newman, there are no comparisons between Newman and Abraham's work. Ford, Review of *Crossing the Threshold of Divine Revelation*, 184.

60. Jay Newman, "Epistemic Inference," 327–39.

61. Maddox, "Newman, Certain Knowledge," 69–86.

62. Abbreviated hereafter as *OCP*.

Summary of Contents

This book is divided into six chapters. The aim of chapter 2 is to provide a historical overview of Newman's philosophical reception during the last two hundred years. It examines a variety of different philosophers; including pragmatists, personalists, phenomenologists, and others. This includes any references and citations made to Newman in order to offer a broad picture as to where he shows up in the general philosophical discussion. Where the philosophers who engage with Newman are identifiable by a philosophical movement, the chapter focuses on Newman's reception by this group. In cases where there is no identifiable philosophical movement the general branch of philosophy will be discussed. The chapter also seeks to give a background to the historical context in which the philosophers who engaged with Newman lived. Thus, the purpose of this second chapter is to determine the degree to which Newman's general philosophical legacy has been underestimated by Newman commentators.

Chapter 3 concentrates on one aspect of Newman's philosophical reception. Following a definition of the term "epistemological particularism" the chapter introduces the relevant Newman literature discussing his relationship with epistemological particularism. It then explores the historical background to epistemological particularism in order to investigate whether these writers share philosophical sources with Newman. This question of shared influences is examined in order to see whether or not the parallels suggested by commentators are the result of a common philosophical heritage. Chapter 4 examines the extent to which Newman's work anticipates the epistemological orientation of particularist writers by exploring whether the similarities that commentators identify permeate the whole of Newman's writing or whether they are isolated to a few minor cases.

Chapter 5 explores whether or not the *Grammar of Assent* has tendencies that might be described as epistemological particularist. It also examines the reception of this work by particularist writers. This includes a study of Chisholm's references to Newman. It also involves an analysis of the way in which Newman's work was received by the forerunners of this particularist approach. The chapter provides a detailed examination of Marty Maddox, who contends that the *Grammar* manifests epistemological tendencies that are contrary to particularism, and Jay Newman, who indicates that this work has the potential to enhance the particularist approach to knowledge. Finally, chapter 6 argues that the philosopher of religion William J. Abraham utilizes Newman's writing in his particularist approach to the epistemology of Christian belief. Since a direct connection between Newman and Abraham is documented—Abraham studied Newman under Basil Mitchell at Oxford and has commented on him at length—this chapter will examine whether Abraham is shaped by Newman.

2

The Underestimation of Newman's Philosophical Reception

Newman's Philosophical Reception in the Nineteenth Century

The state of nineteenth-century philosophy in England

At the beginning of the nineteenth century, philosophy was a subject in decline in England.[1] Kerr's thesis, that in his time Newman was an isolated philosophical figure, needs to be set within this context. A key source used in support of Kerr's argument is Anthony Quinton's (1925–2010) essay "Oxford Philosophy."[2] In this article, Quinton describes Newman as being an "isolated" and "uninfluential" figure. Kerr's incorporation of this description into the title of his essay—"'In an Isolated and, Philosophically, Uninfluential Way' Newman and Oxford Philosophy"—indicates that Quinton's analysis is important for Kerr. Moreover, Kerr's decision to highlight these terms—"isolated" and "uninfluential"—implies that he views Quinton's description as being some kind of official philosophical verdict on Newman. While Kerr latches onto Quinton's description in order to support his thesis, that there has been a general failure on the part of philosophers to recognize Newman's contribution, his analysis

---

1. Quinton, "English Philosophy," 234; Sorley, *A History of British Philosophy to 1900*, 239.
2. Quinton, "Oxford Philosophy," 640.

does not give significant attention to the general condition of philosophy as a subject in nineteenth-century England. Quinton's other contribution to *The Oxford Companion*, an article entitled "English Philosophy," emphasizes that professional English philosophy remained dormant from the Middle Ages until the late nineteenth century.[3] When viewed from within this context it is possible that Quinton's reference to Newman's "isolation" may relate more to the general state of nineteenth-century philosophy than to his person.[4] From this perspective, Kerr's narrative of Newman's "philosophical isolation" may not actually correspond with the facts.

The German philosopher Georg Wilhelm Friedrich Hegel (1770–1831) throws light on the condition of philosophy in England at the beginning of the nineteenth century. In his work on *Logic* (1817) he expresses considerable shock at discovering the following notice in an English Newspaper: "The Art of Preserving the Hair, on Philosophical Principles." Hegel felt that the use of the term "philosophy" in English had an exaggerated empirical focus, which was quite different from its application on the Continent.[5]

Though Newman is influenced by the empiricism, which perturbed Hegel, his understanding of philosophy follows Aristotle in that he considers the aim of this discipline to be universal: to obtain a comprehensive view of things.[6] He states that "Philosophy is to view all things in their mutual relations, and its object is truth."[7] Elsewhere, he describes philosophy as: "Reason exercised upon Knowledge; or the Knowledge not merely of things in general, but of things in their relations to one

---

3. Quinton, "English Philosophy," 234.

4. Though Kerr acknowledges that Oxford was "philosophically infertile" for much of the nineteenth century, he fails to appreciate the depth of this crisis. Kerr, "Newman and Oxford Philosophy," 160.

5. Hegel writes: "Newton continues to be celebrated as the greatest of philosophers: and the name goes down as far as the price lists of instrument makers. All instruments such as the thermometer and barometer . . . are styled philosophical instruments. Surely thought, and not a mere combination of wood, iron [and] ought to be called the instrument of philosophy!" Hegel, *Logic*, 13.

6. Newman's conception of philosophy is influenced by Aristotle: "This is the concept of liberal knowledge or "philosophy" . . . the means of understanding the relations between the different aspects of knowledge." For further discussion, see Hardman, *Six Victorian Thinkers*, 126; Anagnostopoulos, "Aristotle's Works," 19; Aristotle, *Metaphysics*, 4 [982ab].

7. *Ess*, 1:29.

another."[8] In sum, he defines philosophy as "universal knowledge."[9] He writes:

> Philosophy, which I have made to consist in a comprehensive view of truth in all its branches, of the relations of science to science, of their mutual bearings, and their respective values. What the worth of such an acquirement is, compared with other objects which we seek,—wealth or power or honour or the conveniences and comforts of life, I do not profess here to discuss; but I would maintain, and mean to show, that it is an object, in its own nature so really and undeniably good, as to be the compensation of a great deal of thought in the compassing, and a great deal of trouble in the attaining.[10]

Newman considers that an individual who is taught philosophy (universal knowledge) "never views any part of the extended subject-matter of Knowledge without recollecting that it is but a part, or without the associations which spring from this recollection. It makes everything in some sort lead to everything else."[11] Newman concludes that the purpose of a "university" education, by its very definition, should be to teach this universal knowledge.[12]

Newman's classical conception of philosophy, and its place within university education, set him apart from nineteenth-century trends. Though there were others who shared this view, including the philosopher Herbert Spencer,[13] the rise of utilitarianism gave nineteenth-century philosophy an increasing empirical focus. For example, Jeremy Bentham (1748–1832), generally recognized as the founder of this movement,[14]

---

8. This extract is taken from the Oxford University sermon on "Wisdom, as Contrasted with Faith and with Bigotry" (1841). He continues: "It is the power of referring every thing to its true place in the universal system,—of understanding the various aspects of each of its parts." *US*, 290–91.

9. *Idea*, 137.

10. *Idea*, 103.

11. Newman believed that people educated in this way would be intellectually healthy. *Idea*, 124, 137.

12. In the preface to this publication Newman emphasizes that the "view taken of a University in these Discourses is the following:—That it is a place of teaching universal knowledge." *Idea*, ix.

13. "To bring the definition to its simplest and clearest form:—Knowledge of the lowest kind is un-*unified knowledge*; Science is partially-*unified knowledge*; Philosophy is completely-*unified knowledge*." Spencer, *First Principles*, 134.

14. "Though similar ideas go back at least to Democritus (460–370 BC) of Ancient

argued that all knowledge should have its basis in the proofs of physical science.[15] Bentham's limitless faith in Locke's empiricism[16] led him to the following conclusion: "Experience, observation, experiment; in these three words may be seen the sources of all our knowledge."[17] This reduction of knowledge to the disciplines rooted in physical science lead Bentham to view disciplines outside these parameters as fictitious—rendering religion and metaphysics groundless superstitious nonsense.[18] Bentham considered that the only subjects worthy of study were those that have a basis in experience. All of this had a profound impact upon his educational theory. Bentham used the Greek term *Chrestomathia* as the title for his thesis on utilitarian education (1816) because he understood this word to mean things conducive to useful learning.[19] In this work Bentham omitted subjects that had no practical use, such as religion, from the curriculum altogether. This excessive empirical emphasis meant that subjects with a metaphysical object no longer had a place within education.

In view of the above, it is perhaps unsurprising that there was a general sense of apathy felt towards the subject of philosophy in the early part of the nineteenth century. In 1832 the Scottish philosopher William Hamilton (1788–1856) also mourned the "state of philosophical learning in this country."[20] Henry Sidgwick (1838–1900), Professor of Moral Philosophy at the University of Cambridge (1869–1900), indicates the

---

Greece, Jeremy Bentham (1748–1832) has generally been considered the founder of utilitarianism." Duemler, *Bringing Life to the Stars*, 2; Troyer, *Classical Utilitarians*, ix.

15. Bentham stressed that "it is from physical science alone" that humankind is capable of deriving "proof" against "groundless" errors. For further discussion see Bowring, *Works of Jeremy Bentham*, 7:348–49.

16. According to Crimmins, Bentham conveniently ignored Locke's own admissions about the limitations of his theory. See Crimmins, *Secular Utilitarianism*, 46.

17. Bowring, *Works of Jeremy Bentham*, 8:28.

18. "In knowledge in general, and in knowledge belonging to the physical department in particular, will the vast mass of mischief, of which perverted religion is the source, find its preventive remedy. It is from physical science alone that a man is capable of deriving that mental strength and that well-grounded confidence which renders him proof against so many groundless terrors flowing from that prolific source, which, by enabling him to see how prone to error the mind is on this ground, and thence how free such error is from all moral blame, disposes him to that forbearance towards supposed error, which men are so ready to preach and so reluctant to practise." Bowring, *Works of Jeremy Bentham*, 8:13.

19. Bentham, *Chrestomathia*.

20. Hamilton, "Johnson's Translation of Tennemann's History of Philosophy," 160.

great contrast between the utilitarianism pervasive within the academy and Newman's conception of philosophy:

> John Henry Newman set before the world an ideal of University education, in which all students, whatever else they learnt, should give the first place to the royal and ruling study of philosophy—universal knowledge of things mundane and divine, sought as its own end, in disregard of all sordid utilities. We all know how the development of all sciences and studies, and especially the expansion of our ideas of the preparation required for different professions and callings, have inevitably driven English University education to develop in the direction opposed to Newman's view.[21]

Here Sidgwick observes that Newman's classical conception of philosophy (universal knowledge) and its place within the academy has not obtained support within the "English University," which has become focussed upon preparing people for specific professions. This reinforces the notion that Newman's isolation from professional philosophy reveals more about the low estimation of that discipline within English universities than it does about his philosophical credibility.

The "torpid state of the national mind" was even lamented by utilitarian thinkers. For example, John Stuart Mill (1806–73) states that:

> England once stood at the head of European philosophy. Where stands she now? . . . Out of the narrow bounds of mathematical and physical science, not a vestige of a reading and thinking public engaged in the investigation of truth as truth, in the prosecution of thought for the sake of thought. Among few except sectarian religionists—and what they are we all know—is there any interest in the great problem of man's nature and life.[22]

While this extract from Mill's essay indicates the subject's level of decline it also raises an important point. Mill indicates that the only group interested in philosophy are "sectarian religionists." Regardless of Mill's theological opinions, it is demonstrable that a number of nineteenth-century religious thinkers wrote about important philosophical issues. Quinton, who also describes the philosophical situation as being "torpid," acknowledges that philosophy was still "pursued by independent men of

---

21. Sidgwick, *Miscellaneous Essays*, 358–59.
22. Mill, "Professor Sedgwick's Discourse—State of Philosophy in England," 95.

letters" and "philosophically active clergymen."[23] The sources referenced in Quinton's essay reinforce this point. For example, in their examination of nineteenth-century philosophy, John Seth's, *English Philosophers* (1912), William Sorley's *A History of English Philosophy* (1920), John Muirhead's *The Platonic Tradition in Anglo-Saxon Philosophy* (1931), and Meyrick Carré's *Phases of Thought in England* (1949) each discuss the philosophical ideas of non-professional philosophers. Their respective analyses attend to intellectuals from a wide variety of disciplines and interestingly all of these writers discuss "John Henry Newman."[24] Hence, if the relevant literature is not restricted to the contracted scope of professional philosophy during this period then the present enquiry will also widen its examination so as not to be limited in this way. An authentic examination of Newman's philosophical reception should attend to the judgment of nineteenth-century thinkers who, though they were not exactly professional philosophers, have made a valid contribution to the subject. Quinton's article, and other texts pertaining to this period of English philosophy, will serve as a guide for determining the parameters of philosophical discourse during Newman's lifetime. In summary, figures mentioned within the relevant literature who may not be professional philosophers but, nevertheless, have made important contributions will be included where pertinent to Newman.

Newman and nineteenth-century philosophy

There is evidence to suggest that a number of nineteenth-century professional philosophers engaged with Newman. For example, Thomas Fowler (1832–1904), Harriet Martineau (1802–76), James M'Cosh (1811–94), Grant Allen (1848–99), and Thomas Davidson (1840–1900) read Newman.[25] Furthermore, in his work on *Idealism* (1872), William Graham (1839–1911) numbers Newman alongside the religious philosophers F. D. Maurice (1805–72), James Martineau (1805–1900), and the Hegelian philosopher James Hutchison Stirling (1820–1909).[26] James A.

23. Quinton, "English Philosophy," 234.

24. Seth, *English Philosophers*, 321; Sorley, *A History of English Philosophy*, 265–66; Muirhead, *Platonic Tradition*, 221; Carré, *Phases of Thought in England*, 339.

25. Fowler, *Corpus Christi College*, 199; Martineau, *A History of the Thirty Years' Peace*, 4:270; M'Cosh, *Method of The Divine Government*, 510; Allen, *The Incidental Bishop*, 204; Davidson, *A History of Education*, 228.

26. Graham, *Idealism*, ix–x.

Picton (1832–1910) includes him alongside Kepler, Newton, Descartes, Spinoza, and Leibniz.[27] The political philosopher and barrister James Fitzjames Stephen (1829–94) identifies Newman as "the man of genius"[28] and finally Sidgwick, the moral philosopher mentioned above, calls Newman "a fine intellect."[29]

Newman's works are also treated philosophically by a number of nineteenth-century intellectuals. Newman's *Tracts for the Times* (1833–41), which argued that the doctrines and practices of Anglicanism should be grounded in the tradition of the early church, were criticized by the philosopher and nonconformist minister Henry Rogers (1806–77),[30] the logician Richard Whately (1787–1863),[31] and his colleague Baden Powell (1796–1860).[32] The focus of these writers's criticism is that Newman's *Tracts* justified theological beliefs using the authority of the early church instead of proportioning beliefs to reasoned evidence. Despite their criticisms, they refer to Newman's writings as being "philosophical" and go to considerable lengths to show the folly of his position.

Newman's contribution to the Oxford Movement was also discussed in an article on "Philosophy at Oxford" in the very first issue of *Mind: a Quarterly Review of Psychology and Philosophy* (1876).[33] The title of this

---

27. Picton describes Newman as a "seer in the true sense of the word and [a] saint." Picton, *Pantheism*, 16.

28. Stephen, *Essays by a Barrister*, 239.

29. Sidgwick, *Miscellaneous Essays*, 358–59.

30. The notion that Newman's contemporaries deemed his writings philosophical is also underlined by the fact that Rogers spends over fifty pages forming a "systematic exposition" of Tractarian doctrines in order for "[his] readers" to "decide whether or not it is their duty to accept them." If Rogers really thought Newman was irrelevant to philosophy he would not spend nearly as much time rebuking his work. Rogers argues that Newman's Tracts were guilty of "begging the question." For further discussion, see Rogers, "Puseyism," 501–4. After three years as an assistant pastor in Poole (1829–32) Henry Rogers began his lecturing career at Highbury College on logic (1832–36). After a brief period lecturing on linguistics at University College London (1836–39) he spent over twenty years lecturing on mental philosophy at Spark Hill College, a dissenting academy in Birmingham (1839–58). His works include: Rogers, *Reason and Faith* and Rogers, *The Eclipse of Faith*.

31. Whately, *Essays*, 109–10.

32. Powell, *Tradition Unveiled*, 67–68. Powell was a proponent of positivism in philosophy. For further discussion, see Corsi, *Science and Religion*. Powell was a contributor to the very controversial *Essays and Reviews* (1860) and was the father of the famous Robert Baden-Powell; founder of the scouting movement.

33. "Dr. Newman was directed to produce a principle which should counteract the popular prejudices.... In an honest endeavour to get nearer to the truth of things than

article contradicts the notion that Newman's philosophy was ignored at Oxford. That the very first issue of this periodical contains an article criticizing Newman's "Oxford Philosophy," indicates that while Newman may have been unpopular, his "Oxford Philosophy" was viewed as an adversarial piece which needed to be addressed. It should also be stressed that Newman's writing is considered relevant enough to be discussed in the first edition of *Mind*; a journal which went on to publish several groundbreaking philosophical essays including: Bertrand Russell's article "On Denoting" (1905) and Alan Turing's essay "Computing Machinery and Intelligence" (1950).[34]

Newman's *Sermons Chiefly on the Theory of Religious Belief* (1843),[35] were discussed by the Unitarian philosopher James Martineau (1805–1900).[36] In his *Essays Philosophical and Theological* (1865) Martineau explains that instead of believing doctrines on the basis of the evidence in their favor[37] with "Dr. Newman the order is reversed."[38] Newman "begin[s] with faith, and develop[s] it by inquiry; reverently taking the divine instincts, and drawing out their hidden oracles into the symmetry

---

the conventional Philistinism of liberal politicians, Dr. Newman dug down and found a little below the surface the disused principle of authority. Disgusted with the cant phrases of reform oratory of his day, he missed the deeper principle of Reason, which all the while lay below the surface of the Whig political tradition. He broke not only with the constitutional principles of 1688, but with reason. He threw off not only the scum of democratic lawlessness, but the allegiance which the individual understanding owes to the universal reason, and too hastily concluded that authority could supply a basis for a philosophic belief. Long before Dr. Newman gave in his adhesion to the Papal Church, the philosophic basis of his mind had anticipated the Syllabus and the Encyclical." Pattison, "Philosophy at Oxford," 85.

34. Russell, "On Denoting," 479–93; Turing, "Computing Machinery and Intelligence," 433–60.

35. Newman, *Sermons Chiefly on the Theory of Religious Belief*. With the exception of the first and last sermon, most of these were preached during his incumbency at St Mary's Oxford (1828–42).

36. James Martineau was a Unitarian Philosopher. He was Professor of Mental and Moral Philosophy at Manchester New College. "The College, now Manchester College, Oxford, was one of those nonconformist institutions founded to cater for men barred from the universities because of their inability to subscribe to the Articles." LD 7:400.

37. Martineau, *Essays Philosophical*, 352.

38. Martineau believes that in order to attain the "purest religious insight [one must] quit superficial and derivative beliefs, and seek the primitive roots where the finite draws life from the Infinite. The direct contact of the human spirit with the Divine." Martineau, *Essays Philosophical*, 346.

of a holy philosophy."[39] Martineau declares that: "on every account we object to this statement of the ultimate grounds of religion."[40] While Newman is criticized by Martineau for his position, it is easy to lose sight of the fact that this philosopher also credits Newman with the understanding necessary to deliberately communicate a sophisticated philosophical position.[41] Martineau recognizes that the "radical scepticism," which he detects in Newman's writings, is not merely implied "second-hand" but "receives direct and repeated statement as a philosophical principle."[42]

Newman's *Essay on Miracles* (1843), in which he argues that belief in miracles is reasonable, was strongly condemned by Thomas Huxley (1825–95); a biologist whom Quinton describes as an "occasional philosopher."[43] Huxley's discussions concerning the rationality of religious belief are very critical of Newman's contention that it is necessary to believe before we have proved.[44] The work on *Miracles* was also sharply criticized by the *Westminster Review* for "begging the question" because the point that Newman should have proved, that supernatural interventions exist, was assumed from the beginning of *Miracles*—for he takes for granted that God interfered in human history by bringing the church into existence.[45] Whether or not this assessment is correct, Newman's inclu-

---

39. "In the sermons we seem to understand the statements . . . that 'faith must venture something;' [to mean] that in order to finish by knowing, you must commence by trusting; that self-surrender in the dark to conscience clears up into open-eyed wisdom . . . . Thus is the word 'faith' degraded to the sense of 'trying the experiment of an unknown religion, and obeying it at hazard.'" Martineau, *Essays Philosophical*, 352, 354–55.

40. Martineau, *Essays Philosophical*, 350.

41. These sermons were also viewed as a philosophical work by other writers. For example, *The Ecclectic Magazine of Foreign Literature* described these sermons as the "embodiment of Newman's philosophy." Unknown author, "Some Aspects of Newman's Influence," 707.

42. "His own faith is an escape from an alternative scepticism, which receives the veto not of his reason, but of his will. He seems to say within himself, 'There is no bottom to these things that I can find; we must therefore put one there; and only mind that it be sufficient to hold them in, supposing it to be real.' He deals, in short, with the first truths of religion as hypotheses, not known or knowable in themselves." Martineau, *Essays Philosophical*, 346–47.

43. Quinton, "English Philosophy," 235. For further discussion, see Sorley, *British Philosophy*, 275.

44. "There is something really impressive in the magnificent contempt with which, at times, Dr. Newman sweeps aside alike those who offer and those who demand such evidence." Huxley, "Agnosticism and Christianity," 65, 71.

45. Newman "seems to admit that the credibility of miracles rests wholly on our

sion in the *Westminster Review* shows that his work provoked attention from a journal that was set up as the official organ for the "philosophical radicals," the "Benthamites," who were adherents of utilitarian philosophy.[46] The fact that Newman's work is discussed in this periodical indicates that it was deemed significant enough to be contested.

Newman composed his *Essay on Development* (1845) immediately before his conversion to Catholicism in order to try and explain how Roman Catholic doctrine could both represent and yet appear different from the teaching of the early church.[47] The *Westminster Review* describes the *Essay* as a "philosophical" work.[48] In addition to this, Matthew Piers Watt Boulton (1820-94) cites the *Essay* in his philosophical work on the *Examination of the Principles of Kant and Hamilton* (1866).[49] The philosopher John Henry Bridges (1832-1906) compares Newman's *Essay* with the French positivist philosopher August Comte's law of development,[50] and the Scottish philosopher Alexander Bain cites the *Essay* to support his contention that theological doctrines can be revised.[51] The *Vocabulary of the Philosophical Sciences* uses the *Essay's* definition of rationalism in religion.[52] In addition, the clergyman and philosopher W. A. Butler (1814-48)—author of the *History of Ancient Philosophy* (1849)[53] and Professor of Moral Philosophy at Dublin—describes Newman as a "philosophical historian."[54] Nevertheless, Butler argues that Newman's es-

---

previous belief in the Divine omnipotence . . . What the author alleges is then manifestly no answer to the objection, but only reproduces it in other words . . . to what purpose will it be to go on asserting that the Church is altogether a 'supernatural ordinance,' and thus that we are reverently to receive the wonders to which she lays claim . . . in what way will this help to establish the divine origin of Christianity, or to refute the objections of the professed sceptic . . . What is such a defence but merely begging the question, that the Church has that supernatural character, or that there is any such thing, which is the very point to be proved." Powell, "Tendency of Puseyism," 339.

46. Troyer, *Classical Utilitarians*, ix.
47. Newman, *Essay on Development*.
48. Powell, "Tendency of Puseyism," 334-35.
49. Boulton, *Inquisitio Philosophica*, 36.
50. Bridges, *Discourses on Positive Religion*, 21-24; 76.
51. Bain, *Practical Essays*, 277-79.
52. Flemming writes: "'Rationalism, in religion,' more restrictedly, the acceptance of the teaching of revelation only in so far as reason can explain its doctrine. See J. H. Newman Developm. of Christ. Doctrine, ch. i., sect. iii." Flemming, *Vocabulary of the Philosophical Sciences*, 832.
53. Butler, *Lectures on the History of Ancient Philosophy*.
54. Butler, *Letters on Romanism*, 16-18.

say involves "a plain surrender of the claims of Romanism to satisfactory evidence" because it begins by assuming the validity of the Catholic doctrines. Butler considers that by starting with this foregone conclusion, Newman's theory is "utterly destitute of evidence." He concludes, therefore, that Newman's decision to join the Catholic Church was governed by his feelings and imagination.[55]

Newman's *Lectures on the Present Position of Catholics* (1851) were designed to challenge anti-Catholic prejudice. What is interesting is that this work is cited by the logician William Stanley Jevons (1835–82) in his work on *Logic*:

> *Argumentum ad hominem* or appeal to the individual; when we do not defend our position in itself, but merely show that our opponent is not the man to attack it. This is a perfectly legitimate argument on many occasions. . . . When Dr. Newman answered the calumnies of the apostate Achilli against the Church by enumerating a few of his crimes, he was doing a service to truth as well as to religion . . . . But if we seek to divert the minds of our hearers from the force of a solid argument by an

---

55. Butler summarizes Newman's essay in the following way: Newman's "imagination and feelings were irreparably engaged; and reason, as usual, was soon busily active in devising subtle argumentative grounds to justify his choice . . . . Such was the 'theory of development,'—a hypothesis in many respects brilliant, attractive, imposing; having against it only such objections as these,—that it was utterly destitute of evidence beyond its utility for the explanation of the (unnecessary) difficulty that suggested it." Butler, *Letters on Romanism*, 16–18, 34–36. Similar accusations are made towards the *Essay on Development* by the *New Quarterly Review*: "[The Essay] is wholly ineffective of its object. As, from the first, there was no desire into an unrestricted examination of the cases respectively put forward by the two churches . . . a book was put forth to explain [an inconsistency], and there is little in the book but what the circumstances of the case require; and that case has more to do with expediency than truth. There is no independence of thought; (that was out of the reach of possibility); there was a foregone conclusion to support, and all that was thought of was, whence that support was to be drawn: no other idea seems to have once entered the author's contemplation . . . the work is directed towards the removal of an obstacle, which he had before spoken of as lying in the way of communion with the Church of Rome. . . . For, had not the inquiry been founded on a foregone conclusion, . . . something like demonstration would have been attempted . . . something would have been brought forward to prove." Unknown author, "Mr Newman's Theory of Development," 301–2. Although the focus of this periodical is not philosophy, it is interesting that the *Essay on Development*, like many of Newman's works, is accused of "begging the question" by Newman's contemporaries.

irrelevant attack on the character of the man using it, we incur the charge of offending at once against Logic and against common fairness.[56]

Here Jevons commends Newman for his creative use of the *Argumentum ad hominem* in order to undermine the anti-Catholic statements of Achilli (Giacinto); a former Dominican friar.[57]

On becoming the rector of the Catholic University in Ireland, Newman delivered a set of lectures which were published as *Discourses on the Scope and Nature of University Education* (1852).[58] As was noted earlier, Sidgwick observes how Newman's work differs from conventional understandings of university education. Despite this he views Newman as a "man of genius."[59] The feminist and moral philosopher, Edith Simcox (1844–1901), reflects favorably on these *Discourses*[60] as does the biologist George John Romanes (1848–94). Romanes, who examined the intellectual basis of faith in his *Candid Examination of Theism* (1878),[61] affirms Newman's contention that an excessive focus on one particular subject can inadvertently lead one to apply its principles to subjects on which it has no bearing.[62]

Newman's *Apologia* (1864) provides a history of his religious opinions in order to show he attained them both sincerely and reasonably.[63]

---

56. Jevons, *Logic*, 449–51.

57. Jevons, *Logic*, 449–51. Interestingly, Newman is accused of the logical fallacy *Argumentum ad hominem* by the essayist Walter Bagehot (1826–77). For further discussion, see Bagehot, *Literary Studies*, 2:267–69.

58. Newman, *Discourses on the Scope and Nature*.

59. Sidgwick, *Miscellaneous Essays*, 358–59. Sidgwick wrote a number of philosophical works including: *Philosophy Its Scope and Relations*; *Lectures on the Philosophy of Kant*; *Lectures on the Ethics of T. H. Green*. For further discussion, see Schultz, "Henry Sidgwick."

60. Simcox, *Natural Law*, 279.

61. Romanes, *A Candid Examination of Theism*, 29.

62. Romanes, *Christian Prayer And General Laws*, 126. Newman states that "specimens of this peculiarity occur every day. You can hardly persuade some men to talk about any thing but their own pursuit; they refer the whole world to their own centre, and measure all matters by their own rule, like the fisherman in the drama, whose eulogy on his deceased lord was, that 'he was so fond of fish.'" Newman, *Discourses on the Scope and Nature*, 359–60.

63. Newman, *Apologia*. It is unfortunate that later commentators have sometimes concluded that the *Apologia* is mainly intended to meet Kingsley's charge of "mendacity." While much attention has also been given to Newman's style, literary and rhetorical, the value of this work as a contribution to apologetics has often gone

The reaction given to the *Apologia* indicates that his contemporaries viewed it as a logical and in some cases philosophical piece of work. For example, while the *Westminster Review* (1864) disapproved of Newman's *Apologia* for preferring papal authority to the evidence of reason as a foundation for his faith, it nevertheless acknowledged the logical coherence of Newman's position.[64] In his book *Recent British Philosophy* (1866) David Masson (1827–1907), the historian and philosophical commentator, argues that the *Apologia* presents the opportunity for an interesting philosophical study by arguing that Newman's religious opinions are a coherent development of his adherence to "Berkleyan" metaphysical principles.[65] Alexander Campbell Fraser (1819–1914), "the leading Berkeley scholar of the nineteenth century" and editor of the *North British Review* (1850–57), read the *Apologia* closely.[66] In his intellectual autobiography *Biographia Philosophica* he describes Newman as one of his "heroes."[67] Fraser also discusses Newman's writing in relation to John Locke[68] and

---

unnoticed by later commentators. For further discussion, see Abbot, *The Anglican Career of Cardinal Newman*, 2:287–88; Cross, *John Henry Newman*, 30; Houghton, *The Art of Newman's Apologia*; Svaglic, "The Structure of Newman's Apologia," 138; Colby, "The Poetic Structure of Newman's Apologia Pro Vita Sua," 44–57; Connolly, "The Apologia: History, Rhetoric, and Literature," 105–24; Ker, *John Henry Newman*, 549; Jost, "On Concealment and Deception," 51–74; Kreller, "The New Rhetoric," 80–102; Boyce, *Mary*, 10; Ondrako, *Progressive Illumination*, 28; Lams, *The Rhetoric of Newman's Apologia*; Turner, "Newman," 130.

64. Cox, "Dr Newman's Apologia," 357–77.

65. "In Dr. Newman's case, we have a splendid instance over again of the power of a purely metaphysical notion once formed and dwelt in, to dominate a man's whole life, and determine the nature of his practical activity. Dr. Newman had apparently at no time of his life concerned himself with philosophy, except in and through Theology; but he tells us, in his Apologia Pro Vita Sua, how he recollects that from his very "boyhood he carried with him a certain constitutional frame or condition of mind, resembling, if I do not misinterpret his description of it, the Berkeleyan Idealism." Masson, *Recent British Philosophy*, 197–99.

66. McCracken, "Berkeley's Realism," 24–33; Fraser, *Biographia Philosophica*, 264.

67. "The atmosphere of Oxford in 1842 was densely charged with Newmanism, and the "Tracts" had formerly brought me for a time under this influence. Reverence led me to touch the hem of his academic robe. He was then living at Littlemore, and three years later he went over to Rome. I always regret that I missed an opportunity long years after of visiting him at Birmingham." Fraser was very conscious of Newman's absence from the metaphysical society. Fraser, *Biographia Philosophica*, 78, 97–98, 243.

68. Fraser, *Locke*, 139–40.

compares him with the eighteenth-century Scottish philosopher Thomas Reid (1710–96). He writes:

> Reid's appeal to divinely inspired data in what he called the "common sense" of mankind: now seen in the wider light of theistic philosophy, and not merely as inductive philosophy of mind in man. The theistic postulate on which human experience rests could be compared with Reid's dogmatic assumption of uncriticised "necessities to believe." His weapon for war against Hume, not unlike the *securus judicat orbis terrarium* (the deliberate judgment, in which the whole Church at length rests and acquiesces, is an infallible prescription and a final sentence against such portions of it as protest and secede. *Apol* 211), which in another interest was the watchword of Newman.[69]

Here Newman's discussion, in the *Apologia*,[70] of how the collective judgement of the Catholic Church is infallible is compared with Reid's conception of common sense.[71]

Newman's *Grammar of Assent* (1870), which provides a detailed account of why it may be deemed rational to believe propositions that fall short of demonstration, provoked considerable philosophical comment in the periodical press. This is indicated in an article published in the *Christian Observer* (1870):

> ... on hearing that Dr. Newman had written a work upon "Assent," we could not help fearing that it would be composed of ingenious arguments to prove the advisability of believing many things which were ill-supported and absurd; and after we had once succeeded in believing them, of never admitting a doubt about them in future .... [On the contrary] The work is thoroughly philosophical in every way ....[72]

While surprised by the rigour of the *Grammar*, this article clearly identifies the work as one that is "thoroughly philosophical in every way." The *Grammar of Assent* (1870) was described as a "philosophical" work by nineteenth-century periodicals in general.

The *Saturday Review, Fortnightly Review, Contemporary Review, Edinburgh Review, London Quarterly Review,* and the *Journal of the*

---

69. Fraser, *Biographia Philosophica*, 231.
70. Newman, *Apologia*, 211–12.
71. For further discussion, see Wolterstorff, *Thomas Reid*.
72. Unknown author, "Dr Newman's Grammar of Assent," 727.

Transactions of the Victoria Institute or Philosophical Society of Great Britain all describe the *Grammar* as a philosophical work. Nevertheless, these reviewers can be heavily critical of Newman's refusal to proportion assent to inference.[73] For example, in the *Fortnightly Review* the author and philosophical commentator[74] Leslie Stephen (1832–1904) describes Newman and John Stuart Mill as "the two greatest masters of philosophical English in recent times."[75] Nevertheless, while Stephen acknowledges Newman's contribution in this periodical, he is scathingly critical of the *Grammar*, a point well illustrated in his private correspondence:

> I finished old Newman's book [*Grammar*] coming down and as the book is too metaphysical to give you pleasure I will tell you what it comes to, it is an elaborate apology for the morality of persuading yourself that a thing is absolutely certain when you really know that it is not certain at all—e.g. for working yourself up to believe that I (L.S) am a gentleman when you have a strong reason for thinking that I am in the habit of picking pockets, telling lies and getting beastly drunk. This is supported by a lot of metaphysics [which] prove that Newman is grossly ignorant of modern reading. Why shouldn't I say that such a creature is a liar and that I despise him? I do most heartily.[76]

Though this extract is heavily critical, it is important to appreciate the fact that Stephen's contention that the *Grammar* is "too metaphysical" reveals as much about the presuppositions of this utilitarian commentator as it does about Newman.

As this survey of the nineteenth-century reception of Newman's publications comes to a close it is clear that the same motif persists. The above shows that throughout the nineteenth century Newman's writings were viewed as "philosophical" and were discussed and often critiqued by both philosophers and academics who wrote upon philosophical issues. Newman was not ignored by the philosophers of his day. While a number

---

73. Tulloch, "Dr Newman's Grammar of Assent," 382; Rigg, "Newman's Grammar of Assent," 363; Stephen, "Dr. Newman's Theory of Belief," 680–810; Fairbairn, "Catholicism and Religious Thought," 667–69; Row, "Dr. Newman's Essay in Aid of a Grammar of Assent," 60.

74. Leslie Stephen's most famous works concerning philosophical ideas include: *The History of English Thought in the Eighteenth Century*; *An Agnostic's Apology*; *The English Utilitarians*.

75. Stephen, "Dr. Newman's Theory of Belief," 680.

76. Letter sent to Anne Isabella Thackeray in April 1870. See: Bicknell, *Selected Letters of Leslie Stephen*, 81.

of writers were heavily critical of him, the idea that Newman was an ignored philosophical figure is not justified by the literature. Nevertheless, it is also clear that Newman's repeated attempts to justify Christian faith are frequently met with hostility because he does not proportion his beliefs in accordance with conventional forms of evidence. Having indicated that the empirical focus of nineteenth-century philosophy prevented Newman's contemporaries from appreciating the value of his proposals it is important, before proceeding to an analysis of his relationship to twentieth-century philosophy, to briefly examine the reasoning behind this negative reception.

The ethics of belief

Throughout the nineteenth century writers from a variety of disciplines emphasized the importance of proportioning one's beliefs, religious or otherwise, in accordance with the available evidence. The most famous advocate of this evidentialist[77] principle was the philosopher William K. Clifford (1845–79). In an article entitled "The Ethics of Belief" (1877) Clifford states that "it is wrong always, everywhere, and for anyone, to believe anything upon insufficient evidence."[78] The general popularity of this ethic of belief is indicated by its near omnipresence in nineteenth-century academic literature.[79] During the course of the century many writers used this criterion to challenge religious authority. For example, the philosopher Charles Barnes Upton (1831–1920) criticized "established religions" for their failure to conform to the standards of evidence appropriate to scientific understanding.[80] Utilitarian writers such as Bentham and Mill argued that religious doctrines were undermined by their failure to stand up to this principle.[81] Even biologists, such as Huxley and

77. Evidentialism is the position that a belief is only acceptable if it has decisive evidence in its support. Forrest, *The Epistemology of Religion*, §1.

78. Clifford, "The Ethics of Belief," 2:186.

79. For example, see Jamieson, *A Grammar Of Logic and Intellectual Philosophy*, 157; Davies, *An Estimate of the Human Mind*, 204–5; Taylor, *Elements of Thought*, 80; Flemming, *The Vocabulary of Philosophy*, 48; Mill, *On Liberty*, 37; Bain, *The Emotions and the Will*, 560. It should be noted here that although this view was dominant in the nineteenth century it was propounded much earlier by figures such as John Locke. For further discussion, see van Leeuwen, *The Problem of Certainty in English Thought*.

80. Upton, *Lectures on the Bases of Religious Belief*, 128–29.

81. Mill, *Three Essays on Religion*, 138–39. For further discussion, see Schofield, *Bentham*, 120.

Romanes, argued that this ethic of belief demonstrated the subjectivity of religious beliefs.[82]

The above indicates that the evidentialist ethic of belief, typified in Clifford's work, was widespread in Newman's lifetime. The survey of Newman's nineteenth-century philosophical reception, above, indicates that his works were repeatedly criticized for what commentators interpreted as his failure to abide by this rule. However, the precise manner in which he fell foul of this criterion is illustrated in the following extract from the philosopher John Beattie Crozier's (1849–1921) *Civilization and Progress* (1885):

> The degree of belief or assent we give to any proposition is strictly proportioned to the probabilities in its favour, and the evidence by which it is supported. Cardinal Newman contends, on the contrary, that there are no degrees to a man's, assent, and that it may be often yielded when the reasons adduced for the belief would be far from carrying conviction. Accordingly, in his Grammar of Assent, his first object is to get rid of Science as an instrument of the highest truth; and this being done to replace it by an instrument of his own, which shall command men's full conviction and assent . . . . The above is a rough outline of Cardinal Newman's doctrine of "assent," . . . by which he would replace and supersede Science as an organon or instrument of the highest truth. When thus plainly stated, its weakness and absurdity seem, to me at least, so palpable, that I should have passed it by unheeded, but for the great ability and eminence of the author, and the influence he exercises on all hands over men outside the Roman Catholic Communion—men . . . very glad of his assistance in beating off the atheist and infidel.[83]

Here, Crozier criticizes Newman for his refusal to proportion assent to a proposition to the evidence in its support. This, and the other criticisms surveyed above, illustrates the way in which the empirical focus of

---

82. Huxley, "Agnosticism and Christianity," 64; Romanes, *Darwin and after Darwin*, 6. Romanes writes: "Therefore, the difference between science and speculation is not a difference of spirit; nor, thus far, is it a difference of method. The only difference between them is in the subsequent process of verifying hypotheses. For while speculation, in its purest form, is satisfied to test her explanations only by the degree in which they accord with our subjective ideas of probability—or with the 'Illative Sense' of Cardinal Newman—science is not satisfied to rest in any explanation as final until it shall have been fully verified by an appeal to objective proof. This distinction is now so well and so generally appreciated that I need not dwell upon it."

83. Crozier, *Civilization and Progress*, 53, 70, 75.

nineteenth-century philosophy impacted upon Newman's philosophical reception. Newman's philosophical "isolation" was largely due to his divergence from the prevailing evidentialist current in nineteenth-century thought. Despite this, the above survey demonstrates that, although his work was often criticized, he was by no means absent from nineteenth-century philosophical discourse. As Crozier himself states: "the great ability and eminence of the author" meant that he could not be ignored.

Newman's Philosophical Reception in the Twentieth and Twenty-First Centuries

The history of twentieth- and twenty-first-century philosophy is difficult to narrate. Nevertheless, a number of writers have attempted to provide a history of this complex philosophical period. These include Paul Gomer's *Twentieth-Century German Philosophy* (2000), Avrum Stroll's *Twentieth-Century Analytic Philosophy* (2000), Tom Baldwin's *Contemporary Philosophy* (2001), Christian Delacampagne's *History of Philosophy in the Twentieth-Century* (2001), and Brian Shanley's *One Hundred Years of Philosophy* (2001). Though the efforts of these writers cannot be underplayed, Moran laments that there is, as yet, no integrated account connecting the different strands of philosophy during this period.[84] It may take several years before a comprehensive view of philosophy during the last hundred years can be properly formed. All this has implications for our understanding of Newman's philosophical reception.

One of the problems is the sheer increase in the number of professional philosophers during the course of the last century, not to mention the volume of their output. Though it is possible to obtain a reasonably clear picture of the philosophical movements active during the early 1900s, the contours of philosophical debate during the course of the century become increasing blurred. According to Moran, "there probably has never been a time when there have been so many professional philosophers at work in universities across the world."[85] Nevertheless, despite the difficulties this complexity creates for understanding Newman's philosophical reception, it is essential that the great diversity in this subject over the last century be kept in view. Therefore, where it is difficult to identify him with specific philosophical movements, Newman

---

84. Moran, "Towards an Assessment of Twentieth-Century Philosophy," 3.
85. Moran, "Towards an Assessment of Twentieth-Century Philosophy," 1–3.

will be discussed more generally in relation to the different disciplines within philosophy.

Newman, logical positivism, and linguistic philosophy

Earlier it was noted that Newman commentators believe that he has been neglected by professional philosophers during the twentieth century. Though they supply different reasons as to why they believe this to be the case they view the dominance of logical positivism in the early part of the twentieth century to be one of the main reasons for this neglect. The prevalence of logical positivism during this period in Anglophone philosophy as argued by Garcia:

> From the 1920s to the 1960s, large tracts of English-speaking philosophy laboured under the shadow of logical positivism and its verification criterion of meaning. Positivism is evidentialism for the twentieth-century; empirical certitude extends only to what is immediately presented to sense experience (sense-data), and statements that cannot be verified or falsified by such evidence are . . . meaningless.[86]

Thus, while in the nineteenth century Newman's philosophical reception was impaired by the ethic of belief typified in Clifford's work, Newman commentators consider that the prevalence of a different kind of evidentialism within linguistic philosophy, logical positivism, delayed Newman's recognition as a philosopher up until the late 1960s. Many view the posthumous publication of Ludwig Wittgenstein's *On Certainty* (1969), in which Wittgenstein cites an "H. Newman,"[87] as a turning point for Newman's philosophical recognition. For example, Cyril Barrett, a Roman Catholic philosopher who wrote extensively on Wittgenstein,[88] considers that: "since the appearance of that book in 1969 quite a number of papers on Newman as a philosopher, many of them comparing him

---

86. Garcia, "Catholic Philosophical Theology," 530.

87. In this work Wittgenstein writes: "1. If you do know that here is one hand, we'll grant you all the rest. When one says that such and such a proposition can't be proved, of course that does not mean that it can't be derived from other propositions; any proposition can be derived from other ones. But they may be no more certain than it is itself. (On this a curious remark by H. Newman.)" Wittgenstein, *On Certainty*, 3. The consensus among Newman scholars is that this reference is to John Henry Newman.

88. For further discussion, see Barrett, *Wittgenstein on Ethics and Religious Belief*.

with Wittgenstein, have appeared."[89] Though not all commentators mention Wittgenstein's reference to "H. Newman" it is implied by the fact that the date of this publication is often mentioned.[90]

In an article discussing "Newman as a Philosopher" (1990) Basil Mitchell argues that in the century following his death (1890) Newman has been seen as irrelevant to the dominant concerns of both British and Continental philosophy.[91] He indicates that the logical positivist tradition within British empiricist philosophy had "been predominantly hostile" to religious belief.[92] From this Mitchell concludes that Newman, and indeed the philosophy of religion in general, has not been of interest to professional philosophers; that is not until the late 1960s.[93]

One real weakness in Mitchell's analysis is that he only discusses Newman's philosophical reception within Europe. Antony Kenny's assessment of "Newman as a Philosopher of Religion" (1990) is broader in that he appears to take the analytic tradition within the United States more seriously. Nevertheless, he likewise believes that "in the analytic tradition, which is dominant here [in the UK] and in much of the United States"[94] Newman's work has had almost no "progeny" in the century after the publication of the *Grammar* (1870–1969). He also views Wittgenstein's reference to "H. Newman" in *On Certainty* as the turning point

---

89. Barrett, "Newman and Wittgenstein on the Rationality of Belief," 93.

90. Though logical positivism was severely undermined in the early 1950s by Willard Quine's (1908–2000) "Two Dogmas of Empiricism" (1951) and Wittgenstein's *Philosophical Investigations* (1953) commentators tend to focus on the publication date of *On Certainty* (1969). For further discussion, see Quine, "Two Dogmas of Empiricism," 20–47; Wittgenstein, *Philosophical Investigations*.

91. Mitchell, "Newman as a Philosopher," 241.

92. Another reason given by Mitchell is that the tendency toward idealism in continental philosophy detached Newman, who he describes as being "firmly rooted in the Empiricist tradition," from the affairs of European philosophers. Mitchell, "Newman as a Philosopher," 223.

93. Mitchell contends that: "For much of the period that has elapsed since his death it must have seemed that his predominant concerns were simply irrelevant to the development of philosophy. Philosophy of religion was itself increasingly peripheral to the interests of professional philosophers and, within the philosophy of religion, the central question was taken to be that of the meaning of theological utterances. The outstanding challenge to the whole theological enterprise was taken to consist in the problematic character of theological claims as judged by the standards of scientific thought [evidentialism]. Whether these were articulated crudely in terms of verifiability or in more sophisticated ways, it was generally taken for granted that theology could not satisfy them." Mitchell, "Newman as a Philosopher," 236–37.

94. Kenny, "Newman as a Philosopher of Religion," 98–100.

and considers that "in recent decades professional philosophers in the analytic tradition have become interested" in the issues that preoccupied Newman.[95]

Though Kenny's analysis appears to take more interest in developments within anglo-analytic philosophy it was noted in the introduction that Fergus Kerr is focused upon Newman's relationship to Oxford philosophy. Kerr argues that interest in Newman's work was eclipsed when Ayer began his tenure at Oxford (1959–78). Despite this, Kerr wonders why the demise of Ayer's positivism did not make Newman "a precursor of the many Oxford philosophers (not to mention Wittgenstein . . . and others elsewhere) who were resistant, precisely, to such verificationist scientism."[96] Though Kerr is correct to feel abashed at the disinterest in Newman by logical positivists—no mention is made of him in Moritz Schlick (1882–1936), Rudolf Carnap (1891–1970), or A. J. Ayer (1910–89)—it should be borne in mind that this bias is not against Newman but against *any* metaphysical orientation.[97] Moreover, Kerr's suggestion that after the decline of logical positivism Newman remained an isolated figure in philosophy is also incorrect. One example that disproves this assertion is that even in the debate surrounding the philosophy of language, the views of Newman are discussed.

A decade before Wittgenstein's reference to "H. Newman" in *On Certainty* (1969), the Oxford trained philosopher Ernest Gellner (1925–95) and critic of linguistic philosophy observed parallels between Newman's *Apologia* and Wittgenstein's approach to philosophy in his work *Words and Things* (1959).[98] As was noted above, since the publication of *On Certainty* comparisons between Wittgenstein and Newman have increased considerably. The philosopher Roy Lemoine argues that Wittgenstein's "understanding of certainty owes much to Newman's discussion of certitude" (1975).[99] The Oxford-trained philosopher of religion D. Z.

---

95. Kenny, "Newman as a Philosopher of Religion," 98–100.

96. Kerr, "Newman and Oxford Philosophy," 157–58.

97. In this regard Leslie Armour's (1931–), Professor in Philosophy at the University of Ottawa, comments concerning Ayer's *Dictionary of Philosophical Quotations* are telling, for this work not only fails to mention Newman but its obsession with recent developments in analytic philosopher leads Ayer to virtually ignore the British idealists and the Cambridge Platonists. Armour, Review of *Dictionary of Philosophical Quotations*, §1.

98. Gellner, *Words and Things*, 36–37.

99. Lemoine, *The Anagogic Theory of Wittgenstein's*, 13–14.

Phillips (1934–2006) contends that Newman anticipates Wittgenstein (1988).[100] The Scottish philosopher Duncan Pritchard goes further in his essay "Is 'God Exists' a Hinge Proposition" (2000) by suggesting that aspects of Newman's *Grammar* were "a major influence" on Wittgenstein's *On Certainty*.[101] Other writers, including Newman commentators, recognize parallels between these writers, including: Yearley,[102] Ferreira,[103] McCarthy,[104] McGuinness,[105] and Barrett.[106] Even if Wittgenstein "did not read" a word of Newman,[107] many philosophers have discussed Newman in relation to him. Newman has not been ignored by philosophers of language but has been a relevant dialogue partner for linguistic philosophers and their critics.[108]

The above indicates that Kerr's analysis betrays a narrow conception of the history of twentieth-century philosophy. Though Mitchell's analysis is wider than that of Kerr, and while Kenny's analysis is broader still, the analysis given by these writers is inadequate. The claim that Wittgenstein's reference to "H. Newman" in *On Certainty* (1969) acts as a turning point at which Newman began to be taken seriously by philosophers is problematic. First of all, there is uncertainty as to whether Wittgenstein is referring to John Henry Newman or to the Cambridge Mathematician, with whom Wittgenstein worked and argued, Maxwell Herman Newman

---

100. Phillips states that these writers are "as one" in that they reject the idea that "we posses a [basic] concept of reason which justifies all knowledge. Phillips, *Faith after Foundationalism*, 85.

101. Pritchard, "Is 'God Exists' a 'Hinge Proposition' of Religious Belief?" 132.

102. Yearley, *The Ideas of Newman*, 85 & 161n45.

103. Ferreira, *Doubt and Religious Commitment*, 69. Ferreira (a philosopher and Newman commentator) compares Wittgenstein's understanding of religious language with that of Newman.

104. McCarthy, "Newman and Wittgenstein: The Problem of Certainty," 98–120.

105. McGuinness, *Wittgenstein: a Life: young Ludwig 1889–1921*, 153.

106. Barrett argues that the "type of religious reasoning that Wittgenstein favours is very similar to that of John Henry Cardinal Newman in the Grammar of Assent." Barrett, "The Wittgensteinian Revolution," 67.

107. Uncertainty pervades the identity of Wittgenstein's reference to "H. Newman." Despite this a number of writers have attempted to bolster the suggestion that Newman influenced him through an appeal to the contradictory testimony of students, or professors, with whom Wittgenstein worked. For an example of the discrepancies between their accounts, see FitzPatrick, "Newman's Grammar and the Church Today," 128n1; Malcolm, *Ludwig Wittgenstein, A Memoir*, 59.

108. Both proponents and critics of linguistic philosophy cite Newman. For example, Mundle, *A Critique of Linguistic Philosophy*, 107. White, *Misleading Cases*, 129.

(1897–1984). Though Kienzler confidently asserts that any suggestion that the remark in *On Certainty* alludes to Max Newman is "excluded" by the use of the initial H.[109] it is just as possible for Wittgenstein to be referring to Maxwell "H. Newman" as to John "H. Newman." While commentators are correct that this reference has led to numerous comparisons between J. H. Newman and Wittgenstein—and has had a positive effect on Newman's philosophical reception—the uncertainty surrounding the identity of "H. Newman" makes it imprudent to view this reference as a basis for evaluating J. H. Newman's philosophical legacy.

Secondly, it is untrue to suggest that prior to Wittgenstein's *On Certainty* Newman was ignored by philosophers. While the influence of logical positivism and its significance for the philosophy of religion have been considerable,[110] it is demonstrable that Newman was discussed by a wide range of twentieth-century philosophers long before the demise of this form of evidentialism within linguistic philosophy. While Wittgenstein remains one of the most important figures in the history of twentieth-century philosophy, he is not the only philosopher. Important as they are, the history of twentieth-century philosophy cannot be confined to the history of logical positivism or the writings of Ludwig Wittgenstein. Thus, in order to provide an accurate account of Newman's philosophical reception it is essential that the great diversity in twentieth-century philosophy be kept in view. Though it may be too early to process the vast complexities of the last century of philosophical debate, it is possible to examine the way in which a wide variety of philosophers engage with Newman's work.

Newman and the dawn of pragmatism

The dawn of the twentieth century brought with it an attack on Clifford's evidentialist ethic of belief by the pragmatist[111] philosopher, based at Harvard University, William James (1842–1910). In his "Will to Believe" (1896) James argues that because human reasoning cannot be separated

---

109. Kienzler, "Wittgenstein and John Henry Newman on Certainty," 118n6.

110. Moran, "Towards an Assessment of Twentieth-Century Philosophy," 2.

111. In short pragmatists argue that the veracity of a philosophy, or a religion, is determined by its practical efficacy. For further discussion, see "Rescher, "Pragmatism," 710–11.

from passion our beliefs cannot be neatly proportioned in accordance with the available evidence.[112] He writes:

> When the Cliffords tell us how sinful it is to be Christians on such "insufficient evidence" insufficiency is really the last thing they have on their mind. For them the evidence is absolutely sufficient, only it makes the other way. They believe so completely in an anti-Christian order of the universe that there is no living option: Christianity is a dead hypothesis from the start. ... I myself find it impossible to go with Clifford. We must remember that these feelings of our duty about truth and error are in any case only expressions of our passional life. ... [H]e who says, "Better go without belief forever than believe a lie!" merely shows his own preponderant private horror of becoming a dupe. ... I have also a horror of being duped; but I can believe that worse things than being duped may happen to a man in this world.[113]

Here James concludes that the ethic of belief propounded by figures like Clifford is inconsistent because it is not proportional to the available evidence but is actually founded upon the natural inclinations of its author. What is of importance here is that James is highly appreciative of Newman's criticism of evidentialism.[114] In his *Varieties of Religious Experience* (1902) James numbers Newman alongside the philosophers: Zeno, Epicurus, Kant, and Schopenhauer.[115] Moreover, he cites Newman's *Discourses on the Scope and Nature of University Education* (1852) as an antecedent for his own position:

> [Newman's] test of the pretensions of philosophy to found religion on universal reason simplifies my procedure today.

---

112. James attempted to defend the right to believe in religious propositions. He did this by illustrating that: "Our passional nature not only lawfully may, but must, decide an option between propositions, whenever it is a genuine option that cannot by its nature be decided on intellectual grounds; for to say under such circumstances, 'Do not decide, but leave the question open,' is itself a passional decision, just like deciding yes or no, and is attended with the same risk of losing truth." James, "The Will to Believe," 11.

113. James, "The Will to Believe," 14, 18.

114. James, *The Varieties of Religious Experience*, 435.

115. James writes: "Think of Zeno and of Epicurus ... think of Kant and Schopenhauer, of Herbert Spencer and John Henry Newman." James, "The Moral Philosopher, and the Moral Life," 204.

I need not discredit philosophy by laborious criticism of its arguments.[116]

Here James indicates that Newman's writing illustrates the fallacy of the evidentialist principles typified in Clifford's ethic of belief which base religious belief upon supposed universal conceptions of reason. James's considers that Newman's achievements in this domain mean that he himself need not work hard to discredit this belief. This suggests that Newman's contribution to James's pragmatism is significant. James's appreciation is also reflected by the fact that many of his pupils at Harvard, though not all pragmatists, refer to Newman as will be indicated in subsequent sections.

Outside of Harvard, Newman was also recognized as an important thinker by pragmatists. James's colleague F. C. S. Schiller (1864–1937), the Oxford philosopher mentioned in the introduction, claims that Newman's challenge to the notion that reason can remain detached from one's emotional temper paved the way for his and James's pragmatism. John Dewey (1859–1952), a pragmatist based in Chicago, also cites Newman. For example, in his Gifford lectures (1928–29), later published as *The Quest for Certainty* (1929), Dewey cites Newman in order to illustrate the difference between ancient Greek and Christian conceptions of morality.[117] Here he also cites Newman's explanation of the problem of evil:

> There are many versions of this doctrine. The simplest, though not the one which has most commended itself to most philosophers, is the idea of the "fall of man," a fall which, in the words of Cardinal Newman, has implicated all creation in an aboriginal catastrophe.[118]

Later Dewey uses Newman's position in order to illustrate its distinction from that of philosophical *Naturalism* (1940).[119] These references indicate that on a number of occasions Dewey uses Newman in order to illustrate philosophical points. At the very least this indicates that Dewey did not ignore Newman but was aware of his writings. Moreover, like James, Dewey appears to be genuinely impressed with "Cardinal Newman's," *Discourses on the Scope and Nature of University Education* which he describes as "one of the few educational books of the world which are

---

116. James, *The Varieties of Religious Experience*, 436–37.
117. Dewey, *The Quest for Certaint*, 51, 300.
118. Dewey, *The Quest for Certainty*, 51, 300.
119. Dewey, *Naturalism and the Human Spirit*, 14.

neither priggish nor impractical" (1890).[120] The educationalist Malcolm Skilbeck goes further when he suggests that Newman's model of university education may have shaped Dewey's thinking. He states that while "theology had been to Newman the 'Queen of the Sciences,' so scientific studies were given pride of place in Dewey's curriculum."[121] From this it would appear that Newman's work was appreciated by some of the most important pragmatists writing at the beginning of the twentieth century.

This single aspect of Newman's philosophical reception makes it difficult to see why Newman commentators think that his philosophical contribution has been ignored. Throughout the twentieth century, up until the present day, Newman's writings have continued to be discussed in connection with pragmatism: Inge (1909),[122] Keary (1910),[123] Kauffman (1922),[124] Passmore (1957),[125] Rorty (1982),[126] Oppenheim (1987),[127] Wainwright (1995),[128] and Murray (2004).[129] Newman commentators have also examined his similarities with this philosophical movement, including: Gundersen (1952),[130] Hollis (1967),[131] Ferreira (1988),[132] Cosgrove (1995),[133] and Sands (2004).[134] However, although many of these studies discuss Newman's parallels with James's pragmatism they do not mention Dewey's reception of him. In addition, these writers have failed to explore the significance of James's reception of Newman for the development of Harvard philosophy. The recognition of Newman by prominent

---

120. Dewey, "A College Course: What Should I Expect from It?" 28–29. Dewey also cites Newman in his *Lectures in the Philosophy of Education*, 123.

121. Skilbeck, *John Dewey*, 24. For further discussion, see Handschy, "Educational Theories of Cardinal Newman and John Dewey," 129–37.

122. Inge, *Faith and its Psychology*, 234–35.

123. Keary, *The Pursuit of Reason*, 55–56, 83.

124. Kauffman, "The Religion of John Burroughs," 151.

125. Passmore, *A Hundred Years of Philosophy*, 100–101.

126. Rorty, "Keeping Philosophy Pure," 21.

127. Oppenheim, *Royce's Mature Philosophy of Religion*, 376.

128. Wainwright, *Reason and the Heart*, 152.

129. Murray, *Reason, Truth, and Theology in Pragmatist Perspective*, 142.

130. Gundersen, *Cardinal Newman and Apologetics*, 131.

131. Hollis, *Newman and The Modern World*, 181.

132. Ferreira, "Newman and William James on Religious Experience: The Theory and the Concrete," 45.

133. Cosgrove, "We Cannot Do without a View," 32–43.

134. Sands, *The Justification of Religious*, 1.

philosophical figures like Dewey and James has wider implications. For example, Dewey's pupil William Barrett (1913–92), Professor of Philosophy in New York (1950–79), cites Newman on a number of occasions.[135] In fact, a wide range of philosophers who studied under James at Harvard refer to Newman.

Newman, Harvard philosophy, and beyond

The influence of Francis Bowen

A number of philosophers educated at Harvard in the late nineteenth and early twentieth centuries engaged with Newman's work. Their appreciation is possibly due to the high estimation given to him by James and also by his tutor Francis Bowen (1811–90). Bowen writes:

> Newman, in his "Grammar of Assent," has admirably illustrated the truth, that Assent and conduct, which is merely practical Assent to the Reasons for such conduct, are not necessarily determined by inferences.[136]

In his article on "Harvard Philosophy," in *The Oxford Companion to Philosophy*, Quinton describes Bowen as the "first capable Harvard philosopher."[137] According to Quinton, the philosophers "C. S. Peirce, William James, and their early associate Chauncey Wright were all Bowen's pupils."[138] Whether or not Bowen is responsible for James's appreciation for Newman, it remains clear that soon after its publication the *Grammar of Assent* was required reading for students studying in the philosophy department at Harvard (1872).[139] It is documented that

---

135. Though it is not clear that Barrett upheld pragmatist views. Barrett, *Time of Need: Forms of Imagination in the Twentieth-Century*, 295; Barrett, *The Truants: Adventures among the Intellectuals*, 180; Barrett, *Death of the Soul: From Descartes to the Computer*, 18.

136. Bowen, *Modern Philosophy: From Descartes to Schopenhauer and Hartmann*, 169, 220.

137. Quinton, "Harvard Philosophy," 335–36.

138. Quinton, "Harvard Philosophy," 335–36. Though Peirce doesn't mention Newman, Chauncey Wright (1830–75) was aware of Newman's conception of the different forms of reason operative in science and religion. Wright, "The Genesis of Species," 77.

139. Harvard University, *A Catalogue of the Officers and Students of Harvard University for the Academical Year 1871–1872*, 43.

several of James's pupils discuss Newman's writing. Therefore, even if Quinton and Kerr were correct about Newman's "isolation" at Oxford it is apparent that several prominent Harvard philosophers recognized the importance of Newman's contribution and that several of their pupils were introduced to his writing.

Newman and new realism

A number of James's students became part of the new realism philosophical movement emanating from Harvard. Essentially these philosophers argued that "direct perception furnished true knowledge."[140] Of importance here is that several of these philosophers engaged with Newman's work. James's pupil Ralph Barton Perry (1876–1957), who became a leading figure in the new realism movement at Harvard, commends Newman's distinction between science and religion:

> It is true that the believer's assurance is not consciously rational. ... Cardinal Newman fairly expressed the difference between the method of religion and the method of science when he said that "ten thousand difficulties do not make one doubt," that "difficulty and doubt are incommensurate."[141]

Here Perry, contrary to evidentialists like Clifford, argues that religious believers do not need to be conscious of the reasons for their beliefs, and cites Newman as an example of this view. James's pupil, and Harvard graduate, the New Realist William Pepperell Montague (1873–1953)[142] also discusses Newman's response to religious skepticism in his *The Ways of Knowing Or the Methods of Philosophy* (1925).[143] The recognition of Newman's thought by New Realist philosophers exceeds Harvard-trained philosophers. The New Realist philosopher Walter Marvin (1872–1945), based at Rutgers University, mentioned Newman in his *History of*

---

140. Reck, "Walter Taylor Marvin," 1630–31. New realism rejected the idea that we cannot know reality as it really is in itself. It thus rejected the idea that in perception, that which is perceived is separate from the object in itself. Holt, *The New Realism*, 277. For further discussion, see Beck, "New Realism," 618.

141. Perry, *The Moral Economy*, 220–21.

142. Montague was also connected with the "new realism" movement. Beck, "New Realism," 618.

143. Montague, *The Ways of Knowing Or the Methods of Philosophy*, 218–19.

42   NEWMAN IN THE STORY OF PHILOSOPHY

European Philosophy (1917) and described him as a "great English thinker."[144] The above indicates that Newman was discussed by proponents of an important philosophical movement originating in Harvard at the beginning of the twentieth century.

Newman and critical realism

Opponents of new realism also recognized Newman's contribution. For example, in contrast to "New" and other earlier forms of direct realism, critical realists acknowledged that the world is perceived through representations.[145] What is interesting here is that the majority of its early proponents discuss Newman. With the exception of Arthur K. Rogers (1868–1936), who did his doctoral research with John Dewey in Chicago,[146] all of these were trained at Harvard under William James. For example, James's pupil James Bissett Pratt (1875–1944) refers to Newman's sermons in his work *Adventures in Philosophy and Religion* (1931).[147] Durant Drake (1878–1933) compares Newman with Immanuel Kant in *Problems of Conduct* (1921).[148] Arthur Oncken Lovejoy (1873–1962) contrasts Newman's philosophical position with scientific materialism.[149] George Santayana (1863–1952) refers to Newman on several occasions[150] and indicates in his correspondence that he had read most of Newman's writings.[151] Finally Roy Wood Sellars (1880–1973) discusses Newman's relationship to the Catholic Modernists.[152] The above reinforces the idea

144. Though Marvin was not trained at Harvard it is possible that his connection with James" pupils, Perry and Montague exposed him to Newman's ideas. Marvin, *The History of European Philosophy*, 370.

145. Beck, "Critical Realism," 171. For further discussion, see Drake, *Essays in Critical Realism*.

146. Reck, "Arthur Kenyon Rogers," 2067.

147. Pratt, *Adventures in Philosophy and Religion*, 163; Pratt, *Reason in the Art of Living*, 9.

148. Drake, *Problems of Conduct*, 100. He also cites Newman's *Certain Difficulties* and his *Apologia*. For further discussion, see Drake, *Problems of Religion*, 212, 251.

149. Lovejoy, *Essays in the History of Ideas*, 232.

150. Santayana, *Some Turns of Thought in Modern Philosophy: Five Essays*, 50; Santayana, *Winds of Doctrine: Studies in Contemporary Opinion*, 189; Santayana, *The Idea of Christ in the Gospels*, 18. Santayana, *The Works of George Santayana*, 6:169.

151. In his correspondence Santayana indicates that he had read "most of Newman." Holzberger, *The Letters of George Santayana: Book Seven*, 93.

152. Sellars, *The Next Step in Religion*, 182; Sellars, *Religion Coming of Age*, 127.

that James's favorable reception of Newman impacted upon his students. The same also appears to be true of Dewey whose pupil, the critical realist A. K. Rogers, goes so far as to liken his philosophical position with that of Newman.[153]

Though Rogers cannot be described as a Harvard philosopher, his estimation of Newman appears to be quite significant. For example, in an article in *The Journal of Philosophy Psychology and Scientific Methods* on "Belief and the Criterion of Truth" (1916), Rogers likens his own approach to Newman's *Grammar of Assent*. He states that:

> Truth for me is that which I can not help believing.... We have, in other words, to start with the psychological existence of a certain peculiar attitude of mind, not with a reasoned definition or an objective fact. We have the belief before the question of truth arises at all, and we have to go back to the fact of belief to determine whether any truth is left at the end of the inquiry.... [M]y position here is very similar, up to a point, to that of Newman in his "Grammar of Assent"; the disclaimer will rule out, however, certain uses to which Newman puts his theory which are plainly illegitimate.[154]

In beginning with the propositions he cannot help believing it is clear that Rogers's position is the reverse of evidentialism, which demands sufficient evidence prior to the acceptance of a proposition. This interpretation of Rogers's reading of Newman is supported by an earlier essay in the *Philosophical Review* (1904) in which Rogers states that:

> Great changes in belief, epochs in our intellectual history, are seldom due primarily to mere argument, but, rather, to the half unconscious ripening of experience, the transforming, and suffusing with new meaning, of the old facts, brought about by processes lying back of anything we can put, at the time, in syllogistic form. What Newman says of his own development is true normally: "For myself, it was not logic that carried me on; as well might one say that the quick-silver in a barometer changes the weather. It is the concrete being that moves; paper logic is but the record of it."[155]

---

153. Rogers, "Rationality and Belief," 44.
154. Rogers, "Belief and the Criterion of Truth," 393–94, 406n2.
155. Rogers, "Rationality and Belief," 44.

These references indicate that Rogers, whose work contrasts sharply with the evidentialism of figures like Clifford, offers yet another example of a philosopher who recognized Newman's contribution to philosophy.

From this it is already apparent that Newman's work is appreciated by three important philosophical movements originating in Harvard at the dawn of the twentieth century. Though the impact of Bowen and James's appreciation for Newman may never be fully known, it is clear that, even if he were an "isolated" philosophical figure elsewhere, Newman's philosophical legacy was not underestimated by several philosophers connected with Harvard, and their colleagues in other institutions at the start of the twentieth century. Moreover, the arrival in Harvard (1924) of a philosopher trained in a Cambridge (UK) far away from Massachusetts ensured that Newman continued to be an important person of interest in Harvard philosophy; though it is clear that this appreciation had nothing to do with either Bowen or James.

Newman and process philosophy

The great British Cambridge mathematician and process philosopher Alfred North Whitehead (1861–1947) refers to Newman frequently. His friend and colleague Bertrand Russell recounts that "as a young man, [Whitehead] was all but converted to Roman Catholicism by the influence of Cardinal Newman."[156] After a period of agnosticism (1890–1912) Whitehead later embraced theism.[157] Whitehead's interest in theism grew during his time as Professor at Harvard (1924–37).[158] Whether being in Harvard reawakened Whitehead's interest in Newman, or not, it is documented that during this period he cites Newman several times. For example, in his Lowell Lectures (1925), published in his *Science and the Modern World*—a "landmark in the history of philosophy,"[159] Whitehead indicates his hope of a conciliation between science and religion and affirms Newman's understanding of theological development.[160] Moreover, in his work on the *Adventures of Ideas* (1933), he commends the conclusion of Newman's *Grammar of Assent, non in dialectica complacuit*

---

156. Russell, *Portraits from Memory: and Other Essays*, 103.
157. Ford, *The Emergence of Whitehead's Metaphysics*, 103.
158. Kuklick, *A History of Philosophy in America 1720–2000*, 225.
159. Whitehead, *Alfred North Whitehead: An Anthology*, 361.
160. Whitehead, *Science and the Modern World*, 115, 255.

Deo salvum facere populum, as "the motto of every metaphysician"[161] and acknowledges the seminal importance of Newman's *Essay on the Development of Doctrine* for his understanding of the development of ideas.[162] Barrett[163] argues that Newman's ideas on development are like a "clerical" undercurrent within Whitehead's work.[164] Barrett believes that Whitehead's proposals could have accommodated Newman's ideas more fully were he born a "generation earlier."[165] Whether or not this would have been the case, Barrett's observations indicate that Newman's work shaped Whitehead's ideas.

Whitehead's doctoral student, the Harvard-trained philosopher Charles Hartshorne (1897–2000), also refers to Newman.[166] For example, Hartshorne's book *Man's Vision of God and the Logic of Theism* (1941), which applies Whitehead's work on metaphysics to the subject of theology, quotes this extract from Newman's Dublin University Sermons (1856–57):

> Order and harmony must be of His very essence. To be many and distinct in His attributes, yet, after all, to be but one,—to be sanctity, justice, truth, love, power, wisdom, to be at once each of these as fully as if He were nothing but it, as if the rest were not,—this implies in the Divine Nature an infinitely sovereign and utterly incomprehensible order, which is an attribute as wonderful as any, and the result of all the others. He is an infinite law, as well as an infinite power, wisdom, and love. Moreover, the very idea of order implies the idea of the subordinate. If order exists in the Divine Attributes, they must have relations one to another, and though each is perfect in itself, it must act so as not to impair the perfection of the rest, and must seem to yield to the rest on particular occasions. . . . There is an understanding between attribute and attribute, so that one does not interfere with the other, for each is supreme in its own sphere; and thus an infinitude of infinities, acting each in its own order, are combined together in the infinitely simple unity of God.[167]

---

161. "It is not by Logic that it has pleased God to bring about the salvation of his people." Whitehead, *Adventures of Ideas*, 294.

162. Whitehead, *Adventures of Ideas*, 7.

163. Dewey's pupil mentioned above.

164. Barrett, *Illusion Of Technique*, 6.

165. Barrett, *Illusion Of Technique*, 6.

166. Hartshorne, *Man's Vision of God*, 218.

167. *OS*, 184–85.

Reflecting on this passage from Newman's sermon Hartshorne argues that "Cardinal Newman" illustrates the way in which "variety" may be imputed to God "without departing" from traditional conceptions which hold that God is "in all respects absolutely perfect or unsurpassable, in no way and in no respect surpassable or perfectible."[168] Hartshorne's use of this passage indicates that the way in which Newman understands "perfection" and "change" anticipates certain aspects of process theism, which holds that divine perfection does not necessitate divine immutability.[169]

Newman is also cited by the Harvard-trained process philosopher Paul Weiss (1901–2002), another of Whitehead's doctoral students. In his work *Philosophy in Process* (1964), Weiss states that he has "only one objection to Cardinal Newman: he writes like an archbishop. By turns he is solid, stolid, and tedious, as if he were hoping to be made a Cardinal."[170] Weiss presents yet another example of a Harvard-trained philosopher who was aware of Newman's work. Moreover, though Whitehead, Hartshorne, and Weiss differ from Newman theologically they view him as an important interlocutor in the history of process philosophy.

Newman and other Harvard philosophers

Before closing this section on Newman and Harvard philosophy, it is important to note that several other Harvard trained philosophers discuss Newman's work. In *A Philosophy of the Real and the Possible* (1954) the philosopher Harry Todd Costello (1885–1960), who studied under Josiah Royce at Harvard (1909–11), expresses his admiration for Newman's "*Grammar of Assent*," even though he does "not agree with the conclusion at all."[171] Whitehead's doctoral student, the Harvard-trained social philosopher and behaviorist, B. F. Skinner (1904–90) cites Newman in his work *Contingencies of Reinforcement* (1969).[172] Whitehead's pupil Donald Cary Williams (1899–1983), who studied (1928) and taught philosophy at Harvard (1939–67), discusses Newman's *Apologia*

---

168. Hartshorne, *Man's Vision of God*, 11, 218.

169. Hartshorne, *Man's Vision of God*, 218. This is not to suggest that Newman would condone the conclusions of process theology.

170. Weiss, *Philosophy in Process*, 3:129.

171. Costello, *A Philosophy of the Real*, 6. For further discussion, see Kallen and Hook, *American Philosophy Today and Tomorrow*, 100.

172. Skinner, *Contingencies of Reinforcement*, 279.

in relation to philosophical "Personalism" (see below) in his book *Principles of Empirical Realism* (1966).[173] In *Reason, Truth and History* (1981) Hilary Putnam (1926–2016), whose doctoral studies were undertaken at Harvard, describes Newman as a "careful and responsible thinker" and contrasts his conception of rationality with the work of Rudolf Carnap.[174] Finally, William's doctoral student at Harvard, the philosopher Roderick Chisholm (who will be discussed in detail in subsequent chapters) discusses Newman's work. Though the positions taken by these writers differ, their references to Newman demonstrate that he continued to be read by philosophers trained at Harvard throughout the twentieth century.

In summary, it seems that Newman's ideas and writings have a large number of connections with philosophy at Harvard during the first half of the twentieth century. This is not universally the case—it is important to acknowledge, for example, that Clarence Lewis (1883–1964) one of the most significant philosophers to be trained (1910) and teach (1920–53) at Harvard during this time appears to make no mention of Newman. One possible reason for this is that Lewis's proposals had similarities with the logical positivists. Similarly, Lewis's pupil, and successor, W. V. Quine (1908–2000; Harvard professor 1956–78) also makes no mention of Newman. However, while this may appear to support the view that the rise of logical positivism had a detrimental impact upon Newman's philosophical reception, the analysis of Newman's philosophical reception above demonstrates that throughout Lewis's time (1920–69) Newman was viewed as a relevant dialogue partner for a number of philosophers and philosophical movements connected with Harvard. Moreover these were not the only professional philosophers to appreciate Newman in this regard.

Newman and Boston personalism

Another manifestation of Newman's philosophical reception is his connection with the early proponents of American personalism; an approach to philosophy that involves the "general affirmation of the centrality of the person for philosophical thought."[175] Like the pragmatists mentioned

---

173. Williams, *Principles of Empirical Realism: Philosophical Essays*, 168.

174. Putnam, *Reason Truth and History*, 136, 163.

175. "Personalists believe that the human person should be the ontological and epistemological starting point of philosophical reflection. They are concerned to

earlier, this philosophical position challenged the notion that beliefs must be justified by a direct awareness of the evidence in their favor and instead argued that beliefs are the result of a complex interaction of all our faculties: will, feeling, and reason.[176] Led by Borden Parker Bowne (1856-1910), personalism flourished in the early twentieth century at Boston University. What is interesting here is that Bowne[177] and many of his students refer to Newman, including: Francis McConnell (1871-1953),[178] Edgar Sheffield Brightman (1884-1953), George Albert Coe (1861-1951),[179] and Ralph T. Flewelling (1871-1960).[180] For example, in an article published in the *Personalist*, a journal founded by Flewelling which served as a platform for American personalism, Brightman states that:

> In its logical use, the word "personalism" is equivalent to the humanistic form of pragmatism for which not reason alone, but the whole personal life with all its needs, is the guide to truth. It is a reaction against the rigor and vigor of absolutism as well as against the vague excesses of mysticism.... "[P]ersonalism" is an empirical method, aiming at practical certainty; Cardinal Newman's Grammar of Assent illustrates it.[181]

Here Brightman argues that Newman's *Grammar* articulates a form of philosophical "personalism" because he argues that the whole person "not reason alone" is the guide to truth. Here then is another example of the way in which Newman's rejection of the notion that truth is obtained solely through a rationalist criteria of evidence is appreciated by philosophers during the twentieth century.[182]

---

investigate the experience, the status, and the dignity of the human being as person, and regard this as the starting-point for all subsequent philosophical analysis." Williams, *Personalism*, §4.

176. Caldecott, *Philosophy of Religion in England*, 80.

177. Bowne, "Cardinal Newman and Science," 1401-2. Here Bowne also defends Newman's conversion from Anglicanism to Catholicism.

178. McConnell, *The Increase of Faith*, 159; *Public Opinion and Theology*, 42.

179. Coe, *The Religion of a Mature Mind*, 87.

180. Flewelling, *Winds of Hiroshima*, 49.

181. Brightman, "The Use of the Word Personalism," 257.

182. In another article in this same issue of this journal Newman's *Grammar* is credited with articulating "William James" theory of the Will to Believe ... long before James analyzed it." Kauffman, "The Religion of John Burroughs," 151.

Several Newman commentators recognize parallels between Newman's proposals and personalism. These include: Sillem (1969),[183] Crosby (1996; 2004),[184] Dulles (2005),[185] Connolly (2005),[186] and Norris (2009).[187] Unfortunately these particular writers do not explore Newman's connection with early proponents of this approach such as Bowne or the other Boston personalists mentioned above who engaged with Newman's work. At this stage a pattern begins to emerge within Newman scholarship. Though commentators frequently draw parallels with Newman and a particular philosophical figure or movement, they often fail to realize that Newman is discussed by the founders of these approaches to philosophy. This pattern recurs in discussions concerning Newman and phenomenology.

The phenomenologist reception of Newman

Another example of the failure of Newman commentators to properly explore his reception by philosophers is his connection with phenomenology. Although Newman scholars find similarities between his work and the phenomenological movement, his connection with Franz Brentano (1838–1917), a forerunner of phenomenology, is neglected. Brentano visited Newman at the Birmingham Oratory (1872).[188] It is clear that he had read Newman because his publication on *The Origin of Right and Wrong* (1889) describes the *Grammar* as an "interesting work . . . scarcely noticed in Germany."[189] While Brentano uses the term "phenomenology"[190] it is his pupil Edmund Husserl (1859–1938) who is credited with founding this philosophical movement. While Husserl makes no mention of Newman, Husserl's associate, the phenomenologist Max Scheler (1874–1928), makes references to Newman in *Formalism*

---

183. *PN*, 1:19.

184. John Crosby has indicated parallels between Newman and personalism. For further discussion, see Crosby, *The Selfhood of the Human Person*, 51–60; Crosby, *Personalist Papers*, 221–42.

185. Dulles, *John Henry Newman*, 44.

186. Connolly, *John Henry Newman*, 142.

187. Norris, "Faith," 90.

188. Spiegelberg and Schuhmann, *The Phenomenological Movement*, 27–31. Also see LD 26:xiii, 81, 89–91.

189. Brentano, *The Origin of our Knowledge*, 52.

190. Brentano, *Descriptive Psychology*, 137.

and *Ethics* (1913),[191] *Person and Self Value* (1921),[192] and in his essays gathered together as *On the Eternal in Man* (1916–20), which illustrate his engagement with Newman.[193] All of this indicates that Newman's philosophical contribution was appreciated by the early phenomenologists.[194]

It is unfortunate that Newman commentators tend to overlook Brentano's reception[195] of Newman altogether, for example: Boekraad (1955 and 1961),[196] Walgrave (1960 and 1972),[197] Zeno (1965),[198] Pailin (1969),[199] Sillem (1969),[200] Artz (1976),[201] Hammond (1988),[202] Wainwright (2005),[203] Nichols (2006),[204] and Ekeh (2008).[205] While ignorance of Brentano's exposure to Newman's writings might be excused, Laurence Richardson's examination of Newman's *Approach to Knowledge* (2007) mistakenly argues that Newman's thinking was not known by German philosophers like "Brentano." Richardson goes so far as to declare that "no case can be made for thinking that Newman played any direct part whatsoever in the development of this movement."[206] This is odd when

191. Scheler, *Formalism in Ethics*, 231.

192. Scheler, *Person and Self-value*, 151.

193. Scheler, *On the Eternal in Man*, 235, 276, 284, 441.

194. Following on from this, the German theologian and Newman commentator, Erich Przywara (1889–1972) compared Newman's writings with those of Scheler. Przywara, *Religionsbegrundung-Max Scheler-J. H. Newman*. The phenomenologist Karol J'osef Wojtyla, later John Paul II (1920–2005), refers to Scheler and Newman in his writings. Köchler outlines Wojtyla's position as a realist phenomenology: Köchler, "The Phenomenology of Karol Wojtyla," 326–34. For further a discussion of John Paul II's approach to philosophy, see Buttiglione, *Karol Wojtyla*. Also, see Wojtyla, *Valutazioni Sulla Possibilitá Di Costruire L'ética Cristiana*; "Fides et Ratio," 849–915.

195. Despite this, there is a general awareness of Newman's influence on Scheler.

196. Boekraad, *The Personal Conquest of Truth*, 137–44, 139; Boekraad, *The Argument from Conscience*, 154.

197. Walgrave, *Newman the Theologian*, 89; Walgrave, "Religious Experience through Conscience," 110.

198. Zeno, "An Introduction to Newman's Grammar of Assent," 390.

199. Pailin, *The Way to Faith*, 172.

200. *PN*, 1:233.

201. Artz, "Newman as a Philosopher," 283.

202. Hammond, "Imagination in Newman's Phenomenology of Cognition," 21–32.

203. Wainwright, *Religion and Morality*, 30.

204. Nichols, *Scattering the Seed*, 199.

205. Ekeh, "The Phenomenological Context and Transcendentalism of John Henry Newman and Edmund Husserl," 35.

206. Richardson, *Newman's Approach to Knowledge*, 160, 170.

one considers the references that Brentano and indeed Scheler make to Newman's writing. What is even more surprising is that Richardson continues his discussion of *Newman's Approach to Knowledge* with the triumphant declaration that parallels between Newman's thinking and that of the phenomenologists give him "a definite place in the history of contemporary philosophy."[207] As pointed out by the philosopher John Crosby, in the introduction to Richardson's own book: "Scheler was well aware of Newman."[208] Here again it is apparent that while Newman commentators are keen to identify him with a philosophical school it is also clear that they underestimate his direct connection to it.

Newman and other philosophers

Aside from the pragmatist, personalist, or phenomenologist streams of Newman's philosophical reception mentioned above it is demonstrable that, throughout the twentieth century, philosophers from a variety of different disciplines, take an interest in Newman's work. Unfortunately, the richness of twentieth-century philosophical history makes it difficult to assemble the many philosophers who refer to Newman into specific groups. According to Moran:

> Philosophy does seem to have undergone enormous changes in the course of the century, but it also has diversified into many different and competing forms. New disciplines have emerged: from mathematical logic and meta-ethics to philosophy of language, philosophy of mind, and philosophy of psychology: from philosophy of gender and embodiment to environmental philosophy.[209]

The above indicates that a miscellany of different approaches to philosophy have emerged during the last century. This makes an integrated view of Newman's relationship to the different philosophical movements operative during this period difficult to obtain. Nevertheless, it remains the case that the philosophers who do refer to his writings must be documented if Newman's philosophical legacy is to be properly understood. Though it may be difficult to aggregate the array of philosophers who refer to him into coherent philosophical movements, it is still important

207. Richardson, *Newman's Approach to Knowledge*, 160, 170.
208. Crosby, "Introduction," viii.
209. Moran, "Towards an Assessment of Twentieth-Century Philosophy," 1–3.

that these philosophers are mentioned. However, in order to retain a degree of clarity these philosophers will be grouped using their respective branch of philosophy, including: philosophers of education, political philosophers, moral philosophers, and philosophers of religion.

Philosophy of education

Newman's reflections on education have been read by several philosophers. For example, the German philosopher, Karl Jaspers (1883–1969), cites Newman in his discussion of university education *Die Idee der Universität* (1923).[210] In the 1940s Newman's conception of education was discussed in the periodical *Philosophy* (1943).[211] In his work *Education at the Crossroads* (1943) the Catholic philosopher Jacques Maritain (1882–1973) affirms Newman's contention that if there is a God a university cannot be a university if it does not teach theology.[212] Paul Schilpp (1897–1993) discusses Newman's theory of education in his analysis of *The Philosophy of Sarvepalli Radhakrishnan* (1952).[213] The philosopher Martha C. Nussbaum (1947–) cites Newman in her discussion of university education (1997).[214] In an article on "Sidgwick as Philosopher, Professor, and Public Moralist" Stefan Collini contrasts Newman's understanding of education with that of Henry Sidgwick (2001).[215] Anthony O'Hear (1942–), Professor of Philosophy and Head of the Department of Education at the University of Buckingham, refers to Newman in his work *Philosophy in the New Century* (2001).[216] Finally, Gordon Graham, editor of the *Journal of Scottish Philosophy*, cites Newman in *The Institution of Intellectual Values: Realism and Idealism in Higher Education* (2005):

> Newman is one of very few attempts ever made to think directly about the nature and purpose of University. Given the age of the

---

210. Jaspers, *The Idea of the University*, 9.
211. Inge, "The Philosophy of the Wolf State," 9.
212. Maritain, *Education at the Crossroads*, 51, 76, 82.
213. Schilpp, *The Philosophy of Sarvepalli Radhakrishnan*, 325.
214. Nussbaum, *Cultivating Humanity*, 265.
215. Collini, "My Roles and Their Duties," 22–23.
216. O'Hear, *Philosophy in the New Century*, 156. This philosopher also discusses Newman in other publications: O'Hear, *Experience, Explanation, and Faith*, 16–17, 252; O'Hear, *The Landscape of Humanity: Art, Culture and Society*, 144, 148.

> institution, and its importance to the intellectual and cultural life of this country over many centuries, this is a remarkable fact. . . . [Despite] important differences between Newman's time and ours, The Idea of a University (especially Discourses V, VI and VII) still has things to say that are relevant to thinking about contemporary universities.[217]

This relatively recent assessment of Newman indicates that his work continues to offer a "relevant" contribution to contemporary discussions on the theory of education. Moreover, it is clear that, throughout the century, those reflecting philosophically upon education have found Newman to be a relevant dialogue partner.

Political philosophers

A small number of political philosophers also discuss Newman's work. For example, the prominent Oxford philosopher Isaiah Berlin (1909–97) cites Newman in his classic work *Four Essays on Liberty* (1969).[218] The French Philosopher Louis Althusser (1918–90) also mentions Newman in his work *L'Avenir Dure Longtemps* (1992).[219] Finally, Gillian Rose (1947–95), former Professor of Social and Political Thought in Warwick, recognizes the truth of Newman's contention that the removal of theology from public discourse will lead to other disciplines usurping its place. She considers that in this respect Newman anticipates the conclusions of postmodern thinkers such as John Milbank (1952–).[220] To summarize, it seems that although Newman's writing has sparked less interest from political philosophers than it has philosophers of education, writers working within this branch of philosophy have engaged with Newman's work.

Moral philosophers

Several contributions to moral philosophy contain references to Newman. For example, in an essay entitled "Divine Omnipotence and Human Freedom," (1955) Antony Flew (1923–2010) cites Newman's work *Certain Difficulties Felt by Anglicans* (1850) in order to illustrate what he

---

217. Graham, *The Institution of Intellectual Values*, 1–3.
218. Berlin, *Four Essays on Liberty*, 201–2.
219. Althusser, *L'Avenir Dure Longtemps: Suivi De, Les Faits*, 84.
220. Rose, "New Jerusalem, Old Athens from the Broken Middle," 323.

views to be the failings of Roman Catholic understandings of morality. He cites the following passage from Newman's text:

> It were better for the sun and moon to drop from heaven, for the earth to fail, and for all the many millions who are upon it to die ... than that one soul ... should commit one single venial sin. (J. H. Newman).[221]

Though Flew is critical of Newman here in his *Introduction to Western Philosophy* (1971), Flew describes him as a "great Victorian" and cites the *Grammar of Assent* in his discussion of the meaning of Cartesian certainty.[222]

The Moral philosopher Richard Wollheim (1923–2003) cites Newman when discussing the nineteenth-century debate on religion and ethics (1969).[223] Newton Garver (1928–2014) cites Newman's *Apologia* in his essay on "What Violence Is" (1971).[224] The moral Philosopher Richard Mervyn Hare (1919–2002) cites Newman's *Discourses to Mixed Congregations* (1849) in his introductory work on *Plato* (1982)[225] and discusses Newman's conception of liberty in his *Essays on Religion and Education* (1992).[226] The philosopher Derek Parfit (1942–) discusses Newman's conception of sin in relation to consequentialist[227] theories of ethics in his book *Reasons and Persons* (1984).[228]

---

221. Flew, "Divine Omnipotence and Human freedom," 160.

222. Flew, *An Introduction to Western Philosophy*, 320.

223. Wollheim, *F. H. Bradley*, 13, 287.

224. Garver compares Newman with Freud: "This type of Freudian rebuff has the effect of what John Henry Newman called 'poisoning the wells.' It gives its victim no ground to stand on. If he tries to advance facts and statistics, they are discounted and his involvement is attributed to Freudian factors. If he attempts to prove himself free of the aberration in question, his very protest is used as evidence against him. To structure a situation against a person in such a manner does violence to him by depriving him of his dignity; no matter what he does there is no way at all, so long as he accepts the problem in the terms in which it is presented, for him to make a response that will allow him to emerge with honor." Garver, "What Violence Is," 247.

225. *Mix*, 314; Hare, *Plato*, 26.

226. Hare, *Essays on Religion and Education*, 104–6.

227. This position holds that the consequences of an action are the basis for determining whether it is right or wrong. For further discussion, see Sinnott-Armstrong, *Consequentialism*, §1

228. Parfit writes: "Newman believed that pain and sin were both bad, but that sin was infinitely worse. If all mankind suffered 'extremest agony,' this would be less bad than if one venial sin was committed." Parfit, *Reasons and Persons*, 49.

The philosopher Alasdair MacIntyre (1929–), a convert to Catholicism, acknowledges the seminal influence of Newman and refers to him in his works *Whose Justice? Which Rationality* (1988) and *Three Rival Versions of Moral Enquiry* (1990).[229] Finally, Roman Catholic philosopher, Professor Robert O'Donnell, compares Kant's discussion of the "categorical imperative" (the notion that the divine law commands human freedom) with Newman's discussion of how conscience is an evidence for the existence of God (1996).[230] These references to Newman indicate that he was a person of interest to a variety of moral philosophers as well as to others whose work contributes to this area of philosophy.

Philosophers of religion

Though chapter 6 will examine Newman's contribution to the field of the philosophy of religion it is helpful to briefly survey philosophers of religion who have engaged with Newman in order to demonstrate that, as with the other areas of philosophy discussed, Newman has not been ignored by them. On the contrary, throughout the twentieth century, philosophers of religion have engaged with Newman's work. As noted earlier, the Roman Catholic Philosopher Martin D'Arcy (1888–1978) gives Newman's *Grammar of Assent* substantial treatment in his work, *The Nature of Belief* (1931).[231] The Quaker philosopher Elton Trueblood's (1900–1994) *Logic of Belief* (1942) considers that "John Henry *Newman's Grammar of Assent* is still challenging after many years."[232] Newman is discussed in the appendix to Frederick Copleston's (1907–94) *History of Philosophy* (1946)[233] and in Fulton John Sheen's (1895–1979) *Philosophy of Religion* (1948).[234] Newman receives a chapter in John Hick's (1922–2012), *Faith and Knowledge: A Modern Introduction to the Problem of Religious Knowledge* (1953).[235] The Catholic existentialist philosopher Gabriel Marcel (1889–1973) cites Newman's *Essay on Development* in

---

229. MacIntyre, *Whose Justice? Which Rationality?* 8, 353–54, 362; MacIntyre, *Three Rival Versions of Moral Enquiry*, 69.

230. O'Donnell, *Hooked on Philosophy*, 30.

231. D'Arcy, *Nature of Belief*.

232. Trueblood, *The Logic of Belief*, 323. Trueblood was also a Harvard graduate.

233. Copleston, *History of Philosophy*, 8:510–25.

234. Sheen, *Philosophy Of Religion*, 293, 357.

235. Here Hick examines Newman's conception of the illative sense. Hick, *Faith and Knowledge*, 86–105.

his work *The Decline of Wisdom* (1955).²³⁶ The philosopher of religion, and Oxford graduate, Roderick Ninian Smart (1927–2001) cites Newman in his work *The Religious Experience* (1969).²³⁷ The Roman Catholic philosopher Bernard Lonergan (1904–84) refers to Newman on several occasions.²³⁸ For example, in *Understanding and Being* (1980), Lonergan examines Newman's concept of the illative sense and describes Newman's *Grammar of Assent* as "a classic" discussion of the concept of judgement.²³⁹ In *Divine Revelation* (1982) Paul Helm, Oxford graduate and Professor of the History and Philosophy of Religion at Kings college London (1993–2000), discusses Newman's understanding of the development of ideas alongside those of Immanuel Kant and roots Newman within the British empiricist tradition of David Hume and Bishop Butler.²⁴⁰ Yet another Oxford graduate, the philosopher of religion Louis Paul Pojman (1935–2005), discusses Newman's work in relation to the question of free will in his book *Religious Belief and the Will* (1986).²⁴¹ Following Pojman the philosopher William Alston (1921–2009), a former professor of philosophy at Syracuse University (1979–92), links Newman to several philosophers in his work *Epistemic Justification* (1989). Alston argues that like Descartes, Kierkegaard, and Carl Ginet Newman is a proponent of the voluntary control thesis (the notion that our beliefs are under our control).²⁴²

The Canadian philosopher of religion Leslie Armour (1931–), professor in philosophy at the University of Ottawa, recognises Newman's critique of evidentialism (1993).²⁴³ The Roman Catholic philosopher John E. Thiel cites Newman in both his work *Nonfoundationalism* (1994), and

236. Marcel, *The Decline of Wisdom*, 35.

237. Smart, *The Religious Experience of Mankind*, 364–65.

238. Lonergan, *Method in Theology*, 316; Lonergan, *Collected Works*, 5–6, 37, 237.

239. Lonergan, *Understanding and Being*, 109. Moreover several writers identify parallels between Newman and Lonergan: Egan, "Lonergan on Newman's Conversion," 437–55; Egan, "John Henry Newman and Bernard Lonergan", 295–315; Bosco, *Finding God in All Things*, 216; Savage, *The Subjective Dimension of Human Work*, 210.

240. Helm, *The Divine Revelation*, 117.

241. Pojman, *Religious Belief and the Will*, 87.

242. Alston, *Epistemic Justification*, 120.

243. He writes: "Newman in his *Essay in Aid of a Grammar of Assent* . . . argues that logic can never compel any belief; we can question any proposition and any argument. Whatever the standard for accepting a proposition or accepting the validity of an argument, we can ask for more evidence. We can always ask for new premises." Armour, *Infini Rien*, 72.

Senses of Tradition (2000). In the former, he discusses Newman in relation to nonfoundational approaches to philosophy; in the latter he describes the *Grammar of Assent* as a "philosophical study of the nature of faith that possesses interesting theological implications."[244] Thomas Carr, an Oxford-trained philosopher of religion whose contention that Newman has been ignored by philosophers was mentioned in the introduction, compares Newman's work with the philosophy of Hans-Georg Gadamer (1900–2002).[245] In *Reason and the Heart* (1995) William Wainwright, Professor of Philosophy at the University of Wisconsin, cites Newman extensively in support of his contention that purity of heart enhances the reasoning faculty.[246] Following Wainwright, Kelly James Clark, Professor of Philosophy at Calvin College, argues that Newman is correct to assert that "our intellectual and moral character affect our ability to see the truth" in his essay "Fiction as a Kind of Philosophy" (2002).[247]

The president of the Society of Christian Philosophers Peter Van Inwagen (1942–), Professor of Philosophy at the University of Notre Dame, cites Newman's university discourses in his essays on metaphysics (2001).[248] The Catholic philosopher Martin Moleski observes a number of similarities between Michael Polanyi (1891–1976) and Newman in his work *Personal Catholicism* (2000).[249] In an article entitled "Reason and Philosophy in the Anglican Tradition" (2012) Newman is mentioned in relation to philosophical realism.[250] Finally Newman is included in the

---

244. Thiel, *Senses of Tradition*, 172; Thiel, *Nonfoundationalism*, 116.

245. Carr, *Newman and Gadamer*, 12. Several writers have examined similarities between Newman and Gadamer, including: Kasper, *Die Methoden der Dogmatik*, 40–41; Norris, *Newman and His Theological Method*, 121; Paul Crowley, "Catholicity, Inculturation and Newman's Sensus Fidelium," 161–74.

246. Wainwright, *Reason and the Heart*, 55–83.

247. Clark, "Fiction as a Kind of Philosophy," 287.

248. Van Inwagen, *Ontology*, 15.

249. Moleski observes similarities between: the emphasis these writers place on the personal dimension of knowledge, their respective understanding of the manner in which the human mind determines "reasons sufficient for a proof," and their understandings of the indemonstrable nature of first principles. Moleski, *Personal Catholicism*, vii, 120–30. There are several philosophical comparisons have been made between Newman and Polanyi, including: Norris, *Newman and His Theological Method*, 46; Ferreira, *Doubt and Religious Commitment*, 38; Torrance, *Reality and Scientific Knowledge*, 99; Moleski, "Illative Sense and Tacit Knowledge," 189–224; Dulles, *John Henry Newman*, 47n44.

250. Avis, "Reason and Philosophy in the Anglican Tradition," 82.

Stanford Encyclopaedia of Philosophy in an article on "The Epistemology of Religion" (2013):

> Although pre-dating the current debate, Newman's rejection of Locke's and Paley's evidentialism is relevant to the problematic of contemporary epistemology of religion. First he quite clearly rejected the hegemony of epistemology. His procedure was to examine how in fact people made up their minds on non-religious issues and argue that by the same standards religious beliefs were justified. As a result he qualified evidentialism by insisting that an implicit and cumulative argument could lead to justified certainty.[251]

In this relatively recent publication, the Oxford-trained philosopher of religion Peter Forrest (1948–)[252] recognizes the relevance of Newman to contemporary philosophical debate. In sum, a plethora of twentieth- and twenty-first-century philosophers of religion view Newman as a significant thinker.

Summary of Chapter

This chapter has examined Newman's philosophical reception from his lifetime up until the present. Having indicated that Newman's general philosophical legacy is potentially far greater than is generally envisaged we will not explore Newman's possible contribution to all of the aforementioned philosophical disciplines or movements but will instead concentrate upon whether Newman's writing has made a contribution to one philosophical movement in particular, "epistemological particularism," and its manifestations within two different branches of philosophy: epistemology and the philosophy of religion.[253]

---

251. Forrest, *The Epistemology of Religion*, §1.

252. Forrest also cites Newman in other publications. For further discussion, see Forrest, *God without the Supernatural*, 20, 130.

253. Another potential line of inquiry would be whether Newman's similarities with the German philosopher Hans-Georg Gadamer (1900–2002) are due to the latter having read Newman's work. Though Thomas Carr writes his doctoral thesis on the similarities between these writers he argues that Gadamer does not make any references to Newman. Nevertheless, several writers identify parallels between these writers. For further discussion, see Kasper, *Die Methoden der Dogmatik*, 40–41; Norris, *Newman and His Theological Method*, 121; Crowley, "Catholicity, Inculturation and Newman's Sensus Fidelium," 161–74; Carr, *Newman and Gadamer*, 12.

3

Newman Considered in Relationship to Epistemological Particularism

Introducing Epistemological Particularism

WILLIAM ABRAHAM'S ADMISSION THAT his particularist account of the epistemology of theology is shaped by Newman raises the question of Newman's wider significance for this epistemological position. The phrase "epistemological particularism" first appears in Roderick Chisholm's (1916-99) lecture on the *Problem of the Criterion* (1973).[1] Here Chisholm introduces this theory of knowledge by illustrating that to which it is opposed. He explains that particularism is intended to counter a form of classical skepticism called Pyrrhonism.[2] The Pyrrhonists defended their skeptical position using an argument called the *diallelus*—which Chisholm describes as the problem of the criterion. The problem goes something like this: if in order to know something it is first necessary to have a rule that specifies when a piece of knowledge is authentic (a criterion), and if it is impossible to know if this criterion works unless one already knows what true knowledge is, then one should be skeptical about claims to knowledge. Chisholm summarizes the argument in the following way:

---

1. Chisholm, *Problem of the Criterion*, 1–2.
2. Hankinson, "Pyrrhonism," 727.

> To know whether things really are as they seem to be, we must have a *procedure* for distinguishing appearances that are true from appearances that are false. But to know whether our procedure is a good procedure, we have to know whether it really *succeeds* in distinguishing appearances that are true from appearances that are false. And we cannot know whether it does really succeed unless we already know which appearances are *true* and which ones are *false*. And so we are caught in a circle.[3]

This circle—what Chisholm calls the problem of the criterion—is the basis for Pyrrhonian skepticism. The Pyrrhonists concluded that if it is impossible to know without a criterion, and if it is impossible to know if a criterion works without already having true knowledge, then the most logical response to this impasse is skepticism.[4]

Essentially, the problem of the criterion illustrates the inability of humankind to find a procedure for demarcating true knowledge from error. This is the problem against which Chisholm's theory of epistemological particularism is set. Epistemological particularism is Chisholm's proposed solution to this quandary. He suggests that epistemology should not begin with a criterion determining what counts as knowledge. He argues that we should begin with knowledge, with what we think we know, and then work out criteria for how we know.[5] Chisholm's doctoral student, Ernest Sosa (1940–), provides a helpful introduction to epistemological particularism in his article "The Foundations of Foundationalism" (1980):

> The ancient problem of the *diallelus* or "the wheel", most recently given prominence by Roderick Chisholm as "the problem of the criterion." Which should come first: a method or set of criteria for determining when we have a bit of knowledge, or particular examples of knowledge, in terms of which we can determine criteria? Those who give pre-eminence to method or criteria may be called methodists, and those who give pre-eminence to particular examples (e.g., my knowledge that I have two hands) may be called particularists. Note that whereas a methodist can be a skeptic, a particularist is anti-skeptical on principle.

---

3. Chisholm, *Problem of the Criterion*, 3.

4. Hankinson, "Pyrrhonism," 727.

5. Chisholm considers that we should begin with what we know and ensure that the procedures which we develop to measure these truths do not rule out beliefs that are considered quite obviously true (like our having two feet). Chisholm, *Theory of Knowledge*, 16.

> Moreover, whereas a skeptic might be a methodist and cannot be a particularist, he might be a radical skeptic, rejecting both methodism and particularism. Some Pyrrhonic Skeptics were radical in their skepticism.[6]

Here Sosa points out that a particularist begins epistemology with instances of knowledge that are already in their possession and then examines how they know these things. This position is contrasted with that of epistemological methodism, which begins epistemology with a criterion of how accurate knowledge is attained.[7] One of the problems with epistemological methodism, according to Chisholm, is that the chosen criterion can render sensible knowledge claims irrational (such as our belief in the external world).[8] A similar point is made by the particularist philosopher of religion, and Newman commentator, William J. Abraham (1947–).

In his account of the epistemology of theology Abraham believes that "particularism is to be preferred to methodism" because he considers there is a danger, if we begin with theories of how knowledge is attained, that these methods will be too narrow in scope and thus exclude beliefs which "most people would take to be intellectually permissible." Abraham considers that it is better to start "with particular claims to knowledge and then work up from there to proposals about method or theories of knowledge." In *Crossing the Threshold of Divine Revelation* he applies this particularist approach to his account of the epistemology of Christian belief.[9]

The decision of these particularist writers to begin with instances of knowledge rather than an epistemological criterion does not prohibit a reflexive examination of the epistemological status of the initial knowledge claims. On the contrary, both Abraham and Chisholm maintain that

---

6. Sosa, "The Foundations of Foundationalism," 158.

7. Not to be confused with the Methodist Church—the name given to John Wesley's religious societies.

8. Put simply, if one began epistemology with a criterion that stated that only the places discussed in the Sheffield A to Z are real, this would render belief in the existence of Leeds incorrect. Chisholm considers that we should begin with what we know and ensure that the procedures which we develop to measure these truths do not rule out beliefs that are considered quite obviously true. Chisholm, *Theory of Knowledge*, 16.

9. Abraham, *Crossing*, 30–31.

epistemological rules may be formed retrospectively.[10] However, citing Aristotle's contention that different levels of precision are required for different subject matter,[11] both maintain that we should begin with what we know and that we should ensure that the procedures which we develop to measure these truths do not rule out beliefs that are considered quite obviously true. Thus the epistemic rules formed retrospectively are appropriate to the cases of knowledge in hand. Abraham describes this principle as Aristotelian Epistemic Fit.[12]

In summary, three epistemological tendencies may be identified in this introduction to particularism. First of all, in opposing "epistemological methodism" Chisholm and Abraham are challenging writers who presuppose an enquiry with rules concerning when a belief is legitimate (P1). Second, in advancing "epistemological particularism," these writers assume certain beliefs to be valid prior to examining the epistemological evidence in their favor (P2). Third, citing Aristotle's contention that different subjects demand different kinds of precision, these writers formulate epistemological rules appropriate to the cases of knowledge already in hand so as to ensure that these established instances of knowledge are not ruled out; Abraham terms this the "Aristotelian epistemic fit" (P3).[13] While chapter 4 will explore whether or not Newman's writing manifests these three tendencies (P1–3)[14] it is now necessary to examine whether other scholars have discussed Newman's work in relation to these particularist writers.

Newman, Newman Commentators, and Epistemological Particularism

There are only a handful of articles comparing Newman with epistemological particularist writers. With the exception of Collins and Ford these studies have all been epistemological approaches to Newman's

---

10. Chisholm, *Problem of the Criterion*, 35–36; Abraham, *Crossing*, 30.
11. Aristotle, *Nicomachean Ethics*, 4–5 [I.3 1094b13–28].
12. Abraham, *Crossing*, 45.
13. Abraham, *Crossing*, 45.
14. If he does manifest such tendencies this could explain why particularist writers find his work interesting and would also indicate his wider significance to other writers who take this approach but do not, as yet, engage with Newman.

thought.[15] To date, all of them have originated in the United States.[16] In an article on "Newman, Foundationalism, and the Ethics of Belief" (1981), Gerald D McCarthy (1946–) argues that Newman's approach to knowledge has similarities with Chisholm.[17] He maintains that Newman and Chisholm "derive the characteristics of evidence and epistemic norms from an examination of what we consider to be established instances of knowledge."[18] Here McCarthy indicates that both Newman and Chisholm reject the idea that knowledge must be preceded by a criterion and instead assess the evidence in favor of knowledge claims retrospectively. McCarthy believes Newman's similarity with Chisholm in this regard indicates that "the apologetic strategy advocated with such considerable philosophical and rhetorical skill by Newman still continues to bear fruit."[19]

The potential contribution offered by Newman to particularist approaches to epistemology is also discussed by the philosopher and Newman scholar Jay Newman (1948–2007). In an article entitled "Epistemic Inference and Illative Judgment" (1981), Jay Newman suggests that J. H. Newman's conception of reason enhances Chisholm's particularist approach to epistemology.[20] Like McCarthy, Jay Newman observes how J. H. Newman and Chisholm both consider that, rather than beginning with criteria, our spontaneous claims to knowledge (our convictions) should be taken on trust. Moreover, he observes how both these writers consider that these spontaneous convictions may, in retrospect, be reflected upon in order to investigate their validity.[21] However, though noting these similarities, Jay Newman observes that while J. H. Newman believes that the rational causes of our initial beliefs cannot be accommodated within the confines of formal logical argument, Chisholm's approach is different in

---

15. While Collins discusses Newman in relation to the philosophy of education Ford, as noted above, is simply reviewing Abraham's book. For further discussion, see Collins, "Newman, Foundationalism and Teaching Philosophy," 147–48; Ford, Review of *Crossing the Threshold of Divine Revelation*, 184.

16. Though Ford's article is published in *Religious Studies* he is an American writer.

17. McCarthy believes that Newman has similarities with Chisholm's contention that "contemporary epistemology is a form of 'special pleading.'"

18. McCarthy, "Newman, Foundationalism, and the Ethics of Belief," 74–75.

19. McCarthy, "Newman, Foundationalism, and the Ethics of Belief," 79.

20. Jay Newman, "Epistemic Inference," 327–39.

21. A comparison of this aspect of Newman's thought, his discussion of "reflex assent" in the second part of the *Grammar*, and Chisholm's particularist approach to knowledge occurs in chapter 5.

that he actually attempts to extrapolate the formal principles governing the formation of these spontaneous convictions.[22] At this juncture, Jay Newman indicates that J. H. Newman's malleable account of natural reason has a contribution to make to Chisholm's epistemology, for it allows miscellaneous probabilities to be considered as a part of the validation of spontaneous beliefs. Though these points will be examined in more detail in chapter 5, it is apparent that if Jay Newman is correct J. H. Newman's work could have wider significance for the development of epistemological particularism.

A number of other articles briefly mention Newman in connection with the particularist approach. For example, in "Newman, Foundationalism and Teaching Philosophy" (1991) Collins notes similarities between Newman and Chisholm.[23] Likewise Grimm's "Cardinal Newman, Reformed Epistemologist?" (2001) observes similarities between Newman and Chisholm's criticisms of John Locke.[24] While these studies notice a resemblance between these writers, the most detailed comparison, Maddox's article on "Newman, Certain Knowledge and 'The Problem of the Criterion'" (2007), actually contrasts Newman's position with that of Chisholm.[25]

Maddox argues that Newman's discussion of reason in his *Grammar of Assent* (1870) indicates that he is an epistemological methodist because he presupposes a process of informal reasoning (to be introduced later) antecedently to knowledge.[26] While Maddox's analysis remains the fullest to date, it leaves the following questions unanswered. First of all, is it not anachronistic to interpret Newman as an epistemological methodist? Second, did Chisholm read or refer to Newman? Third, did Newman engage with any of the sources that are acknowledged by Chisholm as being instrumental to his proposals?[27] Fourth, how does Maddox's interpretation of Newman's conception of reason compare with other relevant literature on this subject?[28] Fifth, does Maddox's focus on the *Grammar*

---

22. Chisholm, "Epistemic Principles," 343.
23. Collins, "Newman, Foundationalism and Teaching Philosophy," 147–48.
24. Grimm, "Cardinal Newman, Reformed Epistemologist?" 504.
25. Maddox, "Newman, Certain Knowledge," 69–86.
26. Maddox, "Newman, Certain Knowledge," 86.
27. Floridi argues that Joseph Désiré Mercier Cardinal Mercier's *Critériologie* is an important text in the transmission of the problem (and its solution) to Chisholm. For further discussion, see Floridi, *Sextus Empiricus*.
28. Casey, *Natural Reason*.

of Assent lead him to overlook particularist tendencies within Newman's earlier works? Sixth, how does Maddox's methodist interpretation of J. H. Newman's conception of reason relate to Jay Newman's contention that it is precisely this aspect of J. H. Newman's thought which enhances Chisholm's approach to epistemology? Throughout the course of this book the questions raised by Maddox's interpretation will be addressed.

In addition, it is also necessary to ask how Maddox's analysis would explain John Ford's contention that Newman's conception of reason permeates Abraham's particularist account of the epistemology of theology.[29] According to Ford, Abraham is influenced considerably by Newman's conception of reason. In a review of Abraham's work *Crossing the Threshold of Divine Revelation* (2006), Ford observes that the tone and mode of Newman's conception of reason "reverberate throughout this book."[30] Prior to the publication of this work (2003) Abraham envisages that his account of "the epistemology of religious belief," *Crossing the Threshold*, will "follow through on the lines of inquiry brilliantly opened up by John Henry Newman."[31] This acknowledgment indicates that Abraham is constructively operating out of the epistemological framework implicit within the writings of John Henry Newman. If this is the case then Newman has made a contemporary contribution to the philosophy of religion. However, before exploring this question further (chapter 6), it is helpful to examine whether or not Newman engaged with some of the key historical texts acknowledged as important by particularist writers, so as to further understand Newman's work in relation to the development of this philosophical position.

Newman and the sources of particularism

Chisholm and Abraham identify a number of key sources that have been important to the development of their epistemological proposals. For example, Chisholm acknowledges the influence of neo-scholastic writers on his work. His essay on *The Problem of the Criterion* forms the published version of a lecture he was invited to deliver to the Society for Philosophy at Marquette University in honor of St Thomas Aquinas

---

29. Abraham, *Crossing*.
30. Ford, Review of *Crossing the Threshold of Divine Revelation*, 184.
31. Abraham, *Logic of Renewal*, 166.

(1973).³² At the outset, Chisholm explains that his reason for discussing the problem of the criterion on St Thomas's Feast day is that he first came across this Pyrrhonian problem when reading the works of the following neo-scholastic philosophers: Peter Coffey and his "great" teacher Cardinal Mercier.³³ Chisholm credits Mercier with rediscovering this ancient skeptical problem and, moreover, with finding a solution to it. This indicates that texts by neo-scholastic philosophers like Mercier and Coffey are an important source for Chisholm's work. Chisholm also contends that the eighteenth-century common sense philosopher Thomas Reid (1710–96) anticipates the epistemological particularist approach.³⁴ Moreover Chisholm indicates the importance of Aristotle's (384–322 BC) *Nicomachean Ethics* to this approach.³⁵

Conversely Chisholm cites a number of sources that differ from him but which, nevertheless, have been important to the development of this epistemological position. In addition to Pyrrhonian skepticism, Chisholm cites Michel de Montaigne's (1533–92) theological reception of the problem of the criterion. Furthermore, using two empiricist writers as counter examples, Chisholm explains how the particularist position sharply contrasts with that taken by John Locke and David Hume who he describes as methodists; in the sense that they stipulate, in advance, what conditions must be in place before knowledge can occur.³⁶

In *Crossing the Threshold of Divine Revelation* (2006) the philosopher of religion William J. Abraham utilizes Chisholm's epistemological particularist approach in his account of the epistemology of theology. Though he rarely makes reference to neo-scholastic writers, where he does he is critical of them,³⁷ Abraham stresses the fundamental importance of Aristotle to this approach. Though Abraham recognizes Reid's importance to the development of this epistemological orientation he acknowledges Newman, as opposed to Reid, as being the key inspiration for his account of the epistemology of theology.³⁸

32. Chisholm, *Problem of the Criterion*, iii.
33. Chisholm, *Problem of the Criterion*, 1.
34. Chisholm, *Problem of the Criterion*, 19.
35. Chisholm, *Problem of the Criterion*, 35.
36. Chisholm, *Problem of the Criterion*, 15–16.
37. Abraham, *Canon and Criterion*, 18n19. Abraham is also heavily critical of St Thomas. Abraham, *Canon and Criterion*, 84–110.
38. Abraham's use of Newman's work will be examined in chapter 5. For further discussions, see Abraham, *Crossing*, 34; Abraham, *Logic of Renewal*, 166.

Abraham also discusses Pyrrhonism, in his work *Canon and Criterion* (1997), and explores the way in which this form of skepticism was transmitted by theologians during the counter-reformation. This is important to Abraham because it illustrates the way in which this form of skepticism has impacted upon theological discourse.[39] Like Chisholm, Abraham is also critical of Locke's epistemological methodism.[40] Unlike Chisholm, however, Abraham devotes considerable attention to the manner in which Locke's epistemological position negatively affects theological claims.

Having introduced some of the key sources cited by Chisholm and Abraham, it is important to examine whether or not Newman engaged with these historical sources. This is necessary because an incorrect assessment of the sources that shaped Newman could obscure his wider relevance to this philosophical position.

Skeptical sources

Pyrrhonism

It was noted that Maddox contrasts Newman's work with that of Chisholm. Maddox interpretation has a number of problems. The most relevant to the present discussion is his contention that Newman did not have an explicit or a direct knowledge of the Pyrrhonist problem of the criterion.[41] Maddox cites Sextus Empiricus" (c.160–210) *Outlines of Pyrrhonism* as one of the "key texts" for understanding this problem.[42] Here it is important to clarify that Maddox's contention that Newman was not explicitly aware of Pyrrhonism refers not only to classic Pyrrhonian texts, like Sextus, but to the problem itself.[43] Were it the case that Newman had not engaged with Pyrrhonian skepticism then his relevance to particularism would be diminished.

In his *Outlines of Pyrrhonism*, Sextus writes:[44]

---

39. Abraham cites Montaigne, Gentian Hervet (1499–1584) and others. Abraham, *Canon and Criterion*, 167–69.
40. Abraham, *Canon and Criterion*, 215.
41. Maddox, "Newman, Certain Knowledge," 70.
42. Maddox, "Newman, Certain Knowledge," 70n5.
43. Maddox, "Newman, Certain Knowledge," 70.
44. Sextus, *Outlines of Scepticism*, 72 [II. 4, 19–20].

> We neither possess an agreed standard nor even know if there is one . . . in order for the dispute that has arisen about standards to be decided, we must possess an agreed standard through which we can judge it; and in order for us to possess an agreed standard, the dispute about standards must already have been decided. Thus the argument falls into the reciprocal mode and the discovery of a standard is blocked—for we do not allow them to assume a standard by hypothesis, and if they want to judge the standard by which we throw them into an infinite regress.[45]

In this extract, Sextus describes the Pyrrhonist "problem of the criterion" (*diallelus*). The issue is this: if truth or knowledge is dependent upon having a "standard" (criterion), then it is necessary to have a criterion before searching for truth. However, if truth cannot be known until there is a criterion, how is it possible to tell whether the criterion works? Thus a second criterion is needed to determine whether the first criterion is good, and so on.

It is documented that both Chisholm and Abraham refer directly to Sextus.[46] The importance of Pyrrhonism to the development of Chisholm's position is captured in his declaration that "one has not begun to philosophise until one has faced" the skepticism of the Pyrrhonists. Moreover, he emphasizes that the problem of the criterion is "one of the most important and one of the most difficult of all the problems of philosophy."[47] The significance Chisholm gives to Pyrrhonism illustrates why it is important to determine whether or not Newman before him engaged directly with these ideas, for if Maddox is correct, that Newman had no explicit knowledge of them, then it could diminish his relevance to particularist writers like Chisholm.

My reading suggests that Newman, like Chisholm, began his literary career with an essay discussing the writings of Sextus on "Marcus Tullius Cicero" (1824).[48] Newman's references to Sextus in this article demonstrate his explicit knowledge of Pyrrhonism.[49] Newman's personal

---

45. Sextus, *Outlines of Scepticism*, 72 [II. 4, 19–20].

46. Chisholm, *Problem of the Criterion*, 3; Abraham, *Canon and Criterion*, 169.

47. Chisholm, *Problem of the Criterion*, 3

48. Newman, "Marcus Tullius Cicero," 279–94; Chisholm, "Sextus Empiricus and Modern Empiricism," 371–84. Though the article on Cicero is not mentioned, Terrence Merrigan emphasizes the significance of this period in Newman's life for his thought on faith and reason. For further discussion, see Merrigan, "*Newman's Oriel Experience*," 192–211.

49. Newman, "Marcus Tullius Cicero," 279–94. Newman also cites Sextus in his

library contains a copy of Sextus's works, which was given to him by William Palmer.[50] Furthermore, Newman also refers to Pyrrhonism in his *Lectures on the Present Position of Catholics* (1851).[51] This indicates Newman's direct and explicit awareness of Pyrrhonian skepticism.[52]

In his *Lectures on the Present Position of Catholics* Newman's makes the following observation concerning Pyrrhonism:

> If you trace back your reasons for holding an opinion, you must stop somewhere; the process cannot go on for ever; you must come at last to something you cannot prove; else, life would be spent in inquiring and reasoning, our minds would be ever tossing to and fro, and there would be nothing to guide us. No man alive, but has some First Principles or other. Even if he declares that nothing can be known for certain, then that is his First Principle. He has got his place in philosophy ready marked out for him; he is of the sect called Academics or Pyrrhonists, as the case may be, and his dogma is either "Nothing can be known in itself;" or "Nothing can be known even for practical purposes."[53]

In this citation, Newman mentions Pyrrhonism in order to point out that everyone, even Pyrrhonian skeptics, must assume something. What is interesting here is that this observation resonates with Chisholm, who writes:

---

correspondence: LD 10:416. The notion that Newman was unaware of these issues is mistaken. His *Letters and Diaries* demonstrate that his formative years were spent learning about this period. He received his first Greek book, Aesop's Fables at aged 6, at aged nine he possessed a copy of Ovid's *Metamorphosis*, began learning about Latin verse composition and in his own words "got into Virgil." At aged eleven he began reading Homer and, at age twelve, Herodotus. His copy of Cicero's *De Amicitia* (On Friendship) is inscribed with the date 17th August (1816) suggesting that he read the work prior to leaving school. For further discussion see LD 1:6–7, 10–11, 14, & 43–53. In his *Lectures and Essays* Newman gives a pseudo-autobiographic account of his school education: "At school I was reckoned a sharp boy; I ran through its classes rapidly; and by the time I was fifteen, my masters had nothing more to teach me . . . . at the unusual age I speak of, with some inexact acquaintance with Homer, Sophocles, Herodotus, and Xenophon, Horace, Virgil, and Cicero." Newman, *Lectures and Essays*, 167 [*Idea*, 367].

50. Newman's copy of this work, in the Birmingham Oratory, in inscribed with the words "From William Palmer."

51. Newman, *Lectures on Catholicism in England*, 266–67 [*Prepos*, 279].

52. Newman, "Marcus Tullius Cicero," 279–94; Chisholm, "Sextus Empiricus and Modern Empiricism," 371–84.

53. Newman, *Lectures on Catholicism in England*, 266–67 [LG 279].

> In all of this I have presupposed the approach I have called "particularism." The "methodist" and the 'sceptic" will tell us that we have started in the wrong place. If now we try to reason with them, then, I am afraid, we will be back on the wheel. What few philosophers have had the courage to recognise is this: we can deal with the problem [of the criterion] only by begging the question.[54]

Here Chisholm makes clear that the problem of the criterion can only be handled by assuming, or begging the question in favour of, something.[55] These similar reflections illustrate how Newman's grapple with skepticism resonates with that of particularist writers and indicate his potential relevance to this position.

Before closing this section it is important to note that the transmission of the problem of the criterion by theologians during the sixteenth and seventeenth centuries is an important source for Chisholm and Abraham's engagement with Pyrrhonian skepticism. Sextus's writing was largely unknown during the Middle Ages.[56] However, during the sixteenth and seventeenth centuries his work was rediscovered by a number of French thinkers including Montaigne,[57] Gentian Hervet (1499–1584),[58] François de Sales (1567–1622),[59] François Véron (1575–1650),[60] Pierre-Daniel Huet (1630–1721),[61] and others who employed Pyrrhonism for theological ends.[62] According to Abraham:

> It cannot be stressed enough that the revival of scepticism went hand in hand with an attack on the . . . Reformers. The full Latin

---

54. Chisholm, *Problem of the Criterion*, 37.

55. Abraham likewise argues that when dealing with skepticism one must assume something. Thus, while the skeptic assumes that we cannot know, Abraham argues that he will rather assume a network of beliefs. Abraham, *Crossing*, 32–33.

56. Popkin, *Scepticism*, 17ff.

57. Montaigne's *Apology for Raymond Sebond* (1568) used Sextus to show the futility of human arguments in order to defend the Spanish theologian Raymond Sebond (died 1436) from criticism. Montaigne, *Apology*, 161.

58. Hervet, *Sexti Empirici*, a2–a3.

59. de Sales, *Les Controverses in Oeuvres*, 73–74.

60. Véron, *La Victorieuse Methode*.

61. Huet, *A Philosophical Treatise*, 56.

62. Popkin, *Scepticism*, 17ff

edition of Sextus Empiricus's work was published by the French Counter-Reformer Gentian Hervet in 1569.[63]

Here Abraham observes how Sextus's works were actually rediscovered by Hervet who, after finding a copy of Sextus's works, decided he would try and use the problem of the criterion to undermine Calvinism.[64] According to Popkin, the Counter-Reformation argument centres around who possesses the correct norm for interpreting true faith. The reformers had challenged the church's criterion, its own tradition, and had argued that the criterion of true faith was Scripture. The counter-reformers argued that if the church's interpretation of true faith could err then individual private judgment stood little chance of success.[65]

It is documented that Newman, Abraham, and Chisholm engaged with this theological transmission of Pyrrhonism. Though he discusses Sextus at length in his other works, Chisholm uses Montaigne as a key source for his account of *The Problem of the Criterion*.[66] In addition to Hervet, Abraham discusses Montaigne and examines how his summary of the problem of the criterion was employed by Véron and de Sales to suppress the rise of Calvinism by undermining the Calvinists' use of Scripture as a criterion for true faith.[67] Moreover, citing these sources, Abraham argues repeatedly that an appeal to *sola scriptura* cannot ensure any consensus with regard to Christian doctrine. From this, it seems possible that this theological transmission of Pyrrhonism may have shaped Abraham's view of the Protestant use of Scripture; that his rejection of the idea that theologians can obtain doctrinal propositions from the text of Scripture is connected with his engagement with this theological transmission of Pyrrhonism.[68]

---

63. Abraham, *Canon and Criterion*, 169n8.

64. Hervet, *Sexti Empirici*, a2–a3. For further discussion, see Popkin, *Scepticism*, 37.

65. For further discussion, see Popkin, *Scepticism*, 37.

66. Chisholm, *Problem of the Criterion*, 3n3; Chisholm, *Perceiving*, 96. The significance of Montaigne's reception of Pyrrhonism for Chisholm is indicated in that fact that it is his paraphrase of Montaigne that undergirds his discussion of the problem of the criterion. For further discussion of Montaigne's reception and the transmission of Pyrrhonism generally, see Amico, *The Problem of the Criterion*, 38–45, 87ff; Floridi, *Sextus Empiricus*.

67. Abraham, *Canon and Criterion*, 167–69.

68. Abraham, *Canon and Criterion*, 151; Abraham, *Crossing*, 30.

Newman also engaged with this theological transmission of Pyrrhonism. He is frequently critical of Montaigne's skepticism and observes his connection to Pyrrhonism.[69] In addition to his repeated references to de Sales,[70] Newman states in his *Apologia* (a work that is intended to make transparent the theological influences upon him) that he was given a copy of Véron's *The Rule of Catholic Faith*.[71] This last instance is significant, for Véron's use of Pyrrhonism during the counter-reformation was deemed so formidable that French Protestants were instructed not to converse with him for fear that they would lose their faith.[72] In a manner identical to Abraham, Newman consistently argues that when individuals try to interpret Scripture using their own private judgement the result is a confusing variety of interpretations which leads to theological skepticism. As in the case of Abraham, it is probable, therefore, that Newman's engagement with this theological transmission of Pyrrhonism has shaped his view of Protestantism.[73]

Here it is useful to illustrate briefly Newman and Abraham's similarities with these counter-reformation writers. A good example of how the problem of the criterion was used theologically during the counter-reformation is found in the following extract from de Sales:

> If then the church can err, O Calvin, O Luther, who will help me in my difficulties? Scripture, they say; but what will I do, poor man that I am? It is with the Scriptures themselves that I have difficulty. I do not doubt whether to believe Scripture or not, for who does not know that it is the word of truth? What bothers me is the understanding of Scripture[;] . . . these are numberless, diverse and contrary. How can someone choose between one and the other when out of all there is only one correct one,

---

69. Newman, *Grammar*, 304 [*GA*, 311]; Newman, *Lectures and Essays*, 94 [*Idea*, 315].

70. *Dev*, 429; Newman, *Lectures and Essays*, 188 [*Idea*, 406]; S.N. 25–26. Newman also cites de Sales in his correspondence: LD 5:19; LD 8:50; LD 11:92; LD 12:273; LD 19:539; LD 24:118, 240.

71. Newman, *History of my Religious Opinions*, 194 [*Apo* 194]; Véron, *The Rule of Catholic Faith*.

72. Popkin, *Scepticism*, 68. Newman would have also gained an explicit knowledge of this argument from Huet since the work of this French bishop was saturated with Sextus's ideas. For further discussion, see Huet, *A Philosophical Treatise*, 56; Newman, *Essay on Development*, 333 [*Dev*,332]; LD 9:120.

73. Though Newman clearly acknowledges Hawkin's influence on this aspect of his thinking it is important to observe the similarities between Newman and the counter-reformers on this point. For further discussion, see *Apo* 9.

what will make me know the correct one amidst so many that are bad?[74]

Here de Sales challenges the reformers by arguing that if interpretations can be wrong, such as the interpretation given by the church, how can they know that their interpretation is right—except by using their own interpretation which surely can also fail? This is similar to Newman's argument:

> One man sees the doctrine of absolute predestination in Scripture so clearly, as he considers, that he makes it almost an article of saving faith; another thinks it a most dangerous error. One man maintains, that the civil establishment of religion is commanded in Scripture, another that it is condemned by it . . . . If indeed full information had been promised to individuals from private study of the text of the Scriptures, this indeed might be a reason for dispensing with Antiquity, whatever was its value. But even could it be proved without value, as fully as the persons in question desire, still it must be recollected this would not go one step towards proving that such a promise of guidance from reading Scripture has been given; and it happens most remarkably, as I have already hinted, that satisfied, I suppose, with the simplicity of their theory, they have chiefly employed themselves in assailing the Christian Fathers, without proving what far more nearly concerns them, their own doctrine of the sufficiency of Scripture for teaching the faith; which failing, the Fathers are their sole, even though an insufficient resource.[75]

Here, in a manner similar to the counter-reformers, Newman illustrates how private individuals give different interpretations of Scripture. He points out, moreover, that while these individuals may refuse the interpretation given to Scripture by the early church fathers it is impossible for them to prove that their own interpretation is better than that given in Christian antiquity. Though it cannot be certain that Newman obtained this view of Scripture from counter-reformation writers like de Sales or Véron it is possible that this Pyrrhonian Catholic synergy shaped Newman and Abraham's view of the reformation's emphasis on individual private judgement since this use of the problem of the criterion by the

---

74. de Sales, *Les Controverses in Oeuvres*, 73–74. Translated by Ray Morris-Chapman.

75. Newman, *Lectures on the Prophetical Office*, 180, 195 [VM,1:151, 162–63].

counter-reformers was highly influential.[76] Regardless of this, it is clear that Newman's references to these Pyrrhonian sources challenges Maddox's contention that Newman was not explicitly aware of the problem of the criterion.

Liberalism and methodism

It is documented that Newman, Chisholm, and Abraham are all critical of the empiricism of John Locke; however, they all use different terminology to describe Locke. While Chisholm, for example, calls Locke an epistemological methodist, Newman views Locke as the father of nineteenth-century liberalism.[77] Nevertheless, it is interesting that Abraham views Locke as a representative of both epistemological methodism and liberalism.[78] For this reason the present section will compare Newman's opposition to liberalism with Chisholm's rejection of methodism.

Newman's understanding of the term "liberalism"

Liberalism had an enormous influence on Newman. He declares in a variety of places that for most of his life he has opposed "liberalism in religion."[79] However, while Chisholm's definition of epistemological methodism is concise and clear, Newman's understanding of liberalism is more difficult to pin down.[80]

---

76. Abraham is also consistent on this point, for example: "It was not long, then, before the Reformers themselves began developing radically different proposals . . . which were entirely incompatible with the claim that the teaching of Scripture was clear on these matters either in itself or derivatively." Abraham, *Canon and Criterion*, 151.

77. In fact, Newman states that liberalism was "diffused" throughout the "nation in the writings of the celebrated Mr. Locke." Newman, Review of *The Life of Archbishop Laud*, 368.

78. Abraham, *Canon and Criterion*, 280, 338.

79. For example, see Neville, *Addresses to Cardinal Newman*, 63–64.

80. As noted earlier Chisholm describes epistemological methodism as the position which argues that before we can have knowledge a method or criterion for attaining knowledge is required.

There are a variety of definitions given to liberalism.[81] In the Newman literature there are at least two schools of interpretation.[82] Writers tend narrowly to limit its meaning to rationalism[83] (or in Turner's case to evangelicalism),[84] or fall prey to the opposite extreme by suggesting that it is a general term of disapprobation.[85] In his *History of My Religious Opinions* (1865), Newman provides an eighteen-point definition of liberalism which deserves to be quoted in full:

> 1. No religious tenet is important, unless reason shows it to be so.... 2. No one can believe what he does not understand.... 3. No theological doctrine is any thing more than an opinion which happens to be held by bodies of men.... 4. It is dishonest in a man to make an act of faith in what he has not had brought home to him by actual proof.... 5. It is immoral in a man to believe more than he can spontaneously receive as being congenial to his moral and mental nature.... 6. No revealed doctrines or precepts may reasonably stand in the way of scientific conclusions.... 7. Christianity is necessarily modified by the growth of civilization, and the exigencies of times.... 8. There is a system of religion more simply true than Christianity as it has ever been received.... 9. There is a right of Private Judgment: that is, there is no existing authority on earth competent to interfere with the liberty of individuals in reasoning and judging for themselves about the Bible and its contents, as they severally please.... 10. There are rights of conscience such, that every one may lawfully advance a claim to profess and teach what is false and wrong in

---

81. For example, see de Ruggiero, *The History of European Liberalism*, 347–69.

82. In addition to these two approaches there are a few writers who view the seemingly miscellaneous aspects of liberalism as branches of a common root. For example, in his later publications, Merrigan has attempted to combine a rationalistic understanding of liberalism with the political and social connotations implied by Newman's usage: Merrigan, "Newman and Theological Liberalism," 605–21. For other writers who take this kind of approach, see Kenny, *Political Thought*, 129; Yearley, *The Ideas of Newman*, 94; Hastings, *The Theology of a Protestant Catholic*, 119. For further discussion, see Pratt Morris-Chapman, "The Meaning of 'Liberalism' in the thought of John Henry Newman."

83. Further examples of this interpretation include: Sands, *The Justification of Religious*, 103; Gunton, "Newman's Dialectic," 311–12; Nabe, *Mystery and Religion*, 2–3; Norris, *Newman and His Theological Method*, 7; Fey, *Faith and Doubt*, 2, 10; Merrigan, "Newman's Catholic Synthesis," 40.

84. Turner, *John Henry Newman*.

85. Thomas, *Newman and Heresy*, xiii; O'Connell, "Newman and Liberalism," 80; Cameron, "Newman and Liberalism," 166; Dulles, *Newman*, 14, 73; Chadwick, *Newman*, 71, 73–74.

matters, religious, social, and moral, provided that to his private conscience it seems absolutely true and right. . . . 11. There is no such thing as a national or state conscience. . . . 12. The civil power has no positive duty, in a normal state of things, to maintain religious truth. . . . 13. Utility and expedience are the measure of political duty. . . . 14. The Civil Power may dispose of Church property without sacrilege. . . . 15. The Civil Power has the right of ecclesiastical jurisdiction and administration. . . . 16. It is lawful to rise in arms against legitimate princes. . . . 17. The people are the legitimate source of power. . . . 18. Virtue is the child of knowledge, and vice of ignorance.[86]

It is plain that Newman understood liberalism in religion to contain theological, philosophical, political, and educational dimensions.[87] While point nine indicates an association with Protestantism, Turner's definition of liberalism (as evangelicalism) is too narrow.[88]

Nevertheless, Turner's contention that although Newman scholars are frequently using the term "liberalism" their definitions are "internally inconsistent" is justified by the Newman literature.[89] This failure to adequately define liberalism is indicated in the following citation from Jay Newman:

> The terms "liberal" and "liberalism" are notoriously ambiguous and were already so in Newman's day. Newman himself did not have a clear idea of what he was attacking . . . using liberalism as a general term of disapprobation and abuse.[90]

This extract indicates that Jay Newman has failed to note what J. H. Newman actually meant by liberalism.

Newman's eighteen-point definition of liberalism highlights the manner in which liberalism subordinates religion to the ends of reason, politics, and secular ethics. Essentially Newman opposes the theological reductionism or skepticism that results from the introduction of inappropriate theological, philosophical, political or utilitarian educational principles.[91] Theologically, Newman criticizes evangelicals for limiting

86. Newman, *History of My Religious Opinions*, 294–96.

87. Newman's conception of the philosophical dimensions of liberalism is our chief concern here.

88. Turner, *John Henry Newman: The Challenge to Evangelical Religion*.

89. Turner, Review of *The Cambridge Companion*, 422.

90. Newman, *Mental Philosophy*, 30–31.

91. Terrence Kenny makes similar observations regarding liberalism. For further discussion, see Kenny, *Political Thought*, 129.

doctrinal truth to what reason can infer from the contents of the Bible.[92] Politically, Newman and John Keble (1792–1866), like other members of the Oxford Movement, opposed the state's interference in the Irish dioceses.[93] In education Newman felt that liberalism had attacked the place of theology in the university by measuring the value of this subject using the "Philosophy of Utility."[94] Philosophically, the title of *Tract 73* (1835) demonstrates Newman's opposition to "The Introduction of Rationalistic Principles into Revealed Religion." In this *Tract* Newman opposes something approaching epistemological methodism. Here he accuses Jacob Abbot (1803–79), author of *The Corner Stone* (1834),[95] of liberalism and rationalism, in that Abbot "takes for granted" that:

> [T]he human mind may criticise and systematise the divine revelation . . . that it may limit the uses of the latter to its workings through our own reason and affections, and such workings as we can ascertain and comprehend.[96]

Citing Hume as an example of this rationalist frame of mind, Newman argues that the fault of these writers is that they limit the "range of God's operations" to human principles.[97] From this it would seem liberalism

---

92. Newman, Review of *The Brothers' Controversy*, 171–72 [*Ess*, 1:111].

93. The Oxford Movement began when the Whig government decided to suppress ten Irish Bishoprics, a move considered sacrilegious in view of the fact that Keble, and others like Newman, felt that only the church had the authority to reorder diocese. For further discussion see Keble's Assize Sermon: Keble, *Sermons*, 131ff; Smart, *Nineteenth Century*, 70–72.

94. In his *Discourses* Newman recounts how the University of London decided against having a theology department (because theology was not deemed useful as other sciences) and clearly considers this to be a manifestation of liberalism in religion. For further discussion, see Newman, *Discourses on the Scope and Nature*, 136–40, 192.

95. Abbot, *The Corner Stone*.

96. Newman, *Tracts for the Times*, 3:34, 45. [*Ess*, 2:72] Accordingly, Newman connects "liberalism" to the conception that the human mind through human reason can measure divine revelation.

97. "Mr. Hume openly avows this principle, declaring it to be unphilosophical to suppose that Almighty God can do anything, but what we see He does. And, though we may not profess it, we too often, it is to be feared, act upon it at the present day. Instead of looking out of ourselves, and trying to catch glimpses of God's workings, from any quarter,—throwing ourselves forward upon Him and waiting on Him, we sit at home bringing everything to ourselves, enthroning ourselves as the centre of all things, and refusing to believe anything that does not force itself upon our minds as true. Our private judgment is made everything to us,—is contemplated, recognized, and referred to as the arbiter of all questions, and as independent of everything

in religion is to measure the truths of revelation using inappropriate principles drawn from human rationality. Thus Newman, in a manner paralleled in Chisholm's philosophy, is opposed to the presupposition of unsuitable criteria to measure the validity of theological claims. While Newman uses a different term to describe his adversary each of these writers target the empiricism of Locke as being representative of that which they oppose.

Empiricism

Newman, Chisholm, and Abraham's critical reading of John Locke and David Hume[98] documents their shared knowledge of the empiricist tradition.[99] The empiricists emphasized the point that all knowledge of real existence must be based on the senses, thus we cannot prove the existence of anything without appealing to experience.[100] Locke writes:

> Real existence can be proved only by real existence; and, therefore the real existence of a God can only be proved by the real existence of other things. The real existence of other things without us, can be evidenced to us only by our senses.[101]

As Newman understands him, Locke propounds an arbitrary principle of justification when he maintains that assent to a proposition should always be proportionate to the proof in its favor.[102] As a result Newman feels that Locke's theory of assent begins in the wrong place:

---

external to us. Nothing is considered to have an existence except so far forth as our minds discern it." Newman, *Tracts for the Times*, 3:3–4.

98. Abraham, *Canon and Criterion*, 104, 239; Chisholm, *Problem of the Criterion*, 16, 20; *Mir*, 103–4.

99. While several writers take note of Newman's debt to the empiricist tradition, Sillem opposes the very suggestion that Locke and Hume had any constructive influence upon Newman. Whether or not Sillem is correct it is clear that Newman studied the empiricists and that Locke's *Essay on Human Understanding* (1692) formed a perfect foil for Newman's *Grammar*. For examples of Locke's constructive influence, see Cameron, "Newman and Empiricism," 219–43; Corbett, "A Comparison," 40–49; Mitchell, "Newman as a Philosopher," 223–46; Kenny, "Newman as a Philosopher of Religion," 100; Richardson, *Newman's Approach to Knowledge*, 6–7. Sillem's position is captured in the following citation: "I submit that the positive, constructive influence of Locke on Newman was, if it existed at all, so small as to be negligible." *PN*, 1:198, 203.

100. Meyers, *Empiricism*, 1–2.

101. King, *The Life of John Locke*, 315.

102. Locke, *The Works of John Locke*, 2:272 [4.19.1].

> [Locke] takes a view of the human mind, in relation to inference and assent, which to me seems theoretical and unreal. Reasonings and convictions which I deem natural and legitimate, he apparently would call irrational, enthusiastic, perverse, and immoral; and that, as I think, because he consults his own ideal of what ought to be, instead of interrogating human nature, as an existing thing, as it is found in the world. Instead of going by the testimony of psychological facts, and thereby determining our constitutive faculties and our proper condition, and being content with the mind as God has made it, he would form men as he thinks they ought to be formed, into something better and higher, and calls them irrational and immoral, if (so to speak) they take to the water, instead of remaining under the narrow wings of his own arbitrary theory.[103]

Newman argues that Locke should not begin by measuring our assents with his formula of logic, but ought to examine assent as it is found in real life. Grimm aptly notes Newman's similarity with Chisholm at this point:

> Put in terms of a distinction popularized by Chisholm, Newman thus faults Locke for the excessive methodism of his account, when what is called for, according to Newman, is a careful, particularistic analysis of the actual beliefs which claim our rational assent.[104]

It is here that the most obvious parallel linking Chisholm and Newman may be demonstrated, in the similarity between their criticisms of Locke. While Chisholm describes Locke as an epistemological methodist he criticizes him for the same reasons as Newman:

> John Locke was a methodist.... He said in effect: "The way you decide whether or not a belief is a good belief—that is to say, the way you decide whether a belief is likely to be a genuine case of knowledge—is to see . . . whether it bears certain relations to your sensations." . . . This of course is the view that has come to be known as "empiricism." . . . Empiricism, then, was a form of what I have called "Methodism." The empiricist—like other types of methodist—begins with a criterion and then he uses it to throw out the bad [beliefs;] . . . the criterion is very broad and far-reaching and at the same time completely arbitrary. How can one begin with a broad generalization? It seems especially odd that the empiricist—who wants to proceed cautiously, step by

---

103. Newman, *Grammar*, 157 [*GA*, 164–65].
104. Grimm, "Cardinal Newman, Reformed Epistemologist?" 504.

step, from experience—begins with such a generalization. He leaves us completely in the dark so far as concerns what reasons he may have for adopting this particular criterion rather than some other.[105]

Here Chisholm criticizes Locke for epistemological "methodism" because he begins epistemological enquiry with a broad generalization, an arbitrary criterion, which dictates that all knowledge must have a relationship to the senses. This is the same kind of criticism made by Newman, who upbraids Locke for allowing his arbitrary theory, of what constitutes justified assent, to put perfectly legitimate beliefs in doubt. Thus, Newman and Chisholm condemn Locke for exactly the same thing: allowing his criteria to render sensible beliefs irrational.

In a manner strikingly paralleled in Chisholm, Newman argues that Locke commences enquiry in the wrong place. In Newman's view one should not begin with a theoretical rule delineating when an assent is justified but by examining assent as it occurs in everyday human existence:

> When, then, philosophers lay down principles, on which it follows that our assent, except when given to Objects of intuition or demonstration, is conditional, that the assent given to propositions by well-ordered minds necessarily varies with the proof producible for them, and that it does not and cannot remain one and the same while the proof is strengthened or weakened, are they not to be considered as confusing together two things very distinct from each other, a mental act or state and a scientific rule, an interior assent and a set of logical formulas? When they speak of degrees of assent, surely they have no intention at all of defining the position of the mind itself relative to the adoption of a given conclusion, but they mean to determine the relation of that conclusion towards its premisses [sic]. They are contemplating how representative symbols work, not how the intellect is directed towards the thing which those symbols represent. In real truth they as little mean to assert the principle of measuring our assents by our logic, as they would fancy they could record the refreshment which we receive from the open air by the readings of the graduated scale of a thermometer.[106]

Here Newman opposes those philosophers who try to predetermine the parameters of justified belief with invented formulas that have no real

---

105. Chisholm, *Problem of the Criterion*, 15–17.
106. Newman, *Grammar*, 172 [*GA*, 179–80].

bearing upon the facts. Chisholm makes the same point: "to find out whether you know such a thing as that this is a hand, you don't have to apply any test or criterion." For one to be skeptical about knowledge claims, such as "I know that this is my hand," because they do not cohere with a criterion of knowledge is absurd. Thus, Chisholm concludes that if an epistemological criterion denies beliefs that no sane person would deny then it is the theory, and not the knowledge claim, that is misplaced.[107] Newman likewise argues that it is unreasonable to allow a theory, such as Locke's, to deny beliefs to which the majority of people would unhesitatingly stake a claim. Newman considers that Locke's theory denies people the following certitudes:

> (1) That we exist (2) That we remember what happened yesterday (3) That we are ignorant of many things (4) That other people exist (5) That the universe is carried on by laws. (6) That the future is affected by the past. (7) That the earth is a globe. (8) That there are cities in different places on the earth such as Madrid ... Paris. (9) That we had parents, though we can have no memory of our birth. (10) That we shall die, though we can have no experience of the future.[108]

What Newman does is to list a number of instances in which people would claim to have certain knowledge. Like Chisholm, Newman presents these normal beliefs in order to show that there are several things which "we all believe, without any doubt," that cannot be proved on Locke's theory.[109] While Newman, therefore, opposes Locke's "liberalism" and Chisholm views him as a representative of "epistemological methodism," it is clear that their criticisms are almost identical. Both consider that Locke allows an arbitrary theory to render legitimate beliefs irrational.

Abraham also criticizes Locke for epistemological methodism for he considers that the Lockean project made theological claims subordinate to epistemological criterion.[110] Abraham argues that when theology is preceded by an "epistemological prolegomena" theology becomes subservient to the theory at hand.[111] In such cases crucial theological claims

---

107. Chisholm, *Problem of the Criterion*, 20–22.

108. This is not a quote from Newman but a digested list of the commonsense beliefs which, according to Newman, Locke's theory denies. For further discussion, see Newman, *Grammar*, 169–71 [*GA*, 177–79].

109. Newman, *Grammar*, 169 [*GA*, 177].

110. Abraham, *Canon and Criterion*, 235.

111. Abraham, *Crossing*, 9.

are placed in jeopardy by an epistemological theory. Abraham believes that Locke represents an example of this because Locke became skeptical about Christianity's central doctrines since they did not meet his standards for legitimate knowledge.

> The Nicene Creed, the Chalcedonian Definition, the liturgy, iconography, and the Fathers are not just missing [from Locke]; they are treated with distaste because, both in fact and in principle, any use of them is ruled out by the strictures of the favoured epistemology.[112]

What is interesting here is Abraham's acknowledgment that "this is exactly what Newman found so troubling in the liberal circles of his day."[113] Abraham thus shows that his concerns about the way in which epistemological methodism places theology at the mercy of an arbitrary criterion had been anticipated by Newman's worries about the liberalism in Locke's writings.[114]

Abraham recognizes that what concerned Newman most about Locke was his contention that revelation should not be "contrary to reason." Abraham considers that this was "easily transposed by Locke's disciples in such a way as to make revelation redundant." He writes:

> For if the content of revelation is subject to evaluation by reason and the source of revelation has to be validated by reason, it is a simple, if mistaken, step from this to the claim that . . . the canonical doctrines of the Church were acceptable only in so far as they were warranted by the evidence of reason and experience. Furthermore, once reason was given a free hand to examine the content of revelation, the dimension of mystery in divine revelation was immediately put at risk.[115]

Abraham considers that, like epistemological methodism in theology, "liberalism entailed the introduction of the rationalistic principle into theology."[116] From this it would seem that Newman's conception of the philosophical dimensions of liberalism and Chisholm and Abraham's understanding of epistemological methodism amount to the same

---

112. Abraham, *Canon and Criterion*, 224, 227.
113. Abraham, *Canon and Criterion*, 338.
114. Abraham, *Crossing*, 6; Newman, *Grammar*, 169–71 [*GA*, 177–79].
115. Abraham, *Canon and Criterion*, 338.
116. Abraham, *Canon and Criterion*, 338.

thing: allowing an inappropriate criteria to presuppose epistemology or theology.[117]

In summary, it seems that Newman, Chisholm, and Abraham criticize Locke for the same thing. While Newman calls this liberalism, and Chisholm epistemological methodism, both fault Locke for presupposing an invented criterion that inadvertently rules out commonsensical knowledge claims (such as the certainty of death).[118] These similarities indicate why Newman's reception of Locke and his reflections on liberalism are of interest to Abraham. Moreover it further indicates Newman's potential relevance to the wider particularist discussion.

Thomas Reid

Thomas Reid grounded knowledge in the reliable operation of the human faculties such as memory, sense perception, introspection, and so on. He states that "all knowledge got by reasoning must be built upon first principles. This is as certain as that every house must have a foundation."[119] Reid's first principle is that our faculties are reliable. He considers that this principle ought to be prior to all the others "because in every instance of assent, whether upon intuitive, demonstrative, or probable evidence, the truth of our faculties is taken for granted."[120] He states that this just simply is the way we are.[121] Therefore, Reid emphasized the fact that it is a first principle that our various faculties such as memory, sense

---

117. To be clear, Newman's conception of the *philosophical* dimension of liberalism resonates with Chisholm and Abraham's discussion of epistemological methodism. Thus, while the latter is by no means synonymous with liberalism in its more general form, it might be construed as a philosophical subset of it. For further discussion, see Pratt Morris-Chapman, "Liberalism."

118. One possible reason for the similarity between the criticisms that Newman, Chisholm and Abraham make of Locke is their shared knowledge of Pyrrhonism. As discussed earlier, the Pyrrhonists realized the futility of basing knowledge on a criterion. Hence it is possible that these writers condemn Locke's attempt to make knowledge dependent upon a criterion of experience because they view him through a Pyrrhonian lens. For example, it is also possible that Newman's discussion of liberalism as an "antidogmatic principle" could be related to Sextus' discussion of the antidogmatic writers Arcesilaus and Carneades. For further discussion, see *Ess*, 1:264–71.

119. Reid, *The Works of Thomas Reid*, 435; also see Bergmann, *Justification*, 207.

120. Reid, *The Works of Thomas Reid*, 447.

121. Reid, *The Works of Thomas Reid*, 447–48.

perception, and reasoning are reliable and that this means that the beliefs they produce must also be reliable.

In *The Problem of the Criterion* Chisholm cites Reid as an early example of particularism: "Reid, as I interpret him, was not an empiricist; nor was he, more generally, what I have called a 'methodist.' He was a 'particularist.'"[122] Chisholm considers that Reid would begin with the knowledge claims that are in our possession, and from there decide what are the criteria of knowledge.[123] Therefore, following Reid, Chisholm considers that epistemology should be guided by the propositions that "we all do presuppose in our ordinary activity." Taking these commonsense beliefs seriously is essential to his theory of knowledge.[124]

While Abraham explicitly states that he prefers to use Newman rather than Reid when approaching epistemological questions,[125] he also considers Reid to be a forerunner of epistemological particularism.[126] He writes:

> Rather than begin from a general commitment to a method or criterion for accepting or rejecting a particular belief, Reid insisted that any theory about epistemic method or criterion must be tested by the particular beliefs which were generally accepted as correct. Thus, rather than say that we should give up our belief in the external world because that belief failed to satisfy the canon that all our beliefs be derivable from immediate sense experience, we should appeal to our general belief in the existence of the external world to access the validity of the epistemic claim that all our beliefs be derivable from immediate sense experience. In this particular case the material empiricist principles enunciated by Locke and Hume were to be rejected.[127]

Thus Abraham, like Chisholm, considers that Reid begins epistemological enquiry with generally accepted beliefs and argues that epistemological criterion should by shaped by these particular beliefs and not *vice versa*.

In the above Chisholm and Abraham explicitly acknowledge that epistemological particularism is anticipated by Reid. What is interesting

---

122. Chisholm, *Problem of the Criterion*, 19.
123. Chisholm, *Problem of the Criterion*, 12.
124. Chisholm, *Person and Object*, 15.
125. Abraham, *Logic of Renewal*, 166.
126. Abraham, *Crossing*, 34.
127. Abraham, *Canon and Criterion*, 280.

here is that the philosopher and Newman commentator Jamie Ferreira considers Newman as belonging to the same philosophical tradition as Reid.[128] Prior to Ferreira's extensive comparison, however, the link between Reid and Newman was largely ignored.[129] Although Sillem makes the observation that Newman's copy of Reid's works "is extensively marked" with a "large number of notes . . . pencilled around the text," he contends that there is a lack of evidence to establish a link between the two.[130] However, Ferreira's conclusions seem warranted since Newman cites Reid several times in his papers on *Faith and Certainty* (papers written between 1843 and 1890).[131] Newman's work is also compared to Thomas Reid by Charles Meynell (1869).[132]

Newman himself states that he read Reid, as his annotations obviously prove.[133] Although Newman's early references to Reid are generally critical,[134] it is possible that this negative reception might be explained by the fact that his tutor at Oxford, Richard Whately, sought to defend Aristotelian philosophy against the new logic of Scottish philosophers like Thomas Reid.[135] Ferreira's comparison demonstrates the significance of Reid for Newman's writing. Ferreira, for example, compares the following references from Newman and Reid's works:

> [Reid] That there is such a city as Rome, I am as certain as of any proposition in Euclid; but the evidence is not demonstrative, but of that kind which philosophers call probable. Yet in common language it would sound oddly to say, it is probable there is such a city as Rome, because it would imply some degree of doubt or uncertainty.[136]

---

128. Ferreira, *Scepticism*.

129. Ferreira, *Scepticism*, 145–226.

130. *PN,* 1: 221, 223.

131. *TP,* 1:51, 94, 152, 158.

132. Newman initiated correspondence with Meynell (a priest and a philosopher) in order to ask him if he might use his "experienced eye" to check if Newman's draft chapters of the *Grammar of Assent* "offend" either "doctrinal propriety or common sense." LD 24:279, 306–7. For further discussion, see Mitchell, *Meynell*, §1.

133. LD 4:253.

134. In his early correspondence Newman calls Reid's work "trash" and describes it as "destitute" of imagination. For further discussion, see LD 2:63; LD 4:253.

135. Willam, *Aristotelische*, 19–21. Whately's article on Logic is an example of this. Newman and Whately, "Logic," 1:193–240.

136. Reid, *The Works of Thomas Reid*, 482.

> [Newman] We accept and hold with an unqualified assent . . . that Paris or London, unless suddenly swallowed up by an earthquake or burned to the ground, is today just what it was yesterday, when we left it.[137]

These references indicate that Newman uses arguments very similar to those of Reid. Like Reid, Newman contends that it is better to assume things which we are certain of even if we do not possess demonstrative proof for them (in the sense that he himself is not currently present in France); that it is foolish to entertain doubts about the reality of Rome or Paris simply because one is not currently able to obtain empirical proof for their existence.

Newman's similarities with this writer suggest that Ferreira's analysis is correct to interpret Newman as being a part of the same philosophical tradition as Reid. The implications of this for our present analysis are significant when it is considered that Chisholm and Abraham interpret Reid as a forerunner of the particularist tradition. This suggests that if Newman is part of the same philosophical tradition as Reid he might be considered a part of the same tradition as Chisholm and Abraham. At the very least, Newman's conviction that our commonsense beliefs should be taken on trust makes his writing relevant to these writers and to the wider particularist debate.

Thomistic sources

Newman and the forerunners of the scholastic revival

Abraham is highly critical of neo-scholastic writers.[138] However, Chisholm directly acknowledges that his particularist approach to the problem of skepticism is inspired by a key proponent of the revival of this tradition in the nineteenth century. As indicated above, Chisholm cites Désiré Joseph Cardinal Mercier (1851–1926) and his doctoral student Peter Coffey (1876–1943) as having central influence upon his understanding of the problem of the criterion, and upon what he deems to be necessary for its solution.[139]

---

137. Newman, *Grammar*, 170 [*GA*, 177].
138. Abraham, *Canon and Criterion*, 18n19.
139. Chisholm, *Problem of the Criterion*, 1–2. It should be acknowledged here that neo-scholasticism is not always neo-Thomist as the majority of neo-scholasticists in the nineteenth century, especially those before 1870 were eclecticists. For further discussion, see Aubert, "Aspects," 134.

It is highly unlikely that Newman would have engaged with Mercier's works. Newman died (1890) before Mercier's writings became well known. It is, nevertheless, the case that Mercier makes a number of references to Newman. Thus, while chapter 5 will examine Mercier and Chisholm's engagement with Newman's writing, the current section will examine whether Newman, like Mercier, engaged with what have been described as the pioneers of the scholastic revival: Jaime Balmes (1810–48), Matteo Liberatore (1810–92), Gaetano Sanseverino (1811–65), and Josef Kleutgen (1811–83).[140] If Newman did engage with these sources it suggests that his proposals should not, as has often been the case, be viewed in isolation from neo-scholastic writers. This is important because if Newman is viewed in isolation from the sources that Chisholm acknowledges to have shaped his proposals when in fact Newman interacted with these sources, it supports the notion that he is unrelated to this tradition.

As indicated, any comparison between Newman and neo-scholasticism faces a serious objection: Newman preceded the scholastic revival, as Flanagan points out, "When he [Newman] was writing, the scholastic revival can hardly be said to have begun."[141] This objection is based on the fact that the scholastic revival only gained real momentum when Pope Leo XIII's *Aeterni Patris* (1879) encouraged the church to: "restore the golden wisdom of St. Thomas, and to spread it far and wide for the defense and beauty of the Catholic faith . . . and for the advantage of all the sciences."[142] It must be admitted that the majority of Newman's works, even the *Grammar*, were published before this encyclical.[143] The general state of Thomistic studies prior to *Aeterni Patris* is indicated by Newman

---

140. Van Riet views these writers as important forerunners of the scholastic revival. Van Riet, *Thomistic Epistemology*, 1:5. Like Newman, Mercier was familiar with the writings of Balmes and Kleutgen. For further discussion, see Mercier, *Critériologie*, 71, 89, 90, 91, 92, 96, 97, 98, 99, 101, 103, 105, 113, 261, 262, 263, 343, 374, 376, 387, 389, 425.

141. Flanagan, *Newman*, viii. For a classic example of attempts to differentiate Newman from Aquinas, see Harper, "Dr Newman's Essay," 599–611.

142. Para 31 cited in Vincelette argues that: "Aeterni Patris (1879) . . . helped the Catholic Church recover the Thomistic tradition that had been nearly forgotten since 1650." Vincelette, *Recent Catholic Philosophy*, 121.

143. The impact of *Aeterni Patris* was considerable. It led to the formation of a faculty of philosophy in the Pontifical Roman Academy of Saint Thomas Aquinas (1882) and played a major part in the creation of a chair for Thomistic philosophy (1882) at the Catholic University of Louvain; a position first occupied by Cardinal Mercier who himself later founded Louvain's Higher Institute of Philosophy (1899).

himself who, thirty-four years earlier, was disappointed by a report he heard from a Jesuit Father on the state of Thomistic studies in Rome. In a letter to J. D. Dalgairns (November 1846), he recounts this meeting:

> [A] talk we had yesterday with one of the Jesuit fathers here shows we shall find little philosophy. It arose from our talking of the Greek studies of the Propaganda and asking whether the youths learned Aristotle. "O no—he said—Aristotle is in no favor here—no, not in Rome:—not St Thomas. I have read Aristotle and St Thomas, and owe a great deal to them, but they are out of favor here and throughout Italy. St Thomas is a great saint—people don't dare to speak against him—they profess to reverence him, but put him aside." I asked what philosophy they did adopt. He said none. "Odds and ends—whatever seems to them best—like St Clement's Stromata. They have no philosophy. Facts are the great things, and nothing else. Exegesis, but not doctrine." He went on to say that many privately were sorry for this, many Jesuits, he said; but no one dared oppose the fashion. When I said I thought that there was a latent power in Rome which would stop the evil, and that the Pope introduced Aristotle and St Thomas into the Church, and the Pope was bound to maintain them, he shrugged his shoulders and said the Pope could do nothing if people would not obey him.[144]

This reference supports the idea that Newman precedes the popular revival of Thomistic studies. Van Riet, however, makes clear that although there were periods when Aquinas had "few defenders" the "philosophy of St Thomas was never totally cast aside."[145] McInerny likewise argues that while Aquinas may have been out of favor "things could not have been entirely bad."[146]

McInerny shows how easy it is to miss "the role of the Dominicans in accounts of these antecedents" to *Aeterni Patris*. He questions: "Did Newman meet any Dominicans in Rome?" suggesting that if he had his estimation of the situation would have been different.[147] This is an apt question for it is clear from his subsequent letter to Dalgairns (December 1846) that Newman's increasing contact with the Dominicans in Rome had somewhat allayed his fears about the study of Aquinas:

---

144. LD 11:279.
145. Van Riet, *Thomistic Epistemology*, 1:29.
146. McInerny, "The Thomistic Revival," x.
147. McInerny, "The Thomistic Revival," x.

> Now it has been brought home to us in many ways that the Dominicans are the representative of rigorism among the orders—and that in fact they therefore jump [?] a good deal with the French character and school; and I really do hope that this is the explanation of what we heard, (or at least goes a considerable way to explain,) about the prevalent depreciation of St Thomas.[148]

Hence, while Newman's previous conversation with a Jesuit Father led him to conclude that Aquinas was totally out of favor in Rome, it appears that the Dominicans, "a rising body through Italy,"[149] had continued to uphold his teachings.[150]

Most commentators, including Ventresca, accept that the formal intervention of the Roman pontiff turned the "trickle of interest in Thomism into the torrent of revival witnessed after the 1880s." Ventresca, nevertheless, argues that the "Thomistic revival attributed to Leo's decisive intervention preceded his papal declarations by several decades."[151] He writes:

> Thomism was alive and gathering force, albeit slowly, from about the mid-eighteenth century onward. This was especially the case in Italy, where one can speak of "foyers of neo-Thomism"—albeit only a small handful—at least as early as the mid-eighteenth century. The most notable were the Thomistic academy established in Naples in 1846, inspired by the work of Gaetano Sanseverino, as well as the work of the Collegio Alberoni near Piacenza that predated by a century the Thomistic study group Joachim Pecci (the future Leo XIII) established while he was Bishop of Perugia. Of course, the future Pope Leo's reform of seminary instruction while bishop at Perugia, and his formal sponsorship of the Academy of Saint Thomas Aquinas in 1859 (together with his brother Joseph, who was a Thomist heavyweight destined to teach Thomism in the pontifical academies of Rome) contributed in concrete ways to bolster the gathering momentum of a Thomistic revival.[152]

---

148. LD 11:303.

149. LD 12:25.

150. Fergusson argues that "There had been a continuous tradition of Scholastic theology since the medieval era even with its ebbs and flows." Ferguson, *The Blackwell Companion to Nineteenth-Century Theology*, 380.

151. Ventresca, "A Plague of Perverse Opinions," 151–52.

152. Ventresca, "A Plague of Perverse Opinions" 151. Other writers suggest that pockets of Italian neo-Thomism arose even earlier: Pelzer, "Les initiateurs Italiens

These points are affirmed by Jordan who states that "while *Aeterni Patris* did mobilize large-scale ecclesiastical support for a new Thomism, its programme had been worked out in Catholic educational circles during the previous four decades."[153] Van Riet likewise argues that from "about 1850 Christian thinkers began to effect a restoration of Thomistic philosophy" and cites Balmes, Liberatore, Sanseverino, and Kleutgen as pioneers of this revival.[154]

Newman himself read and referred to Balmes, Liberatore, and Kleutgen; key sources for Mercier and the revival of scholasticism.[155] Despite this Newman studies have until quite recently underestimated the significance of Newman's interaction with these forerunners of the neo-scholastic movement.[156] Sillem strangely argues that despite Newman's possession of (and his annotations in) volumes by these writers, "we cannot possibly regard these manuals as a source for any of his own ideas."[157] This seems odd when one considers the many connections between these writers. For example, Newman read Balmes when preparing papers for his *Grammar*[158] and it is clear that Newman's discussion of assent has parallels with Balmes's discussion in his *Fundamental Philosophy* (1846).[159]

---

du neo-thomisme contemporain," 230–54; and Masnovo, "L'opera del Liberatore dal 1840–1850," 120–29.

153. Among these thinkers Jordan lists Matteo Liberatore and Joseph Kleutgen as being of central importance. Jordan, "neo-Thomism," 614.

154. Van Riet, *Thomistic Epistemology*, 1:5.

155. It is possible that Newman was also in conversation with Sanseverino. For further discussion, see *PN*, 1:237.

156. Sands, *The Justification of Religious*; Wainwright, *Reason and the Heart*; Newman, *Mental Philosophy*; Ferreira, *Doubt and Religious Commitment*; Artz, "Newmans Philosophische Leistung," 190; Norris, *Newman and His Theological Method*; Vargish, *Newman*; Zeno, *John Henry Newman*; Juergens, *Newman on the Psychology*.

157. *PN*,1:239

158. Newman possessed a copy of an English translation of Balmes' *Fundamental Philosophy*. For further discussion, see *PN*, 1:240; *TP*, 1:51. Newman cites Balmes a number of times: Newman, *Lectures on Catholicism in England*, 201 [*Prepos*, 210]; LD 14:327; LD 17:35; LD 31:28; Balmes, *Fundamental Philosophy*.

159. For further discussion, compare Newman's distinction between inference and assent, in the *Grammar*, with the following extract from Balmes: "Experience has in fact shown our understanding to be guided by no one of the considerations made by philosophers; its assent, when it is accompanied by the greatest certainty, is a spontaneous product of a natural instinct, not of combinations; it is a firm adhesion exacted by the evidence of the truth, the power of the internal sense, or the impulse of instinct; not a conviction produced by a series of ratiocinations. These combinations and ratiocinations therefore exist only in the mind of philosophers, not in reality;

Before Newman, who separates assent from formal processes of reason, Balmes argued that our assents are "the spontaneous product of man's nature"; that they are not dependent upon the "pretended foundations" of philosophers.[160]

Newman's discussion of assent also has some similarities with Liberatore, who he mentions in his correspondence.[161] For example, Liberatore argued in his *Institutiones Logicae et Metaphysicae* (1845) that by our nature we are endowed with a natural rational capacity which spontaneously inclines us to assent to a number of judgements or certitudes.[162] Anticipating Chisholm's particularism, Liberatore argues that we acquire this knowledge without first having criteria. He argues that such criteria do not provide us with knowledge.[163]

In addition to the above, Newman's copy of Kleutgen's *La Philosophic Scholastique* (1863) is heavily annotated.[164] This is highly significant for Kleutgen taught Vincenzo Pecci (1810–1903) before he became Pope Leo XIII (1878–1903) and, if Boekraad is correct, composed the first draft of *Aeterni Patris*.[165] Newman, for example, marks several of the pages

---

when, therefore, they attempt to designate the foundations of certainty, we are told what could or should have been, but not what is. If philosophers would only be guided by their own systems, and would not forget them nor set them aside as soon as, or even before, they have finished explaining them, it might be said, that even if no reason can be given for human certainty, one can be given for philosophical certainty; but since these same philosophers make no use of these scientific means save when developing them ex professo, it follows that their pretended foundations are a mere theory, having little or no connection with the reality." Balmes, *Fundamental Philosophy*, 1:14–15, 22–23.

160. This aspect of Balmes work anticipates one of the tendencies (P2) identified above as being characteristic of particularist writers. Balmes, *Fundamental Philosophy*, 1:14.

161. LD 17:397.

162. Liberatore, *Institutiones Logicae et Metaphysicae*, 73–77, 82–85. Liberatore argues that if one does not assume that our capacity for attaining knowledge is reliable then skepticism is inevitable. He does not believe that doubt ought to be the starting point for philosophy.

163. This aspect of Liberatore's work anticipates one of the tendencies (P2) identified above as being characteristic of particularist writers. Liberatore, *Institutiones Logicae et Metaphysicae*, 80–82.

164. Kleutgen, *La Philosophie Scholastique*. All the volumes of Kleutgen in Newman's library are marked with his annotations.

165. Boekraad even argues that Newman cites Kleutgen (but does not say where). For further discussion, see Boekraad, *The Argument from Conscience*, 40–45; King, *Newman*, 222.

in the section on certitude.[166] He marks page 451 in which Kleutgen contends that when philosophers undermine certainties that no mature adult would deny we must not heed this speculation.[167] He maintains that philosophical reason should not be permitted to judge definitively about what we can know.[168] This bears considerable resemblance to (P1), Chisholm's criticism of writers (like Locke) who allow "arbitrary" philosophical theories to determine the extent of our beliefs.

These findings call into question Sillem's contention that Newman should "never" be seen as a forerunner of the scholastic revival:

> To understand Newman it is absolutely essential to recapture the atmosphere of mind which existed amongst Catholics in England before the pontificate of Leo XIII, and never to read him as if he were a forerunner of the Scholastic revival.[169]

Despite Sillem's claim, several books discussing the revival of scholasticism mention Newman. For example, Joseph Rickaby, *Scholasticism* (1908),[170] De Wulf's *Scholasticism Old and New* (1910),[171] Phillips's *Modern Thomistic Philosophy* (1941),[172] Wilhelmsen *Man's Knowledge of Reality* (1956),[173] Eley's *God's Own Image: A Counter-Revolution in Philosophy* (1963),[174] and Van Riet's, *Thomistic Epistemology* (1965) all mention him.[175] More recently Newman scholars have become increasingly aware of the similarities between Newman and neo-scholastic writers.[176]

---

166. Kleutgen, *La Philosophie Scholastique*, 1:431.

167. He contends that if we try to deny our spontaneous certitude, for example that the world exists, it will impose itself upon us spontaneously and make us look foolish. Kleutgen, *La Philosophie Scholastique*, 1:446–47.

168. Kleutgen, *La Philosophie Scholastique*, 1:451.

169. *PN*, 1:239.

170. Rickaby, *Scholasticism*, 89.

171. de Wulf, *Scholasticism*, 202.

172. Phillips, *Modern Thomistic*, 1:8–15.

173. Wilhelmsen, *Man's Knowledge*, 34, 209.

174. Eley, *God's Own Image*, 18.

175. Van Riet, *Thomistic Epistemology*, 1:205.

176. With the exception of Ward, and a few other writers, the similarities between Newman and the neo-Thomists have gone unnoticed until relatively recently. For further discussion, see Benjamin King, *Newman*, 62–63, 222–24; Swindal and Gensler, *The Sheed and Ward Anthology*, 270; Ward, *The Life*, 2:274, 306; Toohey, "Newman on the Criterion of Certitude," 444–53; Ward, "Certitude," 253–74; Ward, "Explicit," 421–42.

King points out that the style of Newman's *Grammar*, particularly his "Introduction," is quite scholastic in character.[177] Aquino, Merrigan, and Thomas also acknowledge that Newman can write "in a fashion reminiscent of the most sound Scholastic Philosopher."[178] Some writers, however, interpret this as a "defensive manoeuvre in which he clothed his thought in the ill-fitting suit of scholastic armor" in order to avoid conflict.[179] Nevertheless, while Newman has often been viewed in isolation from the renewal of scholasticism in the nineteenth century,[180] the *Grammar* clearly engages with the rich epistemological insights found within this tradition.

There are of course differences between Newman and neo-scholastic writers. Nevertheless, they share a similar epistemological orientation (P1 & P2), which many commentators have failed to appreciate.[181] It is possible that the use of Newman's work by Catholic modernist writers, in order to set up an opposition between their own position and scholastic theology, may have also masked this common epistemological framework.[182] As a result, Newman commentators have tended to overlook the evidence connecting these writers. Nonetheless it is evident that Newman, like Chisholm, was immersed in the rising tide of neo-scholasticism and that both these writers were exposed to this philosophical tradition.

Thomas Aquinas

There is also evidence to suggest that Newman, like Chisholm, engaged with Thomas Aquinas's (1225–74) work. While Abraham is largely

---

177. King, *Newman*, 62–65. This point is strengthened by the fact that Phillips begins the second volume of his discussion of *Modern Thomistic Philosophy* with an examination of Newman's distinctions. Phillips, *Modern Thomistic Philosophy*, 1:8–15.

178. Aquino, *Communities*, 31n22; Merrigan, *Clear Heads and Holy Hearts*, 121; Thomas, *Newman and Heresy*, 211.

179. Dulles, "From Images to Truth," 264; Chadwick, *From Bossuet to Newman*, 174.

180. Beads, *Philosophy*, 60; Cowburn, *Personalism*, 35; Connolly, *John Henry Newman*, 124; Barmann, "Theological," 181–208; Lash, "Tides," 454. Ker, *The Achievement of John Henry Newman*, 121; Sparr, *To Promote*, 70; Hollis, *Newman and the Modern World*, 25–26; Kenny, *Political Thought*, 99.

181. A trait characteristic of these writers is to argue that "philosophy should begin by explaining, not by disputing the fact of certainty." Balmes, *Fundamental Philosophy*, 1:8.

182. Weaver, *Letters*, 92–93; Powell, *Three*, 18–22.

critical of St Thomas,[183] Newman and Chisholm refer to Aquinas favorably on a number of occasions.[184] Despite this many Newman commentators conclude that the influence of Aquinas on Newman was minimal.[185] This is partly due to the fact that Newman himself expressed the anxiety that he would never understand "St. Thomas" as well as he did the early church fathers.[186]

Another potential reason is that one of the earliest reviewers of Newman's *Grammar*, Thomas Harper (1821–93), challenged this work for its "seeming dissidence" with Aquinas.[187] The persistence of this interpretation is captured in Abraham's contention that Aquinas and Newman's epistemological proposals are so different that Aquinas's canonical status, as a Father and Doctor of the church, would be called into question if Newman is made a Father or Doctor of the church.[188]

While there are many differences between these writers, Newman certainly came across references to Aquinas in his copy of Pierre Daniel Huet's (1630–1721) *Philosophical Treatise Concerning the Weakness of Human Understanding* (1723). In his *Essay on Development*, Newman uses Huet's references to Aquinas in order to support his understanding of the "Supremacy" of belief (P2); the idea that Christians should not wait

---

183. Abraham, *Canon and Criterion*, 84–110.

184. Newman, *Sermons Chiefly on the Theory of Religious Belief*, 292 [*US*, 295]; Newman, *Essay on Development*, 333 [*Dev*, 332]; Newman, *Certain Difficulties*, 244 [*Diff* 1:298] Newman, *Lectures on Catholicism*, 378 [*Prepos*, 396]; Newman, *Discourses on the Scope and Nature*, 214 [*Idea*, 134]; *Lectures and Essays*, 22, 310 [*Idea*, 263, 384]; LD 4:294; LD 7:11, 162; LD 8:237; LD 11:185; LD 12:7, 30–31, 98, 282; LD 13:336; LD 14:96, 241; LD 17:468; LD 20:543, 551; LD 28:340; LD 29:117, 239.

185. Newman, *Mental Philosophy*; Ferreira, *Doubt and Religious Commitment*; Artz, "Newmans Philosophische Leistung," 190; Norris, *Newman and His Theological Method*; Vargish, *Newman: The Contemplation of Mind*; Zeno, *John Henry Newman*; Juergens, *Newman on the Psychology of Faith*.

186. LD 22:73.

187. Harper, "Dr Newman's Essay," 159.

188. Abraham, *Canon and Criterion*, 354. Exceptions to this interpretation do exist. Gerrard specifically matches Aquinas" *passive* intellect with Newman's discussion of the spontaneous assents of human judgement and Richardson structures his account of *Newman's Approach to Knowledge* (2007) using Aquinas as a "familiar reference frame." Much earlier than this articles published in *The New York Review* (1905–8) frequently attempted to reconcile Newman's writings with Aquinas. For further discussion, see Richardson, *Newman's Approach to Knowledge*, xiv; Gerrard, "Bergson, Newman and Aquinas," 755; Gerrard, "Dichotomy: A Study in Newman and Aquinas," 381–94.

for proof before having faith but should "begin with believing," trusting that "conviction will follow" later:[189]

> [Newman] St Thomas adds "No search by natural Reason is sufficient to make man know things divine, not even those we can prove by Reason. . . . Things which may be proved demonstratively, as the Being of God, the Unity of the Godhead, and other points, are placed among articles we are to believe, because previous to other things that are of Faith; and these must be pre-supposed, at least by such as have no demonstration of them." What St. Thomas says of the cognizance of divine things extends also to the knowledge of humans.[190]

Here Newman cites Aquinas in order to justify his desire to assume the "Supremacy of Faith," the presumption of certain theological beliefs prior to obtaining evidence in their support (P2). Secondly he wants to undermine Locke's contention that "things must be considered true only so far as they are proved" (P1).[191] This supports Newman's objectives in his *Essay on Development* since there he assumes the validity of Roman Catholic doctrines from the beginning of the book, prior to examining the evidence in their support.[192]

The same idea is utilized by Chisholm who directly acknowledges that his decision to presuppose certain propositions, before examining the evidence in their support, has parallels with Aquinas (P2). Chisholm recognizes this similarity with St Thomas in his work *Perceiving* (1957):

> When we set out to solve the problem of the criterion, we already knew which propositions are the ones that are evident; we knew in advance that skepticism with regard to the senses is mistaken. Hence one might say that, if St Thomas's philosophy constitutes "special pleading" for certain propositions of

---

189. Newman, *Essay on Development*, 327 [*Dev*, 332].

190. Newman, *Essay on Development*, 333–34 [*Dev*, 332-33]. Newman's citation of Aquinas is taken from Huet: "St Thomas adds . . . Things which can be demonstrated, such as the Being of a God, his Unity, and the like, are reckoned among those things which we are bound to believe, because they are insisted upon beforehand and must precede those which belong to Faith, and be at least presupposed by those who have no demonstration of them. What Thomas Aquinas says, concerning the Knowledge of divine Things, doth likewise extend to that of human Things." Huet, *A Philosophical Treatise*, 138.

191. Newman, *Essay on Development*, 328 [*Dev*, 327-29].

192. Newman, *Essay on Development*, 24, 27, 333–34 [*Dev*, 27, 29, 332-33].

theology, our philosophy constitutes "special pleading" for certain propositions of science and common sense.[193]

Here Chisholm illustrates how his epistemological particularist approach to knowledge (P2), which presupposes knowledge to criteria, resembles the pre-eminence given to certain propositions of faith in Aquinas.

All this indicates that Newman and Chisholm were exposed to a number of Thomistic sources. While Chisholm explicitly states that his particularist approach to epistemology is influenced by this philosophical tradition, Newman is not usually associated with it. However, the textual evidence in marked personal copies of works by these writers (such as Kleutgen) in Newman's library challenges the idea that Newman's work is incommensurate with St Thomas and his descendants. Though it cannot be demonstrated that the presence of epistemological tendencies (P2) in these Thomistic writers may have shaped the formation of similar tendencies in Newman's work, the notion that Newman's work is disconnected from this philosophical tradition is exaggerated and need not act as a barrier to comparing these writers.[194]

Aristotle

The most significant philosophical connection shared by all of these writers is their knowledge of Aristotle (c. 384–322BC). Most importantly, all these writers cite part of the *Nicomachean Ethics* where Aristotle argues that each subject demands a different kind of precision:

> Our account will be adequate if its clarity is in line with the subject-matter, because the same degree of precision is not to be sought in all discussions, any more than in works of craftsmanship. The spheres of what is noble and what is just, which political science examines, admit of a good deal of diversity and variation, so that they seem to exist only by convention and not by nature. Goods vary in this way as well, since it happens that, for many, good things have harmful consequences: some people have been ruined by wealth, and others by courage. So

---

193. Chisholm, *Perceiving*, 102.

194. While Abraham is critical of both Aquinas and the neo-scholastic writers Chisholm's contention that his epistemological particularism is indebted to this tradition indicates that Abraham may through, his reading of Chisholm, be indirectly indebted to these writers; for Chisholm cites them as a key influence upon the development of his theory of knowledge.

we should be content, since we are discussing things like these in such a way, to demonstrate the truth sketchily and in outline, and, because we are making generalizations on the basis of generalizations, to draw conclusions along the same lines. Indeed, the details of our claims, then, should be looked at in the same way, since it is a mark of an educated person to look in each area for only that degree of accuracy that the nature of the subject permits. Accepting from a mathematician claims that are mere probabilities seems rather like demanding logical proofs from a rhetorician.[195]

In this extract Aristotle argues that different subjects are governed by different kinds of rules.[196]

This extract from Aristotle provides Newman, Chisholm, and Abraham with a very important philosophical link.[197] Chisholm, for example, uses this citation to support his belief that epistemological criterion must be appropriate to the knowledge claims in an individual's possession. Chisholm states that in formulating criteria to justify our antecedent beliefs he "will simply proceed as Aristotle did" and "will fit our rules to the cases." He writes:

> So far as our problem of the criterion is concerned, the essential thing to note is this. In formulating such principles we will simply proceed as Aristotle did when he formulated his rules for the syllogism. As "particularists" in our approach to the problem of the criterion, we will fit our rules to the cases.... Knowing what we do about ourselves and the world, we have at our disposal certain instances that our rules or principles should countenance, and certain other instances that our rules or principles should rule out or forbid.[198]

Therefore, citing Aristotle's *Nicomachean Ethics*, Chisholm advances the thesis that our beliefs should be measured using rules appropriate to the instances of knowledge that are already in our possession. He considers

---

195. Aristotle, *Nicomachean Ethics*, 4–5 [I.3 1094b13–28].

196. By the same token, it follows that, an expert in French grammar will not necessarily be good at Japanese.

197. Sillem points out that "Newman made his first acquaintance with Aristotle when he was an undergraduate at Trinity College.... In preparation for his degree [Newman] studied the three set «books» of Aristotle included amongst those which candidates for honours had to present for their examination, the Rhetoric, the Poetics and the Nicomachean Ethics." *PN*, 1:151.

198. Chisholm, *Problem of the Criterion*, 35.

that the criteria developed to measure these antecedent beliefs should be appropriate to the knowledge claims at hand—in other words: the criteria developed should not deny knowledge claims that the majority of people already believe without any hesitation (such as "I am alive").

Newman likewise studied Aristotle extensively and was particularly shaped by the very same aspect of the *Nicomachean Ethics*.[199] In the *Grammar*, and elsewhere,[200] he acknowledges this work directly:

> That a special preparation of mind is required for each separate department of inquiry and discussion (excepting—, of course, that of abstract science) is strongly insisted upon in a well-known passage of the *Nicomachean Ethics*. Speaking of the variations which are found in the logical perfection of proof in various-subject-matters, Aristotle says, "A well-educated man will expect exactness in every class of subjects, according as the nature of the thing admits; for it is much the same mistake to put up with a mathematician using probabilities, and to require demonstration of an orator. Each man judges skilfully in those things about which he is well-informed; it is of these that he is a good judge ; viz. he, in each subject-matter, is a judge, who is well-educated in that subject-matter, and he is in an absolute sense a judge, who is in all of them well-educated." [201]

Here Newman clearly cites the principle Chisholm admires in Aristotle's writing. Unlike Chisholm, however, Newman applies this rule to the subject of religion. Newman argues that theological claims should not be rendered illogical because they do not conform to mathematical proofs. On the contrary, Newman argues that an analysis of revealed truth should use modes of proof appropriate to its subject matter.[202] Hence, in his *Grammar* Newman argues that all our beliefs, whether religious or otherwise, are supported by proofs peculiar to their subject. In affirming the different levels of accuracy found in different disciplines, Newman opposes the uniform application of a strict formula, such as Locke's, and in a manner similar to Chisholm considers that all of our assents should

---

199. Newman's knowledge of Aristotle's works began early and, was developed considerably as an undergraduate at Oxford (and later under Whately), LD 1:64, 70, 91–92, 139, 144. For further discussion of Aristotle's influence on Newman, see Willam, *Aristotelische*.

200. Newman taught Aristotle at Oxford: LD 2:189. For further discussion, see *US*, 28–29; *Mix*, 244; *HS*, 3:180; *Dev*, 113–14.

201. Newman, *Grammar*, 409 [GA, 414].

202. Newman, *Grammar*, 404ff [GA, 409].

be evaluated appropriately; that their "particular case" and circumstance should be taken into account.[203] From this it seems that Newman's work (including his discussion of the *Grammar of Assent*), and Chisholm's particularist conception of criteria, are shaped by reading the *Nicomachean Ethics*.

Following Chisholm, Abraham also considers that the particularist approach to knowledge "dovetails snugly" with what he refers to as an "Aristotelian epistemic fit." Paraphrasing Aristotle, Abraham stresses that "we do not expect historical claims to be measured by the kinds of arguments that would apply to mathematics." Likewise Abraham argues that each network of beliefs must be taken in its "radical particularity."[204] He writes:

> In exploring the nature of reasoning in science or history, we begin by paying attention to the kinds of moves that are made ... and the kinds of arguments that are deployed.[205]

Abraham considers that each subject matter has its own levels of precision. Abraham believes that this principle applies to theological truth as much as it does to history or science. He writes: "In Theology we can begin from within and then work our way outward and upward." Essentially, Abraham wants to apply this Aristotelian principle to theology. Abraham wants to take faith on its own terms; explaining why he thinks its claims are true by exploring the kinds of proof relevant to its case.

This demonstrates that these writers all emphasize the importance of Aristotle's axiom that each subject demands a different kind of precision. The effect of this principle is to cause each of these writers to measure their chosen field of enquiry using rules appropriate to their topic. Thus Chisholm examines the rationality of claims to knowledge by formulating an epistemological theory that will not deny commonsense beliefs. Abraham and Newman examine the rationality of doctrinal claims by using criteria sensitive to these theological truths. The principle of Aristotelian epistemic fit allows all of these writers to formulate appropriate rules for the knowledge claims they presuppose.

---

203. Newman, *Grammar*, 153 [*GA*, 160].
204. Abraham, *Crossing*, 45.
205. Abraham, *Crossing*, 45.

Summary of Chapter

Having explored Newman in relation to the key sources identified by particularist writers, it is apparent that his interaction with these historical sources make Newman a relevant dialogue partner—even if he is yet to be dialogued with—for writers operating within the particularist perspective. The next chapter will explore Newman's relevance to this tradition further by investigating whether epistemological tendencies comparable to those found in particularist writers are manifest throughout the whole of his corpus or whether they are isolated to a few minor cases. Earlier it was noted that a number of writers make parallels between tendencies in Newman and particularist writers which indicate his wider relevance to this philosophical position. The question as to how extensive these tendencies are within Newman's work will thus be examined in chapter 4. Chapters 5 and 6 will then examine whether Newman's writing shapes that of (Mercier) Chisholm and Abraham.

4

Antecedents of Particularism in Newman's Work

Introduction

IN THE PREVIOUS CHAPTER it was noted that Maddox argues for an epistemological methodist reading of Newman's *Grammar of Assent*. The term epistemological methodism was coined by Chisholm in the 1970s and Newman would not have recognized it. It is anachronistic to say that Newman is a methodist. Nevertheless, if Newman's writing echoes epistemologically with methodism in its orientation, it will be difficult to maintain that Newman's work has shaped philosophical thought in the particularist tradition; that particularist writers like William Abraham gravitate towards Newman because his writings possess particularist tendencies. In short, if the aim of this book is to re-evaluate Newman's philosophical legacy by exploring his relevance for particularist approaches to epistemology, Maddox's analysis presents a difficulty.

It is unfortunate that Maddox focuses almost exclusively upon Newman's *Grammar of Assent*. The danger with this kind of approach is that many of the ideas discussed in the *Grammar* originated much earlier. In order to interpret Newman as accurately as possible this study will take a wider look at his writings. A number of examples will be discussed in order to explore whether or not his approach is predominantly compatible with epistemological particularism. However, since not all of Newman's works bear relevance to the present subject, attention will be given to writings that contain the epistemological trends identified in the previous chapter (P1–P3); in the introduction given to particularism. If such tendencies are predominant throughout Newman's corpus some of the problems raised by Maddox's epistemological methodist analysis will be resolved.

At this juncture it is helpful to recapitulate the three particularist tendencies identified in the previous chapter. The first tendency, P1, is that these writers are opposed to those who presuppose an enquiry with inappropriate rules concerning when a belief is legitimate—what particularists term "epistemological methodism." This tendency is manifest in the aversion these writers have to Locke for presupposing an epistemological criterion to knowledge. The second, P2, is that these writers assume certain beliefs to be valid prior to examining the epistemological evidence in their support—what particularists term "epistemological particularism." This tendency is evidenced in their preference for writers like Reid who presuppose knowledge to epistemological criteria. The third tendency, P3, is that these writers follow Aristotle's contention that different disciplines require different kinds of proof—Abraham terms this "Aristotelian epistemic fit."[1] As a result, particularist writers tend to formulate epistemological rules appropriate to the cases of knowledge already in hand so as to ensure that sensible knowledge claims are not ruled out. Thus, the present chapter will explore whether or not Newman's writing manifests tendencies P1–3. If they do it both challenges Maddox's anachronistic interpretation and, more importantly, it could explain why his work might have relevance for particularist writers.[2]

Before proceeding it is important to emphasize that the present examination, into whether or not Newman's work contains epistemological tendencies that anticipate particularist writers, should not imply that Newman can be defined in an anachronistic way. Neither should this investigation be interpreted as an attempt to use the particularist approach as a model for creating a Newman synthesis.[3] Even if Newman does anticipate certain particularist themes, there are many other ways in

---

1. Abraham, *Crossing*, 45.

2. The previous chapter suggests this is likely since it indicates considerable similarities between Newman, Chisholm and Abraham's engagement with writers like Locke and Aristotle.

3. There are already a number of attempts to synthesize Newman's work using a variety of philosophical models and positions. For further discussion, see Merrigan, *Clear Heads and Holy Hearts*, 1–19.

which his thought feeds into the contemporary debate. As we indicated in chapter 2, Newman's writing was appreciated by personalist, pragmatist, and Wittgensteinian writers. If it can be found that Newman makes a contribution to the particularist philosophical tradition, this would be just one of many other examples of how his philosophical legacy has been underestimated. We will not argue that Newman is a particularist. However, if it is the case that his writings can be read using a particularist perspective then this would both undermine Maddox's assertion that he is a methodist and, more importantly, indicate why certain tendencies in Newman's writing are picked up by particularist writers.

Newman on Adverse First Principles P1

Newman's first ever published work was a letter to the *Christian Observer* "On the Subject of Mathematics" (1821).[4] At this early stage Newman identifies something similar to what he later refers to as liberalism. In a manner that anticipates the criticisms made of Locke[5] in his later work Newman objects to anyone who commences an enquiry by "asserting the falsity of the conclusion from some *a Priori* conception of his own fancy." He writes:

> [T]his very thing is done daily with the Bible. Men begin at the wrong end of the scale of reasoning; and having refuted, as they conceive, a doctrine by arguments resting on the basis of pre-conceived ideas, they proceed up the ladder, and arrive at once at the portentous determination, that all the proofs which have been advanced in support of that doctrine, and the book which contains an avowal of that doctrine, must be erroneous. It is in this spirit they lay down the unphilosophical axiom, "a true religion can have no mysteries;" and then infer either that Christianity is not a true religion, because it contains mysteries—or that it contains no mysteries, because it is a true religion. Nothing can be more illogical, more unworthy of a person of science than such conclusions.[6]

---

4. Newman, "On the Subject of Mathematics," 293–95.

5. Newman's correspondence indicates that he had read Locke before he wrote this letter to *The Christian Observer*: "The Long Vacation of 1818 was the only time when I was completely off College studies. During that four months I was taken up with Gibbon and Locke." LD 1:105.

6. Newman, "On the Subject of Mathematics," 295 [LD 1:104].

In this extract Newman criticizes those who presuppose the outcome of an enquiry by laying down an "axiom" which determines the conclusion of an investigation before it has even begun. Though he does not use the word liberalism here it is apparent that in this instance, as is the case in liberal writers like Locke, an invented criterion such as "a true religion can have no mysteries" renders Christianity false even though the axiom itself is unproved. This criticism suggests that, even at this early stage, Newman understood the way in which presupposed principles of this nature could lead to a denial of Christian belief.

Newman's first major published work, an article on "Logic" for the *Encyclopaedia Metropolitana* (1823), which was co-written with Richard Whately (1787–1863), also examines the way in which the principles that precede an enquiry determine its outcome:

> No proposition . . . can be true, which was not implied in the definitions we set out with, which are the first principles: for since these propositions do not profess to state any matter of fact, the only Truth they can possess, consists in conformity to the original principles; to one, therefore, who knows these principles, such propositions are Truths already implied, since they may be developed to him by Reasoning.[7]

As Newman's letter "On the Study of Mathematics" argues that many of our axioms are determined by our own "fancy" so this article emphasizes that "the rules of Logic" cannot determine "whether the Premises are fairly laid down" since these rules have nothing to do with the "truth or falsity" of first principles. His point is that logic is only able to show whether "the Conclusion follows from the premises or not."[8] Thus, as with his earlier publication, Newman illustrates how even logic itself cannot prevent baseless premises determining our conclusions and beliefs. The recurrence of this theme in this work suggests what Whately himself acknowledges: that "the Rev J. Newman, Fellow of Oriel College, . . . actually composed a considerable portion" of this work.[9] The same emphasis recurs in Newman's subsequent contributions to the *Encyclopaedia*.

---

7. Newman and Whately, "Logic," 234.

8. Newman and Whately, "Logic," 231.

9. In the preface to the first book-length edition of this work, Whately acknowledges "the Rev. J. Newman, Fellow of Oriel College, who actually composed a considerable portion of the work as it now stands, from manuscripts not designed for publication, and who is the original author of several pages." See: Whately, *Elements of Logic*, ix. While it is difficult to determine which portions of this work are "original" to

Newman's article on "Apollonius Tyanaeus" (1825) criticizes Jeremy Bentham (1748–1832) for allowing an arbitrary rule to determine the parameters of Christian experience.[10] In its initial form[11] this essay contained "an extended comparison between the Miracles of Scripture" and the kinds of miracles attributed to extra-scriptural figures like Apollonius.[12] In this comparison Newman notes how Bentham's examination of miracles, using "the strict principle of those legal forms which from their secular object go far to exclude all religious discussion of the question," leads him to conclude that all miracles are illogical.[13] He writes:

> From an apparent impatience of investigating a system [of revealed religion] they esteem the laws of the material system alone worthy the notice of a scientific mind; and rid themselves of the annoyance which the importunity of a claim to miraculous power occasions them, by discarding all the circumstances which fix its antecedent probability.[14]

Newman considers that this "partial and inconclusive mode of reasoning" leads writers like Bentham to infer that religion is "founded in the mere weakness or eccentricity of the intellect."[15] Newman's point here is that if someone begins an examination with premises that rule out the possibility of miracles then they will not believe in them—even if the evidence in their favor is considerable.[16] Though Newman does not explicitly accuse Bentham of "liberalism" here, his criticism amounts to this for he disapproves of Bentham for presupposing theological enquiry with a criteria that is hostile to theological claims.

Newman it is clear that he wrote a draft of this work for Whately and, as acknowledged in the *Apologia*, was influenced by its contents: Whately "emphatically, opened my mind, and taught me to think and to use my reason." Newman, *History of My Religious Opinions*, 11 [*Apo* 11].

10. Newman, "Apollonius Tyanaeus," 619–44 [*Mir,* 3–96].

11. In its later form this essay was published together with Newman's preface to Fleury's *Ecclesiastical History* (to be discussed later) which examined extra-scriptural miracles more favourably. For further discussion, see Newman, *Two Essays on Biblical and Ecclesiastical Miracles*; Newman, *An Essay on the Miracles*; Newman, *The Ecclesiastical History*.

12. Newman, "Apollonius Tyanaeus," 625 [*Mir,* 3].

13. Newman, "Apollonius Tyanaeus," 629 [*Mir,* 21–22].

14. Newman, "Apollonius Tyanaeus," 629 [*Mir,* 21–22].

15. Newman, "Apollonius Tyanaeus," 629 [*Mir,* 21–22].

16. Newman, "Apollonius Tyanaeus," 628 [*Mir,* 13–14].

Newman's Oxford University Sermons[17] also criticize those who begin an enquiry with a theory that they themselves have invented.[18] In a sermon on the "Philosophical Temper" (1826) Newman states that:

> It seems incredible that any men, who were really in earnest in their search after truth, should have begun with theorizing, or have imagined that a system which they were conscious they had invented almost without data, should happen, when applied to the actual state of things, to harmonize with the numberless and diversified phenomena of the world.[19]

Here Newman argues that it is absurd to begin an investigation with an invented theory—especially one that is not informed by data from its subject matter.[20] In a similar manner, Newman's sermon on "Implicit and Explicit Reason" (1840) criticizes John Douglas's (1721–1807)[21] *Criterion; or Rules for Determining the True Miracles Recorded in the New Testament* (1807), which argues that there are only "two ways by which

---

17. This has never been the official title for Newman's publication of these sermons. Nevertheless, the work is commonly referred to in this way. For further discussion, see Newman, *Fifteen Sermons Preached*.

18. When the Oxford University Sermons are viewed collectively it is clear that Newman's conception of the relationship between faith and reason is in a state of development. This produces what Jost describes as an "Indeterminacy in the Oxford University Sermons." It is important to understand the way in which Newman redacted these sermons after his conversion. Moreover, it is necessary to understand how the *Prefaces* to later editions attempt to integrate the themes discussed more systematically. However it is also necessary to appreciate the individual value of these sermons. Here Newman's sermons will be examined individually. While this section will explore whether or not the sermons oppose those who would prioritize rules concerning when a belief is legitimate over and above the beliefs themselves later sections will examine the sermons for the other epistemological tendencies discussed in the introduction to this chapter. For further discussion: Jost, *Rhetorical Thought*, 34ff; LD 12:1–30. An illustration of the unsystematic nature of these sermons is illustrated by the "Avertissment" to the first French edition (1851) of this work: Newman, *Discours sur la Théorie*, v–vi.

19. Newman, *Sermons Chiefly on the Theory of Religious Belief*, 8 [US, 7–8].

20. Newman describes those who allow such preconceptions to determine serious discussions as sacrificing truth to the "mere gratification of the fancy." Newman considers that "in forming any serious theory concerning nature, we must begin with investigation, to the exclusion of fanciful speculation." Newman, *Sermons Chiefly on the Theory of Religious Belief*, 8 [US, 7–8]. Moreover, Newman's contention that we must begin with the facts likewise resembles the particularist position which argues that we should begin with the knowledge claims in our possession.

21. Douglas was an eighteenth-century Anglican bishop who debated with the philosopher David Hume.

God could reveal his will."[22] Newman emphasizes that divine revelation cannot be confined by Douglas's arbitrary theory; that criterion like that of Douglas are unable to appreciate the complexity and subtlety of the rationality of faith.[23]

Newman's *Arians of the Fourth Century* (1833) narrates how the introduction of the principle that theological statements should only contain words used in Scripture actually led the church into heresy:

> This artifice, which, obvious as it is, is curious, from the place which it holds in the history of Arianism, was that of affecting on principle to limit confessions of faith to scripture terms; and was adopted by Acacius of Caesarea.[24]

Newman queries the attempt by Acacius of Caesarea (*d.* 366) to make all theological statements subject to terminology found in Scripture. Later Newman describes this arbitrary rule as liberalism:

> During the residence of the Court at Antioch, A.D. 361, the election of the new prelate of that see came on; and the choice of both Arians and Arianizing orthodox fell on Meletius. Acacius was the chief mover in this business. He had lately established the principle of liberalism at Constantinople, where a condemnation had been passed on the use of words not found in Scripture, in confessions of faith; and he could scarcely have selected a more suitable instrument, as it appeared, of extending its influence, than a prelate, who united purity of life and amiableness of temper, to a seeming indifference to the distinctions between doctrinal truth and error.[25]

Newman's use of the word liberalism here affirms the definition given to this term in chapter 3—since Acacius's decision to limit theological

---

22. Douglas writes: "There are but two ways by which God could reveal his will to mankind—either by an immediate influence on the mind of every individual of every age, or by selecting . . . particular persons to be his instruments in reforming and enlightening the world, and for this purpose vested by him with such powers, as might carry the strongest evidence that they were really divine teachers." Douglas, *The Criterion*, 37–38. Reprinted in Newman, *Sermons Chiefly on the Theory of Religious Belief*, 257 [*US*, 261–62]

23. Newman, *Sermons Chiefly on the Theory of Religious Belief*, 257–58 [*US*, 261–62].

24. Newman, *Arians*, 325 [*Ari*, 304].

25. Newman, *Arians*, 385 [*Ari*, 361–62].

language to words contained within the text of Scripture presupposes theological enquiry with an unworkable criterion.[26]

Newman was editor of the *British Critic* (1838–41), a periodical called the "organ" of the Tractarians.[27] In a review of *The Brothers' Controversy* (1835),[28] a book containing the correspondence between two brothers (one a Unitarian the other an Anglican clergyman) in which they debate the true meaning of the Scriptures as regards the doctrine of the Trinity, Newman contends that the idea that Scripture is the sole basis for Protestant theology leads to liberalism.[29] He writes:

> Does not, in consequence, the theory that Scripture only is to be the guide of Protestants, lead for certain to liberalism? . . . [W]hile belief in the document [Scripture] is made the first thing, and belief in the doctrine but the second, (as this theory would have it,) it inevitably follows in the case of the multitude, who are not clear-headed or unprejudiced, that the definition of a Christian will be made to turn, not on faith in the doctrine, but on faith in the document, and Unitarianism will come to be thought, not indeed true, but as if not unreasonable, and not necessarily dangerous.[30]

Here Newman argues that presupposing the document of Scripture, as the rule of faith, leads to the denial of central theological doctrines such as the Trinity.[31]

Newman revisited the topic of miracles in his Introduction to Fleury's *Ecclesiastical History* (1842)—later published as the *Essay on the*

26. It is interesting to note that in this work Newman refers to a translation of Origen by Pierre-Daniel Huet—the Pyrrhonist bishop introduced in the previous chapter. For further discussion, see Newman, *Arians*, 46, 71, 110, 141 [*Ari*, 42, 128].

27. While Newman was editor for three years his first contribution to this periodical was made in 1836. Although authorship is not given in the *British Critic* itself, lists of authors were drawn up by Newman in 1875 and are both at the Oratory, Birmingham, and at Pusey House, Oxford. For a list of Newman's contributions, see Houghton, "The British Critic and the Oxford Movement," 125. Also, see Houghton and Altholz, "The 'British Critic' 1824–1843," 113–15. Unknown author, "Publications on the Oxford Tracts," 100.

28. Longley, *The Brothers' Controversy*.

29. Newman, Review of *The Brothers' Controversy*, 166–99 [*Ess*, 1:102–37].

30. Newman, Review of *The Brothers' Controversy*, 171–72 [*Ess*, 1:111].

31. Though no mention is made of these writers here, Newman's criticism of the protestant conception of scripture in this contributions to the *British Critic* resemble the way in which the counter-reformers' used Pyrrhonism to undermine the Protestant use of Scripture.

Miracles Recorded in Ecclesiastical History (1843).[32] He argues that the rejection of ecclesiastical miracles is caused by two arbitrary criteria. The first of these being the "inviolability" of nature:

> The force of the presumption against Miracles lies in the opinion entertained of the inviolability of nature, to which the Creator seems to "have given a law which shall not be broken." When once that law is shown to be but general, not necessary, and (if the word may be used) when its prestige is once destroyed, there is nothing to shock the imagination in a miraculous interference twice or thrice, as well as once.[33]

Here Newman illustrates how those, who adopt the principle that the ordinary laws of nature cannot be interrupted, deny the reality of miracles because they believe them to controvert this rule. Newman argues that this denial of the probability of ecclesiastical miracles is also accompanied by another subjective rule (of which his previous essay on the miracles contained in Scripture was also culpable)[34] which denies the validity of miracles occurring after the apostolic age:

> The author [believes] the miracles of the Old and New Testaments . . . and, like a religious man, he feels, contrariwise to Hume, that it is not "convenient," but dangerous to allow of an antecedent test, which, for what he knows, and before he is aware, may be applied in disproof of one or other of those sacred and gracious manifestations. But it is far otherwise when he comes to speak of Ecclesiastical miracles, which he begins with disbelieving without much regard to their evidence, and is engaged, not in examining or confuting, but in burdening with some test or criterion which may avail, in Hume's words, "to silence bigotry and superstition," and to "free us from their impertinent solicitations." He acts towards the miracles of the Church as Hume towards the miracles of Scripture. And surely with less reason than Hume . . . because, in being a believer in the miracles of Scripture, he deprives himself of that strong

---

32. Newman, *The Ecclesiastical History*; Newman, *An Essay on the Miracles*.

33. Newman, *The Ecclesiastical History*, xv–xvi [*Mir,* 103–4].

34. Newman's Advertisement to the combined (1870) edition acknowledges that "in the Essay upon the Scripture Miracles, the Author goes beyond both the needs and the claims of his argument, when . . . he deprecates the purpose and value of the Miracles of Church History." Newman, *Two Essays on Biblical and on Ecclesiastical Miracles*, viii.

antecedent ground against all miracles whatever, both Scriptural and Ecclesiastical, on which Hume took his stand.[35]

In this extract Newman illustrates that the arguments against miracles occurring posterior to the apostolic age beg the question in favor of Hume's "criterion of the antecedent probability of a Miracle." According to Newman, this "criterion" presupposes the argument in denial of ecclesiastical miracles by arguing that "no work can be reasonably ascribed to the agency of God, which is altogether different from those ordinary [biblical] works from which our knowledge of Him is originally obtained."[36] Here Newman criticizes Hume for beginning an enquiry with a rule that excludes the possibility of ecclesiastical (post-Scripture) miracles because this predetermines the outcome against what he now considers to be an important aspect of the Christian revelation.

In his lectures on the *Present Position of Catholics* (1851) Newman criticizes Protestants for narrowing down God's revelation "into one or two meagre sentences."[37] Newman argues that the apostles "left us a number of doctrines, not in writing at all, but living in the minds and mouths of the faithful."[38] He maintains that it is for reasons such as this that Catholics refuse to limit revealed truth to what is contained in the New Testament: "Is nothing true but what has been written down?"[39] He writes:

> Protestants virtually assume the point in debate between them and us, in any particular controversy, in the very principles with which they set out; that those first principles, for which they offer no proof, involve their conclusions; so that, if we are betrayed into the inadvertence of passing them over without remark, we are forthwith defeated and routed, even before we have begun to move forward to the attack.[40]

While Newman acknowledges the right of Protestants to disagree with Catholics concerning the extent of revealed truth, he criticizes them for assuming that their own "unproved" first principle, *Sola Scriptura*, is "self-evident." Thus, Newman concludes that Protestants are skeptical toward

---

35. Newman, *The Ecclesiastical History*, xx–xxi [*Mir*, 110].
36. Newman, "Apollonius Tyanaeus," 630 [*Mir*, 26].
37. Newman, *Lectures on Catholicism*, 308 [*Prepos*, 323].
38. Newman, *Lectures on Catholicism*, 303 [*Prepos*, 317].
39. Newman, *Lectures on Catholicism*, 304 [*Prepos*, 329].
40. Newman, *Lectures on Catholicism*, 301–2 [*Prepos*, 315–16].

Roman Catholic teaching because their unproved first principle, that "all truth is contained in scripture," determines that they will only believe what their private judgement deduces from the Bible.[41] Here Newman is critical of Protestants for presupposing theological enquiry with a principle which he considers leads to the denial of important doctrinal truths.

Newman's discussion of the term "liberal" in his *Discourses on the Scope and Nature of University Education* (1852) is more positive than in his other works. Though "liberal" is an adjective and "liberalism" a noun, Newman's use of these terms to describe his ideal model for education has led some commentators to question whether or not Newman is as consistent in his opposition to "liberalism" as he maintains.[42] Though it may appear to be a diversion, the question as to whether or not Newman constantly opposed liberalism in religion, is of importance for it is related to the question of whether or not Newman consistently evidences P1.

At this juncture it is important to clarify that the question of whether or not Newman advocates liberalism in his *Discourses* centres on his promotion of what he terms a "liberal education." By this phrase Newman means that a university is a place where one should acquire a "liberal" or "universal" knowledge through a wide exposure to a broad range of subjects.[43] However, Newman makes absolutely clear that if the subject

41. Despite his criticisms of Protestants, Newman recognizes that it is impossible for either side to demonstrate the validity of their position without begging the question. This acknowledgment, coupled with Newman's reference to Pyrrhonism in this work, indicates that this form of skepticism has shaped Newman's understanding of theological truth. He writes: "Protestants and Catholics each have their own ground, and cannot engage on any other; the question in dispute between them is more elementary than men commonly suppose; it relates to the ground itself on which the battle is legitimately and rightfully to be fought; the first principles assumed in the starting of the controversy determine the issue." Newman, *Lectures on Catholicism*, 267, 301–2 [*Prepos*, 279, 315–16].

42. Culler believes that this work, particularly the fifth discourse (which was omitted in the Longmans Green edition), is more supportive of humanist liberalism than his other works. For further discussion, see Culler, *The Imperial Intellect*, 149, 222.

43. This interpretation is supported by Newman's wider reference to the term. For further discussion, see *PS*, 2:368; *HS*, 2:99; *HS*, 3:82; Newman, *Select Treatise*, 1:52fn, 2:58. However, as the following citation from William Hamilton (1805–65) illustrates, the phrase also signified a model of education which contrasts with the notion that education must be useful to an individual's future profession. He writes: "liberal education . . . is an education in which the individual is cultivated, not as an instrument towards some ulterior end, but as an end unto himself alone; in other words an education, in which his absolute perfection as a man, and not merely his relative dexterity as a professional man, is the scope immediately in view." Hamilton, Review of *Thoughts*, 409.

of theology is not given its rightful place in the curriculum students will be tempted to view truth solely from a material perspective.[44] Here, in order to clarify this issue, it is important to quote Newman at length:

> Institutions may be perverted into hostility to Revealed Truth, in consequence of the character of their teaching as well as of their end. They are employed in the pursuit of Liberal Knowledge, and Liberal Knowledge has a special tendency, not necessary or rightful, but a tendency in fact, when cultivated by beings such as we are, to impress us with a mere philosophical theory of life and conduct, in the place of Revelation. I have said much on this subject already. Truth has two attributes—beauty and power; and while Useful Knowledge is the possession of truth as powerful, Liberal Knowledge is the apprehension of it as beautiful. Pursue it, either as beauty or as power, to its furthest extent and its true limit, and you are led by either road to the Eternal and Infinite, to the intimations of conscience and the announcements of the Church. Satisfy yourself with what is only visibly or intelligibly excellent, as you are likely to do, and you will make present utility and natural beauty the practical test of truth, and the sufficient object of the intellect. It is not that you will at once reject Catholicism, but you will measure and proportion it by an earthly standard. You will throw its highest and most momentous disclosures into the background, you will deny its principles, explain away its doctrines, re-arrange its precepts, and make light of its practices, even while you profess it. Knowledge, viewed as knowledge, exerts a subtle influence in throwing us back on ourselves, and making us our own centre, and our minds the measure of all things.[45]

From this extract it seems that while Newman is keen to promote a liberal or universal education he argues that if a liberal education is pursued without theology it leads us to an unbalanced view of things.[46]

---

44. Newman writes: "any one who thinks that the doctrines of Revelation are true in the same sense that scientific principles and historical facts are true,—that the idea of a University in fact external to the Catholic Church is both unphilosophical and impracticable, supposing, that is, by University is meant a place of education in general knowledge." Newman, *Discourses on the Scope and Nature*, 337 [*Idea*, 214]. The Longmans Green edition differs slightly replacing "revealed truth" with "Catholic faith": "If the Catholic Faith is true, a University cannot exist externally to the Catholic pale, for it cannot teach Universal Knowledge if it does not teach Catholic theology."

45. Newman, *Discourses on the Scope and Nature*, 340–41. [*Idea*, 216–18]

46. It is this materialistic view of the world which blinds the person from understanding the truths of revelation.

Newman believes that when theology is not given its due students may begin to subordinate revealed truth to earthly standards:

> This then is the tendency of that Liberal Education, of which a University is the school, viz., to view Revealed Religion from an aspect of its own,—to fuse and recast it,—to tune it, as it were, to a different key, and to reset its harmonies,—to circumscribe it by a circle which unwarrantably amputates here, and unduly developes there; and all under the notion, conscious or unconscious, that the human intellect, self-educated and self-supported, is more true and perfect in its ideas and judgments, than that of Prophets and Apostles, to whom the sights and sounds of Heaven were immediately conveyed. A sense of propriety, order, consistency, and completeness gives birth to a rebellious stirring against miracle and mystery, against the severe and the terrible. First and chiefly, this Intellectualism comes into collision with precept, then with doctrine, then with the very principle of dogmatism. A perception of the Beautiful becomes the substitute for faith. External to the Church, it at once runs into scepticism or infidelity; but even within it, and with the most unqualified profession of her Creed, it acts, if left to itself, as an element of corruption and debility.[47]

This makes clear that while Newman is supportive of a broad exposure to knowledge, he is resolutely opposed to the subordination of revealed truth. He warns that if left unchecked a liberal education leads to a liberalism in which people "measure" and "proportion" Catholicism "by an earthly standard." Hence, Newman argues that a curriculum which excludes theology could lead students to view everything from a materialistic perspective. He fears that, over time, this disposition could lead people to reject theological truth.

In his unpublished "Papers of 1853 on the Certainty of Faith"[48] Newman criticizes "Protestant" writers for making religious certainty dependent upon an impractical rule:

> The protestant notion of our duty towards our religious sentiments. A man is bound to have his reasons so in hand, if not before him, as to believe only what he can tell over his reasons, if called upon to do so, and in proportion as he can do so.[49]

---

47. Newman, *Discourses on the Scope and Nature*, 340–41. [*Idea*, 216–18]

48. Though these *Papers* were not published during Newman's lifetime they have been published posthumously: Newman, *Faith and Certainty* [*TP*].

49. *TP*, 1:3.

Here Newman argues that a first principle for Protestants is that their religious beliefs must be proportionate to a direct awareness of the evidence in their support. He continues:

> Let us look at the [Protestant] principle more closely still. We ought to able to show our reasons, if questioned; who can show his reasons? Who in the whole world on questions . . . not mathematical, can give the reasons . . . on which he holds a truth. Why do you believe Louis Napoleon is on the French Throne? The plainer and more obvious a thing is, the more difficult often is it to give reasons.[50]

In this passage Newman criticizes the principle that maintains that before an individual can be certain one has to be aware of the reasons for their belief.[51] Newman argues that making knowledge, religious or otherwise, dependent upon this premise inevitably leads to a denial of many sensible knowledge claims; such as Louis Napoleon is King.[52] Thus as in his other works Newman's criticism of Protestantism centres on what he interprets as that of allowing an unsuitable criteria to presuppose belief.

---

50. *TP*, 1:4.

51. In the case of Protestantism this principle involves an awareness of the scriptural support for a doctrine.

52. Newman's contrast of the "Protestant" approach with the Catholic understanding of religious certainty also anticipates particularist tendencies, for example: "Now we turn to consider the Catholic side of the question; and first, by certainty I suppose is meant a firm reception (simple acceptance) of a fact or truth existing; and it has two degrees—First by the very word, is implied the absence of doubt; if a person doubts ever so little, he is not certain; and if he does not doubt, he may be called, and is truly called, certain . . . . [Yet a] man may [fear] whether there is not some faulty principle at the bottom of this . . . . When he has determined that it would be irrational to entertain any such [fears], or, in other words, not only concludes from particular grounds, but is clear that these grounds can never substantially fail him, he is said to be certain without fear." *TP*, 1:4–5. Here Newman distinguishes between subjective and objective certainty. The first subjective certainty is spontaneous. It does not doubt, but is the simple acceptance of a truth. However, on reflection there is fear that it may not be adequately founded. Thus it is only after a reflex examination that one is able to conclude that the grounds of this belief are valid; then the person becomes objectively certain. This has parallels with a particularist approach to knowledge because Newman considers that certain pieces of knowledge (certainty without doubt) occurs antecedent to an examination of their validity. Likewise particularist writers argue that knowledge occurs prior to epistemological enquiry. In like manner, Newman contends that in order for these spontaneous knowledge claims to be justified (certainty without doubt or fear) it is necessary to examine the reasons in their support anticipates the particularist approach; which examines the epistemological validity of a belief retrospectively.

In a contribution to *Month Magazine*, a review of John Seeley's (1834–95) *Ecce Homo* (1866),[53] Newman criticizes Seeley for making "our Lord's Life, as recorded in the Gospels, [the] logical ground of faith."[54] Newman feels that this will condense Christianity into a formula:

> He deems it important to disclaim, in the outset of his work, all reference to the theology of the Church. He eschews with much precision, as something almost profane, the dogmatism of former ages. He wishes "to trace" our Lord's "biography from point to point, and accept those conclusions—not which Church doctors or even Apostles have sealed with their authority—but which the facts themselves, critically weighed, appear to warrant."[55]

Here Newman interprets the main problem with Seeley's work to be that it reduces Christianity to the limits of his own invented criterion. As a result Newman feels that Seeley abandons the deposit of revealed knowledge in exchange for his own formula. In short, here as elsewhere, Newman criticizes Seeley for making theological belief subject to an arbitrary principle.

Towards the end of his life, Newman was criticized by A. M. Fairbairn in the *Contemporary Review* (1885) for separating religion and reason.[56] In response to this Newman points out that he is not averse to examining the kinds of reasons that are in fact at work in religious faith, but that he opposes the introduction of the "world's" narrow conception of reason, and its unproven first principles, into the subject of religion:

> The partisans and spokesmen of Society, when they come to the question of religion, seem to care so little about proving what they maintain, and, on the warrant of their philosophy, are content silently and serenely to take by implication their first principles for granted, as if, like the teachers of Christianity, they were inspired and infallible. To the World, indeed, its own principles are infallible, and need no proof. Now, if its representatives would but be candid, and say that their assumptions, as ours, are infallible, we should know where they stand; there would be an end to controversy.... The World, then, has its first principles of religion, and so have we. If this were understood, I

---

53. Seeley, *Ecce Homo*.
54. Newman, "Ecce Homo," 620 [*DA*, 367].
55. Newman, "Ecce Homo," 629 [*DA*, 387–88].
56. Fairbairn, "Catholicism and Religious Thought," 667–69.

> should not have my present cause of protest against its Reason as corrosive of our faith. I do not grudge the World its gods, its principles, and its worship; but I protest against its sending them into Christian lecture-rooms, libraries, societies, and companies, as if they were Christian—criticizing, modelling, measuring, altering, improving, as it thinks, our doctrines, principles, and methods of thought, which we refer to divine informants.[57]

Here, once again, Newman points out that the introduction of the "World's" unsuitable, and unproven, principles into the subject of theology inevitably leads to a reductionist account of theological truth.

In each of the works examined above Newman recognizes something approaching what Chisholm terms epistemological methodism. It seems that Newman understands how presupposing criteria to knowledge predetermines our beliefs to be in accordance with those criteria. His criticism of liberalism—the employment of narrow premises in religious enquiries—is that it begs the question in favor of unproven criteria, which lead invariably to the denial of religious beliefs. The frequent manifestation of this tendency within Newman's work indicates that he consistently evidences P1.[58] The prevalence of this tendency throughout Newman's works indicates that Maddox's suggestion that Newman's work is epistemologically methodist need not prevent his writing being taken seriously by particularist writers.

Newman on the Priority of Faith P2

Earlier it was noted that a focus upon the *Grammar* has inhibited studies of Newman's epistemology from giving due attention to his other works. This point is duly emphasized by Miller's article "The Reasonableness of Faith" (2010) which draws particular attention to the *Parochial and Plain Sermons* and argues that several themes which reappear later in his *Grammar* are contained within.[59] Here Newman repeatedly asserts that knowledge comes first, prior to reasoned reflection upon it. For

---

57. Newman, "The Development of Religious Error," 463.

58. Though it remains beyond the scope of this book, Mervyn Davies has suggested that Newman's aversion to liberalism offers a way in which his occasional writings might be unified. For further discussion, see Neville, *Addresses to Cardinal Newman*, 63–64; Merrigan, *Clear Heads and Holy Hearts*, 2.

59. Miller, "The Reasonableness of Faith," 42–43. Compare *PS*, 1:194–95 with Newman, *Grammar*, 287–90 [*GA*, 294–96].

example, in his sermon "Religious Faith Rational" (1829) Newman writes that: "from reliance on others we acquire knowledge of all kinds, and proceed to reason, judge, decide, act, form plans for the future."[60] Here Newman maintains that the acquisition of knowledge usually precedes a demonstration of the reasons in its support.[61] Newman's sermon on "Faith without Sight" (1834) develops the theological implications of this idea further when he states that religion is not founded upon reason:

> [W]e speak of religion being built upon faith, not upon reason; on the other hand it is as common for those who scoff at religion to object [to] this very doctrine against us; as if in so saying, we had almost admitted that Christianity was not true.[62]

Despite objections to this conception of the relationship between faith and reason Newman contends that "a mind that believes readily" is blessed.[63] For reasons such as this another of Newman's sermons upholds the "The Mind of little Children" (1833) for their implicit trust in accepting knowledge that is handed down to them.[64] He writes:

> Christ has so willed it, that we should get at the Truth, not by ingenious speculations, reasonings, or investigations of our own, but by teaching... those who in the first place receive [the church's] words, have the minds of little children, who do not reason but obey their mother.[65]

The mind attains truth not by formal "reasonings" and "speculations" but by trusting what it receives from others.

In a sermon on "Faith without Demonstration" (1837) Newman suggests that it is much more rational for us to assume the validity of the beliefs we take upon trust than to doubt them. He considers that if we were to withhold our assent until all these beliefs were proven to our

---

60. *PS*, 1:195–96. According to Miller "Religious Faith Rational," demonstrates Newman's "serious reflection on types of trust that are acceptable not only in faith, but in 'every hour of our lives.'" Miller, "The Reasonableness of Faith," 43.

61. *PS*, 1:195–96

62. *PS*, 2:17.

63. *PS*, 2:17.

64. "The simplicity of a child's ways and notions, his ready belief of everything he is told... I would only have a person reflect on the earnestness and awe with which a child listens to any description or tale; or again, his freedom from that spirit of proud independence, which discovers itself in the soul as time goes on." *PS*, 2:65.

65. *PS*, 2:66.

satisfaction "all our life would be spent in proving things ... we should have no time for action; we should never get so far as action." He considers that many things must be taken for granted, unless we wish to "fritter away life, doing nothing."[66]

In this sermon Newman commends his hearers "to walk by faith; that is, not to ask jealously and coldly for strict arguments."[67] He writes:

> Let us not then seek for signs and wonders; for clear, or strong, or compact, or original arguments; but let us believe; evidence will come after faith as its reward, better than before it as its groundwork.[68]

Thus, Newman argues that demonstrative reason, evidence, and formal proof can only come *after* faith is secured:

> Faith and humility consist, not in going about to prove, but in the outset confiding on the testimony of others. Thus afterwards on looking back, we shall find we have proved what we did not set out to prove. We cannot control our reasoning powers, nor exert them at our will or at any moment ... the more you set yourself to argue and prove, in order to discover truth, the less likely you are to reason correctly and to infer profitably. You will be caught by sophisms, and think them splendid discoveries.[69]

Newman maintains that arguments designed to prove the Christian faith are only useful in confirming what is already believed:

> [B]ooks written to prove to us (as they profess) the being of an Almighty, Infinite, Everlasting God ... do not strictly prove it; they do but recommend, evidence, and confirm the doctrine to those who believe it already.... They are, doubtless, useful to Christians, as far as they tend to enliven their devotion, to strengthen their faith, to excite their gratitude, and to enlarge their minds; but they are little or no evidence to unbelievers.[70]

These extracts indicate that Newman understands reason to play a retrospective role in that it only serves to justify beliefs that are already in

---

66. *PS*, 6:335–36.
67. *PS*, 6:339.
68. *PS*, 6:341.
69. *PS*, 6:340–41.
70. *PS*, 6:338.

place. Newman repeatedly states that formal arguments cannot produce faith:

> Using argumentative forms will ... enable you to dispute acutely and to hit objections, but not to discover truth. There is nothing creative, nothing progressive in exhibitions of argument. The utmost they do is to enable us to state well what we have already discovered. ... Faith and obedience are the main things; believe and do, and pray to God for light, and you will reason well without knowing it.[71]

Thus, according to Newman, formal arguments do not precede knowledge, but are useful after we have attained faith in enabling us to meet objections to it.

In each of the sermons mentioned above, Newman argues that knowledge of God is not dependent upon demonstrative reason.[72] On the contrary, he repeatedly maintains that *faith has priority*, "comes first," *demonstrative reason follows after*; "as its reward." He is adamant that reason is not the "ground" of faith.[73] Therefore, although Newman is discussing theological knowledge, Miller is correct to draw attention to the epistemological significance of these sermons.

From 1833 up until the publication of *Tract* 90 (1841) Newman made a significant contribution to the Oxford Movement. Like his sermons, these writings also prioritize theological belief over and above investigations into its evidence. For example, in *Tract* 73 (1835) Newman outlines what he believes to be a "Catholic" approach to truth:

> [W]e should be very reverent in dealing with revealed truth; next, that we should avoid all theorizing and systematizing as relates to it, which is pretty much what looking into the ark was under the Law: further, that we should be solicitous to hold it safely and entirely; moreover, that we should be zealous and pertinacious in guarding it; and lastly, which is implied in all

---

71. *PS*, 6:341.

72. Newman's correspondence with his mother (1829) reinforces this point: "As each individual has certain instincts of right and wrong, antecedently to reasoning, on which he acts and rightly so, which perverse reasoning may supplant, which then can hardly be regained, but, if regained, will be regained from a different source, from reasoning, not from nature, so, I think, has the world of men collectively." LD 2:130

73. Many of the themes touched upon in these Sermons echo the writings of the common sense philosopher Thomas Reid. Though he doesn't mention Reid in these sermons it is clear that Newman had read his works by this point in his life (before March 1828). For further discussion, see LD 2:63.

> these, that we should religiously adhere to the form of words and the ordinances under which it comes to us, through which it is revealed to us, and apart from which the revelation does not exist, there being nothing else given us by which to ascertain or enter into it.[74]

Newman considers that we should accept revealed truth "entirely" as it "is revealed to us." Moreover, in this *Tract* Newman emphasizes that we should not reject revealed truths because they cannot be "accounted for [by] some existing system."[75] A similar epistemological tendency is present in *Tract* 85 (1838) where Newman argues that we attain many truths before we are able to prove them:

> Let us maintain, before we have proved. This seeming paradox is the secret of happiness. Why should we be unwilling to go by faith? We do all things in this world by faith in the word of others. By faith only we know our position in the world, our circumstances, our rights and privileges, our fortunes, our parents, our brothers and sisters, our age, our mortality. Why should religion be an exception? Why should we be unwilling to use for heavenly objects what we daily use for earthly?[76]

Here Newman indicates that knowledge in many areas of life antecedes proof and suggests that if this is a day-to-day reality then it applies as much to religious belief as it does to commonsense beliefs. Both of these *Tracts* manifest the idea that religious beliefs should be given priority and thus may be assumed valid before investigating the evidence in their

---

74. Newman, *Tracts for the Times*, 3:12–13. [*Ess*, 1:44–47].

75. Here Newman calls this theological reductionism "liberalism" and rationalism: "To rationalize is to ask for reasons out of place; to ask improperly how we are to account for certain things, to be unwilling to believe them unless they can be accounted for, i.e. referred to something else as a cause, to some existing system as harmonizing with them or taking them up into itself. Again, since whatever is assigned as the reason for the original fact canvassed, admits in turn of a like question being raised about itself, unless it be ascertainable by the senses, and be the subject of personal experience, Rationalism is bound properly to pursue onward its course of investigation on this principle, and not to stop till it can directly or ultimately refer to self as a witness, whatever is offered to its acceptance. Thus it is characterized by two peculiarities; its love of systematizing, and its basing its system upon personal experience, on the evidence of sense. In both respects it stands opposed to what is commonly understood by the word Faith, or belief in Testimony; for which it deliberately substitutes System (or what is popularly called Reason,) and Sight." Newman, *Tracts for the Times*, 3:2, 27 & 45. [*Ess*, 1:31, 85].

76. Newman, *Tracts for the Times*, 5:84–85 [*DA*, 214–15].

support. Newman considers this to be true not only of theological beliefs but of knowledge in general.[77]

Newman's *Lectures on the Prophetical Office of the Church* (1837) were designed to resolve some misunderstandings about the spirit of the Oxford Movement. A number of satirical attacks insinuated that the movement had tendencies toward "Romanism."[78] The level of suspicion felt concerning the movement is captured by the following extract from the *Eclectic Review*: "We had long been aware that Popery lurks, like a malaria, in the marshes of the Isis."[79] Newman's lectures in fact attempted to steer a middle course between Protestantism and Roman Catholicism.[80] Of interest here is the way in which Newman views the relationship between theological belief and the evidence in its support. For example, the following extract from Newman's lecture on "Scripture as the Record of Faith," which examines how the Thirty-Nine Articles were formed, argues that the truth of these articles was perceived before any reason was formulated to defend them:

> Which, or whether any of the reasons already mentioned, or presently to be mentioned, was adopted as the ground of the Article by its framers, matters not; or whether we can ascertain it, or adopt it ourselves .... They had no time for theories of any kind; and to require theories at their hand, argues an ignorance of human nature, and of the way in which Truth is struck out in the course of life. Common sense, chance, moral perception, genius, the great discoverers of principles, do not reason. They have no arguments, no grounds; they see the Truth, but they do not know how they see it; and if at any time they attempt to prove it, it is as much a matter of experiment with them, as if they had to find a road to a distant mountain which they see with the eye, and they get entangled, embarrassed, and perchance overthrown in the superfluous endeavour.[81]

Here Newman argues that the authors of the Thirty-Nine Articles did not use any agreed formula or theory to determine Anglican doctrine

77. Here, again, Newman's work reflects that of Thomas Reid who emphasized that the majority of a persons knowledge claims are intuitively obtained through common sense.

78. Dickinson, *A Pastoral Epistle*. For further discussion, see LD 9:61.

79. Unknown author, "Oxford Popery," 45.

80. The work was later republished as: Newman, *The Via Media of the Anglican Church*.

81. Newman, *Lectures on the Prophetical Office*, 338–39. [VM, 1:283–84]

but simply saw the truth.[82] Moreover, Newman contends that one must initially accept the articles of Christianity in faith. He argues that rational assessment should only begin once faith is in place. He writes:

> It is popularly conceived that to maintain the right of Private Judgment, is to hold that no one has an enlightened faith who has not, as a point of duty, discussed the grounds of it and made up his mind for himself. But to put forward such doctrine as this, rightly pertains to infidels and sceptics only, and if great names may be quoted in its favour, and it is often assumed to be the true Protestant doctrine, this is surely because its advocates do not weigh the force of their own words. Every one must begin religion by faith, not by reasoning; he must take for granted what he is taught and what he cannot prove; and it is better for himself that he should do so, even if the teaching he receives contains a mixture of error. If he would possess a reverent mind, he must begin by obeying; if he would cherish a generous and devoted spirit, he must begin by venturing some what on uncertain information; if he would deserve the praise of modesty and humility, he must repress his busy intellect, and forbear to scrutinize.[83]

In this extract Newman criticizes those who would make knowledge of the grounds (evidence) of Christianity into a prerequisite for faith. In order to challenge this view Newman argues that faith comes first, then reason. Newman explains that this is why "subscription to the Thirty-Nine Articles . . . is in this place [Oxford] exacted of those who come hither for education." His point is that people should have faith before studying and reflecting on the articles of religion at university.[84] Thus, Newman is not excluding the role of reason in faith. Rather, he maintains

---

82. Newman's use of the term "Common Sense" here, to imply that the framers of the Thirty-Nine Articles could simply "see" their truth, mirrors Reid's conception of common sense. This similarity between Newman and Reid is also noted by Ferreira. For further discussion, see Ferreira, *Scepticism*, 173–78.

83. Newman, *Lectures on the Prophetical Office*, 161–62 [*VM*, 1:135].

84. Newman, *Lectures on the Prophetical Office*, 162 [*VM*, 1:136] In Newman's day the compulsory university subscription to the Thirty-Nine Articles caused considerable controversy. Chadwick argues that the most important feature of this debate "was the effort to prevent formulas, devised in an age believed to be less well-instructed, from hindering modern 'improvements' . . . to tie [someone] to a particular form of theology which will exclude his subsequent intellectual development." Chadwick, *From Bossuet to Newman*, 80.

that reflection upon the reasons in its support should not begin until one possesses faith:

> [One] may go on to examine the basis of the authority of Scripture or of the Church; and if so, he will do it, not (as is sometimes irreverently said) "impartially" and "candidly," which means sceptically and arrogantly, as if he were the centre of the universe, and all things might be summoned before him and put to task at his pleasure, but with a generous confidence in what he has been taught or rather it ought, according to its opportunities, to exercise itself upon all of these, by way of finding out God's perfect truth.[85]

Thus, while Newman allows for someone to study the evidence in support of their beliefs, he is adamant that they must first accept them in faith and, furthermore, must examine their justification reverently. From this it is apparent that in these lectures Newman maintains that theological knowledge is obtained before one understands the evidence in its support. It is only retrospectively, when knowledge of Christian doctrine is in place, that a reasoned reflection upon its grounds should begin.

Newman wrote a series of letters to the *Times* newspaper (1841) in criticism of Sir Robert Peel's address at the opening of the Tamworth reading room, later republished in his *Discussions and Arguments* (1872).[86] In the sixth of these Tamworth Reading Room letters Newman argued that knowledge precedes reason:

> First comes knowledge, then a view, then reasoning, and then belief. This is why science has so little of a religious tendency; deductions have no power or persuasion. The heart is commonly reached, not through the reason, but through the imagination,

---

85. Newman, *Lectures on the Prophetical Office*, 162–63 [*VM*, 1:136–37].

86. LD 8:555 [*DA*, 254–305]. Newman's criticisms centred upon Peel's insinuation that education, rather than religion, could hold the fabric of society together. For example, Peel states that: "I cannot help thinking that, by bringing together, in an institution of this kind [The Tamworth Reading Room], intelligent men of all classes and all conditions in life, by uniting together, as we have united, in the committee of this institution, the gentleman of ancient family and great landed possessions with the skilful mechanic and artificer of good character; I cannot help thinking that we are all establishing a bond of social connexion that will derive more than common strength from the pure motives that influence us, and from the cause in which we are engaged. (Applause.) I cannot help believing that we are harmonizing the gradations of society, and binding men together by a new bond, which, as I said before, will have more than ordinary strength on account of the object which unites us." Peel, *An Inaugural Address*, 18.

> by means of direct impressions, by the testimony of facts and events, by history, by description. Persons influence us, voices melt us, looks subdue us, deeds inflame us. Many a man will live and die upon a dogma; no one will be a martyr for a conclusion. A conclusion is but an opinion; it is not a thing which is, but which we are certain about; and it has often been observed, that we never say that we are certain, without implying that we doubt. To say that a thing must be, is to admit that it may not be. No one, I say, will die for his own calculations; he dies for realities.[87]

In this extract Newman emphatically states that *knowledge precedes reason*. Once more, this indicates that Newman's writing consistently maintains that one obtains knowledge prior to understanding the evidence in its support.

Newman's Oxford University sermons were examined earlier for their tendency to oppose (P1) writers who prioritize theories concerning when a belief is legitimate above the beliefs themselves. The present section will examine these sermons individually to determine the extent to which they assume beliefs to be valid prior to an examination of the evidence in their support. For example, the first edition of these Sermons was criticized heavily for renouncing the "assistance of reason" (1843).[88] A famous example of this is Charles Kingsley's (1819–75) *What Then Does Dr Newman Mean?* (1864):

> But what, after all, does Dr. Newman teach concerning truth? What he taught in 1843, and what he (as far as I can see) teaches still, may be seen in his last sermon in a volume entitled, "Chiefly on the Theory of Religious Belief," called a sermon "On the Theory of Developments in Religious Doctrine." I beg all who are interested in this question to read that sermon (which I had overlooked till lately); and to judge for themselves whether I exaggerate when I say that it tries to undermine the grounds of all rational belief for the purpose of substituting blind superstition.[89]

Here Kingsley criticizes Newman for substituting reason with faith in "superstitious" beliefs. Though Kingsley is highly critical of Newman's

---

87. LD 8:555.

88. Unknown author, "Oxford Theology," 158.

89. Kingsley, *What, Then, Does Dr. Newman Mean?* 38. Reprinted in: Newman, *Newman's Apologia Pro Vita Sua*, 54–54.

emphasis on faith he is wrong to insinuate that Newman is an advocate of superstition.[90] While Newman's sermons uphold the idea that knowledge of God antecedes formal philosophical speculation concerning its veracity, Newman maintains that the church has always provided a rational defence of its beliefs.

In his sermon on the "Usurpations of Reason" (1831), Newman argues that in the early church reasoned reflection upon the evidences for Christian doctrine began as a form of "self-defence" when heretics called the church's doctrines into question:

> Henceforth the Church was obliged, in self-defence, to employ the gifts of the intellect in the cause of God, to trace out (as near as might be) the faithful shadow of those truths, which unlearned piety admits and acts upon, without the medium of clear intellectual representation.[91]

In this passage, Newman indicates that faith precedes an explicit intellectual comprehension of questions pertaining to its rational justification. He maintains that "exercises of Reason are either external, or at least only ministrative," to faith. Thus, while such questions are "useful in their place, they are not of the 'essense' of faith, not "necessary" to its existence.[92] Newman argues that the example of the early church proves that faith may exist independently from a conscious awareness of the reasons in its defence. He writes:

> Faith, establishing itself by its own inherent strength, ruled the Reason as far as its own interests were concerned, and from that

---

90. Kingsley's biased reading of this work illustrates how easy it is to obtain an unbalanced interpretation of Newman's conception of faith and reason. It cannot be stressed enough that these sermons were preached on a variety of different occasions by a man who was himself in a state of development. It is to be expected that hermeneutical issues will arise when these sermons are interpreted collectively. Moreover, Newman's conversion to Catholicism gave these sermons a new and different readership. Though these questions remain beyond our present scope, it is quite possible that Newman's concerns about censorship for fideism had an impact upon his prefaces, and proposed prefaces, to later editions of this work. For further discussion, see LD 12: 9, 33–34; Bautain, *Philosophie*; Vargish, *Newman: The Contemplation of Mind*, 42; Newman, *Fifteen Sermons Preached*, 237–51; Sheaat, "Newman, Perrone and Möhler," 45–55.

91. Newman, *Sermons Chiefly on the Theory of Religious Belief*, 50 [*US*, 64–65].

92. Newman, *Sermons Chiefly on the Theory of Religious Belief*, 52 [*US*, 67].

time has employed it in the Church, first as a captive, then as a servant; not as an equal, and in nowise (far from it) as a patron.[93]

This presentation of the role of reason in relation to Christian faith indicates once more that theological knowledge is not dependent upon formal reason but is rather "established" in and of itself, before reason is explicitly engaged.

Similar themes are also present in the Sermon entitled "Wisdom, as Contrasted with Faith and with Bigotry" (1841). Here Newman states that reasoned reflection does not begin until knowledge of Christian doctrine is attained:

> What is the true office, and what the legitimate bounds, of those abstract exercises of Reason which may best be described by the name of systematizing. They are in their highest and most honourable place, when they are employed upon the vast field of Knowledge, not in conjecturing unknown truths, but in comparing, adjusting, connecting, explaining facts and doctrines ascertained. Such a use of Reason is Philosophy.[94]

Here Newman argues that when the theological doctrines in question "are all known . . . Reason does but connect fact with fact; instead of discovering it does but analyze."[95] In other words, formal reason does not create theological knowledge, it retrospectively "systematizes" the evidence in its support.[96]

The same tendency manifests itself in the Sermon on "Developments in Religious Doctrine" (1843). Here Newman holds Mary as an exemplar of the right relationship between faith and reason:

> Mary is our pattern of Faith, both in the reception and in the study of Divine Truth. She does not think it enough to accept, she dwells upon it; not enough to possess, she uses it; not enough to assent, she develops it; not enough to submit the Reason, she reasons upon it; not indeed reasoning first, and believing afterwards, with Zacharias, yet first believing without reasoning, next from love and reverence, reasoning after believing. And thus she symbolizes to us, not only the faith of the unlearned,

---

93. Newman, *Sermons Chiefly on the Theory of Religious Belief*, 43 [US, 58].

94. Newman, *Sermons Chiefly on the Theory of Religious Belief*, 292 [US, 294].

95. Newman, *Sermons Chiefly on the Theory of Religious Belief*, 292 [US, 294].

96. Newman definition of philosophy is also significant here for he states that "Philosophy is reason exercised upon Knowledge." Newman, *Sermons Chiefly on the Theory of Religious Belief*, 292 [US, 294].

but of the doctors of the Church also, who have to investigate, and weigh, and define, as well as to profess the Gospel; to draw the line between truth and heresy; to anticipate or remedy the various aberrations of wrong reason; to combat pride and recklessness with their own arms; and thus to triumph over the sophist and the innovator.[97]

In this extract Mary is praised because she begins with faith and then reasons upon it. Newman emphasizes that she does not reason first, but first believes "without reasoning." Yet out of her "love and reverence" she engages in reasoned reflection. Here again Newman approaches the justification of religious belief in a manner that evidences the epistemological tendency of presupposing (theological) knowledge to philosophical contemplation.[98]

In his *Essay on Development* (1845) Newman also sought to show that the doctrines and practices of the Roman Catholic Church of his day were an authentic development of those held by the apostles.[99] However,

97. Newman, *Sermons Chiefly on the Theory of Religious Belief*, 312–13 [*US*, 313–14].

98. Before progressing it is important to acknowledge that in these sermons Newman also describes faith as being an "implicit" form of reasoning. Though Maddox does not utilise this dimension of Newman's sermons to support his epistemological methodist interpretation of the *Grammar* it is possible that Newman's conception of spontaneous forms of reasoning could be viewed in this way. Nevertheless, it should be emphasized that Newman's understanding of the mind's spontaneous modes of reasoning, in the original publication of these sermons, is quite different from formal conceptions of inference. Newman clarifies that there is no "distinct act of reason" which comes before faith. "Instead of there being really any . . . process of reasoning first, and then believing . . . the act of Faith is sole and elementary, and complete in itself." It depends on "no process of mind previous to it." Hence, while indicating that faith is a kind of reason, Newman believes faith to be a spontaneous operation of the mind different in kind to the popular conception of formal inference dominant in nineteenth-century thought. These themes will be taken up in more detail in chapter 4 where Maddox's analysis of the *Grammar*—which argues that Newman's conception of the role of natural inference in assent makes him an epistemological methodist—will be examined in detail. Newman, *Sermons Chiefly on the Theory of Religious Belief*, 194 [*US*, 202]. Also, see Maddox, "Newman, Certain Knowledge," 80.

99. Prior to writing the *Essay on Development* (1845), Newman had given his assent to the idea that the Roman Catholic Church is the true Church. "I had nothing more to learn; what still remained for my conversion, was, not further change of opinion, but to change opinion itself into the clearness and firmness of intellectual conviction." Newman, *History of My Religious Opinions*, 200 [*Apo* 200]. Walgrave therefore gives the wrong impression when he states that Newman "yielded to the evidence" in favor of Catholicism after examining the evidence in its support. Walgrave, *Newman the Theologian*, 37; Bouyer, *Newman*, 243.

while the *Essay* argues in support of this point, Newman begins, not with proof, but with belief.[100] At the outset Newman expresses his conviction that the Christianity of the Roman Catholic Church "is in its substance the very religion which Christ and his Apostles taught in the first."[101] He writes:

> The Roman Catholic communion of this day is the successor and representative of the Medieval Church[.] . . . [T]he Medieval Church is the legitimate heir of the Nicene[.] . . . . [O]f all existing systems, the present communion of Rome is the nearest approximation in fact to the Church of the Fathers, possible. . . . Did St. Athanasius or St. Ambrose come suddenly to life, it cannot be doubted what communion they would mistake for their own.[102]

Therefore, the *Essay* begins with the presupposition that nineteenth-century Catholicism is the true successor to the primitive church.[103] Newman considers that if physicists can presuppose Newton's theory of gravity to be correct because the theory is generally received then he too can assume that the nineteenth-century Roman Catholic Church is the successor of the primitive church.[104] Citing Aquinas as a license for this

---

100. Lash considers, rightly, that it "is imperative, when analysing and assessing the arguments in the *Essay*, never to lose sight of the fact that they stand in that relationship of consequence and subordination to the conviction they seek to articulate." Lash, *Newman on Development*, 9–10.

101. Newman, *Essay on Development*, 3 [*Dev*, 5].

102. Newman, *Essay on Development*, 137–38 [*Dev*, 97–98].

103. This interpretation is also corroborated by Newman's nineteenth-century reviewers, for example: "The reader of Mr. Newman's book will seek in vain for the arguments by which the author was led away from the [Anglican] faith. It seems sufficiently manifest that he first chose his new part, and then cast about for reasons to keep him in countenance. He first decided that Romanism was true, and then looked out for evidences that it was plausible." Unknown author, "Newman on the Development of Christian Doctrine," 113. Similar criticisms are made by other reviewers: unknown author, "An Essay on the Development of Christian Doctrine," 388–89; unknown author, "Mr Newman's Theory of Development," 301–2; Butler, *Letters on Romanism*, 34.

104. In taking this assumption for granted Newman believes he is proceeding in the same way that "physical philosophers" do with "Newton's theory of gravitation." Newman writes: "physical philosophers take Newton's theory of gravitation for granted, because it is generally received, and use it without rigidly testing it first, each for himself, by phenomena; and if phenomena are found which it does not satisfactorily solve, this does not trouble them, for they are sure that a way must exist of explaining them, consistently with that theory, though it does not occur to themselves." Newman, *Essay on Development*, 149 [*Dev*, 101–2].

approach Newman emphasizes that "we must begin with believing," and argues that "the reasons for believing" will follow later.[105] Thus Newman became assured of the veracity of Catholicism and then tried to examine the evidence in support of this belief.[106]

Newman's unpublished paper on the certainty of faith was referred to earlier to indicate his opposition to what he calls the principle of Protestantism, which made theological knowledge dependent upon an awareness of the available evidence. These papers also evidence the tendency to assume the validity of one's beliefs prior to obtaining evidence in their support. For example, Newman discusses two levels of certainty subjective and objective. He writes:

> [B]y certainty I suppose is meant a firm reception (simple acceptance) of a fact or truth existing; and it has two degrees—First by the very word, is implied the absence of doubt; if a person doubts ever so little, he is not certain; and if he does not doubt, he may be called, and is truly called, certain. . . . [Yet a] man may [fear] whether there is not some faulty principle at the bottom of this . . . . When he has determined that it would be irrational to entertain any such [fears], or, in other words, not only concludes from particular grounds, but is clear that these grounds can never substantially fail him, he is said to be certain without fear.[107]

Here Newman distinguishes between subjective and objective certainty.[108] According to Newman, the first subjective certainty is spontaneous.[109] It does not doubt, but is the simple acceptance of a truth. However, if on reflection one is able to confirm that the grounds of this belief are valid then the person becomes objectively certain. These themes are also

---

105. Newman, *Essay on Development*, 327, 333 [*Dev*, 326, 332].

106. The *Essay* proposes a solution to "a number of the reputed corruptions of Rome" which allege that the Roman Catholics have perverted, even contradicted, the doctrines of the apostolic faith. Newman, *Essay on Development*, 29 [*Dev*, 31–32]. Newman cites the words of William Chillingworth (1602–44) as an example of this objection: "There are popes against popes, councils against councils, some fathers against others, the same fathers against themselves, a consent of fathers of one age against a consent of fathers of another age, the Church of one age against the Church of another age." Chillingworth, *The Works*, 2:410.

107. *TP*, 1:4–5.

108. This distinction resonates with that of the neo-Thomistic writers introduced in the previous chapter

109. *TP*, 1:15.

taken up in another preparatory paper for the *Grammar* on "Assent and Intuition" (1860). In contrast to his discussion of the "Protestant principle," Newman maintains that humankind, without an awareness of "any actual proof of it," is "naturally capable" of giving "absolute assent" to pieces of knowledge.[110] He writes:

> Absolute or simple assent is my recognition of the truth of a thought on its own account, and independently of everything else, . . . whether it actually admits of proof or no; that is, it is assent to what I see to be self-evident . . . . When the assent which I give to a truth, (that is to a thought which faithfully represents a thing) is simple and absolute, I shall call it an intuition, as being an insight into things as they are . . . . [It is] my assent to what is self-evident specially to me, though I have not before my mind any actual proof of it: accordingly, it is relative both to me and to my circumstances, and these two may be called its conditions.[111]

Here Newman argues that humankind is able to intuitively attain knowledge prior to having consciousness of its epistemological status. This indicates that, like the Thomistic writers already discussed, Newman considers that knowledge occurs prior to epistemological enquiry.

Newman's article "On Consulting the Faithful" (1859), published in the *Rambler* during Newman's editorship,[112] argues that the laity is inspired to know the truth of God and is unconsciously aware of this truth.[113] He argues that it is then the duty of the teaching office of the church, the pope, and the bishops,[114] to test that truth, "discriminating"

---

110. *TP,* 1:69.

111. *TP,* 1: 64–65.

112. The *Rambler* was a periodical designed for free-thinking lay converts who were critical of the excessive Ultramontanism of the day. Newman said he felt the "extreme mortification" and misfortune of becoming editor. LD 19:96. For further discussion, see Holmes, *More Roman Than Rome,* 112.

113. "They are witnesses to the antiquity or universality of the doctrines which they contain, and about which they are 'consulted.' And, in like manner, I certainly understood the writer in the *Rambler* to mean (and I think any lay reader might so understand him) that the *fidelium sensus* and *consensus* is a branch of evidence which it is natural or it necessary for the Church to regard and consult, before she proceeds to any definition, from its intrinsic cogency; and by consequence, that it ever has been so regarded and consulted." Newman, "On Consulting the Faithful in Matters of Doctrine," 199–200, 211.

114. Newman considers that it is by consulting the laity that the church's hierarchy see what it is they really believe: "It is a curious phenomenon in the philosophy of the human mind, that we often do not know whether we hold a point or not, though we

and "discerning"[115] whether or not it is correct interpretation of the deposit of faith.[116] As in the other examples given above, Newman considers that the truth is instinctively obtained (in this case by the laity) before any formal evaluation of it occurs (by the church authorities).

Newman's *Philosophical Notebook* also maintains that beliefs should be assumed to be valid prior to investigating the evidence in their support. In 1859 Newman, received a copy of Ward's lectures *On Nature and Grace* (1859), delivered at St Edmunds Seminary (Ware), for comments.[117] Here Ward, citing Thomas Reid, argues that "we may most reasonably trust those faculties which [God] has implanted" in us.[118] In his notebook (November 1859) Newman reflects upon this Reidian notion that we should have faith in our faculties of sense, reasoning, and memory. He writes:

> I am conscious of my own existence. That I am involves a great deal more than itself. I am a unit made up of various faculties, which seem to me parts of my being and to be as much facts as that being itself—and, as it would be improper to say I believe in my being . . . so it seems to me an improper use of terms and a play upon words to say that I have faith in those faculties, their exercise & their dictates.[119]

Newman considers these faculties to be contained within our existence. In addition to these basic belief-forming capacities, such as sensation, reason, and memory, Newman speaks of conscience as a power innate to human beings:

---

hold it; but when our attention is once drawn to it, then forthwith we find it so much part of ourselves, that we cannot recollect when we began to hold it, and we conclude (with truth), and we declare, that it has always been our belief." Newman, "On Consulting the Faithful," 227–28.

115. Newman, "On Consulting the Faithful," 205.

116. He summarizes that: "Its *consensus* is to be regarded: 1. as a testimony to the fact of the apostolical dogma; 2. as a sort of instinct, or [*phronema*], deep in the bosom of the mystical body of Christ; 3. as a direction of the Holy Ghost; 4. as an answer to its prayer; 5. as a jealousy of error, which it at once feels as a scandal." Newman, "On Consulting the Faithful," 199, 211.

117. Ward, *On Nature and Grace*, 10.

118. For example Reid writes: "When a man in the common course of life gives credit to the testimony of his senses, his memory, or his reason, he does not put the question to himself, whether these faculties may deceive him; yet the trust he reposes in them supposes an inward conviction, that, in that instance at least, they do not deceive him." Reid, *The Works of Thomas Reid*, 448.

119. *PN*, 2:31, 33.

> In the same way that sensation, consciousness, reasoning, memory are part of myself, and it is unmeaning to say that I have faith in it, or blind faith in it, or that it is a law of the mind, as to say that existence is a law of the mind [so Conscience] is bound up in the very idea or fact of my existence[,] ... we one & all ever recognise it, I mean as a sanction or command.[120]

Here Newman holds that conscience, which he describes as a "feeling" of right or wrong,[121] is intrinsic to human existence. From this Newman contends that, because all possess the faculty of conscience, belief in God is a natural belief:

> If then our knowledge of our existence is brought home to me by my consciousness of thinking, and if thinking includes as one of its modes conscience or the sense of an imperative coercive law, & if such a sense, when reflected on, involves an inchoate recognition of a divine being, it follows that such recognition comes close upon my recognition that I am, and is only not so clear an object of perception as is my own existence. This being of a God being at once brought home to me illuminated, as it will be in its various aspects by reflection, tradition, &c &c., I have a guiding truth, which gives a practical direction to my judgment & faith as regards a variety of other truths or professed truths which encounter me, as the trustworthiness of the senses, our social & personal duties, the divinity of Christianity.[122]

Thus Newman argues that this native impression of appropriate conduct, conscience, leads him to believe that Something (God) has inscribed this moral law upon our souls. Newman considers it right that theism flows naturally from conscience because it makes belief in God accessible to "all, to high and low, from the earliest infancy." Thus Newman contends that our belief in God, rather than being the result of reliable belief forming capacities, is intrinsic to us since it is bound up with human existence itself.[123] Once again this aspect of Newman's discussion indicates that he

---

120. *PN*, 2:49.

121. "This feeling of a law, whatever its dictates, & which I call Conscience, is not a law of the mind, but one of the phenomena which like thought or consciousness are bound up with or convey to me the idea & the fact of my being. Now I say that, our consciousness of thought is a reflex act implying existence ... so this sensation of conscience is the recognition of our obligation involving the notion of an external being obliging." *PN*, 2:59.

122. *PN*, 2:63.

123. *PN*, 2:69–71.

considers that knowledge of God is natural-occurring prior to any kind of formal reasoned reflection.[124]

The recurrence of P2 throughout Newman's writing indicates that there is much in his work that could be exploited by particularist writers. While this potential will be explored in more detail in chapters 5 and 6 the present chapter will examine Newman's works for what Nicholas Lash describes as Newman's "methodological pluralism": Newman's recognition of the truth of Aristotle's contention that different levels of precision are demanded by different subjects (P3).[125]

Newman's "Methodological Pluralism" P3

Newman's Oxford University sermons manifest the Aristotelian notion that different subjects require different kinds of proof. For example, in a sermon on "The Usurpations of Reason" (1831) Newman criticizes Christians who use the Bible as a criterion for determining scientific questions:

> It would be an absurdity to attempt to find out mathematical truths by the purity and acuteness of the moral sense. It is a form of this mistake which has led men to apply such Scripture communications as are intended for religious purposes to the determination of physical questions.[126]

Here Newman is challenging the way in which some Christians misuse the text of Scripture as a scientific method. His point is that every subject has its own level of proof—thus he argues that Scripture is an inappropriate criterion for determining questions relating to science.

Newman's *Essay on Development* was introduced earlier in order to indicate the way in which this work evidences P2—since Newman presupposes the legitimacy of the doctrines and practices of nineteenth-century Roman Catholicism prior to assessing the evidence. The present section will discuss the *Essay* in relation to P3 by examining whether the way in which Newman retrospectively examines the evidence for Roman

---

124. Though it is impossible to demonstrate it is possible that Newman's engagement with Ward's reception of Reid shaped his discussion of the existence of spontaneous claims to knowledge. Moreover, it is possible that Chisholm and Abraham interaction with this common sense philosopher explains some of the similarities between these writers.

125. Lash, *Newman on Development*, 22, 26.

126. Newman, *Sermons Chiefly on the Theory of Religious Belief*, 44, [US, 59].

Catholicism resonates with the Aristotelian notion that different subjects require different levels of precision.[127]

In this *Essay*, under the heading "Character of the Evidence,"[128] Newman makes clear that he will test the legitimacy of Roman Catholic doctrine using reasons appropriate to the case in hand. Citing Aristotle he states that:

> There is a well-known remark of Aristotle's, that "it is much the same to admit the probabilities of a mathematician and to ask demonstration from an orator." Some things admit of much closer and more careful handling than others; and we must look for proof in every case according to the nature of the subject-matter which is in debate, and not beyond it. Evidence may have an air of nature even in its deficiencies; and it recommends itself to us, when it carries with it its explanation why it is such as it is, not fuller or more exact.[129]

The reference to Aristotle at this juncture is significant for it emphasizes that Newman's desire is to use rules appropriate to the present case. Newman clarifies that the arguments that he will produce in support of the authenticity of Roman Catholic doctrine will be drawn from the "history of eighteen hundred years" of the Catholic tradition.[130] He writes:

> History is not a creed or a catechism; it gives lessons rather than rules; it does not bring out clearly upon the canvass the details which were familiar to the ten thousand minds of whose combined movements and fortunes it treats. Such is it from its very nature; nor can the defect ever fully be remedied. This must be admitted: at the same time, principles may be laid down with

---

127. Newman, *Essay on Development*, 147–49 [*Dev*, 100–101].

128. In the third (Longmans Green) edition this heading, and the text following it, is edited to read "State of the Evidence" *Dev*, 110.

129. Newman, *Essay on Development*, 99 [*Dev*, 60]. The text for the third edition is also different: "The same principle is involved in the well-known maxim of Aristotle, that 'it is much the same to admit the probabilities of a mathematician, and to look for demonstration from an orator.' In all matters of human life, presumption verified by instances, is our ordinary instrument of proof, and, if the antecedent probability is great, it almost supersedes instances. Of course, as is plain, we may err grievously in the antecedent view which we start with, and in that case, our conclusions may be wide of the truth; but that only shows that we had no right to assume a premiss which was untrustworthy, not that our reasoning was faulty." [*Dev*, 113–14].

130. Newman, *Essay on Development*, 27 [*Dev*, 29].

considerable success as keys to its various notices, enabling us to arrange and reconcile them.[131]

These extracts indicate that in measuring the validity of Roman Catholic doctrine Newman is shaped by Aristotle's contention that different subjects require different levels of precision. This leads him to assess the validity of nineteenth-century Catholicism using principles appropriate to the historical subject in hand.

The way in which Newman applies this Aristotelian principle is to formulate seven "tests" or "notes" to serve as indicators of authentic doctrinal development.[132] These are: (1) Preservation of Type, (2) Continuity of Principles, (3) Power of Assimilation, (4) Early Anticipation, (5) Logical Sequence, (6) Preservative Additions, and (7) Chronic Continuance. It is necessary to briefly introduce these tests if Newman's relevance to Abraham is to be fully understood (in chapter 6).[133]

The first test is that later developments of an idea must preserve the "essential idea of the doctrine or polity which it represents."[134] Newman maintains that Catholicism fulfils this requirement because it is despised by the world for the same reasons that the heathen world hated the early Christians.[135] The second test holds that a development must remain faithful to the "principle with which it started."[136] He argues that the central principle operative in all ages of the church is the "special preference of faith to reason."[137] He concludes that, because nineteenth-century Catholicism holds faith higher than reason, it maintains a continuity of principles with the primitive church.[138]

---

131. Newman, *Essay on Development*, 7 [*Dev*, 7].

132. In the original version of Newman's *Essay* (1845) Newman uses the word "tests." In his reworked edition (1878), Newman provides seven "notes" of authentic doctrinal development. Newman, *Essay on Development*, 58, 63 [*Dev*, 169–71].

133. These tests are relevant for understanding Newman's influence upon Abraham (treated in chapter 5).

134. Newman, *Essay on Development*, 66 [*Dev*, 178].

135. Newman, *Essay on Development*, 204–42. In the third edition Newman uses different examples to illustrate this test. For further discussion, see *Dev*, 171.

136. Newman, *Essay on Development*, 69, 72 [*Dev*, 178–85].

137. Newman, *Essay on Development*, 328.

138. Newman, *Essay on Development*, 323–24. It is clear that many writers, William Abraham among them, would disagree with Newman on this point. Although Abraham's similarities with Newman will be discussed in chapter 5 it is apparent that, while he agrees with Newman that faith should precede an evaluation of the rationality of religious belief, his work *Canon and Criterion* (1997) argues that the Roman

Newman argues that the third test of a genuine development is its ability to assimilate alien thoughts "into its own substance."[139] He considers that throughout its history Catholicism has been prepared "to adopt, or imitate, or sanction the existing rites and customs of the populace, as well as the philosophy of the educated class."[140] Therefore, Newman concludes that Catholicism is consonant with the early church because it has always been able to absorb local cultural practices; permitting "much variety and change, in the Sacramental issues and instruments which the Church has used."[141] The fourth test of the faithfulness of a development is "its definite anticipation at an early period in the history" of the church.[142] In this regard, Newman argues that the Catholic developments of his day are true because their roots can be traced back to the first centuries of the church.[143]

His fifth test is that a development must be the logical outcome of doctrines held by the early church.[144] This test enabled Newman to view the doctrine of purgatory[145] as a logical development from the conception of baptism held by the early church, which believed that sin committed after baptism could affect one's salvation.[146] His sixth test holds

---

Catholic Church has often allowed epistemological concerns to supersede devotion. For further discussion, see Abraham, *Canon and Criterion*.

139. Newman, *Essay on Development*, 73–74 [*Dev*, 185].

140. Newman, *Essay on Development*, 358 [*Dev*, 372].

141. Newman, *Essay on Development*, 365 [*Dev*, 379]. This test was important for reassuring Newman because he had for a long time held that real ideas are capable of incorporating alien concepts. For further discussion, see Merrigan, *Clear Heads and Holy Hearts*.

142. Newman, *Essay on Development*, 79 [*Dev*, 189].

143. Newman, *Essay on Development*, 369 [*Dev*, 383]. Newman's correspondence demonstrates that the Marian doctrines had long been a stumbling block to his embrace of Catholicism. His ability to account for these using this, and other, tests resolved many of the difficulties surrounding his admission to the Catholic fold. For further discussion, see LD 8:172–74, 180–82, 186–88; LD 9:154–56, 164–65; LD 10:110.

144. Newman, *Essay on Development*, 86 [*Dev*, 195].

145. Prior to his conversion Newman had considered the doctrine of purgatory to be one of Rome's worst "inventions." LD 3:265, 293.

146. Newman considers that this logical connection between the doctrine of baptism and the doctrine of purgatory thus acts as evidence in favor of this Roman Catholic doctrine. He explains that because baptism is the "plenary forgiveness of sins past" Christians often "delayed the rite" to the end of life, raising the problem for people who had received this "one remission of sins, and had sinned since." Newman contends that here "we see how, as time went on, the doctrine of purgatory was opened upon the

that a development should act conservatively upon its past.[147] By way of illustration Newman argues that the title "Mother of God," given to Mary at the Council of Ephesus (431 AD), was designed "to protect the doctrine of the incarnation."[148] Since Mary's veneration was intended to be preservative of previous doctrines it passes his sixth test for authentic doctrinal development.[149]

Newman's final test for determining true doctrinal development presupposes that the "duration" of an idea is an indication of a legitimate development.[150] Newman holds that were Catholicism a corrupt form of Christianity it would long since "have been broken up" nevertheless "it is still living."[151] In other words, whilst a real development endures, heretical doctrine is short lived.[152] Therefore, Newman takes the fact that Catholicism has endured many trials to be yet another form of evidence in support of his belief that the Roman Catholicism of his day is the true heir of the primitive church.

Before closing it is important to clarify that in no way does Newman intend these "tests" to act as criteria for future doctrinal developments.[153]

---

apprehension of the Church as a portion or form of penance due for sins committed after baptism." Newman, *Essay on Development*, 410–17.

147. Thus "a corruption is a development" that "ceases to illustrate, and begins, to prejudice, the acquisitions gained in its previous history." Thus development consists in "addition and increase," not in contradiction or "destruction." Newman, *Essay on Development*, 86–88 [*Dev*, 199].

148. Newman argues that this addition was preservative in intent, in that it was not designed to obscure the divinity of Christ but to secure the doctrine of the incarnation. For this reason Newman believes that the objection, commonly raised, that the elevation of Mary has in fact obscured the divinity of the Godhead in the Roman Catholic faith is incorrect and that this addition serves only to preserve existing Christian doctrine. Newman, *Essay on Development*, 436.

149. Newman, *Essay on Development*, 90. The fact that Newman identifies two tests to resolve his struggle, concerning Marian devotion, illustrates the magnitude of this difficulty. This is emphasized by Newman's declaration that Charles Russell (1812–80), who attempted to resolve this issue for him, "had, perhaps, more to do with my conversion than any one else." Russell was a professor of church history in the Irish Seminary at Maynooth. Newman, *History of My Religious Opinions*, 194–95 [*Apo* 194–95]. For further discussion of Newman's correspondence with Russell, and its background, see Macaulay, *Dr Russell of Maynooth*, 75–98.

150. Newman, *Essay on Development*, 91 [*Dev*, 203ff].

151. Newman, *Essay on Development*, 446–49.

152. Newman, *Essay on Development*, 90.

153. The International Theological Commission misuses Newman's essay when it suggests that it offers "a criteriology for dogmatic development"; for the "ongoing

However, it is clear that while Newman did not outline criteria in order to stipulate the conditions under which future developments should occur, he did outline tests or notes in order to illustrate why he believed the doctrines of the Catholic Church of his day to be continuous with those upheld by the apostles. Moreover, whatever criticisms may be made of these notes of doctrinal development,[154] they are clearly modelled upon Aristotle's contention in the *Nicomachean Ethics* that different subject matters require different levels of precision. Thus, Newman's *Essay* clearly evidences P3 since he deliberately applies this Aristotelian principle to the history of Roman Catholicism in order to argue that an implicit "logic," or grammar, governs the story of this church. It was this "logic" which Newman believed justified him in his antecedent conviction that the doctrines of this church were legitimate developments of those held by the primitive church.[155] Having examined the *Essay on Development* in detail it is necessary to briefly examine whether or not Newman's later writings uphold the principle of "methodological pluralism."

Newman's lectures on *Certain Difficulties Felt by Anglicans* (1850) lament that, because Anglicanism is an established church in England, the rulings of the state have considerable impact upon ecclesiological

---

contemporary interpretation of dogmas." This totally misrepresents his concept of criteria. Newman considers that developments should be left to occur in a "spontaneous" and "gradual" way. He states emphatically that developments are not "intentional and arbitrary deductions" from "existing opinions." Newman's correspondence suggests that he began using the term "Notes" in order to highlight this point. For further discussion: Newman, *Essay on Development*, 337 [*Dev*, 336]; LD 29:165, 193; International Theological Commission, "On the Interpretation of Dogmas," 1–14, at 13. de Wiles also misunderstands Newman's intentions: de Wiles, *The Making of Christian Doctrine*, 168.

154. These will be discussed in more detail in chapter 6. Lash, *Newman on Development*, 37. Cameron, "Newman and the Empiricist Tradition," 92.

155. Many commentators argue that Newman's replacement of the word "tests" with the less ambitious term "notes" should "drive the point home" that the *Essay* does not attempt to provide criteria for development. This is not entirely correct. While Newman does not intend for these criteria to act as a standard by which future developments can be measured, he clearly states (in 1845) that these tests act as "criteria." What, then, are these criteria for? They are intended to operate retrospectively—to reinforce Newman's sense that nineteenth-century Roman Catholic developments are true. For further discussion, see McCarren, "Development of Doctrine," 125; Nichols, *From Newman to Congar*, 47; Coulson, "Was Newman a Modernist?" 78; Cameron, "Newman and the Empiricist Tradition," 92.

matters. Newman explains that, because the life of the church is different from that of other organizations, it requires different regulatory principles:

> One principle has not the life of another. The life of a plant is not the same as the life of an animated being, and the life of the body is not the same as the life of the intellect; nor is the life of the intellect the same in kind as the life of grace; nor is the life of the Church the same as the life of the State.[156]

As stated earlier, Newman believes that each subject matter requires different principles. In saying that the "life of the Church" is not "the same as the life of the State" Newman's point is that the state cannot determine the value of the church's doctrines.[157] As a result Newman concludes that, because the Anglican Church has been governed by the rules of the state, the "Anglo-Catholic teaching" promoted by Tractarian writers had not been evaluated properly.[158]

Newman's article "On Consulting the Faithful in Matters of Doctrine" was introduced in the previous chapter to illustrate the way in which it anticipates the particularist tendency to begin with knowledge claims, prior to investigating how they are obtained. Here the article is discussed in relation to P3. However, before elaborating this, it is necessary to note how Newman's suggestion that the judgement of the laity influenced the development of Christian doctrine brought many objections.[159] In "On Consulting the Faithful" Newman subtly levels a complaint about the way in which his periodical, *The Rambler*, has been subjected to unreasonable levels of scrutiny, inappropriate for essayists like himself:

> Now I know every one will be particular on his own special science or pursuits. I am the last man to find fault with such

---

156. Newman, *Certain Difficulties*, 38 [*Diff*, 1:44].

157. Newman, *Certain Difficulties*, 33–4 [*Diff*, 1:39–40].

158. Newman writes: "in nearly twenty years that movement, though certainly it exerted great influence over the views of individuals, nevertheless has created a mere party in the National Church, having had the least possible influence over the National Church itself; and no wonder, if that Church be simply an organ or department of the State, for in that case, all ecclesiastical acts really proceeding from the supreme civil government, to influence the Establishment, is nothing else than to influence the State, or even the Constitution." *Diff*, 1:34–35.

159. John Gillow, Professor at Ushaw college, and Bishop William Ullathorne both expressed concerns about this. LD 19:129–37.

particularity. Drill-sergeants think much of deportment; hard logicians come down with a sledge-hammer even on a Plato who does not happen to enumerate in his beautiful sentence all the argumentative considerations which go to make up his conclusion; scholars are horrified, as if with sensible pain, at the perpetration of a false quantity. I am far from ridiculing, despising, or even undervaluing such precision; it is for the good of every art and science that it should have vigilant guardians. Nor am I comparing such precision (far from it) with that true religious zeal which leads theologians to keep the sacred Ark of the Covenant in every letter of its dogma, as a tremendous deposit for which they are responsible.... I conceive the force, the peremptoriness, the sternness, with which the Holy See comes down upon the vagrant or the robber, trespassing upon the enclosure of revealed truth, is the only sufficient antagonist to the power and subtlety of the world... I grant, I maintain all this; and after this avowal, lest I be misunderstood, I venture to introduce my notice[.] ... [E]ven a saint's words are not always precise enough to allow of being made a dogmatic text, much less are those of any modern periodical.[160]

Here Newman argues that each subject has its own level of precision, thus one should not expect a periodical to be *ex cathedra* a proponent of Catholic truth—this is not the purpose of a periodical.[161] Newman stresses that it is wrong to measure a contribution to a periodical, whose object is to facilitate research, in the same way as one would a papal encyclical.

Towards the end of his life (1877), when reflecting upon some of the objections made against the Catholic religion, Newman attempts to

160. Newman, "On Consulting the Faithful," 203–4.

161. This brought further objections to the editor. Worse still the bishop of Newport, Thomas Joseph Brown, reported Newman for heresy; arguing that he was "deserving of censure." LD 19:175, 204–5; 240–41. Reflecting on such trials, in a letter to Emily Bowles (May 19 1863) Newman laments what he sees as the extreme centralization of the church. He writes: "In former times, primitive and medieval, ... if a private theologian said any thing free, another answered him. If the controversy grew, it went to a Bishop, a theological faculty, or to some foreign university. The Holy See was but the court of ultimate appeal. *Now*, if I as a private priest, put any such thing into print, *Propaganda* answers me at once. How can I fight with such a chain on my arm? It is like the Persians driven on to fight *under the lash*. There was true private judgment in the primitive and medieval schools—there are no schools now, no private judgment ... no freedom, that is, of opinion. That is, no exercise of the intellect of former times ... calling me to Rome. Call me to Rome! What does that mean? ... [I]t means to oblige him to dance attendance on Propaganda week after week and month after month—it means [an old man's] death." LD 20:447–48.

formulate the principles and indeed the rationality governing the church. These reflections are found in his preface to the third edition of his *Via Media of the Anglican Church*. This preface is of particular interest here because in this essay Newman points out that the rules governing secular enquiries cannot be applied to theological research:

> Here we see the necessary contrast between religious inquiry or teaching, and investigation in purely secular matters. Much is said in this day by men of science about the duty of honesty in what is called the pursuit of truth,—by "pursuing truth" being meant the pursuit of facts. It is just now reckoned a great moral virtue to be fearless and thorough in inquiry into facts; and, when science crosses and breaks the received path of Revelation, it is reckoned a serious imputation upon the ethical character of religious men, whenever they show hesitation to shift at a minute's warning their position, and to accept as truths shadowy views at variance with what they have ever been taught and have held.[162]

In this passage Newman illustrates how "secular" enquiries pursue the facts at whatever costs, even if this means a break with received interpretations; whether these be historical or scientific. In contrast, he maintains that in theological subjects the principles governing enquiry are quite different. He writes:

> But the contrast between the cases is plain. The love and pursuit of truth in the subject-matter of religion, if it be genuine, must always be accompanied by the fear of error, of error which may be sin. An inquirer in the province of religion is under a responsibility for his reasons and for their issue. But, whatever be the real merits, nay, virtues, of inquirers into physical or historical facts, whatever their skill, their acquired caution, their experience, their dispassionateness and fairness of mind, they do not avail themselves of these excellent instruments of inquiry as a matter of conscience, but because it is expedient, or honest, or beseeming, or praiseworthy, to use them; nor, if in the event they were found to be wrong as to their supposed discoveries, would they, or need they, feel aught of the remorse and self-reproach of a Catholic, on whom it breaks that he has been violently handling the text of Scripture, misinterpreting it, or superseding it, on an hypothesis which he took to be true, but which turns out to be untenable.... A man ought to be very sure of what he is

162. *VM,* 1:liii–liv.

saying, before he risks the chance of contradicting the word of God. It was safe, not dishonest, to be slow in accepting what nevertheless turned out to be true. Here is an instance in which the Church obliges Scripture expositors, at a given time or place, to be tender of the popular religious sense.[163]

Therefore, Newman maintains that theology is governed by principles different in kind from those undergirding secular research. Newman's clarifies that the "conservative" respect theologians have for the traditions of the past results from the church's pastoral concern that it should not put a stumbling block in the way of another's faith (Mark 9:42). Newman's separation of the very different principles governing these two different subject-matters indicates that he believes different subjects require different methods of evaluation.[164]

Summary of Chapter

This survey indicates that the majority of Newman's works contain the epistemological tendencies identified in the introduction to this chapter (P1–3). This challenges Maddox's contention that Newman's work is epistemologically methodist in orientation. Contrary to those views expressed by Maddox, this chapter has argued that Newman consistently opposes the presupposition of adverse principles in theological enquiry (P1), that he repeatedly argues that theological knowledge occurs antecedent to a reasoned reflection upon its grounds (P2), and the Aristotelian principle (P3) that holds that different subjects demand different levels of precision—what Lash describes as "methodological pluralism"—is widely evidenced in his writing. The occurrence of these tendencies throughout Newman's corpus indicates that, rather than being epistemologically methodist in orientation, his work is of relevance to the particularist tradition. Moreover, the presence of these tendencies indicates that his work has the potential to shed light upon this philosophical position. Having argued for the prevalence of these epistemological tendencies, the next chapter will investigate the way in which Newman's work might be of further relevance to particularist approaches to epistemology. Chapter 6

163. *VM*, 1:liv–lv.

164. In fact, Newman's preface to the third edition of the Via Media may be viewed as an application of this Aristotelian principle to the whole of the Catholic religion, for Newman seeks to uncover the principles at work across its vast history. For further discussion and comparison, see Abraham, "Church," 177–78; *VM*, 1:xv–xciv.

will then explore the way in which some of these particularist tendencies have been picked up in Abraham's particularist approach to the philosophy of religion.

5

The Grammar of Assent and the Development of Epistemological Particularism

Particularist Tendencies in Newman's Discussion of Assent

WHEN STUDYING THE *GRAMMAR* it is important to bear in mind that this work has two parts and two objectives. Part one examines whether people can believe what they do not understand. Part two examines whether people should believe what they cannot prove.[1] Interestingly, this is the same kind of question which initiates Chisholm's particularist enquiry: why is it that "our beliefs far transcend" what can really be proved?[2] Here the focus will be upon Newman's answer to this second question, as discussed in the second part of the *Grammar*. Thus Newman's discussion of "simple" and "reflex" (also described as complex) assent will be

---

1. In the Longmans Green edition of this work Newman clarifies that "The Essay begins with refuting the fallacies of those who say that we cannot believe what we cannot understand.... This portion of the work finished, I proceed to justify certitude as exercised upon a cumulation of proofs, short of demonstration." *GA*, 495–96. Edward Caswall, Priest of the Birmingham Oratory, discussed the object of the book with Newman who told him that: "the first part shows you can believe what you cannot understand ... the second part that you can believe what you cannot absolutely prove." Dessain, *John Henry Newman*, 148.

2. Chisholm, *Problem of the Criterion*, 5.

examined in order to determine whether or not these components of his analysis manifest epistemological particularist tendencies.[3]

Particularist tendencies in Newman's discussion of simple assent (P1–3)

Newman uses the terms simple assent to describe the reality in which people give credence to many things without being explicitly conscious of the reasons in their favor. He writes:

> Such are the assents made upon habit and without reflection; as when a man calls himself a Tory or a Liberal, as having been brought up as such; or again, when he adopts as a matter of course the literary or other fashions of the day, admiring the poems, or the novels, or the music, or the personages—, or the costume, or the wines, or the manners, which happen to be popular.[4]

Here Newman illustrates that many beliefs made by human beings are made naturally, without even doubting their validity. This implicit acceptance of propositions is "simple assent."[5]

At the outset, three aspects of Newman's discussion of simple assent appear to be resonant with particularist tendencies in that simple assent is "unconditional" and "spontaneous" (P2); in addition his criticisms of Locke for requiring assent (beliefs) to be dependent upon his theory of knowledge (P1) anticipate the critique of Locke made by Chisholm and Abraham.

Newman's conception of simple assent was crystallized following an epiphany he received while on vacation in 1866.[6] In a letter to a friend

---

3. In the second part the *Grammar* Newman considers whether it is possible to believe what cannot be demonstrated. It is necessary, at this stage in the discussion, to focus attention on this claim in order to examine whether this view anticipates a particularist approach to knowledge. The chapter will include aspects of the discussion in part one where these elucidate part two. Newman's earlier works will also be referred to where pertinent.

4. Newman classes this form of simple assent "under the head of Profession." Newman, *Grammar*, 40 [*GA*, 42].

5. "That mode of assent which includes this unconscious exercise, I may call simple assent." During this spontaneous form of assent "propositions pass before us and receive our assent without our consciousness." Newman, *Grammar*, 181–82 [*GA*, 188–89].

6. Though this epiphany was clearly an important moment for Newman, his

(Ann Mozley) Newman states that, although he had struggled for "thirty or forty years" to find a starting point for his work on assent, it was in Switzerland that he recognized "a clue to the treatment of my subject; and my first pages stand pretty much as I wrote them" on return from holiday; these "first pages" written in August of that year form the chapter entitled "Simple Assent."[7] What, in fact, led Newman to view this new insight as the "open sesame" of the "whole subject"?[8] It appears, from the chapter on "Simple Assent," that this insight convinced Newman that assent is not dependent upon inference;[9] that Newman grasped what he describes as the conditional nature of inference and the "unconditional" character of assent.[10] In consequence, the *Grammar* defines inference as a conditional act, because a conclusion implies the assumption of premises. Moreover, it defines assent as an unconditional acceptance of a proposition, independent of premises.[11] This distinction indicates the presence of the second basic particularist tendency identified earlier (P2) which holds that knowledge occurs naturally and independently to an examination of the evidence in its support.

In his discussion of simple assent Newman maintains that there are "many truths in concrete matter, which no one can demonstrate, yet every one unconditionally accepts."[12] Starting with assents that "of course we all believe without any doubt" Newman shows how individuals acquire spontaneous certainty all of the time; without even realizing it has happened. In doing so, Newman illustrates that many certainties arise naturally, without effort or consciousness, and are seldom questioned.[13]

---

discussion of the difference between inference and assent is anticipated in his "Papers of 1865 in Preparation for A Grammar of Assent" (1865), and in his Sermon on "Faith and Doubt" (1849). For further discussion, see *TP,* 1:123–24; Newman, *Discourses Addressed to Mixed,* 249 [*Mix,* 234–35].

7. LD 25:35; Newman, *Grammar,* 152–80 [*GA,* 157–88].

8. LD 25:199.

9. Though it may be commensurate with natural inference.

10. Newman, *Grammar,* 152–53 [*GA,* 157–58].

11. This distinction is stated at the beginning of this work: Newman, *Grammar,* 3 [*GA,* 6]. Newman emphasizes throughout that an "act of Inference includes in its object the dependence of its thesis upon its premises, that is, upon a relation, which is an abstraction; but an act of Assent rests wholly on the thesis as its object, and the reality of the thesis is almost a condition of its unconditionality." Newman, *Grammar,* 38 [*GA,* 40].

12. Newman, *Grammar,* 153 [*GA,* 160].

13. He writes: "We all believe . . . that we exist; that we have an individuality and

Newman illustrates how belief in the existence of cities such as Paris is accepted without question, without any awareness of the reasons in their support. He considers that it would be absurd to doubt such certainties.[14] He argues that "on all these truths we have an immediate and an unhesitating hold, nor do we think ourselves guilty" because we cannot prove them.[15] Moreover, Newman believes life, without the natural occurrence of these spontaneous certainties, would be impracticable. This also anticipates P2 in that particularist writers argue that people are able to know far more than they are able to demonstrate.[16]

Newman emphasizes that it would be impossible to function normally if people did not accept the knowledge that is attained spontaneously: "None of us can think or act without the acceptance of truths, not intuitive, not demonstrated, yet sovereign."[17] For this reason, he protests against philosophers like "Locke" who "lay down principles" to determine when an assent is legitimate.[18] Newman criticizes Locke because he believes he is "confusing together two things very distinct from each other, a mental act or state [such as assent] and a scientific rule."[19] This is indicative of P1 in that Newman is opposed to limiting knowledge to the

---

identity all our own; that we think, feel, and act, in the home of our own minds; that we have a present sense of good and evil, of a right and a wrong, of a true and a false, of a beautiful and a hideous, however we analyze our ideas of them. We have an absolute vision before us of what happened yesterday or last year, so as to be able without any chance of mistake to give evidence upon it in a court of justice, let the consequences be ever so serious." Newman, *Grammar*, 169 [*GA*, 177].

14. He writes: "We are sure beyond all hazard of a mistake, that our own self is not the only being existing; that there is an external world . . . that the earth, considered as a phenomenon, is a globe; that all its regions see the sun by turns; that there are vast tracts on it of land and water; that there are really existing cities on definite sites." Newman, *Grammar*, 170 [*GA*, 177]. This has similarities with Balmes who writes: "Man is inclined, by a natural instinct, to believe. . . . Who doubts the existence of Rome? And yet, the greater part of us only know it upon the authority of other men." Balmes, *Fundamental Philosophy*, 1:224.

15. Newman, *Grammar*, 171 [*GA*, 179].

16. The particularist writer William Abraham states that: "The default position is . . . that we know far more than we are able to show that we know. This is the great merit of Particularism." Abraham, *Crossing*, 33.

17. Newman, *Grammar*, 171 [*GA*, 179].

18. Newman, *Grammar*, 152–59, 171 [*GA*, 160–65, 179].

19. Newman, *Grammar*, 171 [*GA*, 179].

confines of arbitrary human theories instead of taking our spontaneous mental acts of assent as they are.[20] He writes:

> If our nature has any constitution, any laws, one of them is this absolute reception of propositions as true, which lie outside the narrow range of conclusions to which logic, formal or virtual, is tethered; nor has any philosophical theory the power to force on us a rule which will not work for a day.[21]

As noted in chapter 3, Grimm indicates the possibility that Newman is criticizing Locke for a similar reason to Chisholm: allowing his arbitrary theory to place sensible knowledge claims in doubt.[22] It appears Grimm's remarks are warranted since Newman, and Chisholm after him, considers that we acquire many sensible beliefs prior to obtaining evidence that can justify them. For this reason Newman criticizes Locke for allowing his invented theory (of when an assent is legitimate) to deny people the right to believe something. This indicates the presence of P1 and moreover is very similar to Chisholm's criticism of Locke, which states that writers like Locke are wrong to deny people the right to believe sensible things simply because they can not be supported by an epistemological theory.

In summary it seems Newman's discussion of simple assent indicates the presence of both P1 and P2. In a manner similar to particularist writers, who contend that knowledge occurs prior to epistemological reflection (P2), Newman illustrates how he considers that human beings attain knowledge spontaneously and maintains that these simple assents are unconditionally independent of demonstration. In a manner similar to Chisholm's criticism of Locke, which argues that Locke's theory of knowledge denies commonsense beliefs (P1), Newman denounces Locke for requiring that assents (that no one would deny) meet certain "principles" before they can be deemed legitimate.

20. While most of Cardinal Mercier's writings, whom Chisholm cites as a key representative of this movement, were published after Newman's death it is clear that both Mercier and Newman were both influenced by the nineteenth-century pioneers of neo-scholasticism. For example, compare Newman's section on simple assent with: Dmowski, *Institutiones Philosophicae*, 1:27; Liberatore, *Institutiones logicae et metaphysicae*, 73–77, 82–85; Balmes, *Fundamental Philosophy*, I, 14, 22–23; Kleutgen, *La Philosophie Scholastique*, 1:431. Mercier often refers to Liberatore, Balmes and Kleutgen in his writings. See for example: *Critériologie*, 96ff, 103, 113; Mercier, *Les Origines de la Psychologie Contemporaine*, 439.

21. Newman, *Grammar*, 171–72 [*GA*, 179].

22. Grimm, "Cardinal Newman, Reformed Epistemologist?" 504.

Particularist tendencies in Newman's discussion of reflex assent

In his discussion of simple assent, Newman argues that people believe a number of things without knowing how they came to do so. However, he accepts that because many of these assents are made unconsciously they can be incorrect.[23] Newman does not consider that this propensity for error warrants "universal doubt,"[24] rather, he argues that a retrospective analysis of these spontaneous assents is necessary in order to uncover the reasons in their support.[25] He terms this assent, which entails an individual's self-contemplation upon their simple assents, reflex (or complex) assent. This reflex assent is the deliberate conscious assent to a proposition as true.[26] Thus, while simple assent describes the reality of spontaneous instances of belief, reflex assent is to know what we believe and why.[27]

This shows that, for Newman, it is possible to investigate the reasons in favor of our spontaneous beliefs without doubting or being unfaithful to them.[28] If the belief investigated is later confirmed then that reflex assent results in certitude.[29] Newman clarifies here that he defines certitude as a confirmation of what is already assented to. In short, certitude is to assent to the proposition that our spontaneous beliefs are true.[30] Here Newman is adamant that reflex assent constitutes an "investigation" and not an "inquiry." This is because he understands the term "inquiry" to denote someone who has not yet come to assent to the proposition they are examining. In contrast, he understands "investigation" to signify the

---

23. Newman, *Grammar*, 186–87 [*GA*, 194].

24. Newman considers that "Doubt itself is a positive state." Newman, *Grammar*, 371–72 [*GA*, 377–78].

25. Newman, *Grammar*, 183–4 [*GA*, 190–91].

26. Newman, *Grammar*, 182 [*GA*, 189].

27. It is apparent from Newman's earlier writings that he was aware of this "reflex" dimension of assent long before the publication of the *Grammar*. For further discussion, see *PS*, 2:171; Newman, *Sermons Chiefly on the Theory of Religious Belief*, 251 [*US*, 255–56]; Newman, *History of my Religious Opinions*, 215–16 [*Apo* 215–16]. These references indicate that while Newman's notion of reflex (complex) assent is crystallized in the *Grammar* he began thinking about the role of self reflection in certainty much earlier.

28. Newman, *Grammar*, 181–87 [*GA*, 188–94].

29. *TP*, 1:122.

30. Newman, *Grammar*, 203ff [*GA*, 210ff].

action of those, for example, who have already given their assent to a doctrine but wish to investigate its credibility.[31]

Newman acknowledges that the process of investigating the validity of our spontaneous beliefs often causes a reversal of the very assents we intended to confirm. The key point for Newman is that during the investigation the initial belief is given our full assent: there is no fear or doubt or expectation, within the person's mind, that the belief will be abandoned. This is not to suggest that Newman considers such beliefs ought to remain in place even if they are incorrect. On the contrary, he acknowledges that many of these beliefs are little more than prejudice. Despite this he is adamant that the attitude of the person's mind, throughout, should be one of assent rather than doubt. After the investigation, if the original assent continues, our new reflex assent will be stronger than the old. It is explicit and considered and is not mere prejudice.[32]

At this juncture it is helpful to summarize the key components of Newman's discussion of reflex (complex) assent. First of all, he recognizes that our first simple assents can be incorrect; secondly, he maintains that this propensity to error does not warrant universal skepticism; finally, he accepts that a retrospective examination of our spontaneous assents is necessary. Having examined Newman's idea of reflex assent it is apparent that the introduction given to particularism in chapter 3, which identified three basic particularist tendencies (P1–3), is insufficient to facilitate the more detailed analysis that is now required. Therefore, the position taken by Chisholm will be explained further in order to facilitate an in-depth consideration of the *Grammar* in relation to particularism.

Our spontaneous judgments can be incorrect

Newman's contention that some of the beliefs we obtain spontaneously can be incorrect has similarities with views held by Chisholm. Compare, for example, the following extracts:

---

31. Newman, *Grammar*, 184ff [*GA*, 191ff]. Newman also states that: "It is possible then, without disloyalty to our convictions, to examine their grounds, even though they are to fail under the examination, for we have no suspicion of this failure. And such examination, as I have said, does but fulfil a law of our nature." Newman, *Grammar*, 186–87 [*GA*, 194].

32. Newman states that this is an assent not just to a "given proposition, but to the claim of that proposition on our assent as true; it is an assent or what is commonly called a conviction." Newman, *Grammar*, 186–88 [*GA*, 193–96].

> [Newman] Our first assents, right or wrong, are often little more than prejudices.... As time goes on, by degrees and without set purpose, by reflection and experience, we begin to confirm or to correct [them].[33]

> [Chisholm] There are things we believe that we don't in fact know. And we can say of many of these things that we know that we don't know them.... There are other things that we don't know, but they are such that we don't know that we don't know them. Last week, say, I thought I knew that Mr. Smith was honest, but he turned out to be a thief. I didn't know that he was a thief, and, moreover, I didn't know that I didn't know that he was a thief; I thought I knew that he was honest.[34]

These passages indicate the way in which these writers concede the fact that part of what we think we know is actually mistaken. Despite recognizing this fact, both writers reject the notion that because people can be mistaken about what they think they know it is necessary to be suspicious about all (spontaneous) claims to knowledge.

Our potential for error does not warrant skepticism

These writers reject the idea that, because people come to believe things that are not correct, it is necessary to begin by doubting our beliefs:

> [Newman] There are writers who seem to have gone far beyond this reasonable scepticism, laying down as a general proposition that we have no right in philosophy to make any assumption whatever, and that we ought to begin with a universal doubt. ... I would rather have to maintain that we ought to begin with believing everything that is offered to our acceptance, than that it is our duty to doubt of everything.[35]

> [Chisholm] To be sure, there are hallucinations and illusions.... But from this fact—that our senses do sometimes deceive us—it hardly follows that your senses and mine are deceiving you and me right now. And one may say similar things about what we remember.... If on any occasion, you think you remember that

---

33. Newman, *Grammar*, 186–87 [GA, 194].
34. Chisholm, *Problem of the Criterion*, 5–6.
35. Newman, *Grammar*, 371–72 [GA, 377–78].

such-and-such an event occurred, then the wise thing is to assume that that particular event did occur.³⁶

Here both reject the idea that the possibility of human error warrants universal skepticism regarding our initial beliefs.

It is important to emphasize that Chisholm's particularist approach to knowledge is intended to steer a middle way between the universal skepticism indicated above and what he calls dogmatism. He writes:

> We are all acquainted with people who think they know a lot more than in fact they do know. I'm thinking of . . . dogmatists. And we have all heard of people who claim at least to know a lot less than what in fact they do know . . . "skeptics." . . . If you have a healthy common sense, you will feel that something is wrong with both of these extremes and that the truth is somewhere in the middle.³⁷

Here Chisholm criticizes those who would presume to know things they don't actually know: what he calls dogmatism. He also, nevertheless, opposes the suggestion that because people can be mistaken it is necessary to be suspicious about all claims to knowledge: skepticism. Instead, he argues for a middle way between these extremes in which what we think we know is subject to an examination. The question is, does Newman's contention that he would rather "begin with believing everything" than "doubt of everything" indicate that his approach may be classified under what Chisholm views to be an excessive form of dogmatism? If these extracts are taken out of context it would be possible to interpret Newman as a dogmatist. When compared with other references, however, Newman's discussion of reflex assent may be interpreted as an attempt to forge a middle way between those who would blindly accept all their spontaneous assents and those who would reject all such beliefs out of hand.³⁸ While rejecting universal doubt Newman is adamant that it is necessary for people to examine the assents to which they have spontaneously given credence in order to investigate their validity.

---

36. Chisholm, *Problem of the Criterion*, 23–24.

37. Chisholm, *Problem of the Criterion*, 4–5.

38. An interesting but different interpretation of Newman's middle way between dogmatism and skepticism is found in: McCarthy, "A Via Media between Scepticism and Dogmatism?" 57–81.

A retrospective examination of spontaneous belief is necessary

Newman and Chisholm both maintain that investigating the reasons in support of our spontaneous beliefs is necessary. For example, Newman states that:

> The intellectual assents, in which they have . . . been instructed from the first, have to be tested, realized, and developed by the exercise of their mature judgment.[39]

This citation shows that while Newman considers it would be far better to accept all the beliefs that the human mind spontaneously adopts than to begin with a principle of universal doubt he nevertheless stresses the importance of testing these simple assents. Chisholm also considers that things we think we know need to be confirmed:

> We consider things that we know to be true, or think we know to be true, or certain things which, upon reflection, we would be willing to call *evident*. With respect to each of these, we then try to formulate a reasonable answer to the question, "What justification do you have for counting this thing as something that is evident?"[40]

These passages show that both Newman and Chisholm recognize that our spontaneous beliefs need to be tested. Nevertheless, while they do not consider these initial knowledge claims to be guaranteed certainties they recognize that the mind's propensity to error does not legitimate skepticism concerning our spontaneous beliefs. On the contrary, they maintain that these beliefs should be held, even while the investigation into their validity is underway:

> [Newman] I say, there is no necessary incompatibility between thus assenting and yet proving[;] . . . to set about concluding a proposition is not *ipso facto* to doubt its truth; we may aim at inferring a proposition, while all the time we assent to it. We have to do this as a common occurrence, when we take on ourselves to convince another on any point in which he differs from us. We do not deny our faith, because we become controversialists.[41]

---

39. Elsewhere he states that "it is a necessity formally to undertake a survey and revision of [simple assents]." Newman, *Grammar*, 183–87 [*GA*, 192–94].

40. Chisholm, *Theory of Knowledge*, 17.

41. Newman, *Grammar*, 183 [*GA*, 190].

> [Chisholm] In beginning with what we think we know to be true . . . we are assuming that the truth we are seeking is . . . implicit in the mind which seeks it, and needs only to be elicited and brought to clear reflection.[42]

Though there are differences in style and expression here both these writers consider that what we think we know should be upheld during the retrospective process of examining regardless of whether what we think we know is correct. Though they accept that false judgements occur, they maintain that, rather than doubting spontaneous beliefs, we should seek to uncover the reasons in their support—while continuing to hold on to them.

From these references it is fair to conclude that Newman and Chisholm evidence the following tendencies which we will label T1–3:

> (T1) An acknowledgment that our spontaneous certitudes can be incorrect.
> (T2) A potential for error does not warrant skepticism towards all spontaneous certitudes
> (T3) An acceptance that a retrospective examination of these certitudes is necessary.

The presence of these tendencies in both of these writers raises the following question: has Newman shaped Chisholm's work? Here it is important to stress that these epistemological tendencies (T1–3) resonate with Thomistic thought. This suggests that both Newman and Chisholm have been shaped by a common philosophical tradition. While Newman has generally been viewed in isolation from this approach chapter 3 documented his engagement with Aquinas and a number of neo-scholastic writers.[43] Moreover, Newman himself is discussed by important nineteenth-century representatives of this approach, including Cardinal Mercier and Peter Coffey. Considering the importance of Mercier to Chisholm's proposals it is necessary, if Newman's historical relevance to this position is to be investigated, to examine Newman's reception by these writers.

---

42. Chisholm, *Theory of Knowledge*, 17.

43. Newman's first beginning to the *Grammar* was shaped by St Thomas. For further discussion, see Evans, "Newman and Aquinas on Assent," 202–11; *AW,* 269–70; Aquinas, *Scriptum Super Sententiis*, Lib III, Dist. 23, q.2. a.2.qc.1 co.

Chisholm's reception of the Grammar of Assent

It has been argued that the *Grammar of Assent* anticipates a number of tendencies found in Chisholm's work. It is known that Chisholm read the *Grammar*. In his work on *Perceiving* (1957) Chisholm reflects upon the following extract from Newman's *Grammar*: "Whatever a man holds to be true, he will say he holds for certain."[44] In response to this, Chisholm writes:

> If I *see*-if I *perceive*-that it's cutlery, I wouldn't say "I take it to be cutlery." I'm not likely to say, "I take it to be cutlery" unless I feel some doubt or hesitation.[45]

Here Chisholm maintains that if we think something is true, such as the presence of cutlery on a table, we are unlikely to express any doubt concerning it. This reflects Newman's contention that when we see something to be true we will consider ourselves sure of its reality. Moreover, Chisholm's contention, that unless he feels some doubt concerning the presence of the cutlery he will be sure, reflects Newman's belief that assent is unconditional, that a doubt is a different attitude of mind toward a proposition than that of assenting to it.[46]

However, while this extract engages with Newman's conception of certainty, Chisholm clarifies that just because we may think we know something "we need not say, as Cardinal Newman did, that certitude is 'indefectible' and permanent—'that whoever loses his conviction on a given point is thereby proved not to have been certain of it.'"[47] By this Chisholm means that because our knowledge is always restricted by temporal considerations it is unlikely that we could ever attain the level of certainty that Newman holds to be possible concerning the doctrines of the church. This indicates that Chisholm engages with Newman's conception of the unconditional nature of assent. While he does not accept Newman's idea of certitude, the preceding has demonstrated that Chisholm's particularist approach resonates strongly with aspects of Newman's thought, although Chisholm does not acknowledge this.

Chisholm also engages with Newman's account of how the validity of our spontaneous beliefs can be judged in an article on "Epistemic

---

44. Newman, *Grammar*, 191 [*GA*, 197].
45. Chisholm, *Perceiving*, 76.
46. Newman, *Grammar*, 3 [*GA*, 6].
47. Chisholm, *Perceiving*, 20.

Principles" (1981). This essay is in fact a response to criticisms levelled at Chisholm by the Newman commentator Jay Newman who, in an article entitled "Epistemic Inference and Illative Judgment" (1981), argued that Chisholm's conception of the principles of epistemic justification was too rigid. Jay Newman's central criticism is that Chisholm's analysis is not sufficiently malleable to explain how individuals come to be certain.[48] He argues instead that J. H. Newman's account is far more appropriate to the task of exploring the relevant considerations in support of our spontaneous certitudes. If Jay Newman is correct, it is possible that J. H. Newman's work can actually enhance Chisholm's theory of knowledge. Hence, while it is necessary at this point to focus on Chisholm's reception of this dimension of J. H. Newman's work Jay Newman's views will be examined in more detail later in this chapter.

In his reply to Jay Newman, Chisholm states that his overriding intention is to identify the general principles governing our spontaneous certitudes.[49] He argues that if we are justified in accepting the kinds of conclusions that J. H. Newman validates by recourse to the judgement of *phronesis* (the illative sense)[50] "then, as philosophers, we should be able to make explicit the epistemic principles that such inductive conclusions presuppose."[51] In this manner it might be argued that Chisholm hopes to go further than Newman by identifying what he believes to be the general principles governing the unconscious processes of simple assent. Either way it is clear that Chisholm has considered the *Grammar's* proposals.

It has been argued that Newman's discussion of simple and reflex assent in the *Grammar of Assent* anticipates particularist tendencies. Moreover, it is also apparent that Chisholm engages with Newman's work, and, though the details are unclear, his reading of the *Grammar of Assent* shows respect in regard to its potential for development. Having discussed Chisholm's direct engagement with Newman the next section will explore Newman's historical relevance to particularism further by examining his work in relation to Mercier and other neo-Thomistic writers.

---

48. "Unlike the principles of 'ordinary' logic, principles of 'epistemic logic' no matter how general or specific, can never accommodate all those 'circumstances' which are relevant to a determination of the degree of reasonableness of the proposition in question." Jay Newman, "Epistemic Inference," 334.

49. Chisholm, "Epistemic Principles," 343.

50. This dimension of J. H. Newman's discussion will be clarified later in the chapter.

51. Chisholm, "Epistemic Principles," at 345.

The Reception of Newman by Neo-Thomistic Writers

In chapter 3 it was argued that, while preceding the publication of *Aeterni Patris* (1879), Newman's *Grammar* (1870) was shaped by the rising tide of neo-scholastic thought that was present much earlier in the nineteenth century.[52] It was also indicated that Chisholm's proposals are rooted in this neo-Thomist tradition. In particular Chisholm states that it was "Coffey's two-volume work, Epistemology or the theory of knowledge" and "the treatise of Coffey's great teacher, Cardinal D. J. Mercier" which "first" stimulated his particularist response to the problem of Pyrrhonian skepticism.[53] Here Chisholm clearly acknowledges that his theory of epistemological particularism is informed by the writing of Mercier, a key proponent of the revival of Thomism, and his pupil Coffey. What is fascinating is that both these writers who inspired Chisholm read and referred to Newman. Therefore, this section will consider the reception of Newman's work by these writers in order to further our understanding of Newman's connection with the sources and tradition out of which the particularist approach to epistemology has developed.

Cardinal Mercier's reception of Newman

Mercier's philosophical writings have tended to go unrecognized by Newman commentators. Despite this it is evident that Mercier read and referred to Newman in many of his works, including his: *Rapport sur les études supérieures de Philosophie* (1891),[54] *Critériologie Générale ou Théorie Générale de la Certitude* (1884),[55] *Logique* (1894),[56] "La Philosophie Néo-Scolastique" (1894),[57] *Á mes Séminaristes* (1908),[58] his essay on "Criteriology" (1916),[59] and his *Le Christianisme dans la vie Moderne* (1918).[60] In addition to these references, Mercier founded the Philosophical

---

52. As was indicated in chapter two, the author of the first draft of *Aeterni Patris*, Kleutgen, shaped Newman's *Grammar*.
53. Chisholm, *Problem of the Criterion*, 1–2.
54. Mercier, *Rapport sur les études supérieures de Philosophie*, 12–13.
55. Mercier, *Critériologie*, 37.
56. Mercier, *Logique*, 28.
57. Mercier, "La Philosophie Néo-Scolastique," 16–17.
58. Mercier, Á mes Séminaristes, 86.
59. Mercier, *A Manual of Modern Scholastic Philosophy*, 343.
60. Mercier, *Le Christianisme dans la vie Moderne*, 39, 48.

Society of Louvain (1888) on the basis of principles found in Newman's *Discourses on the Scope and Nature of University Education* (1852).[61]

While Newman scholars are largely unaware of Mercier's use of Newman, Mercier is recognized by several twentieth-century philosophers for having rediscovered Sextus Empiricus's critique of dogmatism.[62] Unfortunately Mercier's principal work on this subject, *Critériologie*, has yet to be translated into English. This could explain why Newman scholars have overlooked the philosophical implications of Mercier's references to Newman, his use of terminology from the *Grammar of Assent*, and the parallels between these writers, Chisholm, and Abraham.[63] While Boileau briefly notes that Mercier "was inspired by Newman and strove to imitate the daring, the prudence and the intelligence of the English Master"[64] the only volume solely dedicated to a study of these two figures discusses them in entirely separate sections and considers them "unrelated."[65] This omission cannot be excused by a language barrier, since a translation of Mercier's *Critériologie* has been published in English in an abbreviated form by Coffey.[66] There is, therefore, sufficient material in English to probe Mercier's reception of Newman.

In order for Mercier's reception of Newman to be appreciated it is necessary briefly to introduce Mercier's approach to criteriology

---

61. When Mercier was invited to give a speech before the "Higher Education Section" of the Institute of Louvain he stated that: "We must aim at forming, in greater numbers, men who will devote themselves to science for its own sake." Mercier, *Rapport sur les études*, 12–13, 17. For further discussion, see Peter Coffey, "Philosophy and The Sciences at Louvain," 390; Ward, *The Life of John Henry Cardinal Newman*, 2:502. Ward rightly notes that, in response to Leo XIII Encyclical *Aeterni Patris* (1879) Cardinal Mercier established "in Louvain University a school in close harmony with Cardinal Newman's views."

62. Amico, *The Problem of the Criterion*, 2; Rescher states that "Notwithstanding its intrinsic significance this line of reasoning has lain dormant in Modern Philosophy until D. J. Mercier's monumental *Critériologie Générale ou Théorie Générale de la Certitude*." Rescher, *Methodological Pragmatism*, 17n6.

63. While Abraham refers to Mercier he views him as an example of the epistemological methodism Chisholm opposes. More specifically he argues that Mercier's work has methodist tendencies: "This tendency generally takes the form of a request for appropriate method in the prolegomena to systematic theology. It is worth noting that in Roman Catholic theology it was once common to have a whole field of enquiry devoted to criteriology. See Cardinal Mercier." Abraham, *Canon and Criterion*, 18n20.

64. Boileau, *Cardinal Mercier: A Memoir*, 24.

65. Curiously, it makes absolutely no comparison between them. Boudens, *Two Cardinals*, 27.

66. Mercier, "Criteriology," 1:343–404.

(epistemology) and the way in which it informs Chisholm's work. At the beginning of his essay on "Criteriology" Mercier cites the *Grammar* as recommended reading for those interested in further "study or consultation."[67] From here he examines the nature of human knowledge:

> Criteriology is the reflex study of our certain knowledge and of the grounds upon which its certitude rests.[68]

In the above, Mercier argues that epistemology should begin with the knowledge already in an individual's possession and from there proceed to a "reflex" study of the grounds upon which that knowledge is based. These two stages of knowledge, spontaneous and reflex, form the basic components of his *Critériologie*.

At the outset, it appears that Mercier, like Newman, considers that people (by their natural constitution) are in possession of a number of beliefs; what Newman calls "simple assents." For example:

> [Mercier] we are in possession of a number of propositions of which we think, rightly or wrongly, that we are certain, propositions to which we give a spontaneous and even irresistible assent; spontaneous certitude does exist as a subjective fact.[69]

> [Newman] In proportion then to our ignorance of self, is our unconsciousness of those innumerable acts of [simple] assent, which we are incessantly making. . . . Indeed, I may fairly say, that those assents which we give with a direct knowledge of what we are doing, are few compared with the multitude of like acts which pass through our minds in long succession without our observing them.[70]

Here, both men argue for the reality that the majority of our beliefs occur naturally and are given credence without question.

In addition, Mercier contends that certainty regarding assents that are made spontaneously is more than an emotive disposition. He suspects, at the very least, that truth is at the base of his own certainty concerning these things. Despite this, Mercier acknowledges the truth of the observation made by "le cardinal Newman" that many of the assents which we take for granted are incorrect. Mercier recognizes the reality

67. Mercier, "Criteriology," 343.
68. Mercier, "Criteriology," 343.
69. Mercier, "Criteriology," 350.
70. Newman, *Grammar*, 181–82 [*GA*, 188–89].

that many spontaneous assents, of which he has previously been certain, proved to have no connection to truth.[71] As a result of this, Mercier agrees with Newman that our spontaneous assents must be examined in depth, otherwise they will be rendered subjective, mere viewpoints to which one feels determinedly attached.[72]

From the above it is apparent that Mercier attempts to steer a middle course between accepting spontaneous beliefs without question (exaggerated dogmatism) and skepticism. He calls this *via media* "rational" dogmatism:

> We do not accept that scepticism has the right to affirm *a priori*; before any examination, the essential inaptitude of the mind to succeed in the science of certainty. This is an arbitrary pretension.... Moreover, we do not accord to dogmatism the right to affirm *a priori*, before any examination, the essential aptitude of the mind to reach the truth[;] ... we allow reason to reflect on the judgments about which we are instinctively certain.[73]

This extract from Mercier indicates the manner in which he rejects both the skeptic's unexamined claim that the mind cannot succeed in obtaining knowledge and the dogmatist's unexamined claim that the mind can succeed in obtaining knowledge. Instead, he argues that we should reflect upon what we are instinctively certain about and examine its validity. It is in this middle strategy, between these two extremes, that Chisholm's work takes its inspiration:

> We can know far more than the skeptic says we can know and far less than the dogmatist or the mystic says that he can know. But how are we to decide these things? How do we decide, in any particular case, whether we have a genuine item of knowledge? Most of us are ready to confess that our beliefs far transcend what we really know.... And so the problem is: How are we to distinguish the real cases of knowledge from what only seem to be cases of knowledge? Or, as I put it before, how are we to decide in any particular case whether we have genuine items of

---

71. Mercier, *Critériologie*, 37. Translated by Ray Morris-Chapman. As Newman states elsewhere the "mind is ever exposed to the danger of being carried away by the liveliness of its conceptions, to the sacrifice of good sense and conscientious caution." Newman, *Grammar*, 79 [GA, 82].

72. Mercier, *Critériologie*, 37.

73. Mercier, "Discussion of the Theory of the Three Primary Truths," 280.

knowledge? What would be a satisfactory solution to our problem? Let me quote in detail what Cardinal Mercier says.[74]

This extract indicates the way in which Chisholm's work reflects Mercier's middle path between skepticism and excessive dogmatism.

At the outset it appears that Mercier's account resembles Newman in a number of ways: he argues that we have spontaneous beliefs which should be accepted as true; he contends that our spontaneous certitudes can be incorrect; he rejects the idea that our propensity to error warrants skepticism; he argues that, since we can make mistakes, the most reasonable course of action is for individuals to undertake a process of reflection in order to be sure that their spontaneous convictions are legitimate. From this it is fair to conclude that Newman, Mercier, and Chisholm all evidence the tendencies (T1–3). It is apparent that all three reject what Mercier and Chisholm refer to as dogmatism in which spontaneous beliefs are exempted from criticism. Despite this, their acknowledgment of the possibility of making incorrect assents does not lead them to presuppose skepticism about these initial beliefs. Instead, they advocate a middle way in which the validity of spontaneous beliefs is contemplated.

In evaluating Newman's relevance to the development of the particularist tradition it is helpful to situate Mercier's reception within the wider neo-Thomistic context. References above showed that Mercier describes himself as a rational dogmatist. It is important to recognize that this position is distinct from many[75] of Mercier's forbears who held to an exaggerated "traditional" dogmatism which taught that spontaneous beliefs could be accepted without question.[76] As a result, the third tendency (T3) is absent in many earlier writers working within this tradition.[77]

---

74. Chisholm, *Problem of the Criterion*, 5–6.

75. Joseph Kleutgen may be seen as an exception. Van Riet states that "we do not include among the 'traditional dogmatists' the profound thinker Father Kleutgen[,] ... he is a precursor of rational dogmatism." Van Riet, *Thomistic Epistemology*, 1:123. Also see Boileau, *Cardinal Mercier*, 28.

76. According to Van Riet: "By 'traditional dogmatism' is understood the philosophy of common sense, which has been encountered, under more or less pure forms, in nineteenth-century manuals of Thomistic epistemology. In the philosophy of common sense, the critical problem consists in guaranteeing all our certitudes without distinction. The answer to the problem flows from the incoherence of skepticism: all our means of knowledge; it is said, are infallible, and the same evidence motivates all our convictions." Van Riet, *Thomistic Epistemology*, 1:123.

77. This point is reinforced by Boileau who states that the "Neo-Thomists that Mercier read as a young man" were all traditional (exaggerated) dogmatists in that

James Balmes's *Fundamental Philosophy* may be taken as an example of this traditional dogmatism.[78] Other examples of this excessive form of dogmatism are Salvator Tongiorgi (1820–65) and Domenico Palmieri (1829–1909).[79]

While Mercier is highly critical of Balmes and Tongiorgi's traditional dogmatism,[80] he appears to view Newman's writing as being complementary to his own proposals. For example, he affirms Newman's contention that our spontaneous beliefs can be incorrect (T1):

> A good number of beliefs that I formerly held and which I did not doubt, proved later to me to have no connection to the knowledge of truth as I hold it today, but only viewpoints to which I feel determinedly attached and which I have never examined in depth to see if they are based on truth. . . . "We should be in no doubt," writes Cardinal Newman, "that amongst all these statements in common currency in everyday conversations in everyday life—that no one would dream of challenging—are there not more than a few that should in fact be treated with caution?"[81]

Mercier's reference is significant for it indicates that he recognizes the similarity between his "rational" dogmatism and Newman's *Grammar of Assent*. The relevance of the *Grammar* to this position is indicated further

---

they held that "all our means of knowledge are infallible." Boileau, *Cardinal Mercier*, 28.

78. Though Balmes does distinguish between two kinds of certitude, the spontaneous "certainty of the human race" and "philosophical certitude," he considers these types of certainty to be totally separate. In fact, Balmes believes spontaneous certitude to be impenetrable to philosophical reflection. For further discussion, see Balmes, *Fundamental Philosophy*, I, 7–8, 14–15. As chapter 2 documents, both Newman and Mercier read Balmes.

79. For example, Tongiorgi argues that some truths do not need to be subject to critical reflection: "The Philosopher's task is 1) To inquire what the primitive and fundamental truths on which all certitude and knowledge is based; 2) To show that they not only can, but also must be admitted by the philosopher without demonstration. . . . Now, that these truths can and must be admitted without demonstration by the philosopher, is clear, inasmuch as 1) they need no demonstration; 2) they shun all demonstration; 3) by the very act of denial or doubt they are affirmed." Tongiorgi, cited in Mercier, *Cardinal Mercier's Philosophical Essays*, 271. For further discussion, see Tongiorgi, *Institutiones Philosophicae*, 1:270–71.

80. Mercier viewed Balmes, Tongiorgi, and Palmieri, as exaggerated dogmatists. For example, see Mercier, *Critériologie*, 99–101; Mercier, "Criteriology," 357–58. For further discussion, see de Wulf, *Scholasticism Old and New*, 236.

81. Mercier, *Critériologie*, 37. Translated by Ray Morris-Chapman.

by the description Mercier gives to this retrospective examination of our spontaneous assents (T3):

> The question to be determined is whether this spontaneous assent is justifiable; whether by deliberate reflection upon a proposition to which we spontaneously assent we can show this spontaneous assent to be legitimate, thus obtaining *reflex assent* and true certitude.[82]

What is striking in this passage is Mercier's use of the terms "reflex assent." This terminology appears to be taken from the *Grammar*: "assents as must be made consciously and deliberately, and which I shall call complex or reflex assents."[83] According to Newman, this reflex mode of assent involves an investigation into the reasons for the spontaneous simple assent. In contrast to simple assent, this involves proving what one already believes spontaneously by ascertaining evidence in its favor.[84] Mercier's use of the term "reflex" assent, coupled with his explicit reference to Newman when discussing this point, indicates that the *Grammar* has important historical relevance to the development of this retrospective approach to epistemology.

In summary, it is clear that Mercier's position, particularly his acceptance that a retrospective examination of spontaneous certitudes is necessary (T3), diverges from many of his predecessors. Moreover, Mercier's use of terminology from the *Grammar* (reflex assent) and his reference to Newman in his discussion of the necessity for people to subject their spontaneous certitudes to a reflex examination indicates Newman's importance for Mercier's proposals. [85]

82. Mercier, "Criteriology," 350. Emphasis mine.

83. Newman, *Grammar*, 182 [GA, 189].

84. Newman writes: "I hold absolutely that . . . Great Britain is an island. . . . But it may happen that I forget my reasons for what I believe . . . or I may never have asked my self about them . . . and have been accustomed to assent without a recognition of my assent or of its grounds, and then perhaps something occurs which leads to my reviewing and completing those grounds, analyzing and arranging them, yet without on that account implying of necessity any suspense, ever so slight, of assent, to the proposition that . . . Great Britain is an island. With no suspense of assent at all . . . He does but repeat, after his formal demonstration, that assent which he made before it, or assents to his previous assenting. This is what I call a reflex or complex assent." Newman, *Grammar*, 182–83 [GA, 189–90].

85. The importance of Kleutgen's work to Mercier must not be underestimated. Kleutgen clearly distinguishes between spontaneous and reflex certitudes. For example, he contends that "all that is necessary for the knowledge of certain truths flows

Peter Coffey's reception of Newman

Peter Coffey also shows considerable admiration for Newman. In his *Science of Logic* (1912)[86] and in his *Epistemology* (1917) he makes several references to the *Grammar*; which he believes is "ably conducted on original lines."[87] In addition to this Coffey cites Newman's *Apologia*, the *Idea of a University*, and the *Grammar* in his work *Ontology* (1918).[88] While these references indicate that a number of Coffey's works engage with Newman here we will focus on his work on *Epistemology*.

Like Mercier, Coffey's work on *Epistemology* shows the three tendencies shared by Newman and Chisholm (T1–3). For example, he shares the first tendency (T1), in that he acknowledges the fact that people make incorrect assents.[89] In acknowledging our propensity to make incorrect spontaneous judgements Coffey also evidences the second tendency (T2) in that he emphasizes that our epistemological limitations do not warrant universal skepticism. Citing Newman he states that:

> It is about such that Newman somewhere says "a hundred difficulties do not make one doubt" Such vague and merely subjective misgivings as may arise from the consciousness that we are not infallible . . . are not necessarily incompatible with the fixed or firm assent which constitutes conviction. Men can and do retain multitudes of their spontaneous convictions even after full advertence to, and consideration of, their own mental limitations; and if some philosophers assert that the process of testing critically the grounds of certitude has ended for them in universal skepticism and destroyed their spontaneous convictions, this

---

immediately from the rational nature of man, so that once he has become capable of reflecting, he finds within himself the sufficient reason for affirming these truths." Kleutgen, *La Philosophie Scolastique*, 1:444, 463. Translated by Ray Morris-Chapman. Newman makes a similar point in the *Grammar*: "We judge for ourselves, by our own lights, and on our own principles; and our criterion of truth is not so much the manipulation of propositions, as the intellectual and moral character of the person maintaining them, and the ultimate silent effect of his arguments or conclusions upon our minds." Newman, *Grammar*, 295–96 [*GA*, 302]

86. Coffey, *Science of Logic*, 2:22, 134, 211.
87. Coffey, *Epistemology*, 2:237, 278, 310, 351.
88. Coffey, *Ontology*, 22, 31, 192, 387.
89. He writes: "We never consciously assent to a judgment, *i.e* accept it as true, as knowledge, if we know it to be false. . . . But we can and do accept as true judgments which are really false,—thinking them, of course, to be true." Coffey, *Epistemology*, 1:39.

assertion only proves that like the rest of mankind they too had such convictions.[90]

Here, reflecting on Newman's work, Coffey argues that the fact that we make errors in our spontaneous judgements does not warrant universal skepticism. This reference to Newman, in relation to the second tendency (T2), indicates Coffey's awareness of Newman's relevance to his position.

Coffey's work also evidences the third tendency (T3) in that he argues that, since we can make these errors, a retrospective examination of our spontaneous convictions is necessary. Coffey maintains that in order for us to be sure that our spontaneous certitudes are valid we need to engage in a process of introspection that will confirm whether or not our natural convictions are correct. Moreover, Coffey contends that this kind of epistemological introspection is anticipated in Aquinas's works.[91]

In summary, like Newman, Mercier, and Chisholm, Coffey's works all evidence tendencies T1–3. Coffey's references to Newman in relation to T2 suggest that he views him as being relevant to the neo-Thomistic epistemological orientation he is seeking to articulate. Moreover, his repeated use of Newman's writings throughout his works indicates that he views him as an important interlocutor.

It has been shown that two of Chisholm's most important sources, Mercier and Coffey, were familiar with Newman's works. Like Newman and Chisholm, these writers evidence the epistemological tendencies identified above (T1–3). Though Chisholm and Newman share these tendencies Chisholm does not cite Newman in this regard. Nevertheless, Mercier and Coffey's references indicate Newman's relevance to their own proposals. For example, Mercier cites Newman in relation to the first (T1) and third tendencies (T3)—using terminology from the *Grammar* in this latter case. Moreover, Coffey quotes Newman in relation to the second tendency (T2). The presence of these tendencies (T1–3) in Newman's work, coupled with the references these writers make to him,

---

90. Coffey, *Epistemology*, 1:34.

91. Coffey writes: "Are we justified in entertaining the spontaneous conviction or certitude that we have any such knowledge about? [Aquinas] insists on the need of this introspection for what we may call a reasoned and certain knowledge of truth, implying that this introspection will confirm our fundamental natural conviction. 'We have certain knowledge of the truth,' [Aquinas] says, 'inasmuch as (1) we attain to truth by an act of the intellect, and (2) we know that we do so.'" Coffey, *Epistemology*, 1:41. Here Coffey refers to: Aquinas, *Disputed Questions on Truth*, 1.9; Aquinas, *Quaestiones Disputatae de Veritate*, 1.9.

indicate that they consider his writing to be relevant to their discussion of these points. Secondly, their references suggest that they view Newman as someone sharing a number of similarities with the neo-Thomistic epistemological orientation that they are seeking to convey. Having assessed Newman in relation to these precursors of the particularist position it is necessary to examine the way in which ongoing discussions concerning this approach to epistemology view Newman's work.

Reading the Grammar from a Particularist Perspective

Marty Maddox's methodist interpretation of the *Grammar*

In his assessment of the *Grammar*, Maddox acknowledges that, at first sight, readers of this work may consider it "legitimate to interpret Newman as a particularist."[92] Nevertheless, he believes Newman's account of the natural processes of reasoning which occur antecedently to simple assent reveal what Chisholm calls the "methodist" approach to epistemology.[93] In short, he deems Newman's inferential accompaniment to simple assent to be consonant with epistemological methodism.

It is correct that Newman considers that an "unconscious"[94] mode of reasoning, manifest within the constitution of the mind, attends our simple (spontaneous) assents.[95] He writes:

> This is the mode in which we ordinarily reason, dealing with things directly, and as they stand, one by one, in the concrete, with an intrinsic and personal power, not a conscious adoption of an artificial instrument or expedient; and it is especially exemplified both in uneducated men, and in men of genius, in those who know nothing of intellectual aids and rules, and in

---

92. Maddox concedes that Newman's criticisms of Locke and his emphasis upon the significance of a person's spontaneous assents makes a particularist interpretation of the Grammar "compelling." He writes: 'should Newman be considered a particularist who insists that the answer to the problem of the criterion of truth is to be found first in what the assenter knows.... Newman definitely contends (contra Locke) that there is at least a loose connection between psychological (e.g., imaginative) and epistemological dimensions of a person's judgment regarding a proposition, especially in the quest for certainty." Maddox, "Newman, Certain Knowledge," 79.

93. Maddox, "Newman, Certain Knowledge," 86.

94. Newman, *Grammar*, 324 [*GA*, 331].

95. Newman maintains that as apprehension is "a concomitant; so inference is ordinarily the antecedent of assent." Newman, *Grammar*, 150 [*GA*, 157].

those who care nothing for them, in those who are either without or above mental discipline.[96]

Newman argues that people "ordinarily reason" using an "intrinsic and personal power" that deals with things unconsciously. He emphasizes that this "natural" mode of reasoning does not adopt an external rule or artificial instrument. It is present in educated and uneducated alike.[97] Newman maintains that this natural reasoning is actually part (a "faculty") of the mind,[98] and describes this native inferential aspect to human cognition as the "Illative Sense."[99] It is this spontaneous mode of inference, what Newman terms the illative sense, which causes all our assents conscious or unconscious.[100] Having introduced Newman's understanding of the role of natural inference in simple assent it is important to assess the cogency of Maddox's analysis.

A misunderstanding of natural inference

Maddox considers that because simple assent is a direct result of the judgement of this "illative sense," Newman is an epistemological proceduralist (methodist) because the illative sense is "contoured" by reason:

---

96. Newman, *Grammar*, 324 [*GA*, 331].

97. The description found in the *Grammar* of this natural process of reasoning is anticipated in Newman's University sermons: Newman, *Sermons Chiefly on the Theory of Religious Belief*, 252–53 [*US*, 256–57]. Many commentators argue that Newman's discussion of this form of reasoning has similarities with Joseph Butler's (1692–1752) *Analogy* (1736)—a well-known example of the implementation of "probable" (non-demonstrative) reasoning in support of Christian belief. Though Newman expressly states the influence of Butler's doctrine of probable reason upon him it is clear from the beginning of his *Analogy* that Butler does not believe this kind of reasoning can lead to certitude. In contrast, Newman believes that natural inference is antecedent to assent. In this regard his writing has similarities with David's Hume's (1711–76) contention that an accumulation of non-demonstrative probabilities may lead one to a sense of certainty in belief. For further discussion, see Newman, *History of My Religious Opinions*, 10–11; Newman, *Grammar*, 150. Also, see LD 15:456. Butler, *Analogy*, 3; Hume, *Enquiries*, 56–57 [vi.46]; Cronin, *Theory of Knowledge*, 30; *PN*, 1:170; Norris, *Newman and His Theological Method*, 19; Ferreira, *Scepticism*; Ker, *The Achievement of Newman*, 50–51.

98. Newman, *Grammar*, 331–32 [*GA*, 338–39].

99. Newman, *Grammar*, 335 [*GA*, 342].

100. In simple assent its activity is unconscious but in reflex assent the illative sense enables an individual to judge the reasons in support of a simple assent.

> [Newman] accentuates the illative sense as a faculty of judgment that is oriented toward its "conclusion" by "a method of reasoning," i.e., a rational procedure, not some instantaneous insight or leap of faith. This does not mean that one should attribute to Newman some sort of "rationalism of informal reasoning" that ignores the personal element involved in our assenting to propositions. Rather, it means that, in spite of his numerous appeals to the role of the personal ... he still holds that the illative sense is primarily contoured and designated by its informal inferences (while not identical to them).[101]

Here Maddox argues that the illative sense is "contoured" and "designated" by "informal" inference. This in fact is not Newman's position. Newman argues that the illative sense is contoured and designated by "natural inference." Maddox thus misinterprets Newman's position by conflating two of the different modes of reason discussed in the *Grammar*. For example, in the *Grammar* Newman distinguishes three types of inference: formal, informal, and natural.[102] Formal inference is:

> Verbal reasoning, of whatever kind, as opposed to mental, is what I mean by inference, which differs from logic only inasmuch as logic is its scientific form. And it will be more convenient here to use the two words indiscriminately, for I shall say nothing about logic which does not in its substance also apply to inference.[103]

Thus, Newman understands formal inference to be reason in its verbalized form: ratiocination "restricted and put into [linguistic] grooves." In contrast to this scientific form of reasoning Newman considers that there are two other types, informal and natural inference.[104] Informal and natural inference represent Newman's attempt to describe a form of

---

101. Maddox, "Newman, Certain Knowledge," 79.

102. This analysis of the difference between these forms of reasoning along verbal lines is anticipated in Newman's University Sermons which distinguish between "explicit" and "implicit" reason. This terminology indicates the hidden "unconscious" nature of implicit reasoning. However, in his unpublished papers on *Faith and Certainty* (1853) Newman differentiates two conscious modes of inference "demonstrative" and cumulative" in which the latter represents a conscious "elaborate, circuitous" convergent form of reasoning. By the time Newman came to write the *Grammar* he enumerates three types of reasoning, formal, informal, and natural. For further discussion, see Newman, *Sermons Chiefly on the Theory of Religious Belief*, 246ff [*US,* 251ff]; *TP,*1:20.

103. Newman, *Grammar*, 256–57 [*GA*, 263–64].

104. Newman, *Grammar*, 256 [*GA*, 263].

reasoning which cannot be "arrested and embodied in words."[105] While, however, informal and natural inference are similar, in that both are incommensurate with syllogistic reasoning, there are different levels of consciousness operative within these types of reasoning.[106]

In his chapter on "informal inference" Newman indicates that although informal inference is "more or less implicit" it can, in principle, be described as the accumulation of probabilities. He writes:

> It is plain that formal logical sequence is not in fact the method by which we are enabled to become certain[;] . . . the real and necessary method is . . . the cumulation of probabilities, independent of each other, arising out of the nature and circumstances of the particular case which is under review; probabilities too fine to avail separately, too subtle and circuitous to be convertible into syllogisms, too numerous and various for such conversion, even were they convertible.[107]

Hence, Newman argues that while informal inference cannot be converted into syllogisms it can be recognized as the accumulation of probabilities which enable an individual to become certain. As noted above, Maddox maintains that the illative sense is contoured by this informal process of inference. He argues that, because the illative sense precedes all our first assents, Newman is an epistemological methodist since he presupposes a rational procedure to simple assent. The problem with this analysis is that it is natural, not informal, inference that shapes the operation of the illative sense in simple assent.

Maddox's misunderstanding of this distinction leads him to describe Newman as an epistemological methodist. This is because if Newman considers that an accumulation of probabilities, such as that of informal inference, precedes all our spontaneous assents then this process might qualify as the occurrence of an epistemological procedure prior to simple assent. But Newman's account of natural inference is not synonymous with informal inference. In contrast to informal inference, natural inference is totally "unconscious and implicit." Moreover, he maintains that it is actually an action of the mind itself. Its procedures and processes are in fact the organic operation of the mind.[108] The intrinsic nature of

---

105. Newman, *Grammar*, 256 [GA, 263].
106. Merrigan, *Clear Heads and Holy Hearts*, 213.
107. Newman, *Grammar*, 281 [GA, 288].
108. Concerning natural inference Newman writes: "Reasoning ordinarily shows

this mode of reasoning is captured in his philosophical notebook where Newman states that: "Reasoning is the very breath of my existence."[109] It is this natural form of inference, and not informal inference, which constitutes the illative faculty. This faculty—central to human existence—is the operation of the mind itself.[110]

Therefore, natural inference is identical with the illative sense. When the mind makes spontaneous assents it is the operation of natural inference (the illative sense) which leads the mind to make these judgments:

> This unscientific reasoning, being sometimes a natural, uncultivated faculty, sometimes approaching to a gift, sometimes an acquired habit and second nature, has a higher source than logical rule,—"nascitur, non fit." . . . This divination comes by nature, and belongs to all of us in a measure . . . with a success on the whole sufficient to show that there is a *method* [italics added] in it, though it be implicit.[111]

---

as a simple act, not as a process, as if there were no medium interposed between antecedent and consequent, and the transition from one to the other were of the nature of an instinct,—that is, the process is altogether unconscious and implicit. . . . [T]his natural or material Inference [is] an existing phenomenon of mind[,] . . . [its] inferential processes . . . being the action of the mind itself, that is, by its ratiocinative or illative faculty, not a mere operation as in the rules of arithmetic. . . . [O]ur most natural mode of reasoning is, not from propositions to propositions, but from things to things, from concrete to concrete, from wholes to wholes. . . . [T]he consequents, at which we arrive from the antecedents with which we start . . . are not recognized by us as subjects for analysis; nay, often are only indirectly recognized as antecedents at all. Not only is the inference with its process ignored, but the antecedent also. To the mind itself the reasoning is a simple divination or prediction." Newman, *Grammar*, 323–24 [*GA*, 330–31].

109. *PN*, 2:33–37.

110. In a letter to Richard Hutton (1826–97) Newman compares the operation of the illative sense to the working of human muscles. His point being that it is impossible to quantify the logical force of its proofs. This indicates that it would be impossible for writers like Maddox to isolate any kind of epistemological process or method governing natural inference. He writes: "As to certitude, I should like to lay down as follows;—1. It is, I believe, a fact, that there is no reducing the living power of the muscles to a mechanical scale of force; we only know that a weight of so many pounds exerts more force than a given muscle, and another weight less force. Any how, this will do for an illustration. 2. In like manner the living intelligence of the prudent man decides that a certain conclusion is trustworthy, or imposes on him the duty of believing it. He is not able, be he ever so logical, to express how much and what evidence in a logical shape is just sufficient, neither more or less, to impose a conclusion on his assent." LD 16:40.

111. Newman, *Grammar*, 324 [*GA*, 331].

THE GRAMMAR OF ASSENT 171

Here Newman indicates that, although natural inference is unconscious, the efficiency of this mode of reasoning suggests that there is an "implicit" "method" operative within it. Seizing upon Newman's use of the term "method," Maddox interprets this to mean that Newman presupposes a specific inferential procedure to assent making him an epistemological methodist. Referring to this passage from Newman's discussion of "Natural Inference" Maddox states that:

> Newman's "method of converging probability" is not a procedure that is "beyond our comprehension." We may not be able to outline exactly how this unconscious approach to knowledge works for each person, but we can characterize how the procedure works in principle.[112]

In this extract, when he refers to natural inference as Newman's "method of converging probability," Maddox is applying terminology used to denote informal inference to a passage in which Newman is discussing natural inference. This indicates that Maddox is in fact conflating informal and natural inference. Maddox also confuses these two modes of reasoning in another passage. Citing Newman, Maddox writes:

> Newman's famous analogy of the polygon in a circle is a helpful guide to help us understand how the illative sense proceeds in its method of proof: [Newman writes] "*We know that a regular polygon, inscribed in a circle, its sides being continually diminished, tends to become that circle, as its limit; but it vanishes before it has coincided with the circle, so that its tendency to be the circle, though ever nearer fulfillment, never in fact gets beyond a tendency. In like manner, the conclusion in a real or concrete question is foreseen and predicted rather than actually attained; foreseen in the number and direction of accumulated premises, which all converge to it.... This is what is meant, by a proposition being 'as good as proved,' a conclusion as undeniable 'as if it were proved,' and by the reasons for it 'amounting to a proof,' for a proof is the limit of converging probabilities.*"[113]

This extract from Newman's chapter on "informal inference" is what Newman describes as an attempt to "hazard" what may appear as "a far-fetched or fanciful" description of the method operative in informal

---

112. Maddox, "Newman, Certain Knowledge," 84.

113. Here Maddox cites the chapter on informal inference in Newman's *Grammar of Assent*: Maddox, "Newman, Certain Knowledge," 84; Newman, *Grammar*, 313–14 [*GA*, 320–21].

inference; though Newman himself questions whether "any account can be given of the ratiocinative method in such proofs."[114] Maddox's repeated misapplication of this description of informal inference, to Newman's account of natural inference, betrays his confusion of these two kinds of reasoning.

The implications of this conflation of informal and natural inference lead Maddox to describe Newman's conception of the organic inferential operations of the mind in simple assent as an epistemological methodist approach to knowledge. Even if Maddox were not guilty of this category mistake he insists that despite the organic nature of the reasoning process accompanying simple assent it is, nevertheless, an inferential precursor to assent; a logical procedure that provides proof to the believer. He writes:

> Although such implicit rational procedures are not mechanistic but organic, and in spite of the fact that they are often not amenable to symbolization via formal logical expression ("paper logic"), they are, nonetheless, cognitive movements that give a person the logical force of proof in reference to concrete matters.[115]

Here it is apparent that Maddox's suggestion that informal and natural inference, though "often not amenable" are in principle capable of symbolization, leads him to conclude that Newman presupposes an implicit inferential procedure to assent. This interpretation does not correlate with Newman's discussion of these different terms:

> Taking Logic in the larger sense . . . "Informal" and "Natural Inference" fall under it, as far as exercises of mind can fall under science at all, which are not only beyond syllogism, but partially beyond language.[116]

Here Newman emphasizes that the informal and natural reasoning of the mind is "too subtle and circuitous to be convertible into syllogisms, too numerous and various for such conversion, even were they convertible."[117] This indicates that Newman's understanding of these informal types of inference is that it is impossible to squeeze them into a set formula or method because their processes are incommensurate with formal logic.

---

114. Newman, *Grammar*, 313 [GA, 320].
115. Maddox, "Newman, Certain Knowledge," 79.
116. LD 25:132.
117. Newman, *Grammar*, 281 [GA, 288].

Newman's emphasis on the impossibility of converting informal and natural inference into formal inference differs from Maddox's suggestion that, while "often not amenable," "symbolization" of these forms of reason might be possible. When Maddox's analysis of natural inference is compared with the interpretation given by other Newman commentators it would appear that his methodist interpretation of the *Grammar of Assent* centres upon a misunderstanding of natural inference and its relationship with simple assent.

Several Newman commentators disagree with the suggestion that informal and natural inference are in principle "amenable to symbolization."[118] Klubertanz, for example, emphasizes that informal and natural modes of inference cannot be viewed as "implicit, inchoative formal inference." On the contrary he considers that these two kinds of inference are irreducible; "informal inference cannot be turned into formal inference."[119] Moleski likewise argues that these forms of reasoning operate "without rules" and are thus incapable of being "formalized or articulated."[120] Finally Gerard Casey's study of Newman's notion of *Natural Reason* (1984) argues that Newman's distinction between these different types of inference is indicated by the impossibility of translating natural reason verbally:

> Reasoning which is completely explicit or conscious is formal inference[,] . . . reasoning which is completely inexplicit or unconscious is natural inference.[121]

Here Casey maintains that one of the main points of distinction between formal inference and natural inference is the ability to translate reasoning verbally. Having indicated that within the Newman literature it is generally accepted that natural inference is totally incommensurate with

---

118. An exception to this is Jay Newman who, in one of his early publications, argues that many of Newman's discussions of inference are "no less 'formal' than any other argument." Jay Newman, "Cardinal Newman's Factory-Girl Argument," 77. Nevertheless, as will be indicated shortly in an examination of his more recent work, Jay Newman's later work argues that these informal modes of inference are incapable of formalisation. "Unlike the principles of 'ordinary' logic, principles of 'epistemic logic', no matter how general or specific, can never accommodate all those 'circumstances' which are relevant to a determination of the degree of reasonableness of the proposition in question." Jay Newman, "Epistemic Inference," 334.

119. Klubertanz, "Where is the Evidence for Thomistic Metaphysics," 298.

120. Moleski, *Personal Catholicism*, 5.

121. Casey, *Natural Reason*, 6.

formal inference, never "amenable to symbolization" it is important to question whether or not the natural inference that contours the illative sense really qualifies as inference at all.

Connolly, Ferreira, and Casey all question whether natural inference, if it is not commensurate with formal inference, can be described as inference.[122] This question is relevant to the present enquiry because if it is not really a form of inference then it is difficult to see how Maddox can maintain that its position within Newman's account, prior to assent, makes him an epistemological methodist. A good example of this position is Casey who struggles to see how natural reason can even be considered as a type of inference. He argues that whereas in formal and informal inferences one has a partial awareness of the relationship between the premises and the conclusion natural inference is spontaneous and instinctive.[123] Hence Casey argues that because natural inference operates "as a simple indivisible act" without any awareness of antecedent propositions or premises, it is difficult to see how Newman can class it as an inference when the kernel of inference, according to Newman, is "when we hold this by virtue of that."[124]

Casey argues that natural inference is actually more like an exercise of memory or sense perception since in this natural mode of reasoning we are unconscious of the route we take from the premises to the conclusion.[125] Moreover he maintains that if the premises of natural inference

---

122. Connolly, *John Henry Newman*, 67; Ferreira, *Scepticism*, 205; Casey, *Natural Reason*, 43.

123. Casey writes: "Newman here gives us the first intimation that natural inference differs from both formal inference and informal inference in a significant respect. Both formal and informal inference have . . . a partial awareness of the connection between the premises and the conclusion. Natural reasoning, on the other hand, is apprehended by us as a simple indivisible act. Newman calls the move in natural inference from antecedent to consequent 'instinctive' meaning by this that it is spontaneous and inevitable." Casey, *Natural Reason*, 43.

124. Newman writes: "We reason, when we hold this by virtue of that; whether we hold it as evident or as approximating or tending to be evident, in either case we so hold it because of holding something else to be evident or tending to be evident." Newman, *Grammar*, 252 [*GA*, 259].

125. Casey writes: "The exercise of reason in its natural state can profitably be compared to the exercise of sense or memory. Just as we do not ordinarily know how we sense . . . how we remember, so too, we are not aware of the route we take in passing from antecedent to consequent in a piece of [natural] ratiocination." Casey, *Natural Reason*, 43.

are not expressible in propositions (proponible) then this is not a form of reasoning:

> It seems to me that [natural] inference is no inference at all, . . . if there really is an inference here, then its grounds must be proponible. If this is not the case and it is impossible, in principle, to express these grounds propositionally, then what we have is not an inference.[126]

From this he concludes that natural inference is "really a form of simple assent."[127] He writes:

> If Newman is serious in his claim about the complete non-consciousness of the phenomenal grounds of the inference then what he calls natural inference is not . . . inference. While it too is unconscious, it is also the case that it does not begin from premises, either expressed or unexpressed. This natural inference is really not inference at all. It is rather, some kind of primitive or basic apprehension of a state of affairs and the propositional expression of that apprehended state of affairs. In short, it is, to use Newman's own terminology, an assent.[128]

Casey implies here that certain ambiguities or nuances within Newman's account of natural inference mean that it is not altogether clear whether or not natural inference really qualifies to be inference in the technical sense of that word. Whether or not Casey is correct to view this subtlety within Newman's position as an ambiguity, the implications of Casey's position for Maddox's interpretation are as follows: if natural inference is not inference (as we know it) then the idea that Newman is an epistemological methodist, because he precedes simple assent with natural inference, is seriously undermined.

Natural inference, phronesis, and the neo-Thomist tradition

In addition to the above, it would appear that Maddox's interpretation of Newman's conception of natural inference, as a "rational procedure," is at variance with the tradition upon which Newman's concept is based. According to Willam, Newman's discussion of natural inference possesses

---

126. Casey, *Natural Reason*, 47–48.
127. Casey, *Natural Reason*, 74.
128. Casey, *Natural Reason*, 52–53.

similarities with Aristotle's work.[129] Newman does acknowledge parallels between this "illative faculty" and "what Aristotle calls (*phronesis*)."[130] In his correspondence he states that:

> There is a faculty in the mind ... which, when properly cultivated and used, answers to Aristotle's [*phronesis*,] its province being, not virtue, but the "*inquisitio veri*," which decides for us, beyond any technical rules, when, how, etc to pass from inference to assent, and when and under what circumstances, ... a mental faculty which reasons in a far higher way than that of merely measuring the force of conclusions by the force of premises.[131]

Here Newman applies the term *phronesis* to the innate faculty of reasoning which determine assent.[132] Maddox interprets Newman's use of Aristotle's notion of *phronesis* as being epistemologically proceduralist because Newman presupposes this faculty of natural inference to knowledge. This interpretation conflicts with Nussbaum's understanding of Aristotelian *phronesis* which sharply differentiates this concept from presupposed ethical criteria:

> For teaching and learning, here, do not simply involve the learning of rules and principles. A large part of learning, in turn, requires the cultivation of perception and responsiveness: the ability to read a situation, singling out what is relevant for thought and action. This active task is not a technique; one learns it by guidance rather than by a formula.[133]

---

129. Willam, *Aristotelische*, 307. Translated by Muriel Pilkington. Willam compares Aristotle's notion of συλλογισμός ἀασθενής with Newman's contention that "Faith, then, I have said, does not demand evidence so strong as is necessary for what is commonly considered a rational conviction, or belief on the ground of Reason; and why? For this reason, because it is mainly swayed by antecedent considerations." Newman, *Sermons Chiefly on the Theory of Religious Belief*, 179.

130. LD 30:148. Aristotle, *Nicomachean Ethics*, 110–15 [VI. 811 1141b28–1144a18].

131. LD 29:115–16.

132. Although this aspect of Newman's thought is influenced by Aristotle the difference between them is that while the "illative sense" is connected with whether a proposition is received *phronesis* deals primarily with conduct. Though Aristotle does conceive that *phronesis* has this potential, he does not treat its general relation to truth, and the affirmation of truth, but only as it bears upon things done. For further discussion, see Hochschild, "The Re-Imagined Aristotelianism of John Henry Newman," 333–42.

133. Nussbaum, *Love's Knowledge*, 44.

Here Nussbaum argues that *phronesis* is not governed by presupposed rules or formula but is the ability to "read a situation." If this definition of *phronesis* is correct then it calls Maddox's methodist interpretation of the illative sense into question for Newman is arguing that the human mind itself is able to "read" (comprehend) the veracity of a belief.

Maddox accepts that for Newman natural inference is a "basic" constituent of human judgement. He emphasizes that Newman's description of the inferential components of spontaneous assent nevertheless differs from that of Thomas Reid whom he describes as "the model particularist."[134] He writes:

> For Newman in contrast to Reid, our basic sense of rational judgment is deeply connected with inference. The very word "illation" . . . is not merely a designation of our shared human intuition regarding first principles; it is also, to the degree that it is cultivated toward its own perfection, our main way of insight into the patterns of natural inference which inform and determine the self-evident truths that we rely on in our reasoning about particular subject matters.[135]

Here Maddox argues that Newman, unlike Reid who is generally viewed as a forerunner of epistemological particularism,[136] links spontaneous assent to "illation." On this basis Maddox argues that Newman is an epistemological methodist. In contrast, Maddox interprets Reid as an epistemological particularist because, he argues, Reid separates spontaneous assent from inference altogether.

Ferreira's comparison of this aspect of Reid and Newman's thought indicates that Maddox's sharp differentiation between the two is overly simplistic:

> From Newman's side the contrast between [Reid's] commonsense and the illative sense is mitigated by his understanding of the radical implicitness of informal reasoning for at its extreme the implicitness of informal reasoning renders it nearly indistinguishable from intuition. From Reid's side the contrast is mitigated by the understanding he shares of non-demonstrative certainty—that is, allowing reasoning to be subtle enough to

---

134. Maddox, "Newman, Certain Knowledge," 71.
135. Maddox, "Newman, Certain Knowledge," 80.
136. For example, see de Bary, *Thomas Reid*, 41; Abraham, *Crossing*, 34.

generate certainty from converging probabilities might lesson the need to contrast it radically with intuition.[137]

Here Ferreira argues that the differences between Newman and Reid concerning the inferential dimensions of spontaneous assent are mitigated on both sides. First of all Newman's natural conception of inference verges on being intuition, and secondly Reid's understanding of the role played by probable reasoning in certainty. Thus, Ferreira's conclusions appear to diminish the sharp distinction that Maddox draws between common-sense and the illative sense.

Maddox's contrast between these two writers also fails to appreciate the way in which the neo-scholastic writers who influence Chisholm's work develop this aspect of Reid's thought. As noted earlier, Chisholm states that this theory is highly indebted to "scholastic philosophy."[138] Though Chisholm specifically mentions neo-Thomists like Mercier and Coffey, these writers are shaped by the forerunners of the revival of scholastic philosophy in the nineteenth-century, figures like Balmes and Kleutgen.[139]

Balmes views spontaneous assent to be the result of an "intellectual instinct."[140] He associates Reid's notion of common sense, which Maddox interprets as being separate from inference, with this "intellectual" instinct, which inclines the mind to assent.[141] His conception of an "intel-

---

137. Ferreira, *Scepticism*, 206.
138. Chisholm, *Problem of the Criterion*, 3.
139. Mercier, *Critriologie*; Coffey, *Epistemology*.
140. The French Roman Catholic Philosopher, Victor Cousin (1792–1867), also argues that: "Every man does not give an account to himself of what he knows. To know, without giving an account of our knowledge to ourselves; to know, and to give an account of our knowledge to ourselves—this is the only possible difference between man and man, between the people and the philosopher. In the one, reason is altogether spontaneous; it seizes at first upon its objects; but without returning upon itself and demanding an account of its procedure; in the other, reflection is added to reason; but this reflection, in its most profound investigation, can not add to natural reason, a single element which it does not already possess; it can add to it nothing but the knowledge of itself. Again, I say, reflection well-directed; for if it be ill-directed, it does not comprehend natural reason in all its parts; it leaves out some element, and repairs its mutilations only by arbitrary inventions. First, to omit, then to invent; this is the common vice of almost all systems of philosophy." Cousin, *Elements of Psychology*, 444–45.
141. Balmes writes: "Intellectual instinct is the natural inclination to assent in cases which lie without the domain of consciousness and evidence. The intellectual instinct obliges us to give an objective value to ideas; in this case it mingles with the

lectual instinct" indicates that neo-scholastic writers, and forerunners of this revival like Balmes, construe this Reidian notion to include inference.[142] In a similar manner, Kleutgen argues that a form of reasoning "inherent" within the "human understanding" leads us "from one truth to the knowledge of another" without explicitly "reflecting" on the fact that it has "passed from premises to conclusion at all."[143] Hence Kleutgen, the architect of *Aeterni Patris*,[144] contends that the human mind by virtue of its nature spontaneously infers propositions in a manner similar to Newman's discussion of natural inference.

In an article on "Leo XIII and the restoration of Thomistic Studies" Cardinal Mercier criticizes Reid and argues that the mind's spontaneous acquisition of knowledge is governed by an intelligent principle.[145] Hence, Mercier argues that the "spontaneous inclination" that the human mind has to knowledge "constitutes an intelligent" action.[146] This indicates once more that within the neo-scholastic tradition, by which Chisholm's epistemological particularism is shaped, there is a general acceptance that the mind's spontaneous assents are attained by implicit inferential activity.

Peter Coffey, citing Newman's illative sense, also argues that our convictions are the result of "spontaneous reasonings."[147] He maintains that the human mind "spontaneously thinks, judges [and] believes."[148]

---

truths of evidence, and is, in ordinary language, confounded with evidence. When the intellectual instinct operates upon non-evident objects and inclines us to assent, it is called Common Sense." Balmes, *Fundamental Philosophy*, 1:237.

142. It is possible that writers within the Catholic tradition combined Common Sense with inference in order to avoid charges of fideism. For further discussion, see Chadwick, *From Bossuet to Newman*; Shea, "Newman, Perrone, and Möhler," 49.

143. Kleutgen, *La Philosophie Scolastique*, 4:318–19. Translated by Ray Morris-Chapman.

144. An encyclical promoting the revival of Thomistic studies.

145. Mercier writes: "In man endowed with intelligence and freedom the ideal instinct itself is in solidarity with reason . . . . Far from being blind impulse, as Reid and the Scottish School thought, this inclination constitutes an intelligent and free principle: it belongs not only to the will, to the understanding, and to the imagination, but also to the living and unconscious functions . . . . Man aspires to know and the aspiration of his highest faculties carries him spontaneously to [knowledge]." Mercier, "Leo XIII and the Restoration of Thomistic Studies," 90–92.

146. Mercier, "Leo XIII," 90–92.

147. Coffey, *Science of Logic*, 2:22.

148. Coffey writes: "Just as a man's spontaneous reasonings can be correct without his having previously learned from the science of logic the canons to which they must

Moreover, he offers an interpretation of Reid's notion of common sense in which inference is integral:

> By "Common Sense" Reid meant simply what is sometimes also described as "good sense" or the faculty of sound judgment: in other words human reason or intelligence as brought to bear, in its sane and normal functioning, on the objective evidence whereby a large collection of convictions is borne in upon men generally as objectively true.[149]

Here Coffey reinforces Ferreira's contention that Reid's notion of common sense needn't be separated from inference, moreover, he challenges Maddox's interpretation of Reid which sharply polarizes inference and common sense. In addition to the above, Coffey affirms the inferential dimensions of Newman's illative sense and criticizes those who would separate inference from common sense:

> It is by his intellectual faculty as a rational, reflecting being, that man gives these assents. . . . If this is recognized and admitted there can be no danger of misunderstanding in describing such function of the intellect as "instinctive" or "natural" or "spontaneous," any more than there is in Newman's terminology when in his Grammar of Assent he speaks of "Natural Inference" and the "Illative Sense". But if it is denied that such assents are given by the individual reason, if it is maintained that they are given without any reference to the voice or dictate of reason, that they are not amenable to the bar of reflecting reason, that reason is powerless to pronounce them to be objectively true and valid interpretations of reality, then, in the mind of a being endowed with reason they are inevitably doomed to wither into scepticism.[150]

Here Coffey criticizes writers who separate spontaneous assent from the voice of reason because it prevents reasoned reflection about these spontaneous certitudes. He commends Newman's discussion of the illative sense for preventing this from happening.

---

have conformed, so can he by his spontaneous convictions have attained to true and certain knowledge without his having previously assured himself from the science of epistemology that he was not misled by those convictions." Coffey, *Epistemology*, 1:22–23.

149. Coffey, *Epistemology*, 2:307.

150. Coffey, *Epistemology*, 2:309–10.

If Maddox's contention that any inferential process antecedent to assent denotes methodism is to be refuted it is important to question whether Coffey's inferential interpretation of common sense shows that the epistemological approach taken by Reid, and neo-Thomistic writers like Coffey would be more commensurate with methodism. In his work *Thomas Reid and Scepticism* (2002) De Bary indicates the contrary:

> Perhaps we should concede that the categorization of Reid as a particularist is not quite as clear-cut as we might wish. There is something of a "bird and egg" difficulty . . . in applying Chisholm's notion of a "criterion" to . . . terms in Reid's epistemology. And in the non-technical everyday sense of "method" and its cognates, Reid, like anyone who tackles epistemology (or anything else, if it comes to that), must be counted a methodist. But if we allow that there is a real distinction, and one worth drawing, behind the terms "methodist" and "particularist," we shall find it hard to do anything but classify Reid as the latter.[151]

This extract implies that if the term "method" is interpreted in its "everyday sense" then everyone, including Reid, who writes upon issues related to epistemology must be interpreted as a methodist. Indeed, it seems Maddox's contention that Newman's discussion is epistemologically methodist would, if true, mean that everyone who possesses mental processes, whether conscious or unconscious, is an epistemological methodist. De Bary, moreover, is correct to suggest here that it is anachronistic to ascribe Chisholm's notion of epistemological "methodism" or "particularism" to Reid's understanding of the acquisition of knowledge. The same applies to Newman. Nevertheless, he points out that if anyone predating Chisholm can be viewed as anticipating particularism then it remains apparent that Reid has more particularist tendencies than methodist. In a like manner it seems that although Newman cannot be categorized using these terms his discussion of spontaneous assent may be interpreted as having sufficient particularist tendencies for it to be relevant to the proposals of Chisholm and Abraham.[152]

In summary, Maddox is correct to draw attention to the unconscious inferential antecedents of simple assent. However, his interpretation of this inferential dimension as an epistemological procedure is exposed to be a conflation of Newman's discussion of the method of informal

---

151. de Bary, *Thomas Reid and Scepticism*, 41.

152. Abraham's use of Newman's writings to advance a particularist approach to the epistemology of theology will be discussed in the next chapter.

inference with his account of the spontaneous natural operation of the intellect. Moreover, Maddox's interpretation is undermined further by his failure to attend to the nuances in Newman's understanding of natural inference, which lead several Newman commentators to question whether natural inference can even be viewed as inference in any conventional understanding of this term. Finally, Maddox's insistence that this aspect of Newman's account distinguishes him from Reid overlooks the way in which Reid's work has been interpreted by the neo-scholastic tradition. Maddox fails to appreciate the fact that Newman's conception of the inferential dimension operative in simple assent is commensurate with other sources important for the development of this approach.[153] Maddox's failure to take into account both the impact of the neo-scholastic tradition upon Chisholm, and Newman's similarities with it, impairs his analysis considerably.

Jay Newman: a particularist interpretation of the *Grammar*?

Earlier it was indicated that the philosopher Jay Newman suggests that J. H. Newman's discussion of the role of the illative sense in reflex assent may actually improve Chisholm's account of the formulation of criterion. In this section we will first examine the nature of the role of the illative sense in reflex assent and then explore Jay Newman's contention that this might potentially contribute to Chisholm's epistemology.

The role of the illative sense in reflex assent

Newman's discussion of reflex assent illustrates that the examination of our spontaneous certitudes raises a number of epistemological challenges. For example, Newman suggests that while no sane person would deny that Great Britain is an island[154] he points out that few of the reasons people could offer for this certainty would satisfy philosophers:

> 153. The problems identified in Maddox's interpretation illustrate the dangers of making Reid the sole ancestor of the particularist philosophical approach.
> 154. He writes: "Great Britain is an island. We give to that proposition our deliberate and unconditional adhesion. There is no security on which we should be better content to stake our interests. . . . . This is the position of our minds towards our insularity; yet are the arguments producible for it (to use the common expression) in black and white commensurate with this overpowering certitude about it?" Newman, *Grammar*, 287 [*GA*, 294].

> [F]irst, we have been so taught in our childhood, ... every book we have read, invariably took it for granted.... There is a manifest *reductio ad absurdum* attached to the notion that we can be deceived on such a point as this. However, negative arguments and circumstantial evidence are not ... the highest kind of proof possible. Those who have circumnavigated the island have a right to be certain: have we ever ourselves even fallen in with anyone who has? And as to the common belief, what is the proof that we are not all of us believing it on the credit of each other?[155]

Newman is not insinuating that we should doubt that Britain is an island. Nevertheless, he wished to point out that most people "cannot analyze a proof satisfactorily" for writers such as Locke.[156] Therefore, Newman concludes that the majority of our certitudes are based, not on formal proof, but upon informal reasons. He writes:

> On the whole, I think it is the fact that many of our most obstinate and most reasonable certitudes depend on proofs which are informal and personal, which baffle our powers of analysis, and cannot be brought under logical rule, because they cannot be submitted to logical statistics. If we must speak of Law, this recognition of a correlation between certitude and implicit proof seems to me a law of our minds.[157]

Here Newman states that the informal mode of proof which leads to certitude is incommensurate with strict logic, or formal inference. It should be clarified here that "informal inference" is not altogether unconscious like natural inference. Newman emphasizes that the informal reasons elicited in support of a reflex assent, though they be "more or less implicit," are conscious of their antecedents.[158] Despite this, Newman believes that there is no criterion, measure, or calculus that can evaluate whether or not this mass of informal reasons requires reflex assent. The only standard available is a person's illative judgment, the illative sense:

> We judge for ourselves, by our own lights, and on our own principles; and our criterion of truth is not so much the manipulation of propositions, as the intellectual and moral character of the person maintaining them, and the ultimate silent effect of

---

155. Newman, *Grammar*, 287–88 [*GA*, 294–95].
156. Newman, *Grammar*, 289 [*GA*, 296].
157. Newman, *Grammar*, 294 [*GA*, 301].
158. Newman, *Grammar*, 285 [*GA*, 292].

> his arguments or conclusions upon our minds. It is this distinction between ratiocination as the exercise of a living faculty in the individual intellect, and mere skill in argumentative science, which is the true interpretation of the prejudice which exists against logic in the popular mind, and of the animadversions which are levelled against it, . . . that it never makes converts, that it leads to rationalism, . . . that Laputa is the land of logicians, and the like. Such maxims mean, when analyzed, that the processes of reasoning which legitimately lead to assent, to action, to certitude, are in fact too multiform, subtle, omnigenous, too implicit, to allow of being—measured by rule, that they are after all personal,—verbal argumentation being useful only in subordination to a higher logic.[159]

Here Newman argues that the reasons brought out in support of a reflex assent are incapable of being reduced to a logical rule or method. On the contrary, he considers that it is only a living illative faculty within the mind that is able to judge whether or not these "omnigenous" informal reasons warrant reflex assent (certitude). Thus, whereas simple assent contains what Newman terms natural inference so reflex assent, which is a conscious act, educes the kinds of reasons in support of what one already believes so as to ascertain evidence in its favor.[160] During spontaneous assent natural inference, the illative faculty of the mind, unconsciously judges the legitimacy of a belief. In reflex assent, the illative sense accompanies and "supervises the work of analysis and technical reasoning and pronounces . . . on the correctness of its results, completing by its view of the whole, the work of the impersonal laws of logic."[161] Hence Newman concludes that were a criterion required to appraise whether or not this miscellany of informal reasons are sufficient for a reflex assent to our spontaneous beliefs then it is not a set standard or rule but only human judgment, the illative sense, which ultimately determines whether such diverse and informal reasons warrant certitude.[162] Having indicated

---

159. Newman, *Grammar*, 295–96 [*GA*, 302–3].

160. Newman, *Grammar*, 190–91 [*GA*, 197–98].

161. Walgrave, *Newman the Theologian*, 104.

162. It is important to stress that this innate ratiocinative faculty is not a set standard or rule. For Newman it is the very character of a person which determines the principles and truths to which he or she gives assent. He considers that the judgements of the illative sense are more accurate if an individual is morally pure. He believes that people of good character are able to judge rightly. Newman considers that our illative sense: "is enfeebled, obstructed, perverted, by allurements of sense and the supremacy

how Newman understands the role of the illative sense in reflex assent, it is necessary to explore the way in which Jay Newman considers that this aspect of J. H. Newman's work makes a contribution to Chisholm's approach to epistemology.

The potential contribution of the illative sense

In an article entitled "Epistemic Inference and Illative Judgment," Jay Newman criticizes Chisholm for his account of the justification of belief. Earlier it was noted that Chisholm considers that epistemology begins with what is known and then proceeds to formulate principles of justification appropriate to the knowledge claims in hand. He writes:

> We presuppose, first, that there *is* something that we know and we adopt the working hypothesis that *what* we know is pretty much that which, on reflection, we think we know.... We presuppose, second, that the things we know are justified for us in the following sense: *we* can know what it is, on any occasion, that constitutes our grounds, or reason, or evidence for thinking that we know.... And we presuppose, third, that if we do thus have grounds or reasons for the things we think we know, then there are valid general principles of evidence—principles stating the general conditions under which we may be said to have grounds or reasons for what we believe[;]... our concern, in investigating the theory of evidence, is to find out what these general principles are.[163]

Here Chisholm argues that the general conditions for knowledge—principles of evidence—should be formulated retrospectively, from a position of spontaneous knowledge. One of the general epistemic principles which Chisholm outlines in appraisal of our spontaneous knowledge is (D):

> (D) For any subject S, if S believes, without ground for doubt, that he remembers perceiving something to be F, then the proposition that he does remember perceiving something to be F is one that is acceptable for S.[164]

---

of self, and, on the other hand, quickened by aspirations after the supernal and; so that at length two characters of mind are brought out into shape." Newman, *Grammar*, 304. [*GA*, 311–12].

163. Chisholm, *Theory of Knowledge*, 16–17.
164. Chisholm, *Theory of Knowledge*, 139.

Here Chisholm maintains that if someone (S) can remember perceiving something (F) then they are justified in believing that they remember that perception. However, Jay Newman criticizes Chisholm for making his epistemic principles too general, citing (D) as an example:

> If (D) is to be taken seriously as a "principle" of "logic," then it should be of value to a rather wide range of subjects. Chisholm himself indicates that it should hold "for any subject S." But is (D) equally valid for [someone] S_1, who has a photographic memory, and for [someone else] S_2, who has both a bad memory and a tendency to daydream? ... [Furthermore,] among those who have an excellent memory, some have a better memory than others, and among those who have a bad memory, some have a worse memory than others. So there would seem to be no end to the number of variants of (D) that an adequate epistemic logic would require.[165]

Here Jay Newman illustrates that if the validity of a perception is linked to memory capacity then Chisholm's principle is too broad to account for the fact that some are better at remembering things than others. Jay Newman's purpose in targeting this particular principle is to illustrate that epistemic principles can never account for the plethora of reasons which lead an individual to assent. He writes:

> This short summary does not do full justice to Chisholm's theory ... of which he offers a lengthy exposition; but it does draw our attention to some places in the theory where Chisholm has left himself open to criticism. .... Sometimes Chisholm seems to want us to believe that he is making explicit the actual epistemic principles that real people apply in real epistemic inferences. At other times he seems to be suggesting that he is just trying to give us an idea of the kind of epistemic principles that people apply. ... At still other times he seems to be arguing that his epistemic principles are the principles that a person ought to apply. And usually it is not clear which or how many of these things he is trying to do. ... To me, a theory of epistemic inference which does not ring true phenomenologically cannot be adequate. "But," the critic may insist, "the epistemologist should think" of justification in the way that a logician does and "need not be concerned with extraneous phenomenological considerations." Such a statement begs the question raised in this paper.[166]

---

165. Jay Newman, "Epistemic Inference," 332–33.
166. Jay Newman, "Epistemic Inference," 330, 339.

Here Jay Newman indicates that Chisholm's formulation of epistemic principles to justify a person's antecedent knowledge claims does not do justice to the actual way in which spontaneous assents are obtained.

In sum, Jay Newman believes that the reasons which elicit assent to a proposition cannot be reduced to general principles of "epistemic logic" such as those outlined by Chisholm. Here he suggests that J. H. Newman has something to offer:

> So, as Cardinal Newman observes, the method of concrete inference involves the "cumulation of probabilities, independent of each other, arising out of the nature and circumstances of the particular case." Unlike the principles of "ordinary" logic, principles of "epistemic logic," no matter how general or specific, can never accommodate all those "circumstances" which are relevant to a determination of the degree of reasonableness of the proposition in question.... [Thus] the practical value of (D) as a "principle" of "logic" is completely destroyed.[167]

Here Jay Newman criticizes the rigidity of Chisholm's epistemic principles and argues that the practical value of principles like (D) is nonexistent because it fails to resonate with the diverse ways in which real people attain certitude. At this juncture Jay Newman indicates that J. H. Newman's discussion of the illative sense, or put simply human judgement itself, presents Chisholm's epistemology with a malleable "criterion" that can account for these variants. He writes:

> One must appreciate the importance of what Newman characterizes as the "method of concrete inference" and "illative" judgment. Let us follow Newman's advice and focus our attention on a particular case. While at a cocktail party, I find myself sitting next to a dazzlingly attractive woman whose face looks awfully familiar. I turn to her and say, "Haven't I met you before? I seem to remember meeting you some years back when I was living in Toronto." She replies, as attractive women almost instinctively do in such situations, "Maybe, but I don't think so. You must be confusing me with someone else." ... After reflecting on the matter for a few minutes ... I'm sure that I do remember meeting her ... how did I come to be "sure"? Before attempting to answer this question, I want to tell you about something that did not occur to me in the course of my reflection. Not once did I think to myself that it is not more reasonable to suspend judgment about whether I remember meeting her than it is to

---

167. Jay Newman, "Epistemic Inference," 334.

believe that I do remember meeting her. But in the course of my reflection and conversation with my friends, there was the gradual "*cumulation of probabilities, independent of each other, arising out of the nature and circumstances of the particular case which [was] under review.*" [Italics mine] My reflection may have lacked the orderliness, the coherence, that marks my academic lectures and letters to federal tax officials; but it did its job.[168]

Here Jay Newman cites the *Grammar* and compares the series of informal reasons that lead him to be certain with J. H. Newman's discussion of the same. The way in which he attains this confident judgement, that he remembers the girl, is clearly indebted to the way in which J. H. Newman considers we are justified in holding that Great Britain is an island. In each case the individual gathers a number of reasons which viewed separately appear to have no real bearing on the subject, but when these considerations are taken together the mind's living illative faculty is able to judge that they are sufficient for certitude. The similarity between Jay Newman's account and J. H. Newman's discussion of the reasons sufficient for a reflex assent is further evidenced below:

> In the course of my reflection, some ideas flitted through my mind, almost at random; and they mixed freely with other ideas which were the fruit of the highest degree of mental exertion that a person is capable of at a cocktail party. Now, I cannot list for you all of the things that occurred to me during the course of my reflection; some of them flitted by too quickly (i.e., were "*too fine to avail separately*"), and others cannot be verbalized without very great effort (being "*too subtle*") And there were so many! (I.e., they were "*too numerous*" for "*conversion*" [Italics mine].) . . . . In weighing all of this data, I did not make one basic inference, though I may well have made dozens and dozens of inferences. In the meantime, after wavering for a while, I took note of two things which finally convinced me. I heard the mysterious lady comment on the new local production of La Traviata, and I seemed to remember that the woman that I had met years earlier was also interested in classical music. And that mannerism, the way she brushed back her hair: there was something unique and familiar about it. These two pieces of data were not in themselves all that compelling; but combined with all the other data, they made me realize, made me see, that this was indeed the woman that I had met before, probably at the Gibsons' house. I did not merely come to a conclusion—indeed,

168. Jay Newman, "Epistemic Inference," 337–38.

what could the "premises" of such an "inference" be?—but I came to realize, to see, that I did remember meeting the attractive lady.[169]

In this extract Jay Newman argues that the considerations that lead him to be certain were not capable of being formulated into epistemic principles like those outlined by Chisholm. Citing the *Grammar* he states that these reasons are *"too fine to avail separately."* He thus concludes that the notion of illative judgment found in the *Grammar of Assent* offers a way in which a multiplicity of informal reasonings can be judged sufficient so as to enable someone to attain confidence about their initial beliefs.

The references indicate that Jay Newman's findings have important implications. The notion of the illative sense, and its role in reflex assent, enables an individual to comprehend the diverse phenomenological considerations which lead them to certitude. It is precisely this appreciation for the epistemic value of a miscellany of extraneous inferences which Chisholm's epistemic principles are unable to incorporate. Therefore, Newman offers an inclusive criterion to particularist writers, for illative judgement can encompass an infinite range of epistemological factors. This indicates that Newman's work continues to be of relevance to the ongoing development of particularist approaches to epistemology.

Summary of Chapter

Having compared Newman's ideas with those of Chisholm, and explored the way in which Mercier and Coffey engage with the *Grammar of Assent*, it is apparent that these writers share a similar epistemological outlook. This illustrates Newman's relevance to the particularist approach to knowledge. Moreover, though it would be anachronistic to classify Newman using Chisholm's terminology, his work clearly anticipates the proposals of the latter. Perhaps the most interesting finding is Jay Newman's suggestion that J. H. Newman's conception of the illative sense has the potential to enhance Chisholm's epistemological position. This suggests that the illative sense offers a relevant and needed contribution to the development of this theory of knowledge. This idea is exploited in the work of the particularist writer William J. Abraham and, for this reason, the next chapter will examine the way in which Newman's work shapes Abraham's particularist account of the epistemology of religious belief.

169. Jay Newman, "Epistemic Inference," 338–39.

6

The Justification of Religious Belief in Abraham and Newman

THERE ARE MANY WAYS in which Newman is referenced by philosophers. The question here is whether or not Newman's work has been constructively engaged by the philosopher of religion William J. Abraham. Earlier it was noted that, in his book *The Logic of Renewal* (2003), Abraham indicates that his writing upon the "epistemology of religious belief" follows the "lines of inquiry brilliantly opened up by John Henry Newman."[1] Abraham's subsequent philosophical publication *Crossing the Threshold of Divine Revelation* (2006) clearly makes references to Newman, as does his earlier work *Canon and Criterion* (1998). In order to explore whether or not Newman's thought contributes to Abraham's approach, whether perhaps he is constructively operating out of the epistemological framework implicit within Newman's corpus, we will need to assess the extent to which Abraham really draws upon the insights "brilliantly opened up" by Newman in his particularist account of the rationality of Christian belief.[2] First, however, it is helpful to provide some background to both Abraham and his work.

---

1. Abraham, *Logic of Renewal*, 166.
2. Abraham, *Crossing*, 30–31.

William J. Abraham and John Henry Newman: A Preliminary Comparison

William J. Abraham (1946–) is a member of the United Methodist church.[3] In his early publications he regularly identifies himself with the evangelical tradition. For example, in *The Divine Inspiration of Holy Scripture* (1981) he acknowledges that his position is a continuation of the evangelical tradition.[4] In *Divine Revelation and the Limits of Historical Criticism* (1982) he states that his work should be viewed as a deliberate contribution to the evangelical tradition as expressed in the reformers and the thought of John Wesley.[5]

Abraham notes that a key characteristic of evangelicalism is that "Evangelicals like to rely entirely on Scripture alone."[6] While his subsequent writings continued to contribute to this tradition, Abraham's later works also demonstrate a steady increase in his appreciation for the role of tradition in theology. For example, Abraham's book on the *The Coming Great Revival: Recovering the Full Evangelical Heritage* (1984) counterbalances the authority of Scripture with tradition, reason, and experience.[7] His work the *Logic of Evangelism* (1989) lays even greater stress on the importance of the early church's methods for Christian initiation.[8] Thus while these works are also written from within an evangelical and Methodist perspective there is a gradual departure from the conception of Scripture commonly associated with this position.

In Abraham's later works there is strong criticism of evangelicalism and Protestantism in general. A good example of this is an article entitled "The End of Wesleyan Theology" (2005), which argues that it is impossible to attain a united theological consensus from reading Scripture:

> In my judgment, the very idea of the authority of Scripture . . . has outlived its usefulness .. . . [G]iven that there is no agreed theology in scripture . . . it was inevitable that over time Wesley's

---

3. The Methodist Church (whether American, British or elsewhere) should not be confused with the methodist epistemological position.

4. Abraham, *The Divine Inspiration of Holy Scripture*, 11.

5. Abraham, *Divine Revelation and the Limits of Historical Criticism*, 5.

6. Abraham, *The Divine Inspiration of Holy Scripture*, 32

7. This theological method is often referred to as the "Wesleyan Quadrilateral." Abraham, *The Coming Great Revival*.

8. Abraham, *Logic of Evangelism*.

own reading of Scripture would collapse and be replaced by other readings by his own followers.[9]

In what appears to be a rejection of his spiritual roots Abraham judges that Wesley's emphasis on Scripture would never secure doctrinal unity. Likewise in "Saving Souls in the Twenty-First Century" (2003) Abraham concludes that "we need to abandon the biblicism that was so tempting to Wesley" and draw much more heavily upon patristic theology.[10]

The reasoning behind Abraham's decision to move away from evangelical Protestant conceptions of Scripture is that he believes that "biblicism" has devastated the church.[11] He writes:

> Biblicism . . . has systematically destroyed the canonical faith of the church within modern Protestantism. . . . Bible and doctrine do not function as foundation and superstructure, or as basis and building; Bible and doctrine operate as wonderful gifts of the Holy Spirit to be used delicately as instruments of spiritual formation within a wider network of practices, persons, and materials.[12]

In *Canon and Criterion* (1998) Abraham describes the Protestant emphasis on the authority of Scripture as "the epistemizing of the church's canonical life." He considers that making Scripture into a "norm for testing all theological proposals" led the reformers to "rationalize" the canonical heritage of the church.[13] Abraham believes that this foundation of Scripture, as the rule for all faith, inevitably led the reformers to rationalize the canonical heritage of the church into those elements that had a clear basis in Scripture. He writes: "the propositions of scripture became the premises of a deductive science secured as true by the fact that they were spoken by God. All the teachings of the church were taken as derivable from scripture."[14] Unfortunately this led to the abandonment of many important aspects of patristic faith. He believes that the consequences of this were disastrous because grounding all doctrine in Scripture left them extremely vulnerable to unitarianism: "a radically conservative

---

9. Abraham, "The End of Wesleyan Theology," 16–18.
10. Abraham, "Saving Souls in The Twenty-First Century," 19.
11. Abraham, "The Emergence of Canonical Theism," 148.
12. Abraham, "Saving Souls In The Twenty-First Century," 19.
13. Abraham, *Canon and Criterion*, 157–60.
14. Abraham, "Philosophical Reflection on Revelation and Scripture," 695.

movement" that denied the doctrine of the Trinity because it took *sola scriptura* to its logical conclusion.[15]

What is fascinating here is that Abraham compares this Protestant rationalization of the Christian faith to what Chisholm calls epistemological methodism.[16] In suggesting this, Abraham is saying that the reformers' use of Scripture to determine theological truth limits the content of revelation in order to satisfy an arbitrary criterion:

> Scripture, the biblical canon, it will be said, is the foundation, the criterion for Christian theology; this is the proper epistemology of all good theology.[17]

Here Abraham is suggesting that theologians who believe that from the beginning the church had a criterion in the canon of Scripture to determine the limits of revelation are epistemological methodists. On this interpretation, the reformers, like epistemological methodists, begin with Scripture as a criterion for proper theology and then make doctrines using that criterion—doctrines that are viewed as legitimate only in so far as they act as representative summaries of Scripture.[18]

Abraham is not the first writer to criticize the epistemological conception of Scripture adopted by many Protestants. For example, George Marsden's *Fundamentalism and American Culture* (1980), Mark Noll's *The Scandal of the Evangelical Mind* (1995), and Christian Smith's *The Bible Made Impossible* (2011) all illustrate the way in which evangelicals have imbibed an excessive epistemological foundationalist conception of Scripture. They argue that the methods of Enlightenment philosophy have had an undue influence upon evangelical approaches to theology.[19] However, what is distinctive about Abraham's comparison is that his *Canon and Criterion* (1998) traces this problem further back, arguing that this epistemological methodist conception of Scripture was a

---

15. Abraham, *Crossing*, 113.

16. "Scripture has been systematically epistemized; that is, it has been seen primarily as a criterion of truth in theology. . . . It has been seen as the critical warrant for theological construction. Its primary function is as a foundation and test of the church's teaching." Abraham, *Crossing*, 101–2.

17. Abraham, "Canonical Theism and the Future of Systematic Theology," 290.

18. Abraham, "Canonical Theism and the Future of Systematic Theology," 290–91.

19. Marsden, *Fundamentalism*, 111; Noll, *The Scandal of the Evangelical Mind*, 91; Smith, *The Bible Made Impossible*, 149.

problem during the Reformation—before the Enlightenment's elevation of reason.[20]

Canonical theism

Abraham's later works illustrate a key change in his position. He concludes that the contemporary church should broaden its attention from an excessive focus on Scripture in order for it to be enriched by the great canonical heritage of the undivided church of antiquity. Thus, contrary to usual evangelical thought, Abraham contends that revelation continues after the formation of the canon of Scripture. In his work *Canon and Criterion* (1998) he points out that, prior to the schism between East and West (1054 AD), the early church identified a broad catalogue of material, including rites of passage such as baptism, liturgical traditions, iconographic material, ecclesiastical regulations, persons (such as the fathers, saints, and teachers), creeds, and so on.[21] Abraham emphasizes that these "canons" were not created to be epistemological criteria. On the contrary, he argues that in recognizing certain materials as "canons" the church judged these materials to be the means of grace necessary for immersing new believers into the life of faith.[22]

His *Canonical Theism* (2008)[23] argues that a recovery of all the canons will bring renewal to the contemporary church:

> Canonical theism is intimately tied to the notion of the canonical heritage of the church. The church possesses not just a canon of books in its Bible but also a canon of doctrine, a canon of saints, a canon of church fathers, a canon of theologians, a canon of liturgy, a canon of bishops, a canon of councils, a canon of ecclesial regulations, a canon of icons, and the like. . . . Canonical theism is the theism expressed in and through the canonical heritage of the church.[24]

---

20. Abraham, *Canon and Criterion*, 111–38.
21. Abraham, *Canon and Criterion*, 37–38.
22. Abraham, *Canon and Criterion*, 53, 112; Abraham, *Crossing*, 16.
23. Whilst Abraham is the architect behind the proposal for a "canonical theism," he has developed this vision as a collaborative project. Abraham states that "It is precisely because the ideas pursued are beyond the work of any one scholar" that he has recently enlisted the help of others. See Abraham, "Introduction," xvii.
24. Abraham, "Canonical Theism: Thirty Theses," 2.

Abraham considers that in its identification of these canonical materials the primitive church "was interested primarily in singling out medicine for the soul."[25] He writes:

> The sacraments, the scriptures, the creed, the canon of the fathers, and the like, I am suggesting, were construed as materials and practices which fed the soul, which mediated the life of God, which returned human beings to their true destiny as children of God, and which ultimately led to a life of sanctity. Alternatively we might say that they were seen as gifts of the Holy Spirit in the life of the church, intended to bring about participation in the life of God through the working of the same spirit, who guided the church in their selection and use . . . as medicine to heal the sickness of the world.[26]

Canonical theism is therefore about accepting the entire canonical heritage of the early church. This proposal of a *Canonical Theism* indicates the extent to which Abraham's views have developed over time.[27] Against the traditional evangelical position, Abraham now considers revelation has continued to be at work in the life of the church and that this ongoing revelation of God has, over time, led to the formation of a vast canonical heritage.

Abraham links the recovery of the patristic faith to Chisholm's epistemological particularist approach. In contrast to the reformers, Abraham argues that the early church did not begin theology with a criterion of Scripture designed to limit the scope of Christian faith:

> What the canonical theist asserts is that the church offers no formal theory as to how it knows that it possesses the truth about God. . . . [C]anonical theists insist that the failure to canonize an epistemology was a wise omission both for the good of the church and for the good of epistemology.[28]

---

25. "The Creed is exceptionally useful in catechetical work; the Scriptures are useful in providing agreed texts for preaching; the Eucharist is pivotal in nurturing an intimate communion with the risen Lord; . . . the writings of the fathers are invaluable in pursuing the implications of the scriptural material." Abraham, *Canon and Criterion*, 53, 156.

26. Abraham, *Canon and Criterion*, 112.

27. Abraham states that his "central thesis is relatively simple. . . . We should expand the material identification of canon to take in more than scripture, so it can cover the whole canonical heritage of the early church." Abraham, "I Can See People," at 238.

28. Abraham, *Crossing*, 17.

Here Abraham underlines the point that the process of theological discernment in the patristic period was not governed by an epistemological criterion. He points out that chronologically the creed was accepted by the church prior to the canon of Scripture.[29] He explains that the Nicene Creed was actually used to help the church decide which books should be included in the Bible. He writes:

> The church was doing theology long before it had any fixed canon of scripture. . . . Moreover the church's rule of faith was critical in deciding the content of the canon of scripture, so the relation is the reverse of what we usually claim.[30]

This makes nonsense of the idea that the creed should be extrapolated from Scripture. Instead of beginning with Scripture, or any other criterion, Abraham argues that the church carefully and collectively judged certain materials to be necessary for catechesis.[31] The materials used in Christian initiation were called canons ("lists") and Abraham is emphatic that these means of grace were not epistemological criterion but were rather the means of immersing new Christians into the life of God.

Abraham considers that since the division between East and West, the church has been divided into ever-increasing factions by the formulation of arbitrary criteria that it is believed will secure Christian truth. This emphasis on finding a criterion for theological method has, according to Abraham, led to a reductionist approach to the rich canonical heritage of the church. Over time he believes that this has rendered the church's acceptance of the canons vulnerable to the prevailing opinions in contemporary philosophy.[32]

Exploring Newman's connections with Abraham's proposal

Abraham's proposals have a number of similarities with Newman. At the outset, however, it is important to acknowledge a key difference between

---

29. Building upon the work of Walter Bauer (1877–1960), Ehrman argues the church edited some scriptural texts using the creed so as to ensure that the Bible supported its credal statements. For further discussion, see Bauer, *Orthodoxy and Heresy*; Ehrman, *The Orthodox Corruption of Scripture*. For a criticism of this view, see Köstenberger and Kruger, *The Heresy of Orthodoxy*.

30. Abraham, "Canonical Theism and the Future of Systematic Theology," 291.

31. Abraham, *Canon and Criterion*, 111–38.

32. Abraham, *Crossing*, 6.

these writers. Abraham's profound desire to avoid limiting the canonical heritage leads him to uphold the view that revelation is continuous.[33] Abraham thus holds, contrary to Newman, that divine revelation is continuously being given to the church. In contrast, Newman's position is that the apostles received the deposit of revelation in full.[34] Here our purpose is not to refute Abraham's conception of revelation, neither is it to take up the issue of revelation in Newman,[35] rather our focus is to see how Abraham's account draws upon Newman's discussion generally.

While acknowledging this important difference between Newman and Abraham, their proposals have a number of similarities. For example, Abraham's contention that when theologians begin with epistemological theories Christian doctrine is made subservient to these criteria has similarities with Newman's concerns about liberalism in religion. Abraham acknowledges that "this is exactly what Newman found so troubling in the liberal circles of his day."[36] Abraham considers that, like epistemological methodism, nineteenth-century "liberalism entailed the introduction of the rationalistic principle in theology."[37] In making this statement, Abraham indicates a central theme common to what Newman referred to as liberalism and what Chisholm refers to as epistemological methodism. In both cases theological truth is governed by an antecedent criterion that is unfit to determine the profundity of the Christian revelation. A number of extracts from these writers indicate that Newman's condemnation of liberalism in religion anticipates Abraham's criticisms of epistemological methodism in theology. Nowhere is this more apparent than in their respective criticisms of the reformers.

---

33. Abraham, *Crossing*, 108–109; Abraham, *Canon and Criterion*, 356–57.

34. LD 25:418. Newman maintains that the contemporary church does not have more revelation than the apostles. Nevertheless, he considers that over time, this revelation is progressively realizing itself (like yeast within dough) within the mind of the church. This tension in Newman's account makes it amenable to Abraham's contention that God continuously reveals truth to the church. However, while Abraham indicates that new revelation is given, Newman believes that the church is given inspiration, the grace to illuminate the fullness of the revelation already in its possession. For further discussion, see *TP*, 2:66–67.

35. There are already a number of works discussing this important dimension of Newman's writing. For example: McGrath, *Universal Revelation*, 133–46; Merrigan, "Revelation," 47–65.

36. Abraham, *Canon and Criterion*, 338.

37. Abraham, *Canon and Criterion*, 338.

Abraham's criticism of the reformers for epistemological methodism has a number of similarities with Newman's opposition to "liberalism in religion." Whereas Abraham accuses the reformers of epistemological methodism, because they use Scripture as a foundation for all Christian belief Newman accuses the reformers of liberal rationalism. Both view the Reformation as a kind of rationalism. Each considers that the reformers' attempt to use Scripture as the one true standard of doctrine was actually a shift towards rationalism in that it allowed an inappropriate standard to determine the limits of theology.

As noted earlier, Newman opposed any form of theological reductionism resulting from the introduction of inappropriate first principles into religion.[38] Newman considers that the reformers were guilty of this "rationalism" because they tried to limit Christian doctrine to what human reason could infer from the text of Scripture.[39] Newman likewise perceives the "abundant signs" of "liberalism" in "the writings of the *Evangelicals*"[40] and argues that the Protestant attempt to formulate theology from Scripture leads to liberalism.[41] This aversion to the theological reductionism caused by the Reformation leads to another similarity between these writers. This shared concern has directed both Newman and Abraham towards a greater appreciation of the patristic faith.

Newman does not use the phrase epistemological particularism. Nevertheless, his desire, like that of Abraham, is that the revelation of God be judged on its own terms. His aversion to liberalism indicates that he gives priority to the substance of the Christian faith as opposed to theories about the rationality of this content. Hence, Newman believed that the way to avert the theological reductionism caused by liberalism was for nineteenth-century Anglicanism to embrace the abundant resources supplied by the early church:

> The object of the Movement was to withstand the Liberalism of the day. I found and felt that this could not be done by mere

---

38. Kenny, *Political Thought*, 129.

39. Newman and Keble, *Literary Remains of Richard Hurrell Froude*, 1:389, 2:6. Newman had long since rejected the notion that scripture alone could lead one into doctrinal orthodoxy. His rejection of *sola scriptura* was aided by Hawkins's *A Dissertation upon the Use and Importance of Unauthoritative Tradition*. Here Hawkins had argued that the unsystematic nature of the scriptures meant that it was extremely difficult to extract doctrine from them (from scratch).

40 *AW*, 142.

41. Newman, Review of *The Brothers' Controversy*, 171–72 [*Ess*, 1:111].

negatives. It was necessary for us to have a positive church theory erected as a definite basis.[42]

Thus Newman's calls for a return to the patristic faith were designed to prevent liberalism, theological reductionism, from weakening the theology and ministry of the Anglican church in the nineteenth century. This extract illustrates the way in which Newman envisaged the "primitive" church:

> Its outward forms are but the type of what it is within. Within it is calm and serene, as the sea spread before the throne of God, reflecting in its bosom the stars of heaven and giving to view "the jewels of the great deep" which lie beneath. And such as this is the garb which, at its Master's command, it has put on from the beginning. Though its coat was of many colours, yet it was woven from the top throughout; though made with much cunning work and many a curious device, yet it was "fine linen, clean and white," like the inward "righteousness of saints." Such was the sanctity, the comeliness, the gravity of those ancient forms, which as being imbued with what they represented resembled it, and while they resembled it promised it. The order of the ministry, the descent and relationship of the churches, the ritual of worship, the precepts for governing, evangelizing, protesting, suffering, all spoke of that inward heaven which exists in its degree in the soul of every true Christian, and has its perfect unapproachable prototype in that of his Divine Master .... [I]f we would see what true social religion is, we must betake ourselves to the various forms in which it is presented to us in antiquity.[43]

In the writings of the patristic church Newman perceived a "character and spirit," an "ethos" that could be absorbed into the Anglican church.[44] Newman's belief that the church of antiquity may supply the contemporary church with spiritual riches closely resembles Abraham's vision of a canonical theism that will bring renewal to the contemporary church.

Abraham explicitly links his call for a return to the patristic faith to an epistemological particularist approach to knowledge. He argues that in beginning with the vision of God contained in the canonical heritage of the early church he is able to place knowledge of God before theories of

---

42. Newman, *History of My Religious Opinions*, 146 [*Apo* 146].
43. Newman, Review of *Random Recollections of Exeter Hall*, 193–94.
44. Newman, Review of *The History of the Christian Church*, 210.

rationality and justification. In a manner similar to Newman, Abraham believes that the canonical heritage of the early church offers a vision of God that has not been diminished by epistemological criteria:

> I shall take as our target the vision of theism embodied in the canonical heritage of the church . . . canonical theism. . . . While it is impossible to avoid the shadow of artificiality here, this strategy of highlighting this particular expression of theism . . . [avoids] any form of theism that has been cut back to fit some favored epistemological vision. We allow the theism on offer to stand independently of its defence.[45]

These appeals to the patristic faith show that Abraham like Newman believes that a return to the faith of the early church provides a richer undiminished religion that has not been affected by theological reductionism. While Newman refers to this attenuation as liberalism and Abraham describes it as epistemological methodism the rationale behind Newman's appeals to the church of antiquity clearly resemble the reasoning behind Abraham's calls for the church to embrace the full canonical heritage of the early church.

Aristotelian epistemic fit

Newman and Abraham's shared opposition to theological reductionism leads these writers to take a different approach to epistemological questions. Chapter 2 demonstrated that Roderick Chisholm, Newman, and Abraham all use what the latter terms Aristotelian epistemic fit. As noted earlier, this expression refers to Aristotle's belief that "it is a mark of an educated person to look in each area for only that degree of accuracy that the nature of the subject permits."[46] What these writers infer from this statement is that the validity of a belief should be determined in an appropriate way. The following extract from Abraham illustrates the way in which he wants to apply this principle to Christian belief:

> I want to explore a network of basic observations on the logic of canonical theism that brings into sharp relief the particular insights that relate to the justification of canonical theism. I want to identify features of what is on offer so that we shall have an appropriate sense of the kinds of considerations that are relevant

---

45. Abraham, *Crossing*, 13–14.
46. Aristotle, *Nicomachean Ethics*, 4–5 [I.3 1094b13–28].

to its truth or falsehood. In short, we shall explore what emerges when we apply the principle of appropriate epistemic fit to canonical theism.[47]

This clearly contrasts Abraham's approach with the kind of theological reductionism brought about by figures such as the reformers. Rather than identifying a criterion at the beginning, he attends to the claims of canonical theism and then explores what sorts of rules ought to govern these antecedent theological statements of truth. In order to avoid making theological claims subordinate to a criterion, such as the canon of Scripture, Abraham follows Chisholm in beginning with particular claims to knowledge and then exploring the most suitable way to measure their validity. However, Abraham's application of Aristotelian epistemic fit to religious belief has more in common with Newman than Chisholm.

Chisholm's use of the principle of epistemic fit is entirely philosophical in its application. It is Newman's writings that anticipate Abraham's application of the principle of epistemic fit to Christian belief. Following Abraham's acknowledgment that he will use Aristotelian epistemic fit to explore the rationality of canonical theism he then proceeds to cite Newman as an example of how this should be done:

> My aim is to lay bare the epistemic suggestions that naturally but not necessarily emerge in the exposition of, appropriation of, and engagement with the epistemic proposals that lie below the surface of canonical theism. . . . [W]e need to include in our epistemic narrative softer components like cultivated insights, particular intuitions, specific experiences of God, the intellectual effects of conspicuous sanctity, and the like. Newman captured the tone and mode of this intellectual possibility in a memorable passage.[48]

This demonstrates that Abraham's evaluation of the rationality of Christian belief not only uses the same Aristotelian procedure as Newman but he also considers that Newman's work illustrates how the intellectual tone of canonical theism may be captured. This would imply that Newman's application of this Aristotelian principle to Christian faith gives Abraham's account of the epistemology of canonical theism a clearer articulation.

---

47. Abraham, *Crossing*, 41.
48. Abraham, *Crossing*, 51–52.

The "memorable passage" cited by Abraham refers to Newman's discussion of implicit reason in his Oxford University sermons. Abraham suggests that Newman's account of this natural mode of reasoning is able to reveal the complex intellectual substance that is canonical theism. This would indicate that Abraham views Newman's analysis of this mode of reasoning as an excellent example of how one should evaluate the rationality of Christian belief. The previous chapter illustrated how Newman's conception of reason had the potential to make a real contribution to Chisholm's philosophy. Citing Jay Newman's work it was argued that Newman's pliable account of reason has the potential to facilitate particularist approaches to knowledge with a criterion more malleable than the epistemic principles offered by Chisholm. Abraham cites the same article by Jay Newman in his essay "Cumulative Case Arguments for Christian Theism" (1987). While Abraham does not expand upon Jay Newman's insights it appears that he also recognizes the full potential of J. H. Newman's conception of reason because he believes that the complex factors involved in an individual's coming to faith are commensurate with Jay Newman's account of epistemic judgement.

In a number of other places Abraham cites Newman's work as an ideal example of how to explore the underlying logic governing the development of Christian doctrine. In his philosophical reflection on the "Church" (2010), Abraham describes Newman's account, in *An Essay on the Development of Christian Doctrine* (1845), of the logical continuity of Roman Catholic Christianity with the apostolic church, as a "felicitous articulation."[49] This statement is particularly interesting when it is understood that Newman applies Aristotle's principle, that different disciplines require different levels of precision, to his examination of the evidence supporting the doctrines of the nineteenth-century Catholic church. That Abraham considers Newman's examination of the same to be felicitous indicates that he considers Newman to be adept at applying what Abraham terms Aristotelian epistemic fit to religious belief. Here and elsewhere Abraham recognizes Newman's methods of analysis to be felicitous. For example, Abraham describes Newman's analysis of the historical development of Christianity in this way:

> The interpretation of Canonical Theism . . . is not a static affair. The handing over of the canonical heritage is accompanied by intense discussion . . . . John Henry Newman, with characteristic

---

49. Abraham, "Church," 177–78.

felicity, exaggerates only a little when he writes: "Nor is it an inferior faculty to discriminate, rescue, and adjust the truth, which a fierce controversy threatens to tear in pieces, at a time when the ecclesiastical atmosphere is thick with the dust of the conflict, when all parties are more or less in the wrong, and the public mind has become so bewildered as not to be able to say what it does or what it does not hold, or even what it held before the strife of ideas began. In such circumstances, to speak the word evoking order and peace, and to restore the multitude of men to themselves and to each other, by a reassertion of what is old with a luminousness of explanation which is new, is a gift inferior only to that of revelation itself."[50]

This illustrates how Newman's analysis of the intellectual development of theological truth within the church inspires Abraham. Furthermore, Abraham specifically states that in exploring the epistemic insights contained deep within the dense history of the church he will need to draw upon the labours of Newman.[51]

In summary, while there are differences between these writers, Newman and Abraham share a similar antagonist: theological reductionism. Moreover, it is apparent that Abraham sees a number of resonances between Newman's concerns about liberalism and epistemological methodism. In both instances, revelation is regulated by inappropriate rules. Mutual concerns about theological reductionism lead these writers to the faith of the early church—which they believe to be untarnished by rationalism. Furthermore, both these writers use what Abraham describes as Aristotelian epistemic fit. Abraham's repeated references to Newman's application of this Aristotelian principle to Christianity raise the question as to whether or not Newman informs Abraham's application of this methodology to the justification of religious belief. Thus, having indicated that Abraham may be shaped by Newman's application of what the latter refers to as Aristotelian epistemic fit, it is necessary to examine this possibility by exploring the way in which Abraham incorporates specific aspects of Newman's account of the grammar of faith in his particularist epistemology of Christian belief.[52]

---

50. Abraham, *Crossing*, 15.
51. Abraham, *Crossing*, 129.
52. Abraham, *Crossing*, 44, 51.

The Justification of Individual Christian Faith

As stated, Abraham follows Chisholm and begins with particular claims to knowledge and then explores what is the most suitable way to measure their validity. This operates at both a corporate and an individual level. Therefore, in examining the epistemology of canonical theism, Abraham's approach is to accept the canons of the church as items of knowledge and, retrospectively, to evaluate the considerations relevant to their justification using criteria appropriate to the truth claims at hand. Similarly, in evaluating the validity of an individual's belief, Abraham begins by accepting the believer's claims to revelation before, subsequently, examining the considerations relevant to their justification in a manner that does not diminish or reduce the content of these antecedent beliefs. As will be seen, all this resonates profoundly with Newman's thought.

Abraham's account of the justification of individual Christian faith

Perceiving God

Let us begin by examining Abraham's particularist account of the epistemology of individual belief. Like Chisholm, Abraham argues that people have knowledge without being aware of how they attained it. Applying this principle to religious belief, Abraham argues that people find themselves in possession of beliefs about God but are not always aware of how they have acquired those beliefs. He maintains that all human beings, by their nature, are able to sense God's presence. He considers that everyone is able to perceive God because they have a "spiritual" eye enabling them to recognize divine activity in the world.[53] He compares this innate capacity for divine revelation to a number of other human faculties, including sense perception, memory, and introspection. Abraham is not alone in making this argument. The twelfth-century writer Hugh of St Victor (1096–1141) argued that humankind has the implanted ability to perceive God.[54] While the legitimacy of religious experience has been

---

53. Abraham, *Crossing*, 48, 67.

54. He called this spiritual eye an *Oculus Contemplationis*. This phrase is used to denote the human capacity for a "natural knowledge of God's existence" in which "the soul apprehends God within herself." Copleston, *A History of Philosophy*, 2:177.

heavily criticized during the twentieth century,[55] William Alston and Alvin Plantinga have gone to great lengths to show the reliability of mystical perception.[56]

Abraham accepts that although some human beings believe they have perceptions of God, and as a result form theological beliefs, these initial claims may be bolstered by an accompanying explanation. This is not to say that these initial beliefs require validation but rather that they may be strengthened by explanatory theories. Abraham maintains however, that our initial perceptions of God are able to stand alone, in the absence of proof. He considers that as particularists it is necessary to treat these antecedent beliefs as genuine instances of knowledge.[57] This could leave him vulnerable to the charge of relativism,[58] since he clearly begs the question in favor of the theists' antecedent belief. Abraham anticipates this criticism,[59] but stresses that questions about the justification of beliefs should be discussed "postlegomenon." By this he means that a theist's antecedent experiences of God should not be ruled out because an arbitrary epistemological criterion has been presupposed from the beginning. As a particularist he considers that questions about the epistemology of religious belief should be investigated once the vision of God is secure. That way around, arguments are to be garnered in support of the beliefs already possessed.

---

55. Many writers argue that religious experiences are determined by the recipients cultural context. For a classic example, see Proudfoot, *Religious Experience*. There are also a number of general criticisms of the viability of religious experience: Freud, *The Future of an Illusion*, 51; Mackie, *The Miracle of Theism*, 186; Hear, *Experience Explanation and Faith*, 27; Martin, *Atheism*, Gale, *On the Nature*, 285.

56. Plantinga, *Warranted*; Alston, *Perceiving God*.

57. Abraham, *Crossing*, 73–74.

58. Martin makes a similar criticism of Plantinga for putting religious beliefs "beyond rational appraisal." Martin, *Atheism*, 276.

59. "Plunging straight like this into the content of Christian theology may frustrate even the most sympathetic reader. What about the question of truth? What about the justification of these theological claims? What about the criteria of theological inquiry? Surely, it will be said, it is these questions that ought to be foremost in the work of analytic theology. In fact it seems perverse not to tackle these questions up front." Abraham, "Systematic Theology as Analytic Theology," 66, 69.

Revelation and criticism

When examining the epistemology of an individual's Christian beliefs, Abraham considers that serious attention should be given to the person's testimony. He argues that the standard descriptions of how people come to have beliefs about God are inadequate. It is unlikely that Abraham is referring here to the study of religious conversion for there is an abundance of literature discussing this issue.[60] It seems rather that Abraham is referring to philosophical discussions of conversion for he maintains that the standard view of religious conversion sees coming to believe as a matter of evaluating the evidence for specific theistic propositions. In contrast to this view, Abraham argues that the embrace of religious belief is a world-constituting experience that revolutionizes one's perspective absolutely.[61]

In order to support his dramatic conception of conversion, Abraham employs the Damascene transformation of the apostle Paul as a paradigmatic case.[62] Reciting the transformation of Saul of Tarsus into Paul the apostle, Abraham argues that Saul's acceptance of the revelation of Jesus has irreversible consequences. In the case of Paul, Abraham's analysis is a valid interpretation of the effects of revelation on belief. Paul has a divine revelation, he accepts it immediately, and he acts upon it.[63] Abraham states that "Revelation", in the case of Paul, is clearly a single and absolute event that changes Paul's perception of reality forever.

To illustrate his point further, Abraham compares an experience of revelation to the panoramic vision attained at the summit of a mountain. While one ascends one has a limited view of the landscape. At the top one can see in all directions. He compares this enhanced perspective to the appropriation of revelation. Abraham also compares the acceptance of revelation to the attribution of legal guilt. His point here is that once the court's declaration has been made a new reality must be embraced.[64] In all of these analogies, Abraham is seeking to depict the acceptance of

---

60. There are numerous psychological studies of conversion. For example, see Zygmunt, "Movements and Motives," 449–67; Lofland, "Becoming a World-Saver revisited," 10–23; Rambo, *Understanding Religious Conversion*.

61. Abraham, *Crossing*, 80, 95, 127.

62. Abraham, *Crossing*, 79.

63. This interpretation is not uniform. To take a classic example, Inglis considers that Paul went through a subconscious struggle long before he even had a divine revelation. See Inglis, "The Problem of St Paul's conversion" 228.

64. Abraham, *Crossing*, 86–87.

revelation as a threshold that, once crossed, has transformative effect on one's whole field of vision. Abraham acknowledges that the process of crossing the threshold of divine revelation is difficult to quantify. Nevertheless, he maintains that four features stand out: (1) it is dramatic; (2) it has divine origins; (3) it inspires a faithful response; (4) it involves a cognitive revolution.[65]

Revelation and criticism

The above implies that Abraham views claims to revelation as being above and beyond rational criticism. Many passages in his writing appear to suggest that once attention is given to divine revelation by an individual it somehow takes the host captive. This would imply that its influence is final and absolute, that once an appeal to divine revelation is made, discussion concerning the rationality of a belief is over. Were this interpretation correct it would allow fundamentalists, religious extremists, and terrorists to justify attacks against all who disagree with them using a mistaken appeal to divine revelation.[66] In anticipation of these criticisms, Abraham stresses that those who make claims that they have received a divine revelation must be willing to face legitimate objections.[67]

Abraham holds that when an individual declares that they have received a divine revelation it is their duty to provide a supporting argument in order for this claim to be taken seriously.[68] He clarifies that each religious tradition will have its own internal criterion to measure the validity of these claims.[69] He stresses that these claims should not be measured using alien scientific criterion or a supposed "neutral" method or algorithm. On the contrary, he argues that each of these claims to revelation should be evaluated using the norms of the religious tradition itself.[70]

---

65. Abraham, *Crossing*, 89.

66. Esposito illustrates how readily claims to revelation have been used for the slaughter of innocent people in: Esposito, *Unholy War: Terror in the Name of Islam*, 65. Abraham is highly critical of those who use revelation as a guise to commit acts of terror: Abraham, *Shaking Hands with the Devil*.

67. Abraham, *Crossing*, 151.

68. Abraham, *Crossing*, 153.

69. Abraham, *Crossing*, 130.

70. Alston makes a similar point: "There is a problem of distinguishing the real

Having identified what he believes to be the correct approach to the justification of an individual's religious beliefs, Abraham illuminates his position using a fictional narrative that describes the conversion of "Ms Convert." To begin with, he maintains that Ms Convert had a natural ability to perceive God in creation. In addition he argues that she had a strong sense of God guiding and directing her own life. He explains that as she explored the Scriptures she gradually found herself drawn into the life of faith, eventually being baptized.[71] Abraham moves on from this to discuss the second reflective part of this convert's spiritual pilgrimage. At this stage, she begins to look for a number of reasons, formal and informal, to support her new-found faith. Answers to prayer, a sense of the coherence of Christian doctrine, and study of the traditional arguments for the existence of God all amounted to a confidence regarding the validity of her religious convictions. This assurance gave Ms Convert a sense that her belief in God was justified.[72]

Abraham uses this conversion narrative to capture his account of the epistemology of Christian belief. Essentially, he believes that a native capacity to perceive divine revelation can lead to belief in God. This faith is then reflected upon and strengthened through resources including Scripture and tradition. Abraham also discusses the epistemology of Christian doctrine itself, however, before examining this aspect of his thought it is necessary to explore whether Newman informs Abraham's discussion of the justification of an individual's religious beliefs.

Newman and Abraham's justification of individual faith

Having indicated his debt to both Chisholm and Newman earlier, it is necessary to examine the extent to which Abraham actually makes use of these writers in his account of the rationality of Christian belief. While our focus is upon whether or not Newman shapes Abraham's work it is necessary to elucidate two key ways in which Abraham echoes Chisholm.

First of all, Abraham is using Chisholm's particularist approach to knowledge, as is demonstrated in his decision to begin with the believer's

---

thing from imposters . . . we depend on the background theology and other aspects of the tradition for principles that lay down conditions under which what we are aware of is God." Alston, *Perceiving God*, 294.

71. Abraham, *Crossing*, 116–21.
72. Abraham, *Crossing*, 121–27.

existing network of theistic beliefs. Secondly, Abraham's contention that all human beings have a spiritual sense organ similar to Hugh of St Victor's *Oculus Contemplationis* (spiritual eye) clearly draws upon Chisholm's discussion of this phrase.[73] Chisholm writes:

> Hugh of St. Victor held, in the twelfth century, that in addition to the *oculus carnis*, by means of which we know the physical world, and the *oculus rationis*, by means of which we know our own states of mind, there is also an *oculus contemplationis* by means of which we know the truths of religion.[74]

Citing this passage from Chisholm's work, Abraham contends that human beings simply find themselves aware of the reality of God: "We experience God, as it were, straight off, as we perceive the World around us."[75] Abraham is adamant that these beliefs, and our general awareness of God, occur spontaneously.

This direct awareness of God fits with Abraham's decision to follow a particularist approach to knowledge. He emphasizes that the beliefs produced by the *Oculus Contemplationis* are basic. These beliefs arise naturally and are not preceded by theories of knowledge. They are not produced by a criterion of knowledge. This coheres with a particularist approach to knowledge because these spontaneous experiences of God occur prior to any proofs of theism or criterion.[76]

In *Crossing the Threshold of Divine Revelation* Abraham combines the human capacity for a direct awareness of God (the *Oculus Contemplationis*) with Newman's "illative sense." Abraham contends that a variety of complex explanations may be found to support our antecedent

---

73. Abraham, *Crossing*, 66n6.

74. Chisholm, *Theory of Knowledge*, 33–134.

75. Abraham, *Crossing*, 66–67.

76. Abraham, *Crossing*, 66–67. Though Abraham's conception of this innate ability to perceive God has similarities with Newman's conception of how (in conscience) one can become immediately aware of God, Merrigan is right to point out that, for Newman: "There is no suggestion here of a private revelation or of some sort of mystical encounter with God. God is present as the source of the phenomenon, and the person —most obviously the child . . . spontaneously apprehends Him in the [conscience]. . . . Hence conscience is described as the voice of God, or more accurately, the echo of God's voice in us." Thus Newman's understanding of the apprehension of God in conscience is different from Abraham's account of how individual's can receive new revelations of God. For further discussion, see Merrigan, "Revelation," 50–51.

experiences of God.[77] To illustrate the informal nature of these arguments, Abraham cites the following example:

> One's initial sense that God has spoken in a special way, say, through Jeremiah, may cohere with and thus be strengthened by his avowals about his call, by the way his message dovetails with earlier revelation, by the depth of his message, by the ensuing events, and the like.[78]

There are, therefore, a variety of different reasons that support, cohere with, and strengthen, the conviction that God has spoken through Jeremiah[79] Abraham stresses that these grounds are so multifaceted that it is difficult to commensurate them formally. In order to unravel this complexity Abraham introduces Newman's "illative sense":

> If there is an additional sense, then we can posit an illative sense, that is, a capacity to perceive below the surface of our formal reasoning so as to frame and to test hypotheses informally.[80]

In this extract Abraham indicates how Newman's conception of the illative sense could function in such a way as to validate informal explanations for an individual's claims to divine revelation. What does Abraham mean by this? How does he envisage that Newman's illative sense functions in this context? The answer to these questions is indicated in other texts that will now be considered.

When analyzing Newman's *Grammar* in *Canon and Criterion*, Abraham states that:

> It is not possible to provide a formal calculus of all the factors which rightly have a place in the formation of our judgement as to what constitutes divine reality or divine judgement. We can, and should, seek to analyse the various considerations which play a role in coming to relevant conclusions, but this is a hazardous process. . . . We operate according to our illative sense; this is the heart of the matter from an epistemological point of view.[81]

---

77. Abraham, *Crossing*, 70.
78. Abraham, *Crossing*, 73–74.
79. Abraham, *Crossing*, 76.
80. Abraham, *Crossing*, 70.
81. Abraham, *Canon and Criterion*, 341.

Here Abraham interprets Newman's illative sense as having the potential to enable believers to view the miscellaneous signs, which individually would be insufficient to justify their claim to revelation, as a whole so as to confirm the validity of their initial perception of God:

> Newman's answer to [this] question of the identification of special revelation is that we become aware of divine revelation through a variety of signs which, taken together, constitute entirely sufficient evidence for the claim that God has spoken to us.[82]

Abraham considers that if we are to understand the theists' "deep intellectual structure" it is better to combine the *Oculus Contemplationis* with the illative sense. He writes:

> The best way to think of that deep structure is to see it as positing an initial *oculus contemptationis* complemented by an illative sense that does indeed form complex explanatory theories that are supported by the same experiences that trigger our initial beliefs about God.[83]

The above indicates that in addition to drawing upon Chisholm's discussion of the *Oculus Contemplationis,* Abraham combines this basic theistic belief-forming mechanism with Newman's conception of the illative sense. Thus, he considers that the experiences that trigger our initial beliefs about God are justified by the individual locating informal reasons in their support using their illative sense. Abraham's combination of the *Oculus Contemplationis* with this dimension of Newman's work offers an example of how Newman's work is relevant to particularist writers.[84]

The previous chapter examined Maddox's contention that the role of the illative sense in simple assent rendered Newman vulnerable to the charge of epistemological methodism. This was because of the analytic features of the illative sense. Abraham's approach, above, resolves the difficulty posed by Maddox's analysis. Since Abraham considers that one's initial beliefs about God are acquired through an immediate—"bedrock"—belief-forming mechanism, and the illative sense is only active retrospectively in examining the veracity of these theistic

---

82. Abraham, *Canon and Criterion*, 340–41.

83. Abraham, *Crossing*, 72.

84. It should be stressed here that Newman would not sanction the idea, implied in Abraham's conception of the *Oculus Contemplationis*, that individuals can obtain new "private" revelations from God. Merrigan, "Revelation," 51.

assumptions, then the charge of methodism can no longer be applied. Thus, Abraham shows how an aspect of Newman's thought can be readily incorporated into a particularist account of the epistemology of Christian belief. Abraham acknowledges directly how Newman's felicitous analysis of the reasons that lead one to faith enable him to capture the way in which a convert forms explanatory theories to support the radical particularity of this very personal commitment.[85]

From the above it is clear that Abraham's discussion of believers' direct awareness of God is drawn from Chisholm's references to Hugh of St Victor.[86] While Abraham's contention that believers spontaneously acquire beliefs about God has parallels with Newman's discussion of simple assent, Newman makes no reference to the *Oculus Contemplationis*. Nevertheless, Abraham's account of the formation of complex explanatory theories has parallels with Newman's discussion of reflex assent and his use of the terms "illative sense" is informed by Newman's *Grammar of Assent*.

Abraham's concept of revelation compared with Newman's discussion of assent

Abraham's discussion of revelation as a threshold concept has similarities with Newman's discussion of assent. Though Abraham's conception of revelation differs from Newman his analysis of how individuals interact with divine truth has similarities with Newman's discussion of assent. For example, it was noted that Abraham compares receiving a revelation to crossing a geographical threshold:

> Once revelation is recognized, then the threshold has been crossed. Once one acknowledges the revelation, then everything may have to be rethought and redescribed in the light of what has been found . . . one enters a whole new world that requires extensive unpacking and intense reflection.[87]

The concept of a threshold is spatial but Abraham is using it metaphorically in order to explain that the acceptance of revelation re-orientates an individual's whole field of vision.

---

85. Abraham, *Crossing*, 51–52.

86. Abraham may well have read Hugh of St Victor. Nevertheless, Abraham's epistemological discussion of the *Oculus Contemplationis* refers to Chisholm's work.

87. Abraham, *Crossing*, 86–87.

While Abraham's version of crossing the threshold of divine revelation is informed by the apostle Paul's dramatic conversion, it is clear that Newman's analysis of assent is not quite so "dramatic" as the "Damascus" road experience. However, Abraham acknowledges that "there are other ways to unpack the image of a threshold" and mentions Ferreira's, *Scepticism and Reasonable Doubt* (1986) as an example.[88]

What is notable here is that Ferreira interprets Newman's discussion of assent as a "threshold" concept.[89] On this reading of Newman's *Grammar*, the mind crosses a threshold when it assents to a proposition.[90] Once one gives assent, nothing can make that assent stronger. Ferreira quotes from Newman the following example:

> Certitude does not admit of more or less—but is a state of mind, definite and complete, admitting only of being and not-being. To fancy that it may be strengthened, is to imply that it has never been attained.[91]

Ferreira argues that Newman's notion of certainty indicates that all certainty is equal. Hence, once the threshold of certainty is crossed it is absolute.[92]

From this it seems possible that Ferreira's interpretation of Newman's concept of assent, as a threshold category, impacts upon Abraham's conception of conversion to Christianity as "crossing the threshold of divine revelation." This possibility is strengthened by Abraham's analysis of Newman's *Grammar of Assent* in *Canon and Criterion*:

> In the case of the recognition of divine revelation. Coming to believe that Christianity indeed possesses a divine revelation rests on the exercise of the illative sense on a variety of subtle considerations. However, once we come to the point where we recognize the revelation for what it is, we reach a threshold. While the initial, foundational process is one of probability or plausibility, once we have satisfied ourselves that we are in possession of divine revelation, our commitment to the revelation is unconditional and certain. We pass, as it were, a threshold from probability to infallibility because the content of the identified

---

88. Abraham, *Crossing*, 85n14.
89. Ferreira, *Scepticism*, 186–88.
90. Ferreira, *Scepticism*, 186–88.
91. *TP*, 1:124; Ferreira, *Scepticism*, 186–88.
92. Newman, *Grammar*, 150 [*GA*, 157].

revelation is now guaranteed by God, whose Word merits unconditional and absolute assent.[93]

In this extended quotation Abraham describes Newman's account of an individual's unconditional assent to "God's Word" using the following terms: "we pass as it were a threshold." This indicates that Abraham, like Ferreira, views assent as a threshold concept.

The fact that Abraham discusses assent in terms of *passing* a threshold, also indicates the possibility that his conception of *crossing* the threshold of divine revelation is shaped by Newman's discussion of assent. For example, the similarity between the following quotations from Abraham and Newman is striking:

> [Abraham] The cords that connect us to a divine revelation initially look rather weak and frayed. It is easy to dismiss them as weak and flimsy and ephemeral. Equally it is tempting to bolster them with miracles and other surefire guarantees. Thus we seesaw back and forth between suspicion and intellectual overreach. There is another way. We begin where we are, taking seriously the epistemic capacities and platitudes that lie to hand. In due course we discover that the weak and frayed cords that connect us to divine revelation are but the outward covering for a steel cable with many interconnecting strands that can more than support us. Or at least that is how it turns out for the mature believer who has crossed over the threshold of divine revelation.[94]

> [Newman] The best illustration of what I hold is that of a cable, which is made up of a number of separate threads, each feeble, yet together as sufficient as an iron rod. An iron rod represents mathematical or strict demonstration; a cable represents moral demonstration, which is an assemblage of probabilities, separately insufficient for certainty, but, when put together, irrefragable. A man who said, "I cannot trust a cable, I must have an iron bar," would in certain given cases, be irrational and unreasonable:—so too is a man who says I must have a rigid demonstration, not moral demonstration, of religious truth.[95]

---

93. It is important to emphasize here that Newman's discussion of an individuals recognition of revelation refers to existing revelation, that is revelation that has already been given. Abraham, *Canon and Criterion*, 341–42.

94. Abraham, *Crossing*, 128.

95. LD 21:146.

Though Abraham is discussing revelation and Newman is describing assent both of these descriptions utilise the same image. Each reference depicts the informal evidence accumulated before an assent as the converging cords of a "cable" of certainty. This convergence is designed to capture a critical threshold after which one becomes so convinced of a truth that further evidence is unnecessary. Most important, however, is that Abraham uses an image which Newman employs to describe assent in order to clarify the nature of crossing the threshold of divine revelation. This indicates two things: first, Abraham's discussion of revelation, as a threshold concept, is informed by Ferreira's account of Newman's discussion of assent; second, Abraham's discussion is also shaped by Newman.

In summary, it seems that Abraham's discussion of revelation, as a threshold concept, is informed by Ferreira's interpretation of Newman's concept of assent. Whilst Newman spoke of assent, Abraham speaks of revelation. On this view, the acceptance of Christianity is understood in terms of crossing a metaphorical threshold. While Abraham's account draws heavily upon the experience of St Paul, his discussion of the threshold of revelation being "complete and absolute" has clear parallels with Newman's discussion of assent. Furthermore, Abraham's use of the same illustration, the cable analogy found in Newman's correspondence, indicates that Abraham's conception of crossing the threshold of revelation is influenced directly by Newman.

Revelation, criticism, and complex assent

Abraham and Newman both argue that religious beliefs must be thoroughly investigated. Newman called this process of investigating our simple assents "complex assent" (or reflex assent).[96] What is interesting here is that Abraham discusses this issue using similar terms to Newman:

> [Abraham] To be sure, there are *complex* levels of *assent* in believing.[97]

As noted above Newman discusses this process of investigating our simple assents in the *Grammar of Assent* under the heading "Complex

---

96. Newman, *Grammar*, 188–94.
97. Abraham, *Crossing*, 143. Emphasis mine.

Assent."[98] Abraham's contention that all claims to revelation should be investigated are couched in similar terminology as evidenced from the extract above from *Crossing the Threshold*. This likeness could be swept aside as coincidental were it not the case that further similarities between Newman's discussion of complex assent and Abraham's discussion can be found.

Both writers consider that an investigation into the proofs supporting our beliefs is an obligation:

> [Newman] I consider that, in the case of educated minds, investigations into the argumentative proof of the things to which they have given their assent, is an obligation, or rather a necessity.[99]

> [Abraham] Proponents of divine revelation need to advance in some detail the particular claims they think are secured, the relevant epistemic considerations they deem appropriate, the precise arguments they think strengthen their case, and the way they propose to handle standard defeaters and objections. . . . It is the mark of a serious theological tradition derived from divine revelation to own up to this responsibility and explain itself in public.[100]

Here Abraham and Newman argue that it is a responsibility of people to investigate the evidence supporting their beliefs. Thus, like Newman with regard to assent, Abraham considers that those who make claims that they have received a divine revelation must be willing to face objections.[101] Abraham considers that when a claim to divine revelation is made, the person who made that claim should be encouraged to take seriously their duty to provide a specific argument or backing for it.[102]

Secondly, both Newman and Abraham argue that an examination of the evidence supporting our beliefs can result in loss of faith:

> [Newman] Certainly, such processes of investigation, whether in religious subjects or secular, often issue in the reversal of the assents which they were originally intended to confirm.[103]

98. Newman, *Grammar*, 188–94.
99. Newman, *Grammar*, 185 [*GA*, 192].
100. Abraham, *Crossing*, 153.
101. Abraham, *Crossing*, 151.
102. Abraham, *Crossing*, 153.
103. Newman, *Grammar*, 185 [*GA*, 192–393].

> [Abraham] Claims to divine revelation can be undermined and falsified; they can be subjected to strain; they can be overturned by a review of the status of our cognitive capacities; they can be challenged by the undercutting of the evidence advanced in their favour or by new evidence.[104]

Here both Newman and Abraham argue that an examination of the evidence supporting an individual's religious beliefs can result in them being invalidated.

There is, however, a difference between their respective accounts. Abraham maintains that an individual's commitment to a revelation must always be conditional in character so that a claim may be thoroughly investigated concerning its validity.[105] All this may appear to contrast Abraham with Newman for whom the distinctive characteristic of assent, as contrasted with inference, is that it is an unconditional act (whereas inference is a conditional one); whereas for Abraham commitment to revelation is conditional. Regardless of their semantic differences, however, Abraham's discussion of the commitment to claims to revelation is similar to Newman's discussion of assent. Whilst Newman may have felt that assent was an unconditional act, he is careful to point out that this does not mean it is immune to investigation:

> But the question before us is whether acts of assent and of inference are compatible; and my vague consciousness of the possibility of a reversal of my belief in the course of my researches, as little interferes with the honesty and firmness of that belief while those researches proceed, as the recognition of the possibility of my train's oversetting is an evidence of an intention on my part of undergoing so great a calamity. My mind is not moved by a scientific computation of chances, nor can any law of averages affect my particular case. To incur a risk is not to expect reverse; and if my opinions are true, I have a right to think that they will bear examining.[106]

Hence, Newman makes emphatically clear that it remains possible to unconditionally assent to a proposition, without doubting its validity, while simultaneously investigating its legitimacy. Therefore, like Abraham he believes that all our spontaneous beliefs must be subjected to analysis.

---

104. Abraham, *Crossing*, 143.
105. Abraham, *Crossing*, 143.
106. Newman, *Grammar*, 186 [*GA*, 193].

In summary, Abraham's recommendation that proponents of a revelation should always be prepared to advance their reasons (whether demonstrative or not) for their claims to revelation (being willing also to face objections to their claims), is also similar to Newman's contention that our simple assents should be investigated in order to explore what demonstrative evidences may be favorable to our simple assents. Both use similar terminology to describe this activity; both consider it to be an obligation; both acknowledge that this investigation can result in loss of faith. Although Newman considers our simple assents unconditional acts (whilst Abraham considers commitment to revelation should always remain conditional), he too like Abraham considers that (complex assent) this process of investigation can cause the reversal of the assents which they were intended to confirm.[107] Thus both maintain that all claims to revelation, all assents to propositions, should be investigated in order to ascertain what evidence they have in their favor.

Newman and the story of Ms Convert

As noted above, Abraham uses a conversion narrative in order to illustrate the various components and workings of the theist's intellectual structure before and after crossing the threshold of divine revelation. It is interesting that Abraham depicts the process of conversion in a manner similar to the *Grammar*'s discussion of simple and complex (reflex) assent.[108]

Several features of Abraham's account of the first spontaneous stage of Ms Convert's journey resonate with Newman's illustration of the nature of simple assent using the example of a child's natural assent to faith:

> [Newman] First, it involves the impression on his mind of an unseen Being with whom he is in immediate relation;... next, of One whose goodwill towards him he is assured of, and can take for granted—nay, who loves him better, and is nearer to him, than his parents; further, of One who can hear him, wherever he happens to be, and who can read his thoughts, for his prayer need not be vocal; lastly, of One who can effect a critical change in the state of feeling of others towards him. That is, we shall not be wrong in holding that this child has in his mind the image of an invisible Being, who exercises a particular providence among us, who is present everywhere, who is heart-reading,

---

107. Newman, *Grammar*, 188–94.
108. Abraham, *Crossing*, 129.

> heart-changing, ever-accessible. . . . What a strong and intimate vision of God must he have already attained if, as I have supposed, an ordinary trouble of mind has the spontaneous effect of leading him for consolation and aid to an Invisible Personal Power![109]

This has several similarities with the Ms Convert narrative. First of all both writers argue that before conversion both the child in Newman's story and Ms Convert have an unprompted sense of God's existence.[110] Secondly each of these characters attained a spontaneous impression of God's providence and care.[111] In each case the characters are drawn to believe naturally without knowing the reasons in support of their religious assents. Thus, Newman's discussion of a child's assent to faith matches a number of aspects in the first part of the Ms Convert narrative.

The second stage of Ms Convert's story also indicates similarities with Newman's conception of natural inference and converging probabilities found in the *Grammar*. It has been shown that Abraham engages with this aspect of Newman's thought in his "Cumulative Case Arguments for Christian Theism" (1987).[112] As discussed in the previous chapter, Newman argues that many of our assents are justified by the combination of informal reasons which converge upon the mind leading it to assent:

> The conclusion in a real or concrete question is foreseen and predicted rather than actually attained; foreseen in the number and direction of accumulated premises, which all converge to it, and as the result of their combination, approach it more nearly than any assignable difference, yet do not touch it logically (though only not touching it,) on account of the nature of its subject-matter, and the delicate and implicit character of at least part of the reasonings on which it depends. It is by the strength, variety, or multiplicity of premises, which are only probable . . . . [B]y all these ways, and many others, it is that the practised and experienced mind is able to make a sure divination that a conclusion is inevitable, of which his lines of reasoning do not actually put him in possession.[113]

---

109. Newman, *Grammar*, 109–10 [*GA*, 112–13].

110. It is important to emphasize that for Newman the awareness of God's existence is not a new, private revelation.

111. Abraham, *Crossing*, 116–17.

112. Abraham, "Cumulative Case Arguments," 17–37.

113. Newman, *Grammar*, 313–14.

This extract from the *Grammar* argues that a variety of evidences, which considered individually do not demonstrate a conclusion, can be combined to provide cogency. Newman argues that the combined force of these converging probabilities leads the individual to reflex (or complex) assent. Abraham's account of the way in which Ms Convert sought to come to terms with crossing the threshold of divine revelation utilizes this image of converging probabilities. For example, Abraham lists a number of unrelated informal reasons supporting Ms Convert's spontaneous assent to divine revelation. He argues that initially she found support for divine revelation in answers to prayer. She later found coherence in Christian doctrine. She found the ontological, cosmological, and teleological arguments also bolstered her faith. She also began to resolve obstacles to faith. Finally, she felt that her new-found faith enabled her to see and know more clearly. Abraham acknowledges that considered separately the threads linking Ms Convert with divine revelation do not prove decisive enough to justify her connection to God. Nevertheless, he maintains that while individually these reasons appear insufficient, when the various elements combine together they provide mutual support and give credibility to commitment and faith.[114] Abraham's understanding of converging probabilities, as depicted here, corresponds with Newman's *Grammar*. This indicates that Newman has shaped this dimension of Abraham's account.

In this narrative Abraham illustrates how the constituents of the theist's noetic structure operate in an individual conversion to Christianity. His account captures the way in which coming to believe in divine revelation entails a threshold after which one may still engage in critical reflection upon the experience. This has similarities with the analysis of Newman's *Grammar of Assent* presented in the previous chapter, in which one unconditionally accepts a proposition through simple assent, and yet may reflect upon its veracity retrospectively through complex (reflex) assent.

The above indicates that Abraham's particularist account of the epistemology of Christian belief draws upon Newman's writings in a number of ways. While Abraham is informed by Chisholm's discussion of the *Oculus Contemplationis* he combines this "bedrock" belief forming capacity with Newman's illative sense. This terminology is taken from the *Grammar*. Moreover, it is apparent that this aspect of Newman's thought

---

114. Abraham, *Crossing*, 121–28.

shapes Abraham's discussion of the complex explanatory theories formed retrospectively in order to locate reasons in support of these basic religious experiences. In combining these two senses, Abraham challenges Maddox's (epistemological methodist) interpretation of the illative sense; he also illustrates how Jay Newman's suggestion—that this part of J. H. Newman's thought can enhance the particularist approach—may be realized.

It would also appear that Ferreira's interpretation of Newman's discussion of assent as a threshold category informs Abraham's account of crossing the threshold of divine revelation. Abraham considers that revelation is an absolute experience which, once acquired, changes one's perspective. While there are differences between their conceptions of revelation this clearly has parallels with Newman's discussion of simple assent as something which, once possessed, is also absolute in character. While Newman refers to assent as an unconditional act, Abraham's account of revelation deems it as something that can be accepted conditionally. Nonetheless, both writers consider that crossing the threshold of assent or revelation can be reversed. Furthermore, Abraham allows criticism of revelation. This too has parallels with Newman's discussion of complex (reflex) assent. Finally Abraham's account of conversion is strikingly parallel to Newman's thought. These points indicate that Newman contributes to Abraham's particularist account of the epistemology of religious belief. Therefore, having examined the way in which Newman informs Abraham's discussion of an individual's commitment to Christian faith, it is necessary to explore if Newman informs Abraham's discussion of the epistemic considerations relevant to the justification of Christian doctrine.

The Epistemology of Canonical Theism

The justification of canonical doctrine

In his account of the epistemology of canonical theism, Abraham reiterates that one should adopt an approach which involves epistemological particularism and the Aristotelian principle of appropriate epistemic fit. This approach requires him to measure the rationality of the church's canonical heritage by working out the considerations most suited to such an assessment. As a particularist, Abraham begins with the canonical materials of the church and examines what reasons those who believe in these materials claim as their warrant for believing.[115] He maintains that one of "the epistemic suggestions" that naturally lies "below the surface of canonical theism" is an appeal to divine revelation.[116] Therefore, Abraham examines how the canonical doctrines of the early church might be justified by divine revelation.[117]

Abraham approaches the epistemology of canonical theism in the same way as he discussed the justification of individual Christian faith. As before, he posits an *Oculus Contemplationis,* but here it is corporate: the spiritual senses of the whole church (the *sensus fidelium* or "sense of the faithful"). As with individuals, Abraham argues that the church as a collection of people has a corporate sense of the revelation of God.[118] However, Abraham registers the limitations of this spiritual eye. He stresses that it is not possible to go straight from the "inner witness of the Holy Spirit to the doctrine of the Trinity."[119] He argues that because human beings cannot take in the magnitude of God's revelation all at once doctrines take time to develop. He maintains that this period is needed for the church to contemplate worshipfully and theologically on the divine revelation it has received. Doctrines do not emerge straight away, but can take centuries to come into view.[120] For Abraham, revelation is ongoing.[121] This conception of revelation is thus different from that of Newman whose references to the *sensus fidelium* refer to the inspiration of the church rather than to ongoing revelation.

Abraham concludes that the canonical heritage is created by the accumulated effects of divine revelation upon the church over time.[122] Abraham explains that:

---

115. Abraham, *Crossing,* 44.
116. Abraham, *Crossing,* 51.
117. Abraham, *Crossing,* 95.
118. Abraham, *Crossing,* 108.
119. Abraham, *Crossing,* 97.
120. Abraham, *Crossing,* 102, 105.

121. While Abraham stresses that divine revelation is definitively given in Christ, that there is no ongoing revelation on a par with the incarnation, his decision to privilege the canonical life of the church prior to 1054 implies that revelation is (in some sense) ongoing—at the very least until the schism between East and West. Abraham, *Crossing,* 105.

122. Here he criticizes writers such as Plantinga who, according to Abraham, consider that the doctrines of the church can be justified without appealing to the church's testimony. Abraham, *Crossing,* 49, 106–7.

> From the beginning, special revelation in Israel created a very special people. The soteriological intention embedded in Israel worked itself out in the formation of a community with a long history that culminated in the renewal of Israel in and through the life, death, and resurrection of Jesus of Nazareth . . . . It was within this community that the extra special revelation made through Jesus of Nazareth was effected, recognized and received. It was in the community created by Jesus that this revelation was treasured, recorded preached, mulled over, and transmitted across the generations . . . . [Here] There is an ordered progression of divine revelation in Israel and in the church that operates as pivotal data in the very particular vision of God that emerges over time.[123]

Hence, Abraham believes that the church's canons arose out of the deep interaction of the special revelation of God. He acknowledges that because the canonical heritage takes time to emerge it is difficult to be precise concerning the nature of the connection between divine revelation and the doctrines of the church. He writes: "no matter how we explain the relationship" there is always "a significant gap between the vision of revelation embraced and the doctrines adopted."[124] However, he states that:

> If we must work with . . . summary statements, we might say that the doctrine of the Trinity arose over time out of the deep interaction of the special revelation of God in Israel, the extra special revelation of God in Jesus Christ, experience of God in the Holy Spirit, and sanctified creative imagination and reason.[125]

Thus Abraham concedes that the relationship between revelation and the canonical heritage is "multidimensional, informal, and indirect."[126] On this understanding the canonical heritage of the church is given to the church over time by the Holy Spirit.

Therefore, Abraham concludes that the canons of the church are justified by revelation. He considers that in their own special way all of the church's canons are connected to divine revelation because of a complex interaction between revelation and the church.[127] While he recognizes that it is not easy to describe the character of the relationship between the

123. Abraham, *Crossing*, 105.
124. Abraham, *Crossing*, 102.
125. Abraham, *Crossing*, 106.
126. Abraham, *Crossing*, 106.
127. Abraham, *Crossing*, 110.

doctrines of the church and divine revelation, it is not satisfactory simply to say that the doctrine of the Trinity arose over time because of the guidance of the Holy Spirit. While he believes this doctrine to be justified by divine revelation, this position could be consolidated by showing how this aspect of the canonical heritage is continuous with other canonical materials. In other words, he could apply the principle of Aristotelian epistemic fit more fully to canonical theism in order to uncover the connections between the different aspects of the church's canonical heritage. Were Abraham to do this, it would strengthen his contention that all the canonical materials are inspired by the same source.

Another problem with Abraham's proposal is that he needs to specify which church he is referring to when he states that the canonical heritage is a result of the church's experience of God. Which church does he believe that the revelation of God has interacted with over time? Abraham has explained that canonical theism relates to the canons approved before the schism between East and West in 1054.[128] However, there has not existed a church which only accepts the canons that were approved prior to this schism. Currently, one would either need some sort of time machine in order to enter that church, or one would require all the Christian denominations, including the Roman Catholic, the Orthodox, and the numerous Protestant churches (and the rest) to unite, accept Abraham's conception of revelation, and agree only to hold those canons which were agreed before the schism, and thus abandon any canons adopted since that time. The likelihood of either of these options does not seem too probable.

Despite this, Abraham inextricably links acceptance of the Christian revelation to the initiation into a concrete ecclesial body. He writes:

> To join the body of Christ, one cannot avoid joining some concrete, particular body of believers at some particular place in space and time. To claim that one belongs to the church universal but that this doesn't entail belonging to some specific body of believers is a sham . . . one cannot join the Christian community without being involved in some *particular* Christian community. These particular Christian communities are not just physical entities of brick and mortar; they are expressions of Christian tradition.[129]

---

128. Abraham, *Crossing*, 14–15.
129. Abraham, *Coming Great Revival*, 3–4.

Abraham is adamant that God's grace is mediated through a real concrete ecclesial community. He writes:

> Grace does not . . . [work] in a vacuum. God is free to work as and how he pleases, yet he has covenanted to work in and through baptism, through the Eucharist, through fellowship . . . and so on. To omit these from initiation is to treat grace as unrelated to the concrete, physical character of our existence . . . . [I]nitiation is [thus] intrinsically related to physical incorporation into the church through baptism.[130]

He also states that:

> God in his reign has established his eschatological community. It is therefore incoherent to say that one can enter that reign but remain outside the church. Baptism is inescapable and essential, once one grasps this point, for it is through baptism that one enters the Israel of God, that body where God reigns supreme in worship and praise.[131]

Abraham's understanding of revelation is that its acceptance relates to a "concrete initiation into the flesh and blood of the Christian community."[132] Thus, Abraham's concept of the way in which revelation interacts with the church is linked to the idea of a definite physical community. That is, Abraham's concept of the church as a carrier of revelation is a concept which requires a real ecclesiological root.

The above indicates that the ecclesiological vacuum in Abraham's account poses an epistemological problem. This makes questions about his ecclesiological inclinations pertinent to the present enquiry.[133] Abraham does acknowledge that his vision of "canonical theism" might appear "untidy,"[134] however he does not seem to resolve the implications raised by his contention that the church is a carrier of revelation. Abraham does state that "the eastern wing of the church during and after the schism" has maintained the canonical heritage "in keeping with the canonical vision of the early church."[135] If Abraham modified his conception of

---

130. Abraham, *Logic of Evangelism*, 130.

131. Abraham, *Logic of Evangelism*, 130.

132. Abraham, *Logic of Evangelism*, 128–29.

133. A similar problem was faced by Newman in that he felt that Anglicanism was unable to sustain his theological commitments.

134. Abraham, *Crossing*, 15.

135. Abraham, *Canon and Criterion*, 113–14.

revelation,[136] and became a member of the Orthodox Church, he could coherently argue that the canonical heritage of the Orthodox Church is justified by the mediation of the revelation of God through that institution.[137] However, despite his apparent inclination toward the Orthodox Church, Abraham remains a member of the American United Methodist Church, which by his own admission[138] is far from upholding only the canons held "prior to the great schism" between East and West. Thus, whilst it is clear that Abraham does not see the American United Methodist Church as a bearer of the canonical faith of the church prior to the schism between East and West, it is unlikely that he is about to leave the United Methodist Church and join the Eastern Orthodox Church.

The confusion regarding Abraham's ecclesiology is not abnormal for a United Methodist (or a British one). A number of Methodist theologians display an ambiguity about whether the Methodist church ought really to be regarded as a church at all. Albert Outler,[139] David Chapman;[140] Geoffrey Wainwright;[141] and David Carter[142] among others consider that the Methodist Church would function better as a religious order within the wider Catholic church.[143] Within the context of United Methodism and British Methodism, there is an attempt to look to other traditions for a more robust ecclesial vision. Abraham's attempt to locate his ecclesial identity in the early church is not out of place when this factor is taken into consideration. Nevertheless, this ecclesial quandary clearly undermines the veracity of canonical theism. While Abraham believes that

---

136. The Eastern Orthodox tradition rejects the notion of continuous revelation. For further discussions, see Ware, *Orthodox Church*.

137. Other writers note Abraham's apparent attraction to the Orthodox Church. Moberly, "Scripture as a means of Grace," 119; Griffiths, "Canon and Criterion in Christian Theology," 266; Webster, "Canon and Criterion," 229.

138. Abraham, *Waking from Doctrinal Amnesia*.

139. Oden et al., *The Wesleyan Theological Heritage*.

140. Chapman, *In Search of the Catholic Spirit*.

141. Wainwright, *The Ecumenical Moment*.

142. Carter, *Love Bade Me Welcome*.

143. The great Wesleyan scholar Albert Outler perceives that there is a lack of Methodist consensus regarding ecclesiology and regarding the question of whether Methodists have a doctrine of the church. He considers that Methodism does not work well alone and would function better within a Catholic church as an evangelical order of both witness and worship, discipline and nurture. For further discussion, see Oden et al., *The Wesleyan Theological Heritage*, 212–26.

canonical theism is justified by the interaction of revelation within the church, he fails to explain which church is the carrier of revelation.

In summary, Abraham holds that the canonical heritage is justified by divine revelation. He considers that the church has a natural capacity to perceive revelation collectively. He contends also that the church's doctrines are the result of an accumulation of revelation over the centuries because understanding the nature of this revelation is a process that takes time. These points, however, raise questions about how this interaction takes place and about Abraham's ecclesiological inclinations. Therefore, having introduced Abraham's discussion of the epistemology of canonical theism we now examine whether Abraham's application of the principle of epistemic fit to canonical theism draws upon Newman's work. More specifically we will examine whether: Abraham's discussion of the church's corporate sense of God is informed by Newman's work, if Abraham's account of the church's appropriation of divine revelation has parallels with Newman's *Essay on Development*; if Newman's *Essay* can resolve problems in Abraham's account; and, finally, if Newman offers a solution to the epistemological problem caused by Abraham's ecclesiological predicament.

Newman and the epistemology of canonical theism

Newman and Abraham on the sensus fidelium

In his analysis of the relationship between divine revelation and the church, Abraham specifically acknowledges the importance of Newman's essay "On Consulting the Faithful." Citing Newman, Abraham argues that the doctrines of the church gradually arose over time, as a result of the interaction of divine revelation within the church.[144] Abraham thus views the church as a "charismatic community" that has a "communal" sense of the ongoing revelation of God.[145]

Newman's essay *On Consulting the Faithful* (1859) was introduced in chapter 3. In this work Newman argues that "the Christian people at

---

144. Abraham, *Crossing*, 108n5.
145. Abraham, *Crossing*, 107–8.

large"[146] are witnesses to the "tradition of revealed doctrine."[147] Newman describes them as the "voice" of the Christian tradition.[148] However, Newman would reject the notion, implied in Abraham's work, that revelation is ongoing.[149] Abraham suggests that, after the "once-for-all revelation" of Jesus Christ, the church has continued to receive revelation in some form.[150] For Newman the consensus of the faithful offers a manifestation of the "tradition of the apostles" since the deposit of revelation was given to the church at the beginning.[151] Thus, Newman maintains that the contemporary church "does not know more than the Apostles knew."[152] He believes, nevertheless, that the Holy Spirit continues to "inspire", "breathe" grace into, the church enabling the devout to act as an authentic witness to the revelation that is already in its possession.[153]

It is apparent that Newman holds, simultaneously,[154] that the apostles received the deposit of revelation in full and yet he considers that over time, the laity is given the grace to manifest this revelation.[155] This tension in Newman's account is exploited by Abraham in that he uses

---

146. Newman's essay was originally published as an article during his editorship of a periodical called *The Rambler* In this role Newman aimed to elevate "the intellect in the educated classes," and to "combine devotion to the Church" with "freedom of thought." LD 19: 88, 96, 131.

147. Newman, "On Consulting the Faithful," 205.

148. Newman, "On Consulting the Faithful," 214.

149. Elsewhere, Abraham acknowledges his divergence from Newman on this point: "The idea that all revelation is given completely and fully to the early apostles is artificial and strained. Newman's case at this point is, of course, a subtle and complex one. It is only implicit revelation which has been given to the apostles; this implicit material is then developed in an explicit way under appropriate circumstances. Even in this form the thesis is unconvincing. It is more fitting to allow for genuine development above and beyond what would be recognized by the apostles." Abraham, *Canon and Criterion*, 356–57.

150. While stressing that there is no new revelation on a par with the incarnation, Abraham's work repeatedly suggests that the church has (in some way) continued to receive new revelation. Abraham, *Crossing,* 106–8.

151. Newman, "On Consulting the Faithful," 205.

152. LD 25:418

153. Newman, "On Consulting the Faithful," 211. Newman cites Ullathorne in support of this position. For further discussion see Ullathorne, *The Immaculate Conception*, 172.

154. Merrigan, *Clear Heads and Holy Hearts*, 94–95.

155. Newman states that the laity are "witnesses to the antiquity or universality of the doctrines which they contain." Newman, "On Consulting the Faithful," 199–200.

Newman discussion of the divine inspiration of the laity to support his conception of the way in which new revelation is given to the church. For example, when Abraham argues that the church has an ongoing "communal" sense of the revelation of God he states that "Newman's insightful and controversial essay *On Consulting the Faithful* . . . remains an important text wrestling with this difficult topic."[156] Here Abraham cites Newman's discussion of the divine inspiration of the laity as an example of what he considers to be the way in which revelation continues to be given to the church. Clearly Abraham's account of how the people of God have a corporate sense of revelation is thus stimulated by Newman's discussion of the divine inspiration of the laity.[157]

Newman and Abraham on the appropriation of revelation

Abraham's account of the church's appropriation of divine revelation also appears to be shaped by Newman's conception of the development of Christian doctrine, as is indicated by the following extracts from Newman and Abraham:

> [Newman] At first men will not fully realise what it is that moves them, and will express and explain themselves inadequately. . . . There will be a time of confusion, when conceptions and misconceptions are in conflict, and it is uncertain whether anything is to come of the idea at all, or which view of it is to get the start of the others. New lights will be brought to bear upon the original statements of the doctrine put forward; judgments and aspects will accumulate. After a while some definite teaching emerges . . . . This process, whether it be longer or shorter in point of time, by which the aspects of an idea are brought into consistency and form, I call its development, being the germination and maturation of some truth or apparent truth on a large mental field.[158]

---

156. Abraham, *Crossing*, 108n15.

157. Though the scope of this research does not permit a detailed discussion of these issues it is important to note that for Newman the term "revelation" concerns what is revealed whilst the term "inspiration" denotes the manner in which revelation is transmitted. McGrath, *Universal Revelation*, 138. For further discussion of Newman's understanding of the difference between revelation and inspiration, see *TP*, 2:66–67.

158. *Dev*, 37–38. The original is slightly different: "Let one such idea get possession of the popular mind, or the mind of any set of persons, and it is not difficult to understand the effects which will ensue. There will be a general agitation of thought, and

> [Abraham] First there really was a unique and special revelation given to the world through Israel in Jesus of Nazareth. Second the reception and understanding of this divine revelation is not immediately apparent. Indeed, its initial significance requires the call and commission of Paul as a prophet. We can see that it would be extremely odd for God to go to all these lengths to make known his name and not provide critical assistance to the church as a whole in unpacking what this means . . . . From this angle we can surely see the deep significance of the ongoing work of the Holy Spirit in the church in coming to the truth about God enshrined in its canonical doctrines.[159]

These extracts indicate that, while Abraham believes that revelation is ongoing, both these writers consider that the church's comprehension of divine truth takes time. Thus Abraham's contention, that the meaning of a divine revelation is not immediately recognized resembles Newman's contention that the full implications of a doctrine are not understood at the beginning. Moreover, both writers argue that when fresh insights are brought to bear upon the initial disclosure deeper truths are uncovered.

In addition to the parallels identified above, it is apparent that both men believe that it is impossible to engage with revealed truth without it having a profound effect upon its recipients. Thus Newman argues that powerful ideas, such as those already contained within the Christian revelation, "arrest and possess the mind, [they] may be said to have life, that is, to live in the mind which is its recipient."[160] He states that:

> [When] religion, is carried forward into the public throng of men and draws attention, then it is not merely received passively in this or that form into many minds, but it becomes an active principle within them, leading them to an ever-new

---

an action of mind both upon itself and upon other minds. New lights will be brought to bear upon the original idea, aspects will multiply, and judgments will accumulate. There will be a time of confusion, when conceptions and misconceptions are in conflict; and it is uncertain whether anything is to come of the idea at all, or which view of it is to get the start of the others. After a while some definite form of doctrine emerges . . . . This process is called the development of an idea, being the germination, growth, and perfection of some living, that is, influential truth, or apparent truth, in the minds of men during a sufficient period." Newman, *Essay on Development*, 35–37.

159. Abraham, *Crossing*, 106–7.
160. *Dev*, 36. Newman, *Essay on Development*, 35.

contemplation of itself, to an application of it in various directions, and a propagation of it on every side.[161]

Thus, although the revelation was given to the church at the beginning, Newman implies that this gift is alive.[162] For this reason Newman makes clear that revelation could not be received passively by the church. On the contrary, it has vigorously taken hold of the mind of the church. In a similar manner Abraham considers that revelation cannot be received casually:

> The implications of these observations for divine revelation are clear. Hearing God speak or being confronted by the incarnation is not a casual affair like reading the local newspaper or switching on the television. At one level we are in the long run inevitably confronted by our darkness and rebellion. Our initial natural reaction to divine revelation may not be one of welcome but one of awe and even terror; given our alienation from God.[163]

While there are differences in their conceptions of revelation, both writers argue that revelation is something which changes and shapes the life and mind of the recipient and indeed the church as a whole.

Newman and Abraham also contend that revelation cannot be confined to the books of the Bible, but must inhabit the community which receives that revelation.[164] For example, Newman states that:

> It may be objected that [Christianity's] inspired documents, such as the Holy Scriptures, at once determine its doctrine without further trouble. But they were intended to create an idea, and that idea is not in the sacred text, but in the mind of the reader; and the question is, whether that idea is communicated to him, in its completeness and minute accuracy, on its first apprehension, or expands in his heart and intellect, and comes to perfection in the course of time. Nor could it be maintained

---

161. *Dev*, 36. The original is slightly different: "But when some great enunciation, whether true or false, about human nature, or present good, or government, or duty, or religion, is carried forward into the public throng and draws attention, then it is not only passively admitted in this or that form into the minds of men, but it becomes a living principle within them, leading them to an ever-new contemplation of itself, an acting upon it and a propagation of it." Newman, *Essay on Development*, 35.

162. *Dev*, 57. Newman, *Essay on Development*, 96.

163. Abraham, *Crossing*, 64.

164. Newman, *Essay on Development*, 95 [*Dev*, 56–57].

without extravagance that the letter of the New Testament, or of any assignable number of books, comprises a delineation of all possible forms which a divine message will assume when submitted to a multitude of minds.[165]

Here Newman argues that Scripture does not determine the limits of Christian doctrine because its readers form their own understanding of the text; which itself develops over time as this interpretation interacts with other readings. Thus Newman indicates that the understanding of revelation develops inside the multitude of minds reading that text. Abraham makes a similar statement:

> Acts of revelation, are not performed in a vacuum. . . . The Christian claim about revelation in Christ has to be understood, then, as part of a comprehensive vision of ourselves and our predicament that shapes the very form and character of that revelation. God did not send a library of books for our enlightenment, . . . God sent the Son . . . . For revelation to occur something has to be picked up and received, or could have been picked up and grasped. Hence revelation, to be revelation, has to be in principle subjectively effective. It has to be such that it can find its way into the life of the individuals and communities to which it is directed.[166]

This indicates that Newman's discussion of the way in which different interpretations of the revelation of Scripture lead the mind of the church to new understandings of divine truth has similarities with Abraham's account of the reception of revelation. Like Newman, Abraham argues that revelation has to be understood in relation to a recipient. His point is that divine disclosure cannot be exhausted by a library of books (the canon of Scripture), but includes the effect that this revelation has upon the life and indeed the mind of the individual or community which receives it. This shows that these writers share another common reason for holding that the church's understanding of divine revelation develops over time: the different ways in which the community of believers understand God's truth over the centuries.

Finally, both these writers stress that the full implications of revelation cannot be realized straight away because finite minds cannot fully grasp them all at once. For example, Newman holds that a succession of

---

165. Newman, *Essay on Development*, 95 [*Dev*, 56–57].
166. Abraham, *Crossing*, 63.

generations apprehend the truth of an idea in more detail over time, enabling people to gradually understand an idea more fully. For this reason he believes that development, in the collective (human) perception of an idea, is inevitable.[167] Newman thus proposes that Christianity, considered as an idea, develops over time. For similar reasons Abraham considers that it takes time for the church to take hold of divine revelation:

> The core issue can be approached by thinking of the problem as one of discerning the action of God in creation, in history, and in one's own life. At stake is the recognition of God and his revelatory action. Once we express the issue this way, in terms of discernment and recognition, we do not have to take in the full stretch of God's activity all at once. We can, as it were, enter the circle of revelatory action at various points, selecting relevant revelatory actions, and then move on to explore the full range available to us.[168]

Here Abraham argues that the polymorphous nature of divine revelation means that it is viewed at various points. For this reason it takes time for the church to explore the full range of God's truth because its different aspects are considered gradually.

The extracts suggest that Abraham's diachronic conception of revelation draws upon Newman's discussion of doctrinal development. While there are differences, both these writers hold that revelation is not passive but takes hold of the mind of believers, that the meaning of divine truth is understood gradually, and that the church's comprehension of revelation takes time to come to the surface.

Newman's possible contribution to the epistemology of canonical theism

The beginning of this section introduced Abraham's approach to the justification of canonical theism. Taking an epistemological particularist approach Abraham begins by assuming the veracity of the canonical heritage. He then explores what kind of considerations are relevant to its justification. Abraham maintains that these canonical materials are justified by revelation and that the canonical doctrines developed because of the operation of the Holy Spirit within the life of the church. While

---

167 Newman, *Essay on Development*, 32-36. [*Dev*, 34-35]
168. Abraham, *Crossing*, 65.

Abraham, as a particularist, begins by presuming the authenticity of the church's canonical doctrines it is not satisfactory simply to say that these doctrines developed over time because of an interaction between divine revelation and the church. Abraham himself admits this in his work *Canon and Criterion*:

> The teachers of the Church have to argue for the truth of the Church's doctrine, and they gladly do so in all sorts of ways. For example, a Church teacher may appeal to the historical continuity of the Church's faith with that of the apostles.[169]

In this citation Abraham accepts that it is not sufficient simply to say, for example, that the creed is true. Teachers of the "Church" have a responsibility to argue for the truth of the Christian faith. Why then does he simply state that the canons arose out of the interaction of divine revelation within the church? Why doesn't he also present arguments for their mutual coherence and their relationship with apostolic teaching? If Abraham thinks this is an option, he could clarify these ideas by making further use of Newman's *Essay on Development*.

It was noted above that Abraham commends Newman's *Essay on Development* for its "felicitous" account of the connection between the apostolic faith and the various canonical doctrines of nineteenth-century Catholicism. Chapter 3 introduced the way in which this work exhibits particularist tendencies. It was shown that Newman, presuming the veracity of nineteenth-century Catholicism from the outset, identifies seven tests or notes which he considers act as a key to harmonize nineteenth-century doctrines with the teaching of the primitive church.

One possible reason why Abraham has resisted this option is that he is loath to try and quantify divine revelation:

> It is a mistake to look here for proof, for demonstration, for finalizing deductive arguments. It is equally a mistake to look for surefire guarantees. It was this quest that led to theories of infallibility, whether of scripture or of the church. One worry that drove this development was the feeling that without absolute foundations, without external guarantees, the alternative is subjectivism and arbitrary judgment. This still haunts the discussion in the West.[170]

---

169. Abraham, *Canon and Criterion*, 41.
170. Abraham, *Crossing*, 108–10.

Abraham considers that it was this quest for certainty that drove theologians to seek an external authority, such as the infallibility of Scripture or the pope. He considers that the anxiety caused by the fear of making mistakes has led to an unnecessary emphasis being placed on a book or on an institution.[171]

Further, Abraham believes that it is impossible to formulate a criterion for revelation because it is not possible to determine how a revelation will unfold:

> One cannot say in advance exactly what form a canonical tradition will take or how it will be transmitted. Had we been present in the Christian community in Jerusalem around AD 40, the only canonical material we might have recognized would have been what is now designated as the Old Testament.... We have to piece the story together from the historical record as best we can.[172]

Hence Abraham is adamant that there is no "prior rational scheme" or criterion that can tell us how future developments will unfold.[173] Abraham is right to insist that it is impossible to formulate criteria that will regulate future developments. He is also correct to argue that when many of the canons were formulated the "process was informal."[174] However, this does not prevent him looking back and examining the development of canonical theism retrospectively in order to examine whether there is a "key" that will harmonize these doctrines with other elements of the canonical heritage. Here Newman's writing can add coherence to Abraham's proposals.

While Abraham is concerned to respect the "radical freedom of the Holy Spirit to guide the church into those canonical traditions deemed useful for the community as a whole,"[175] it is clear that an examination of how this process occurred does not oblige us to believe that God will use the same process in the future. In formulating criteria for authentic doctrinal development, Newman himself did not want to determine future developments. Nevertheless, he had no opposition whatsoever to examining retrospectively the implicit reasons that led to the development of

---

171. Abraham, *Crossing*, 108–10.
172. Abraham, *Canon and Criterion*, 28–29.
173. Abraham, *Canon and Criterion*, 28–29.
174. Abraham, *Canon and Criterion*, 35.
175. Abraham, *Canon and Criterion*, 28–29.

established doctrines in order to apologetically defend their continuity with earlier teaching.

Having illustrated the particularist tendencies in Newman's *Essay on Development* in chapter 3 it is necessary to ask: how can canonical theists like Abraham derive epistemological respectability from Newman's criteria? Lash believes that "the arguments in question are, to say the least, inadequate."[176] Cameron asserts that no one would take his criteria "seriously . . . as it stands."[177] This interpretation undervalues the particularist tendencies latent within Newman's proposal. Using Christian history as his informant, Newman outlines a vision of the rationality of Christian doctrine appropriate to the subject matter in hand. The essay, therefore, presupposes Roman Catholic doctrines to be legitimate developments and then formulates suitable arguments in order to justify this belief.

The weaknesses in Abraham's account of the epistemology of canonical theism can be strengthened using Newman's work. The contribution that Newman's tests could make to canonical theism are that they illustrate a way in which it is possible to retrospectively articulate criteria for the authentic development of the canonical heritage. The principle of Aristotelian epistemic fit requires canonical theists like Abraham to provide suitable criteria for analyzing the development of the canonical heritage of the church up to the division between East and West. Therefore, it is not so much Newman's criteria but the "felicitous" manner in which Newman conducts his essay which has the potential to contribute to the epistemology of canonical theism. Newman's criteria need not be applied to Canonical theism. New tests could be formulated, appropriate to this subject matter, in order to justify an antecedent commitment to canonical theism. Thus, using Newman, one could argue for the continuity of the canonical heritage.

The above shows how Newman's writing could make a contribution to the epistemology of canonical theism. Using the pattern found in Newman's *Essay on Development* the canonical theist can formulate an account of the implicit logic governing the development of the canonical heritage. Retrospectively formulating appropriate tests to illuminate the continuity of the canonical heritage over the course of its historic development would reinforce the notion that the canonical doctrines are all inspired by the same source—divine revelation. Even if Abraham

---

176. Lash, *Newman on Development*, 37.

177. Cameron, "Newman and the Empiricist Tradition," 92.

chooses not to do this, Newman's writing has the potential to enhance the epistemology of canonical theism at this point.

An ecclesiological and epistemological dilemma

It was noted that Abraham's canonical theism is not grounded in any ecclesiological institution. This is a problem because Abraham considers that revelation, which he believes justifies the canonical heritage, is mediated through "concrete" ecclesial structures. Were Abraham clearly to define his ecclesiological commitments he could legitimately argue that the canons of the said "church" are justified by its cumulative experience of revelation over time. However, his conception of continuous revelation, and his understanding of the canonical heritage, makes it difficult to integrate his proposals within either the Roman Catholic or Eastern Orthodox traditions.[178] This leaves Abraham's attempt to apply the principle of epistemic fit to theology with a problem. He could change his proposals. He could abandon the notion that the appropriation of revelation is not received in a vacuum. On the other hand, if his conception of revelation were developed he could perhaps join the Roman Catholic Church, and uphold the canonical heritage stored within that church. Were Abraham to take this latter course he could develop Newman's tests so as to justify an adherence to its particular canonical heritage. Although this would make his application of the principle of epistemic fit to theology more coherent, there are further reasons, which will now be considered, that indicate why he would not move in this direction.

Abraham considers that the first major split between the East and the West was caused in part by the decision of the Western church to give primacy to Rome on matters of doctrine. He writes:

> What had originally belonged to the whole Church—namely the right to decide dogmatic questions—was now claimed by one part of the Church. To support this, a monopoly of inspiration was predicated of the Roman tradition. . . . [T]his claim to a special charism fitted nicely with the infallibility of the Pope, who became a kind of oracle.[179]

Abraham sees the Roman Catholic Church as distorting the canonical heritage of the church by making the pope an "epistemic mechanism

---

178. Both the Eastern Orthodox and Roman Catholic Churches reject this notion.
179. Abraham, *Canon and Criterion*, 77–78.

which could . . . be utilized to arrive at genuine knowledge." Abraham considers that in making the pope a "privileged locus of epistemic authority" the West represented an historic shift which turned canons into epistemic criterion.[180] He writes:

> The Roman Catholic tradition involves a deep transposition of the patristic heritage. . . . [T]he whole effort to canonize epistemological materials in the full and official way taken by Rome is a radical departure from the earlier tradition.[181]

In making "epistemological commitments canonical" Abraham believes that the West precipitated schism. Abraham considers this to be the case because making "the church's identity and unity . . . depend on adopting the favoured epistemology" does not only cause division over "the gospel or the creed, but on issues of epistemology as well."[182] Thus, Abraham does not seek a return to the Roman Catholic Church; in fact, he considers that by "epistemizing" the canonical heritage of the church the Roman Catholic Church initiated centuries of division.

Abraham's opposition to joining the Roman Catholic Church does not prevent him from coherently articulating appropriate arguments in support of the canonical heritage. However, his insistence that to be a Christian involves baptism into a physical church means that this ecclesiological question undermines his contention that the canonical heritage is justified by the church's corporate experience of revelation over time.

This discussion indicates that there are a number of epistemological problems posed by the ecclesiological vacuum in Abraham's account. To solve this dilemma Abraham needs to belong to an ecclesial body that both recognizes the canons of the undivided church and identifies itself as being an ongoing recipient of divine revelation. From within this body Abraham could then coherently articulate appropriate arguments in support of its canonical heritage.[183]

180. Abraham, *Canon and Criterion*, 115.
181. Abraham, *Canon and Criterion*, 354–55.
182. Abraham, *Crossing*, 19.
183. Abraham does consider the Orthodox tradition to be more commensurate with his conception of the canonical heritage. If this is the case, Abraham could join the Orthodox Church and begin epistemological enquiry from within a commitment to the canons of this community. If he joined the Orthodox Church he would not have to go back in time to a vision of the Christian faith which was stored in the church's canons before the schism between East and West. He could simply articulate criteria for authentic doctrinal development from within the Orthodox tradition. However, his conception of revelation is at variance with this tradition.

Summary of Chapter

This chapter has shown that Abraham's particularist account of the epistemology of Christian belief is shaped by Newman's writings in a number of ways. To begin with Abraham is inspired by Newman's Aristotelian approach and finds resonances between his own antagonist, epistemological methodism, and Newman's concerns about liberalism. Secondly Abraham incorporates specific aspects of Newman's work into his particularist account of the epistemology of Christian belief. Abraham combines Newman's illative sense with Chisholm's discussion of the *Oculus Contemplationis*. This challenges Maddox's epistemological methodist interpretation of the illative sense and demonstrates how Newman's *Grammar* contributes to his own particularist account of the epistemology of Christian belief. Furthermore, though their understandings of revelation are different, Newman's discussion of assent helps articulate Abraham's conception of revelation as a threshold category which, once accepted, changes one's view absolutely. In addition, Abraham's discussion of the need to subject claims to revelation to critical investigation has a number of parallels with Newman's discussion of complex (reflex) assent.

Finally, this chapter shows how Abraham's particularist account of the justification of canonical theism, using divine revelation, draws upon Newman's writing in number of ways. His description of revelation actively at work within the corporate mind of the church draws upon Newman's *Essay on Consulting the Faithful* and the *Essay on Development*. However, while Abraham believes that canonical theism is justified by the ongoing interaction of revelation within the church, he does not specify which contemporary church is the carrier of revelation. His contention that the canonical doctrines arose as a result of the work of the Holy Spirit in the church could be enhanced were he to retrospectively identify a key for showing how the different elements of the canonical heritage are continuous with each other. Here Abraham faces a problem similar to that addressed by Newman in *An Essay on the Development of Christian Doctrine*. However, Newman's solution to this quandary is much more coherent in terms of the principle of Aristotelian epistemic fit. His seven notes of authentic development offer Abraham a way in which he might retrospectively defend the coherence of the development of the canonical heritage. Furthermore, Abraham's contention that the church is a carrier of divine revelation, and that grace is mediated through concrete physical structures, requires him to outline a real ecclesial body in which one may be initiated—and thus receive revelation. Though his conception of revelation prevents him joining the Orthodox or Roman Catholic Churches, Abraham's proposal is incoherent as it stands without an ecclesiological home.

In summary, Abraham's particularist approach to the justification of Christian belief is in many ways inspired, shaped, and may even be developed by Newman's work. Abraham thus offers a good example of the way in which Newman's writing has made, and continues to offer, a contribution to contemporary approaches to the epistemology of Christian belief and the philosophy of religion in general.

7

Conclusion

Reconsidering Newman's Philosophical Legacy

"It is something to have started a problem, and mapped in part a country, if I have done nothing more."[1]—John Henry Newman

The findings of this work show that there has been a gross underestimation of Newman's philosophical legacy. Throughout the course of this book we have examined the history of Newman's philosophical reception. In contrast to the consensus held by Newman scholars, which argues that his work has largely been overlooked by philosophers, it has been demonstrated that over the last two centuries a wide range of philosophers have engaged with Newman.

Philosophers from a variety of backgrounds and positions discuss Newman's work. Even philosophers trained at Oxford, where Newman's alleged neglect was considered acute, acknowledge his importance. The admission by an Oxford-trained philosopher of religion, William Abraham, that he discovered Newman's writing while studying at Oxford offers a powerful example of this. As shown, Abraham acknowledged that his particularist approach to the epistemology of Christian belief is inspired by Newman; this illustrates Newman's ongoing importance for the philosophy of religion and to epistemology in general.

The work also explored Newman's historical significance. Though commentators often identify parallels between Newman and a variety of

1. *LD*, 25:280.

philosophical positions, there is a general failure to recognize that the founders of these approaches refer to Newman. For example, Maddox's contrast between Newman and the epistemological particularist approach fails to mention Roderick Chisholm's references to Newman and, moreover, their common neo-Thomistic philosophical heritage. Though Newman has often been viewed in isolation from the revival of Thomism, this book has demonstrated Newman's interaction with the neo-Thomist tradition that shaped this theory of knowledge; this underlines his historical connections with the development of epistemological particularism.

Newman's philosophical relevance is also demonstrated by the fact that he shares a number of tendencies with particularist writers. These include his conviction that no subject should be diminished by the presupposition of adverse first principles; the importance he gives to spontaneous beliefs; and his Aristotelian conception of rationality. This common epistemological orientation, particularly his use of Aristotle, has made Newman's writing conducive to particularist writers by offering clarity for the articulation of their ideas. Jay Newman's discussion of the illative sense, which enables individuals to gauge the strength of miscellaneous forms of evidence, represents one instance of this. His contention that this aspect of the *Grammar of Assent* enhances Chisholm's approach illustrates J. H. Newman's relevance to the development of the particularist position. In like manner, J. H. Newman's writing makes a similar contribution to William Abraham.

Several aspects of Abraham's work in the philosophy of religion are informed by Newman's writing. Abraham's analysis of the epistemological factors operative in conversion makes extensive use of Newman's malleable conception of reason. In particular, Jay Newman's observations concerning the illative sense are realized in Abraham's combination of this faculty with Chisholm's conception of the *Oculus Contemplationis*. Abraham's methodology is also informed by J. H. Newman for Abraham's application of Aristotelian epistemic fit to the epistemology of canonical theism is inspired by J. H. Newman's use of this Aristotelian principle.[2] However, weaknesses in Abraham's position stem from his failure to consistently apply this principle. Here Newman's writing models an approach that has the potential to enhance the coherence of the epistemology of canonical theism.

2. Abraham's proposal, for the creation of a new discipline called the epistemology of theology, is clearly informed by Newman's application of this Aristotelian principle to various forms of Christian discourse.

In conclusion, this book has endeavoured to provide a historical re-evaluation of Newman's philosophical legacy. The findings of this investigation demonstrate that Newman's writing has not been ignored by philosophers, but has made, and continues to offer, an important contribution to this discipline. More specifically, this research indicates that Newman's work offers a relevant contribution to two specific branches of the subject of philosophy: epistemology and the philosophy of religion. His many connections with the sources and the tradition out of which epistemological particularism has developed, coupled with his reception by Mercier, Coffey, and Chisholm, indicate that his work is relevant to discussions concerning the origins and development of the particularist approach to epistemology. Moreover, Abraham's extensive use of Newman's writings and his incorporation of Newman's particularist tendencies into his own proposals show that Newman is relevant to contemporary discussions concerning the epistemology of Christian belief.

The implications of this are wider than particularist approaches discussed. At the end of this book it is important to stress the fact that Newman's philosophical legacy is far wider than Newman scholarship has previously imagined. Though it is not possible for the present study to examine Newman's contribution to pragmatism, personalism, or phenomenology, for example, it is clear that there is considerable scope for examining the many philosophers who cite Newman in order to determine whether a connection can be established between his writings and these philosophical traditions. In sum, while this book has investigated one dimension of Newman's philosophical legacy, there is still much work to be done in exploring Newman's place in the story of philosophy.

Bibliography

John Henry Newman Primary Sources

Addresses to Cardinal Newman with his Replies etc 1879–81. Edited by W. P. Neville. London: Longmans, Green, 1905.
Apologia Pro Vita Sua: Being a Reply to a Pamphlet Entitled "What, Then, Does Dr. Newman Mean?" London: Longman, Green, Longman, Roberts, and Green, 1864.
The Arians of the Fourth Century: Their Doctrine, Temper, and Conduct Chiefly as Exhibited in the Councils of the Church between AD 325, & AD 381. London: Rivington, 1833.
"The Benedictine Centuries." *The Atlantis* (1859) 1–43.
"Catholicity of the English Church." *The British Critic* 27 (1840) 40–88.
The Church of the Fathers. London: Rivington, 1840.
Collected Works. Edited by J. Rickaby et al. 41 vols. London: Longmans, Green, 1874–1921.
"The Convocation of the Province of Canterbury." *The British Magazine* 7 (1835) 33–41.
"The Development of Religious Error." *Contemporary Review* 48 (1885) 457–69.
Discourses Addressed to Mixed Congregations. London: Longman, Brown, Green, 1849.
Discourses on the Scope and Nature of University Education. Dublin: J. Duffy, 1852.
Discours sur la Théorie de la Croyance Religieuse Prononcés Devant l'Université d'Oxford. Translated by A. de Ferrië. Liege: Lardinois, 1851.
"Ecce Homo." *New Catholic World Monthly Magazine of General Literature and Science* (1866) 618–34.
The Ecclesiastical History of M. L'Abbe Fleury. Edited by J. H. Newman. Translated by A. Christie et al. 3 Vols. Oxford: John Henry Parker, 1842.
An Essay in Aid of a Grammar of Assent. London: Burns, Oates, 1870.
An Essay on the Development of Christian Doctrine. London: James Toovey, 1845.
Essay on the Miracles Recorded in the Ecclesiastical History of the Early Ages. Oxford: John Henry Parker, 1843.
Fifteen Sermons Preached before The University of Oxford between A.D. 1826 and 1843 by John Henry Newman Sometime Fellow of Oriel College. Edited by J. D. Earnest and G. Tracey. Oxford: Oxford University Press, 2006.
History of My Religious Opinions. London: Longman, Green, Longman, Roberts, and Green, 1865.

John Henry Newman: Roman Catholic Writings on Doctrinal Development. Edited by J. Gaffney. Kansas City, MO: Sheed and Ward, 1997.
"Judgement of the English Bishops on the Royal Commission." *The Rambler* (1859) 117–23.
Lectures and Essays on University Subjects. 2nd ed. London: Longman, Green, Longman and Roberts, 1859.
Lectures on Catholicism in England Delivered in the Corn Exchange. Birmingham, UK: Corn Exchange, 1851.
Lectures on Certain Difficulties Felt by Anglicans in Submitting to the Catholic Church. London: Burns and Lambert, 1850.
Lectures on the History of the Turks in its Relation to Christianity. Dublin: J. Duffy, 1854.
Lectures on Justification. London: Rivington, 1838.
Lectures on the Prophetical Office of the Church Viewed Relatively to Romanism and Popular Protestantism. London: Rivington, 1837.
A Letter Addressed to His Grace the Duke of Norfolk on Occasion of Mr. Gladstone's Recent Expostulation. London: B M Pickering, 1875.
A Letter Addressed to the Rev. R. W. Jelf, D.D. Canon of Christ Church, in Explanation of No.90, in the Series called the Tracts for the Times. London: Rivington, 1841.
Letters and Correspondence of John Henry Newman during His Life in the English Church, with a Brief Autobiography. Edited by A. Mozley. 2 vols. London: Longmans, Green, 1891.
A Letter to the Rev. E. B. Pusey, D.D. on his Recent Eirenicon. London: Longmans, Green, 1866.
"The Life of Apollonius Tyanaeus." In *EM* 10:619–44.
"Logic." In *EM* 1:193–240.
"Marcus Tullius Cicero." In *EM* 10:279–94.
"On Consulting the Faithful in Matters of Doctrine." *The Rambler* (1859) 198–230.
"On the Subject of Mathematics." *The Christian Observer* (1821) 293–95.
"Poetry: With Reference to Aristotle's Poetics." *The London Review* 1 (1829) 153–71.
Remains of the Late Reverend Richard Hurrell Froude Fellow of Oriel College Oxford. Edited by J. H. Newman and J. Keble. 2 Vols. London: Rivington, 1838.
The Restoration of Suffragan Bishops Recommended, as a Means of Effecting a More Equal Distribution of Episcopal Duties, as Contemplated by His Majesty's Recent Ecclesiastical Commission. London: Rivington, 1835.
Review of *The Brothers' Controversy, Being a Genuine Correspondence between a Clergyman of the Church of England and a Layman of Unitarian Opinions,* by B. Longley. *The British Critic* 20 (1836) 166–99.
Review of *The History of the Christian Church, from the Ascension of Jesus Christ to the Conversion of Constantine,* by Edward Burton. *The British Critic* 19 (1836) 209–31.
Review of *The Life of Archbishop Laud,* by Charles Webb Le Bas. *The British Critic* 19 (1836) 354–80.
Review of *Random Recollections of Exeter Hall in 1834-1837,* by unknown author. *The British Critic* 24 (1838) 190–210.
Review of *A Treatise on the Church of Christ, designed chiefly for the use of Students in Theology,* by W. Palmer. *The British Critic* 24 (1838) 347–72.
Sayings of Cardinal Newman. London: Burns and Oates, 1890.
Select Treatise of Athanasius, Archbishop of Alexandria, in Controversy with the Arians. Edited by J. H. Newman. 2 vols. Oxford: James Parker and Co, 1877.

Sermons Bearing on Subjects of the Day. London: Rivington, 1843.
Sermons Chiefly on the Theory of Religious Belief Preached before the University of Oxford. London: Rivington, 1843.
"The State of Religious Parties." *The British Critic* 25 (1839) 395–426.
Tracts for the Times: By Members of the University of Oxford. 6 vols. London: Rivington, 1833–40.
The Works of John Henry Newman. Edited by J. H. Newman. 36 vols. London: B. M. Pickering, 1873–93.

William J. Abraham Primary Sources

Aldersgate and Athens: John Wesley and the Foundations of Religious Belief. Waco, TX: Baylor University Press, 2010.
The Bible Beyond the Impasse. Dallas: Highland Loch, 2012.
Canon and Criterion in Christian Theology: From the Fathers to Feminism. Oxford: Clarendon, 1997.
Canonical Theism. Grand Rapids: Eerdmans, 2008.
"Canonical Theism and the Future of Systematic Theology." In *Canonical Theism*, edited by W. Abraham, 287–302. Grand Rapids: Eerdmans, 2008.
"Canonical Theism: Thirty Theses." In *Canonical Theism*, edited by W. Abraham, 1–7. Grand Rapids: Eerdmans, 2008.
Celtic Fire: Evangelism in the Wisdom and Power of the Spirit. Dallas, TX: Highland Loch, 2012.
"Church." In *The Cambridge Companion to Christian Philosophical Theology*, edited by C. Taliaferro and C. Meister, 170–82. Cambridge: Cambridge University Press, 2010.
The Coming Great Revival: Recovering the Full Evangelical Tradition. San Francisco: Harper and Row, 1984.
Crossing the Threshold of Divine Revelation. Grand Rapids: Eerdmans, 2006.
"Cumulative Case Arguments for Christian Theism." In *The Rationality of Religious Belief*, edited by S. Holtzer, 17–38. Oxford: Clarendon, 1987.
The Divine Inspiration of Holy Scripture. Oxford: Oxford University Press, 1981.
Divine Revelation and the Limits of Historical Criticism. Oxford: Oxford University Press, 1982.
"The Emergence of Canonical Theism." In *Canonical Theism*, edited by W. Abraham, 141–55. Grand Rapids: Eerdmans, 2008.
"The End of Wesleyan Theology." *Wesleyan Theological Journal* 40 (2005) 7–25.
"Epistemological Significance of the Inner Witness of the Holy Spirit." *Faith and Philosophy* (1990) 434–50.
"The Epistemology of Conversion." In *Conversion in the Wesleyan Tradition*, edited by K. Collins and J. Tyson, 175–94. Nashville: Abingdon, 2001.
"The Existence of God." In *The Oxford Handbook of Systematic Theology*, edited by J. Webster, 19–34. Oxford: Oxford University Press, 2007.
"Faraway Fields Are Green." In *God and the Philosophers*, edited by T. Morris, 162–72. Oxford: Oxford University Press, 1994.
"'I can see people but they look like trees walking': A Response to Professor Webster." *Scottish Journal of Theology* 54.2 (2001) 238–43.

An Introduction to the Philosophy of Religion. Englewood Cliffs, NJ: Prentice Hall, 1985.
"Introduction." In *Canonical Theism*, edited by W. Abraham, xii–xix. Grand Rapids: Eerdmans, 2008.
John Wesley for Armchair Theologians. Louisville, KY: Westminster John Knox, 2005.
The Logic of Evangelism. 2nd ed. Grand Rapids: Eerdmans, 2002.
The Logic of Renewal. London: SPCK, 2003.
"Loyal Opposition and the Epistemology of Conscience." *Asbury Theological Journal* 56.1 (2001) 135–47.
"The Offense of Divine Revelation." *Harvard Theological Review* 95.3 (2002) 251–64.
"On How to Dismantle the Wesleyan Quadrilateral." *Wesleyan Theological Journal* 20.1 (1985) 34–44.
"Orthodoxy and Evangelicalism." *Sourozh* 61.3 (1995) 1–14.
"Philosophical Reflection on Revelation and Scripture." In *A Companion to Philosophy of Religion*, 2nd ed., edited by C. Taliaferro et al., 695–701. Oxford: Blackwell, 2010.
"Response to Marc Cortez." *Journal of Analytic Theology* 1 (2013) 25–29.
"A Response to Stanley Grenz." *Wesleyan Theological Journal* 36.2 (2001) 45–49.
"Saving Souls in the Twenty-First Century: A Missiological Midrash on John Wesley." *Wesleyan Theological Journal* 38.1 (2003) 7–20.
"Scripture and Revelation." In *The Blackwell Companion to the Philosophy of Religion*, edited by P. Quinn and C. Taliaferro, 584–90. Oxford: Blackwell, 1997.
Shaking Hands with the Devil: The Intersection of Terrorism and Theology. Dallas: Highland Loch, 2012.
"Some Trends in Recent Philosophy of Religion." *The Theological Educator* 9 (1979) 93–103.
"Systematic Theology as Analytic Theology." In *Analytic Theology: New Essays in the Philosophy of Theology*, edited by O. Crisp and M. Rea, 54–69. Oxford: Oxford University Press, 2009.
"Turning Philosophical Water into Theological Wine." *Journal of Analytic Theology* 1 (2013) 1–16.
Waking from Doctrinal Amnesia: The Healing of Doctrine in the United Methodist Church. Nashville, TN: Abingdon, 1995.
"What Should United Methodists Do with the Quadrilateral?" *Quarterly Review* 22.1 (2002) 85–88.

Roderick M. Chisholm Primary Sources

"Epistemic Principles." *Dialectica* 15 (1981) 341–45.
On Metaphysics. Minneapolis, MN: Minnesota University Press, 1989.
Perceiving: A Philosophical Study. Ithaca, NY: Cornell University Press, 1957.
Person and Object: A Metaphysical Study. London: Allen, 1976.
Philosophy. Englewood Cliffs, NJ: Prentice Hall, 1964.
The Problem of the Criterion. Milwaukee, WI: Aquinas Papers, 1973.
"Sextus Empiricus and Modem Empiricism." *Philosophy of Science* 8 (1941) 371–84.
Theory of Knowledge. Englewood Cliffs, NJ: Prentice Hall, 1966.
Theory of Knowledge. 2nd ed. Englewood Cliffs, NJ: Prentice Hall, 1977.

"Theory of Knowledge in America." In *The Foundations of Knowing*, edited by R. Chisholm, 109–93. Minneapolis, MN: Minnesota University Press, 1982.

Other Sources

Abbot, Edwin. *The Anglican Career of Cardinal Newman*. 2 vols. London: Macmillan, 1892.

———. *Philomythus: An Antidote against Credulity: A Discussion of Cardinal Newman's Essay on Miracles*. London: Macmillan, 1891.

Abbot, J. *The Corner Stone: Or a Familiar Illustration of the Principles of Christian Truth*. Boston: William Peirce, 1836.

Achten, Rik. *First Principles and Our Way to Faith: Fundamental-Theological Study of John Henry Newman*. Frankfurt: Lang, 1995.

Allen, Grant. *The Incidental Bishop*. London: C. A. Pearson, 1902.

Alston, William. *Epistemic Justification: Essays in the Theory of Knowledge*. Ithaca, NY: Cornell University Press, 1989.

———. *Perceiving God*. Ithaca, NY: Cornell University Press, 1993.

Althusser, Louis. *L'Avenir Dure Longtemps: Suivi De, Les Faits*. Paris: Stock Imec, 1992.

Amico, Robert. *The Problem of the Criterion*. Lanham, MD: Rowman Littlefield, 1995.

Anagnostopoulos, Georgios. "Aristotle's Works and the Development of His Thought." In *A Companion to Aristotle*, edited by G. Anagnostopoulos, 14–28. Oxford: Blackwell, 2009.

Annas, Julia. *The Morality of Happiness*. Oxford: Oxford University Press, 1995.

Aquinas, Thomas. *Disputed Questions on Truth*. Translated by R. W. Mulligan. Chicago: Regnery, 1952.

———. *Quaestiones Disputatae de Veritateed*. Edited by R. M. Spiazzi. Turin: Marietti, 1949.

———. *Scriptum Super Sententiis Magistri Petri Lombardi Recognovit Atque Iterum*. Edited by P. M. Fabianus Moos. Paris: Lethielleux, 1933.

Aquino, Frederick. "Broadening Horizons: Constructing an Epistemology of Religious Belief." *Louvain Studies* 30.3 (2005) 198–213.

———. *Communities of Informed Judgment*. Washington, DC: Catholic University of America Press, 2004.

Aristotle. *De Anima*. Translated by D. W. Hamlyn. Oxford: Clarendon, 1968.

———. *Metaphysics*. Translated by J. Sachs. St Des Moines, IA: Peripatetic, 1979.

———. *Nicomachean Ethics*. Translated by R. Crisp. Cambridge: Cambridge University Press, 2004.

Armour, Leslie. *"Infini Rien:" Pascal's Wager and the Human Paradox*. Carbondale, IL: Southern Illinois University Press, 1993.

———. Review of *A Dictionary of Philosophical Quotations*, by A. J. Ayer. https://www.amazon.com/-/es/J-Ayer/dp/0631170154.

Artz, Johannes. "Newman as a Philosopher." *International Philosophical Quarterly* 16 (1976) 263–87.

———. "Newmans Philosophische Leistung." *Newman Studien* 10 (1978) 169–229.

———. "Newman in Contact with Kant's Thought." *Journal of Theological Studies* 31 (1980) 517–35.

Aubert, Robert. "Aspects divers du Ne´o Thomisme sous le pontificat de Le´on XIII." In *Aspetti della Cultura Cattolica nell'Eta` di Leone XIII*, edited by G. Rossini, 149–51. Rome: Edizioni Cinque Lune, 1961.

Avis, Paul. "Reason and Philosophy in the Anglican Tradition." In *Theology and Philosophy*, edited by M. Davies et al., 71–86. London: T. & T. Clark, 2012.

Bagehot, Walter. *Literary Studies*. Edited by R. H. Hutton. 3 vols. London: Longmans, Green, 1905.

Bain, Alexander. *The Emotions and the Will*. 2nd ed. London: Longmans Green and Co, 1865.

———. *Practical Essays*. New York: D. Appleton, 1884.

Baldwin, Thomas. *Contemporary Philosophy*. Oxford: Oxford University Press, 2001.

Balmes, J. *Fundamental Philosophy*. 2 vols. Translated by H. F. Brownson. New York: Sadler, 1856.

Barrett, Cyril. "Newman and Wittgenstein on the Rationality of Belief." In *Newman and Conversion*, edited by I. Ker, 89–99, Edinburgh: T. & T. Clark, 1997.

———. *Wittgenstein on Ethics and Religious Belief*. Oxford: Blackwell, 1991.

———. "The Wittgensteinian Revolution." In *Faith and Philosophical Analysis: The Impact of Analytical Philosophy on the Philosophy of Religion*, edited by H. Harris and C. Insole, 61–71. Farnham, UK: Ashgate, 2005.

Barrett, William. *Death of the Soul: From Descartes to the Computer*. New York: Anchor, 1987.

———. *The Illusion of Technique: A Search for Meaning in a Technological Civilization*. New York: Anchor, 1978.

———. *Time of Need: Forms of Imagination in the Twentieth Century*. New York: Harper and Row, 1973.

———. *The Truants: Adventures among the Intellectuals*. New York: Doubleday, 1983.

Barmann, Lawrence. "Theological Enquiry in an Authoritarian Church." In *Discourse and Context: An Interdisciplinary Study of John Henry Newman*, edited by G. Magill, 181–208. Carbondale, IL: Southern Illinois University Press, 1993.

Bauer, Walter. *Orthodoxy and Heresy in Earliest Christianity*. Philadelphia: Fortress, 1971.

Bautain, Louis. *Philosophie Morale*. Paris: Librairie Philosophique, 1842.

Beards, Andrew. *Philosophy: The Quest for Truth and Meaning*. Collegeville, MN: Liturgical, 2010.

Beck, Lawrence. "Critical Realism." In *OCP*, 171.

———. "New Realism." In *OCP*, 618.

Becker, Werner. "Newman's Influence on Germany." In *The Rediscovery of Newman*, edited by J. Coulson, 174–76. London: Sheed and Ward, 1967.

Bennett, Longley. *The Brothers' Controversy, Being a Genuine Correspondence between a Clergyman of the Church of England and a Layman of Unitarian Opinions*. Edited by R. Davenport. London: B. Fellowes, 1836.

Bentham, Jeremy. *Chrestomathia*. London: Messrs, Payne and Foss, 1816.

Bergmann, Michael. *Justification without Awareness: A Defense of Epistemic Externalism*. Oxford: Oxford University Press, 2006.

Berlin, Isaiah. *Four Essays on Liberty*. Oxford: Oxford University Press, 1969.

Bicknell, John, ed. *Selected Letters of Leslie Stephen, Volume One, 1864–1882*. London: Macmillan, 1996.

Boekraad, Adrian. *The Argument from Conscience to the Existence of God*. Louvain: Nauwelaerts, 1961.
———. *The Personal Conquest of Truth According to J. H. Newman*. Louvain: Nauwelaerts, 1955.
Boileau, David. *Cardinal Mercier: A Memoir*. Louvain: Peeters, 1998.
Bosco, M. *Finding God in All Things*. New York: Fordham University Press, 2007.
Boudens, Robrecht. *Two Cardinals: J. H. Newman / D. J. Mercier*. Edited by L. Gevers. Louvain: Peeters, 1995.
Boulton, Matthew. *Inquisitio Philosophica: An Examination of the Principles of Kant and Hamilton*. London: Chapman and Hall, 1866.
Bouyer, Louis. *Newman: His Life and Spirituality*. Translated by L. Mayl. London: Kenedy and Sons, 1958.
Bowen, Frances. *Modern Philosophy: From Descartes to Schopenhauer and Hartmann*. New York: Scribner, 1877.
Bowne, Borden. "Cardinal Newman and Science." *Independent* 42 (1890) 1401–2.
Bowring, James, ed. *The Works of Jeremy Bentham*. 11 vols. Edinburgh: Simkin, Marshall, 1843.
Boyce, Philip. *Mary: The Virgin Mary in the Life and Writings of John Henry Newman*. Leominster, UK: Gracewing, 2001.
Brentano, Franz. *Descriptive Psychology*. Translated by B. Müller. London: Routledge, 1995.
———. *The Origin of Our Knowledge of Right and Wrong*. Translated by R. Davies. London: Westminster, 1902.
Bridges, John Henry. *Discourses on Positive Religion*. London: Reeves, 1891.
Brightman, Edgar. "The Use of the Word Personalism." *The Personalist* 3 (1922) 254–59.
Brownson, Orestes. "Newman's Development of Christian Doctrine." *Brownson's Quarterly Review*, July 1846, 342–86.
Bunnin, N., and E. P. Tsui-James, eds. *The Blackwell Companion to Philosophy*. Oxford: Blackwell, 1996.
Butler, Joseph. *The Analogy of Religion Natural and Revealed, to the Constitution and Course of Nature*. Oxford: Oxford University Press, 1833.
Butler, William Archer. *Lectures on the History of Ancient Philosophy*. London: Macmillan, 1874.
———. *Letters on Romanism: In Reply to Mr Newman's Essay on Development*. Cambridge: Macmillan, 1858.
Buttiglione, Rocco. *Karol Wojtyla: The Thought of the Man Who Became John Paul II*. Translated by P. Guietti. Grand Rapids: Eerdmans, 1997.
Caldecott, Alfred. *Philosophy of Religion in England and America*. New York: Macmillan, 1901.
Cameron, James. "Newman and Empiricism." In *The Night Battle*, edited by J. Coulson, 219–43. London: Catholic Book Club, 1962.
———. "Newman and the Empiricist Tradition." In *The Rediscovery of Newman*, edited by A. Allchin and J. Coulson, 76–96. London: Sheed and Ward, 1967.
———. "Newman and Liberalism." *Cross Currents* 30.2 (1980) 153–66.
Capps, Donald. "Newman's Truth: Irony and Metaphors of the Self in the Apologia." *Religion and Literature* 29.2 (1997) 1–25.
Carr, Thomas. *Newman and Gadamer: Toward a Hermeneutics of Religious Knowledge*. Atlanta: Scholars, 1996.

Carré, Meyrick. *Phases of Thought in England*. Oxford: Clarendon, 1949.
Carter, David. *Love Bade Me Welcome: A British Methodist Perspective on the Church*. London: Epworth, 2002.
Casey, Gerard. *Natural Reason: A Study of the Notions of Inference, Assent, Intuition, and First Principles in the Philosophy of John Henry Cardinal Newman*. New York: Lang, 1984.
Chadwick, Owen. *From Bossuet to Newman*. Cambridge: Cambridge University Press, 1987.
———. *Newman*. Oxford: Oxford University Press, 1990.
Chalybaeus, H. M. *The History of Speculative Philosophy from Kant to Hegel*. Translated by A. Edersheim. Edinburgh: T. & T. Clark, 1854.
Chapman, David. *In Search of the Catholic Spirit: Methodists and Roman Catholics in Dialogue*. London: Epworth, 2004.
Chillingworth, William. *The Works of William Chillingworth*. 3 vols. Oxford: Oxford University Press, 1838.
Cicero, Marcus Tullius. *On Academic Scepticism*. Translated by C. Brittain. Indianapolis, IN: Hackett, 2006.
Clark, Kelly J. "Fiction as a Kind of Philosophy." In *Realism and Antirealism*, edited by W. Alston, 280–94. Ithaca, NY: Cornell University Press, 2002.
Clifford, William K. *Lectures and Essays*. 2 vols. London: Macmillan, 1879.
Coe, George, A. *The Religion of a Mature Mind*. Chicago: Revell, 1902.
Coffey, Peter. *Epistemology or Theory of Knowledge*. 2 vols. London: Longmans, Green, 1917.
———. *Ontology, or, The Theory of Being; an Introduction to General Metaphysics*. 2 vols. London: Longmans, Green, 1918.
———. "Philosophy and the Sciences at Louvain." *Irish Ecclesiastical Record* 17 (1905) 385–408.
———. *Science and Logic*. 2 vols. London: Longmans, Green, 1912.
Colby, Robert. "The Poetic Structure of Newman's Apologia Pro Vita Sua." *Journal of Religions* 33 (1953) 44–57.
Collini, Stefan. "My Roles and Their Duties: Sidgwick as Philosopher, Professor, and Public Moralist." In *Henry Sidgwick*, edited by R. Harrison, 9–50. Oxford: Oxford University Press, 2001.
Collins, Peter. "Newman, Foundationalism and Teaching Philosophy." *Metaphilosophy* 22 (1991) 143–61.
Conn, Walter E. "Newman Versus Subjectivism: The Context of Liberalism, Evangelicalism, and Rationalism." *Newman Studies Journal* 4 (2007) 83–86.
Connolly, Francis. "The Apologia: History, Rhetoric, and Literature." In *Newman's Apologia: A Classic Reconsidered*, edited by V. Blehl and F. Connolly, 105–24. New York: Fordham University Press, 1964.
Connolly, John. *John Henry Newman: A View of Catholic Faith for the Millennium*. Lanham, MD: Sheed and Ward, 2005.
Copleston, Frederick. *History of Philosophy*. 9 vols. Westminster, MD: Newman, 1946–75.
Corbett, Edward. "A Comparison of John Locke and John Henry Newman on the Rhetoric of Assent." *Rhetoric Review* 1 (1982) 40–49.
Corsi, Pietro. *Science and Religion: Baden Powell and the Anglican Debate, 1800–1860*. Cambridge: Cambridge University Press, 1988.

Cosgrove, Brian. "'We Cannot Do without a View'—John Henry Newman, William James and the Case against Scepticism." *Irish Theological Quarterly* 61 (1995) 32–43.

Costello, Harry. *A Philosophy of the Real and the Possible*. New York: Colombia University Press, 1954.

Coulson, John. *Newman and the Common Tradition*. Oxford: Clarendon, 1970.

———. *Religion and Imagination*. Oxford: Clarendon, 1981.

———. "Was Newman a Modernist?" *Cardinal Newman-Studien* 14 (1990) 74–84.

Cousin, Victor. *Elements of Psychology: Included in a Critical Examination of Locke's Essay on The Human Understanding*. Translated by C. Henry. New York: Ivison, 1856.

Cowburn, John. *Personalism and Scholasticism*. Milwaukee, WI: Marquette University Press, 2005.

Cox, G. "Dr Newman's Apologia." *Westminster Review* 26 (1864) 357–77.

Crosby, John F. *Personalist Papers*. Washington, DC: Catholic University of America Press, 2004.

———. *The Selfhood of the Human Person*. Washington, DC: Catholic University of America Press, 1996.

Crowley, Paul. "Catholicity, Inculturation and Newman's Sensus Fidelium." *Heythrop Journal* 33 (1992) 161–74.

Crozier, John B. *Civilization and Progress*. London: Longmans Green, 1888.

Crimmins, James E. *Secular Utilitarianism Social Science and the Critique of Religion in the Thought of Jeremy Bentham*. Oxford: Clarendon, 1990.

Cronin, John F. *Cardinal Newman: His Theory of Knowledge*. Washington, DC: Catholic University of America, 1935.

Cross, Frank L. *John Henry Newman*. London: Allan, 1933.

Culler, Dwight. *The Imperial Intellect*. New Haven, CT: Yale University Press, 1955.

Cunningham, Francis. "The Second Operation and the Assent versus Judgment in St Thomas." *The New Scholasticism* 31 (1957) 1–33

D'Arcy, Martin. *The Nature of Belief*. London: Sheed and Ward, 1931.

Davidson, Thomas. *A History of Education*. New York: Scribner, 1900.

Davies, Brian. *An Introduction to the Philosophy of Religion*. Oxford: Oxford University Press, 1993.

Davies, John. *An Estimate of the Human Mind: A Philosophical Inquiry into the Legitimate Application and Extent of Its Leading Faculties*. London: J. W. Parker, 1847.

de Bary, Paul. *Thomas Reid and Scepticism: His Reliabilist Response*. London: Routledge, 2002.

de Ruggiero, Guido. *The History of European Liberalism*. Translated by R. G. Collingwood. Boston: Beacon, 1997.

de Sales, François. *Les Controverses in Oeuvres Tome I*. Annecy, France: Imprimerie J. Niérat, 1892.

de Wulf, Maurice. *Scholasticism Old and New*. Translated by P. Coffey. London: Longmans, Green, 1910.

Deen, Leonard W. "The Rhetoric of Newman's Apologia." *English Literary History* 29 (1962) 224–38.

Delacampagne, Christian. *A History of Philosophy in the Twentieth Century*. Baltimore, MD: John Hopkins University Press, 2001.

Delio, David. "A 'Multitude of Subtle Influences:' Faith and Reason in Newman's Thirteenth Oxford University Sermon." *Newman Studies Journal* 5 (2008) 77–86.

Dessain, Charles S. *John Henry Newman.* London: Thomas Nelson, 1966.

Dewey, John. "A College Course: What Should I Expect from it?" *Castalian* 5 (1890) 26–29.

———. *Lectures in the Philosophy of Education.* New York: Random House, 1966.

———. *Naturalism and the Human Spirit.* New York: Colombia University Press, 1940.

———. *Quest for Certainty: A Study of the Relation of Knowledge and Action.* New York: Minton Balch, 1929.

Dickinson, Charles. *A Pastoral Epistle from His Holiness the Pope to Some Members of the University of Oxford, Faithfully Translated from the Original Latin.* London: B Fellowes, 1836.

Dmowski, Josephus-Aloysius. *Institutiones Philosophicae.* 2 vols. Rome: Joannis, 1843.

Douglas, John. *The Criterion; or Rules by which the true miracles recorded in the New Testament are distinguished from the spurious miracles of pagans and papists.* London: T. Cadell, 1807.

Drake, Durrant. *Essays in Critical Realism.* London: Macmillan, 1920.

———. *Problems of Conduct: An Introductory Survey of Ethics.* New York: Houghton Mifflin, 1914.

———. *Problems of Religion.* New York: Houghton Mifflin, 1916.

Duemler, David. *Bringing Life to the Stars.* Lanham, MD: University Press of America, 1993.

Dulles, Avery. "From Images to Truth: Newman on Revelation and Faith." *Theological Studies* 51 (1990) 252–67.

———. *John Henry Newman.* New York: Continuum, 2009.

Egan, Phillip. "John Henry Newman and Bernard Lonergan: A Note on the Development of Christian Doctrine." *Revista Portuguesa de Filosofia* 63 (2007) 295–315.

———. "Lonergan on Newman's Conversion." *Heythrop Journal* 37 (1996) 437–55.

Egner, G. *Apologia Pro Charles Kingsley.* London: Sheed and Ward, 1969.

Ehrman, Bart. *The Orthodox Corruption of Scripture.* New York: Oxford University Press, 1993.

Ekeh, Ono. "The Phenomenological Context and Transcendentalism of John Henry Newman and Edmund Husserl." *Newman Studies Journal* 5 (2008) 35–50.

Eley, Ann S. *God's Own Image: A Counter-Revolution in Philosophy.* New York: White Crescent, 1963.

Empiricus, Sextus. *Outlines of Scepticism.* Translated by J. Annas and J. Barnes. Cambridge: Cambridge University Press, 2000.

Esposito, John. *Unholy War: Terror in the Name of Islam.* Oxford: Oxford University Press, 2002.

Evans, Gillian. "Newman and Aquinas on Assent." *Theological Studies* 30 (1979) 202–11.

Fairbairn, Andrew M. "Catholicism and Religious Thought." *The Contemporary Review* 47 (1884) 652–74.

Ferreira, Jamie M. *Doubt and Religious Commitment: The Role of the Will in Newman's Thought.* Oxford: Clarendon, 1980.

———. "Newman and William James on Religious Experience: The Theory and the Concrete." *Heythrop Journal* 29 (1988) 44–57.

———. *Scepticism and Reasonable Doubt: The British Naturalist Tradition in Wilkins, Hume, Reid, and Newman*. Oxford: Clarendon, 1986.
Fey, William R. *Faith and Doubt: The Unfolding of Newman's Thought on Certainty*. Shepherd's Town, WV: Patmos, 1976.
FitzPatrick, P. "Newman's Grammar and the Church Today." In *John Henry Newman Reason, Rhetoric and Romanticism*, edited by D. Nicholls and F. Kerr, 109–34. Bristol: Classical, 1991.
Flanagan, Philip. *Newman, Faith and the Believer*. London: Sands, 1946.
Flemming, W., ed. *The Vocabulary of Philosophy, Mental, Moral, and Metaphysical*. Glasgow: Richard Griffin, 1857.
Flew, Anthony. "Divine Omnipotence and Human Freedom." In *New Essays in Philosophical Theology*, edited by A. Flew and A. Macintyre, 144–69. London: SCM, 1963.
———. *An Introduction to Western Philosophy*. London: Thames, 1991.
Flewelling, Ralf T. *Winds of Hiroshima*. New York: Bookman Associates, 1956.
Floridi, Luciano. "The Problem of the Justification of a Theory of Knowledge." *Journal for General Philosophy of Science* 24 (1993) 205–33.
———. *Sextus Empiricus: The Transmission and Recovery of Pyrrhonism*. Oxford: Oxford University Press, 2002.
Ford, John T. Review of *Crossing the Threshold of Divine Revelation*, by William J. Abraham. *Religious Studies* 32 (2006) 184.
Ford, Lewis S. *The Emergence of Whitehead's Metaphysics: 1925–1929*. New York: Albany, 1984.
Forrest, Peter. "The Epistemology of Religion." http://www.plato.stanford.edu/entries/religion-epistemology/
———. *God without the Supernatural: A Defence of Scientific Theism*. Ithaca, NY: Cornell University Press, 1996.
Fowler, Thomas. *Corpus Christi College: University of Oxford*. London: F. E. Robinson, 1898.
Fraser, Alexander C. *Biographia Philosophica: A Retrospect*. Edinburgh : W. Blackwood, 1905.
———. *Locke*. Edinburgh: W. Blackwood, 1890.
Freud, Sigmund. *The Future of an Illusion*. New York: Double Day, 1957.
Gale, Richard. *On the Nature and Existence of God*. Cambridge: Cambridge University Press, 1991.
Garcia, Laura. "Catholic Philosophical Theology." In *Routledge Companion to Philosophy of Religion*, edited by C. Meister and P. Copan, 525–34. London: Routledge, 2013.
Garver, Newton. "What Violence Is." In *Moral Problems: A Collection of Philosophical Essays*, edited by J. Rachels, 242–49. New York: Harper and Row, 1971.
Gascoigne, Neil. *Scepticism*. Chesham, UK: Acumen, 2002.
Gellner, Ernest. *Words and Things: An Examination of, and an Attack on, Linguistic Philosophy*. London: Routledge, 2005.
Gerrard, Thomas J. "Bergson, Newman and Aquinas." *Catholic World* 3 (1913) 748–62.
———. "Dichotomy: A Study in Newman and Aquinas." *The New York Review* 3 (1908) 381–94.
Glover, Jonathan. *Responsibility*. Atlantic Highlands, NJ: Humanities, 1970.
———. *Utilitarianism and Its Critics*. London: Macmillan, 1990.
Goetz, L. "Submission Guidelines." http://www.pdcnet.org/nsj/Submission-Guidelines

Gomer, Paul. *Twentieth-Century German Philosophy.* Oxford: Oxford University Press, 2000.
Graham, Gordon. *The Institution of Intellectual Values: Realism and Idealism in Higher Education.* Exeter, UK: Imprint, 2005.
Graham, William. *Idealism: An Essay, Metaphysical and Critical.* London: Longmans Green, 1872.
Granger, H. *Aristotle's Idea of the Soul.* New York: Springer, 1996.
Griffiths, Paul. "Canon and Criterion in Christian Theology: From the Fathers to Feminism." *Modern Theology* 16 (2000) 265–67.
Grimm, Stephen. "Cardinal Newman, Reformed Epistemologist?" *American Catholic Philosophical Quarterly* 75 (2001) 497–522.
Guitton, Jean. *La Philosophie de Newman.* Paris: Boivin, 1933.
Gundersen, Borghild. *Cardinal Newman and Apologetics.* Oslo: I Kommisjon Hos Jacob Dybwad, 1952.
Gunton, Colin. "Newman's Dialectic Dogma and Reason in the Seventy-Third Tract for the Times." In *Newman after a Hundred Years,* edited by I. Ker and A. Hill, 309–22. Oxford: Clarendon, 1990.
Hamilton, William. "Johnson's Translation of Tennemann's History of Philosophy." *The Edinburgh Review* 58 (1832) 160–77.
———. Review of *Thoughts on the Study of Mathematics as a Part of a Liberal Education,* by William Whewell. *The Edinburgh Review* 62 (1836) 409–55.
Hamlyn, David W. "History of Epistemology." In *OCP,* 242–45.
Hammond, David M. "Imagination in Newman's Phenomenology of Cognition." *Heythrop Journal* 29 (1988) 21–32.
Handschy, Harriet W. "Educational Theories of Cardinal Newman and John Dewey." *Education* 49 (1928) 129–37.
Hankinson, Richard J. "Pyrrhonism." In *Routledge Encyclopedia of Philosophy,* edited by E. Craig, 727–28. London: Routledge, 2002.
———. "Stoic Epistemology." In *The Cambridge Companion to the Stoics,* edited by B. Inwood, 59–84. Cambridge: Cambridge University Press, 2003.
Hardman, Malcolm. *Six Victorian Thinkers.* Manchester: Manchester University Press, 1991.
Hare, Richard M. *Essays on Religion and Education.* Oxford: Clarendon, 1992.
———. *Plato.* Oxford: Oxford University Press, 1982.
Harper, Thomas. "Dr Newman's Essay in Aid of a Grammar of Assent." *Month* 8 (1870) 159–84.
———. "Dr Newman's Essay in Aid of a Grammar of Assent." *Month* 12 (1870) 599–611.
Hartshorne, Charles. *Man's Vision of God and the Logic of Theism.* Hamden, CT: Archon, 1964.
Harvard University. *A Catalogue of the Officers and Students of Harvard University for the Academical Year 1871–1872.* Cambridge, MA: Metcalf and Hilliard, 1872.
Hastings, Adrian. *The Theology of a Protestant Catholic.* London: SCM, 1990.
Hauptli, Bruce W. *The Reasonableness of Reason: Explaining Rationality Naturalistically.* Peru, IL: Open Court, 1995.
Hawkins, Edward. *A Dissertation upon the Use and Importance of Unauthoritative Tradition.* London: SPCK, 1889.

Hegel, Georg W. F. *The Logic of Hegel*. Translated by W. Wallace. Oxford: Clarendon, 1904.
Helm, Paul. *The Divine Revelation*. London: Marshall, 1982.
Hervet, Gentien, ed. *Sexti Empirici Viri Longe Doctissimi Adversvs Mathematicos*. Paris: Apud Martinum Iuvenem, 1569.
Hick, John. *Faith and Knowledge: A Modern Introduction to the Problem of Religious Knowledge*. Ithaca, NY: Cornell University Press, 1957.
Hodgson, Shadworth. *The Metaphysic of Experience*. 4 vols. London: Longmans, Green, 1898.
Hollis, Christopher. *Newman and the Modern World*. London: Hollis and Carter, 1967.
Holmes, J Derick. *More Roman Than Rome: English Catholicism in the Nineteenth Century*. London: Burns and Oates, 1978.
Holt, Edwin B, ed. *The New Realism*. New York: Macmillan, 1912.
Holzberger, W., and Herman Saatkamp, eds. *The Letters of George Santayana: Book Seven, 1941–1947*. Cambridge: Massachusetts Institute of Technology, 2006.
Hochschild, Joshua P. "The Re-Imagined Aristotelianism of John Henry Newman." *Modern Age* 46 (2003) 333–42.
Houghton, Esther R. "The British Critic and the Oxford Movement." *Studies in Bibliography* 16 (1963) 119–37.
———. "The 'British Critic' 1824–1843." *Victorian Periodicals Review* 24 (1991) 111–18.
Houghton, Walter E. *The Art of Newman's Apologia*. New Haven, CT: Yale University Press, 1945.
Huet, Pierre-Daniel. *A Philosophical Treatise concerning the Weakness of Human Understanding*. London: Gysbert Dommer, 1725.
Hume, David. *Enquiries Concerning Human Understanding and Concerning the Principle of Morals*. Oxford: Clarendon, 1975.
Huxley, Thomas H. "Agnosticism and Christianity." *The Eclectic Magazine of Foreign Literature, Science and Art* 113 (1889) 63–81.
———. *The Major Prose of Thomas Henry Huxley*. Edited by A. Barr. Athens, GA: University of Georgia Press, 1997.
Inge, William R. *Faith and Its Psychology*. London: Duckworth, 1919.
———. "The Philosophy of the Wolf State." *Philosophy* 18 (1943) 6–16.
Inglis, G. J. "The Problem of St Paul's Conversion." *The Expository Times* 40 (1929) 227–31.
International Theological Com. "On the Interpretation of Dogmas." *Origins* 20 (1990) 1–14.
James, William. "The Moral Philosopher, and the Moral Life." In *The Will to Believe and Other Essays*, edited by W. James, 184–215. London: Longmans, Green, 1910.
———. *The Varieties of Religious Experience: A Study In Human Nature Being The Gifford Lectures On Natural Religion Delivered at Edinburgh in 1901–1902*. London: Longmans, 1908.
———. "The Will to Believe." In *The Will to Believe and Other Essays*, edited by W. James, 1–31. London: Longmans, Green, 1910.
Jamieson, A. *A Grammar of Logic and Intellectual Philosophy*. London: Whittaker, 1819.
Jaspers, Karl, *The Idea of the University*. Translated by H. Reiche and H. Vanderschmidt. London: Owen, 1965.
Jevons, William S. *Logic*. London: Macmillan, 1889.

Jordan, W. "Neo-Thomism." In *OCP*, 614–15.
Jost, Walter. "On Concealment and Deception in Rhetoric: Newman and Kierkegaard." *Rhetoric Society Quarterly* 24 (1994) 51–74.
———. *Rhetorical Thought in John Henry Newman*. Columbia, SC: University of South Carolina Press, 1989.
Juergens, Sylvester P. *Newman on the Psychology of Faith in the Individual*. New York: Macmillan, 1928.
Kallen, Horace, and Sidney Hook, eds. *American Philosophy Today and Tomorrow*. New York: Ayer, 1968.
Kasper, Walter. *Die Methoden der Dogmatik*. Munich: Kosel, 1966.
Kauffman, Reginald W. "The Religion of John Burroughs." *The Personalist* 3 (1922) 149–56.
Keary, Charles F. *The Pursuit of Reason*. Cambridge: Cambridge University Press, 1910.
Keble, John. *Sermons, Academical and Occasional*. 2nd ed. Oxford: John Henry Parker, 1848.
Kenny, Anthony. *A Brief History of Western Philosophy*. Oxford: Wiley-Blackwell, 1998.
———. *A New History of Western Philosophy: Philosophy in the Modern World*. 4 vols. Oxford: Clarendon, 2007.
———. "Newman as a Philosopher of Religion." In *Newman a Man for Our Time*, edited by D. Brown, 98–122. London: SPCK, 1990.
Kenny, Terence. *The Political Thought of John Henry Newman*. London: Longmans, 1957.
Ker, Ian. *The Achievement of Newman*. New York: Continuum, 1991.
———. *John Henry Newman*. Oxford: Oxford University Press, 1990.
———. "John Henry Newman." In *Concise Routledge Encyclopaedia of Philosophy*, edited by E. Craig, 627. London: Routledge, 2000.
Ker, Ian., and Terrence Merrigan, eds. *Newman and Faith*. Louvain: Peeters, 2005.
Kerr, Fergus. "'In an Isolated and, Philosophically, Uninfluential Way' Newman and Oxford Philosophy." In *Newman and the Word*, edited by T. Merrigan and I. Ker, 155–79. Louvain: Peeters, 2000.
Kienzler, Wolfgang. "Wittgenstein and John Henry Newman on Certainty." *Grazer Philosophische Studien* 71 (2006) 117–38.
King, Benjamin. *Newman and the Alexandrian Fathers*. Oxford: Oxford University Press, 2009.
King, Peter. *The Life of John Locke*. London: Henry Colburn, 1829.
Kingsley, Charles. "Froude's History of England." *Macmillan's Magazine* 9 (1864) 211–24.
———. *"What, Then, Does Dr. Newman Mean?": A Reply to a Pamphlet Lately Published by Dr. Newman*. London: Macmillan, 1864.
Kinzer, Bruce. "Flying under the Radar: The Strange Case of Matthew Piers Watt Boulton." *Times Literary Supplement* 5 (2009) 14–15.
Kleutgen, Joseph. *La Philosophie Scholastique Expose´e et De´fendue*. 4 vols. Paris: Gaume, 1868.
Klubertanz, George P. "Where Is the Evidence for Thomistic Metaphysics." *Revue Philosophique de Louvain* 56 (1958) 294–315.
Knoll, Mark. *The Scandal of the Evangelical Mind*. Grand Rapids: Eerdmans, 1995.

Köchler, Hans. "The Phenomenology of Karol Wojtyla: On the Problem of the Phenomenological Foundation of Anthropology." *Philosophy and Phenomenological Research* 42 (1982) 326–34.
Köstenberger, Andreas J., and Michael Kruger, eds. *The Heresy of Orthodoxy: How Contemporary Culture's Fascination with Diversity Has Reshaped Our Understanding of Early Christianity*. Wheaton, IL: Crossway, 2010.
Kreller, Paul. "The New Rhetoric and the Reception of Newman's 'Apologia.'" *Victorian Periodicals Review* 32 (1999) 80–102.
Kuklick, Bruce. *A History of Philosophy in America 1720–2000*. Oxford: Clarendon, 2001.
Laertius, Diogenes. *The Lives and Opinions of Eminent Philosophers*. Translated by C. Yonge. London: Henry, 1853.
Lams, Victor J. *The Rhetoric of Newman's Apologia pro Catholica 1845–1864*. New York: Lang, 2007.
Langhorne, John, William Langhorne, eds. *Plutarch's Lives: Translated from the Original Greek; with Notes Critical and Historical; and a Life of Plutarch*. 6 vols. Edited and translated by J. Langhorne and W. Langhorne. London: Printed by Richards and Co, 1823.
Lash, Nicholas. *Newman on Development: The Search for an Explanation in History*. London: Sheed and Ward, 1975.
———. "Tides and Twilight: Newman since Vatican II." In *Newman after a Hundred Years*, edited by I. Ker and A. Hill, 447–64. Oxford: Clarendon, 1990.
Lemoine, Ray E. *The Anagogic Theory of Wittgenstein's "Tractatus."* The Hague: Mouton, 1975.
Liberatore, Matteo. *Institutiones Logicae et Metaphysicae*. Napoli: Typis, 1847.
Lilly, William S. *Studies in Religion and Literature*. London: Chapman, 1904.
Locke, John. *The Works of John Locke*. 12th ed. 9 vols. London: Rivington, 1824.
Lofland, John. "Becoming a World-Saver Revisited." In *Conversion Careers*, edited by J. Richardson, 10–23. Beverly Hills, CA: Sage, 1978.
Lonergan, Bernard. *Collected Works of Bernard Lonergan: Philosophical and Theological Papers*. Edited by F. Crowe. Toronto: University of Toronto Press, 1996.
———. *Method in Theology*. London: Herder, 1972.
———. *Understanding and Being*. 1980. Reprint, Toronto: University of Toronto Press, 1990.
Long, D. Stephen. *Speaking of God: Theology Language and Truth*. Grand Rapids: Eerdmans, 2009.
Lovejoy, Arthur O. *Essays in the History of Ideas*. New York: George Braziller, 1955.
Lowndes, W. "Plato." In *EM* 10:72–90.
Lucas, John R. *Freedom and Grace*. Grand Rapids: Eerdmans, 1976.
———. *Butler's Philosophy of Religion Vindicated*. London: SPCK, 1978.
Lynch, Thomas. *The Newman-Perrone Paper on Development*. Southsea, UK: Coasby, 1935.
Macaulay, Ambrose. *Dr Russell of Maynooth*. London: Darton, Longman and Todd, 1983.
MacIntyre, Alasdair C. *Three Rival Versions of Moral Enquiry*. London: Duckworth, 1990.
———. *Whose Justice? Which Rationality?* London: Duckworth, 1988.
Mackie, J. L. *The Miracle of Theism*. Oxford: Clarendon, 1982.

Mackinnon, Donald M. *A Study in Ethical Theory*. London: Adam, 1957.
Maddox, Marty M. "Newman, Certain Knowledge and 'The Problem of the Criterion'." *Newman Studies Journal* 4 (2007) 69–86.
Malcolm, Norman. *Ludwig Wittgenstein, a Memoir*. Oxford: Oxford University Press, 1984.
Marcel, Gabriel. *The Decline of Wisdom*. New York: Philosophical Library, 1955.
Masson, David. *Recent British Philosophy: A Review with Criticisms*. London: Macmillan, 1867.
Maritain, Jacques. *Education at the Crossroads*. New Haven, CT: Yale University Press, 1969.
Marsden, George M. *Fundamentalism and American Culture*. Oxford: Oxford University Press, 1980.
Martin, Michael. *Atheism: A Philosophical Justification*. Philadelphia: Temple University Press, 1990.
Martineau, Harriet. *A History of the Thirty Years" Peace, A.D. 1816-1846*. 4 vols. London: Bell, 1878.
Martineau, James. *Essays Philosophical and Theological*. London: Trubner, 1865.
———. "Personal Influences on Our Present Theology: Newman-Coleridge-Carlyle." *The National Review* 3 (1856) 449–94.
Marvin, Walter T. *The History of European Philosophy*. New York: Macmillan, 1917.
Masnovo, Amato. "L'opera del Liberatore dal 1840–1850." *Rivista di Filosofia Neo-Scolastica* 1 (1909) 120–29.
McCarren, Gerrard. "Development of Doctrine." In *The Cambridge Companion to John Henry Newman*, edited by I. Ker, 118–36. Cambridge: Cambridge University Press, 2009.
McCarthy, Gerald. "Newman, Foundationalism, & the Ethics of Belief." *Horizons* 8 (1981) 62–79.
———. "Newman and Wittgenstein: The Problem of Certainty." *Irish Theological Quarterly* 49 (1982) 98–120.
———. "A Via Media between Scepticism and Dogmatism? Newman's and Macintyre's Anti-Foundationalist Strategies." *Newman Studies Journal* 6 (2009) 57–81.
McCracken, Charles J. "Berkeley's Realism." In *New Interpretations of Berkeley's Thought*, edited by S. H. Daniel, 24–33. New York: Humanity Books, 2008.
McConnell, John F. *The Increase of Faith: Some Present-Day Aids to Belief*. New York: Eaton, 1912.
———. *Public Opinion and Theology*. Nashville, TN: Abingdon, 1920.
McGrath, Francis. *John Henry Newman: Universal Revelation*. Wellwood, UK: Burns and Oates, 1997.
McGuinness, Brian. *Wittgenstein: A Life: Young Ludwig 1889-1921*. Berkeley, CA: University of California Press, 1988.
McInerny, Ralph. "The Thomistic Revival." In *Cardinal Mercier's Philosophical Essays*, translated by D Boileau, ix–xviii. Louvain: Peeters, 2002.
M'Cosh, James. *Method of the Divine Government*. New York: Robert Carter, 1860.
Mercier, Désiré-Joseph. *Le Christianisme dans la vie Moderne*. Paris: Perrin, 1918.
———. *Critériologie Générale ou Théorie Générale de la Certitude*. 5th ed. Louvain: Institut Supérieur de Philosophie, 1906.
———. "Criteriology." In *A Manual of Modern Scholastic Philosophy*, vol. 1, edited by D. J. Mercier, 343–404. Translated by P. Coffey. London: Keegan, Paul, 1916.

———. "Discussion of the Theory of the Three Primary Truths." In *Cardinal Mercier's Philosophical Essays*, translated by D Boileau, 267–81. Louvain: Peeters, 2002.

———. "Leo XIII and the Restoration of Thomistic Studies." In *Cardinal Mercier's Philosophical Essays*, translated by D Boileau, 55–120. Louvain: Peeters, 2002.

———. *Logique*. Louvain: Institut Supérieur de Philosophie, 1922.

———. *A Manual of Modern Scholastic Philosophy*. 2 vols. Edited by D. J. Mercier. Translated by P. Coffey. London: Keegan, Paul, 1916.

———. *Á mes Séminaristes*. Paris: Beauchesne, 1908.

———. *Les origines de la psychologie contemporaine*. Louvain: Institut Supérieur de Philosophie, 1925.

———."La Philosophie Néo-Scolastique." *Revue Néo-Scolastique* 1 (1894) 5–18.

———. *Rapport sur les études Supérieures de Philosophie, Présenté au Congrés de Malines, le 9 Septembre 1891*. Louvain: Institut Supérieur de Philosophie, 1891

Merrigan, Terrence. *Clear Heads and Holy Hearts: The Religious and Theological Ideal of John Henry Newman*. Louvain: Peeters, 1991.

———. "Newman's Catholic Synthesis." *Irish Theological Quarterly* 60 (1994) 39–48.

———. "Newman's Oriel Experience: Its Significance for His Life and Thought." *Bijdragen* 47 (1986) 192–211.

———. "Newman and Theological Liberalism." *Theological Studies* 66 (2005) 605–21.

———. "Revelation." In *The Cambridge Companion to John Henry Newman*, edited by I. Ker, 47–65. Cambridge: Cambridge University Press, 2009.

Metz, Rudolf. *A Hundred Years of British Philosophy*. Translated by J. W. Harvey. London: Allen, 1938.

Meyers, Robert G. *Empiricism*. Chesham, UK: Acumen, 2006.

Middleton, Conyers. *A Free Inquiry into the Miraculous Powers Which are Suppose to Have Subsisted in the Christian Church from the Earliest Ages through Several Successive Stages*. Dublin: Smith, 1749.

Mill, John S. *On Liberty and Other Writings*. Cambridge: Cambridge University Press, 1998.

———. "Professor Sedgwick's Discourse—State of Philosophy in England." *London Review* 1 (1835) 94–135.

———. *Three Essays on Religion: Nature, the Utility of Religion and Theism*. London: Longmans, Green, 1874.

Miller, Alexander. "The Reasonableness of Faith and Assent in Newman's Parochial and Plain Sermons and Grammar of Assent." *Newman Studies Journal* 7 (2010) 42–54.

Miller, Michael. *The Encyclicals of John Paul II*. Huntington, IN: Our Sunday Visitor, 1996.

Mitchell, Basil. *The Justification of Religious Belief*. Oxford: Oxford University Press, 1973.

———. "Newman as a Philosopher." In *Newman after a Hundred Years*, edited by I. Ker and A. Hill, 223–46. Oxford: Clarendon, 1990.

Mitchell, Rosemary. "Meynell, Charles (1828–1882)." In *The Oxford Dictionary of National Biography*. https://doi.org/10.1093/ref:odnb/18638

Moberly, Walter. "Scripture as a Means of Grace." *The Expository Times* 110 (1999) 119.

Moleski, Martin. "Illative Sense and Tacit Knowledge: A Comparison of the Epistemologies of John Henry Newman and Michael Polanyi." In *John Henry Newman: Theology and Reform*, edited by M. Allsopp and R. Burke, 189–224. New York: Garland, 1992.

———. *Personal Catholicism: The Theological Epistemologies of John Henry Newman and Michael Polanyi*. Washington, DC: Catholic University of America Press, 2000.

Moncho, José R. *La Unidad de la Vida Moral Segun Aristoteles*. Valencia: Université Catholique de Louvain, 1972.

Montague, William P. *The Ways of Knowing or the Methods of Philosophy*. London: Allen, 1925.

Montaigne, Michel. *Apology for Raymond Sebond*. Translated by R. Ariew and M. Grene. Indianapolis, IN: Hackett, 2003.

Moran, Dermot. "Towards an Assessment of Twentieth-Century Philosophy." In *The Routledge Companion to Twentieth-Century Philosophy*, edited by D. Moran, 1–40. London: Routledge, 2008.

Moser, Paul, ed. *Human Knowledge: Classical and Contemporary Approaches*. Oxford: Oxford University Press, 1995.

Muirhead, John H. *The Platonic Tradition in Anglo-Saxon Philosophy*. London: Allen, 1931.

Mundle, Clement W. *A Critique of Linguistic Philosophy*. London: Glover, 1979.

Murray, Paul D. *Reason, Truth, and Theology in Pragmatist Perspective*. Leuven: Peeters, 2004.

Nabe, Clyde. *Mystery and Religion: Newman's Epistemology of Religion*. Lanham, MD: University Press of America, 1988.

Newman, Jay. "Cardinal Newman's Factory-Girl Argument." *Proceedings of the American Catholic Philosophical Association* 46 (1972) 71–77.

———. "Epistemic Inference and Illative Judgment." *Dialectia* 35 (1981) 327–39.

———. *The Mental Philosophy of John Henry Newman*. Waterloo, ON: Wilfrid Laurier University Press, 1986.

Nichols, Aidan. *Conversation of Faith and Reason: Modern Catholic Thought from Hermes to Benedict XVI*. Chicago: Liturgy Training, 2011.

———. *From Newman to Congar: The Idea of Doctrinal Development from the Victorians to the Second Vatican Council*. Edinburgh: T. & T. Clark, 1990.

———. *Scattering the Seed*. New York: Continuum, 2006.

Nockles, Peter. *The Oxford Movement in Context: Anglican High Churchmanship, 1760–1857*. Cambridge: Cambridge University Press, 1994.

———. "Oxford Tract 90 and the Bishops." In *Reason, Rhetoric and Romanticism*, edited by D. Nichols and F. Kerr, 28–87. Bristol: Classical, 1991.

Norris, Thomas. *Newman and His Theological Method*. Leiden: Brill, 1977.

———. "Faith." In *The Cambridge Companion to John Henry Newman*, edited by I. Ker, 73–97. Cambridge: Cambridge University Press, 2009.

Northropp, Filmer, and Martin Gross, eds. *Alfred North Whitehead: An Anthology*. Cambridge: Cambridge University Press, 1953.

Nussbaum, Martha C. *Cultivating Humanity: A Classical Defense of Reform in Liberal Education*. Cambridge: Harvard University Press, 2003.

———. *Love's Knowledge: Essays on Philosophy and Literature*. New York: Oxford University Press, 1990.

O'Connell, Marvin R. "Newman and Liberalism." In *Newman Today. Papers Presented at a Conference Sponsored by the Wethersfield Institute New York City, October 14–15, 1988*, edited by S. Jaki, 79–94. San Francisco: Ignatius, 1989.

O'Donnell, Robert A. *Hooked on Philosophy*. New York: Alba House, 1995.

Oden, Thomas C., and Longdon Leicester, eds. *The Wesleyan Theological Heritage: Essays of Albert C. Outler*. Grand Rapids: Zondervan, 1991.
O'Hear, Anthony. *Experience, Explanation, and Faith: An Introduction to the Philosophy of Religion*. London: Routledge, 1984.
———. *Philosophy in the New Century*. New York: Continuum, 2001.
———. *The Landscape of Humanity: Art, Culture and Society*. Exeter, UK: Imprint, 2008.
Ondrako, Edward L. *Progressive Illumination: A Journey with John Henry Cardinal Newman, 1980–2005*. Binghamton, NY: Global, 2007.
Oppenheim, Frank M. *Royce's Mature Philosophy of Religion*. Notre Dame, IN: University of Notre Dame Press, 1987.
Owen, Huw P. *The Moral Argument for Christian Theism*. London: Allen, 1965.
Pailin, David. *Groundwork of Philosophy of Religion*. London: Epworth, 1986.
———. *The Way to Faith: An Examination of Newman's Grammar of Assent as a Response to the Search for Certainty in Faith*. London: Epworth, 1969.
Parfit, Derek. *Reasons and Persons*. Oxford: Oxford University Press, 1984.
Passmore, John A. *A Hundred Years of Philosophy*. London: Duckworth, 1957.
Pattison, Mark. "Philosophy at Oxford." *Mind: A Quarterly Review of Psychology and Philosophy* 1 (1876) 82–97.
Peel, Robert. *An Inaugural Address Delivered by the Right Hon. Sir Robert Peel, Bart. M.P., President of the Tamworth Library and Reading room on Tuesday 19th January 1841*. London: James Bain, 1841.
Pelzer, Auguste. "Les initiateurs Italiens du neo-thomisme contemporain." *Revue Neo-Scolastique de Philosophie* 70 (1911) 230–54.
Perrone, Giovanni. *L'Ermesianismo*. Roma: Salviucci, 1838.
Perry, Ralph B. *The Moral Economy*. New York: Scribner, 1909.
Phillips, Dewi Z. *Faith after Foundationalism*. London: Routledge, 1988.
Phillips, Richard P. *Modern Thomistic Philosophy*. 2 vols. London: Burns, Oates, 1941.
Phipps, David J. "John Henry Newman's Adoption of Baptismal Regeneration, and the Relative Importance of John Bird Sumner, Richard Mant and William Beveridge to His Development." *New Blackfriars* 76 (1995) 500–510.
Picton, James A. *Pantheism: Its Story and Significance*. London: Constable, 1905.
Plantinga, Alvin. *Warranted Christian Belief*. Oxford: Oxford University Press, 2000.
Pojman, Louis P. *Religious Belief and the Will*. London: Routledge, 1986.
Polansky, Ronald. *Aristotle's De Anima*. Cambridge: Cambridge University Press, 2010.
Popkin, Richard H. *The History of Scepticism: From Savonarola to Bayle*. Oxford: Oxford University Press, 2003.
Powell, Baden. "Tendency of Puseyism." *Westminster Review* 45 (1846) 304–43.
———. *Tradition Unveiled or an Exposition of the Pretensions and Tendency of Authoritative Teaching in the Church*. London: John W. Parker, 1839.
Powell, Jouett L. *Three Uses of Christian Discourse in John Henry Newman*. Missoula, MT: Scholars, 1975.
Pratt, James B. *Adventures in Philosophy and Religion*. New York: Macmillan, 1931.
———. *Reason in the Art of Living*. New York: Macmillan, 1949.
Price, Henry H. *Belief: The Gifford Lectures*. London: Routledge, 2002.
Pritchard, Duncan. "Is 'God Exists' a 'Hinge Proposition' of Religious Belief?" *International Journal for Philosophy of Religion* 47 (2000) 129–40.

Proudfoot, Wayne. *Religious Experience*. Berkeley, CA: University of California Press, 1987.
Przywara, Erich. *Religionsbegrundung–Max Scheler–J. H. Newman*. Freiburg: Herder, 1923.
Pusey, Edward B. *An Eirenicon, in a Letter to the Author of the "Christian Year": The Church of England a Portion of Christ's One Holy Catholic Church, and a Means of Restoring Visible Unity*. London: Rivington, 1865.
———. *An Historical Enquiry into the Probable Causes of the Rationalistic Character Lately Predominant in the Theology of Germany*. London: Rivington, 1828.
Putnam, Hilary. *Reason Truth and History*. Cambridge: Harvard University Press, 2004.
Quine, Willard V. "Two Dogmas of Empiricism." In *From a Logical Point of View*, edited by W. Quine, 20–47 Cambridge: Harvard University Press, 1964.
Quinn, Phillip., Charles Taliaferro, eds. *A Companion to the Philosophy of Religion*. Oxford: Blackwell, 1997.
Quinton, Anthony, "English Philosophy." In *OCP*, 232–36.
———. "Harvard Philosophy." In *OCP*, 335–36.
———. "Oxford Philosophy." In *OCP*, 640.
Radhakrishnan, Sarvepalli. *The Idealist View of Life*. London: Allen, 1981.
———. *The Reign of Religion in Contemporary Philosophy*. London: Macmillan, 1920.
———. *Religion in a Changing World*. London: Allen, 1967.
Rambo, Lewis. *Understanding Religious Conversion*. New Haven, CT: Yale University Press, 1993.
Randall, John H. *Readings in Philosophy*. New York: Barnes and Noble, 1940.
Reck, Andrew J. "Arthur Kenyon Rogers." In *The Dictionary of Modern American Philosophers*, edited by John Shook, 2067. New York: Continuum, 2005.
———. "Walter Taylor Marvin." In *The Dictionary of Modern American Philosophers*, edited by John Shook, 1630–31. New York: Continuum, 2005.
Reid, Thomas. *The Works of Thomas Reid: Now fully collected with selections from his unpublished letters*. 5th ed. Edited by W. Hamilton. Edinburgh: Maclachan and Stewart, 1858.
Rescher, Nicholas. *Methodological Pragmatism: A Systems-Theoretic Approach to the Theory of Knowledge*. Oxford: Blackwell, 1977.
———. "Pragmatism." In *OCP*, 710–11.
Richardson, Lawrence. *Newman's Approach to Knowledge*. Leominster, UK: Gracewing, 2007.
Rickaby, Joseph. *Scholasticism*. London: Constable, 1908.
Rigg, James H. "Mr Kingsley and Dr Newman." *The London Quarterly Review* 23 (1864) 115–53.
———. "Newman's Grammar of Assent." *London Quarterly Review* 30 (1871) 363–89.
Rogers, Arthur K. "Belief and the Criterion of Truth." *The Journal of Philosophy Psychology and Scientific Methods* 13 (1916) 393–410.
———. "Rationality and Belief." *The Philosophical Review* 13 (1904) 30–49.
Rogers, Henry. *The Eclipse of Faith, or, A Visit to a Religious Sceptic*. London: Longman Brown, 1853.
———. "Puseyism, or the Oxford Tractarian School." *Edinburgh Review* 77 (1843) 501–62.
———. *Reason and Faith: Their Claims and Conflicts*. London: Longman Brown, 1850.

Romanes George J. *A Candid Examination of Theism*. Boston: Houghton, Osgood, 1878.
———. *Christian Prayer and General Laws*. London: Macmillan, 1874.
———. *Darwin and after Darwin: An Exposition of the Darwinian Theory and a Discussion of Post-Darwinian Questions*. Chicago: Open Court, 1892.
Romaine, William. *Triumph of Faith*. New York: Williams and Whiting 1809.
Rorty, Richard. "Keeping Philosophy Pure." In *The Consequences of Pragmatism*, edited by R. Rorty, 19–36. Minneapolis, MN: Minneapolis University Press, 2003.
Rose, Gillian. "New Jerusalem, Old Athens from the Broken Middle." In *The Post Modern God*, edited by G. Ward, 318–40. Oxford: Blackwell, 1997.
Row, Charles A. "Dr. Newman's Essay in Aid of a Grammar of Assent." *Journal of the Transactions of the Victoria Institute or Philosophical Society* 6 (1872) 45–91.
Rule, Phillip C. *Coleridge and Newman: The Centrality of Conscience*. Oxford: Clarendon, 2004.
Russell, Bertrand. "On Denoting." *Mind* 14 (1905) 479–93.
———. *Portraits from Memory: and Other Essays*. London: Allen, 1956.
Ryan, James H. *An Introduction to Philosophy*. New York: Macmillan, 1924.
Sands, Paul F. *The Justification of Religious Faith in Søren Kierkegaard, John Henry Newman, and William James*. Piscataway, NJ: Gorgias, 2004.
Santayana, George. *The Idea of Christ in the Gospels*. New York: Scribner's Sons, 1946.
———. *Some Turns of Thought in Modern Philosophy: Five Essays*. New York: Scribner's Sons, 1933.
———. *Winds of Doctrine: Studies in Contemporary Opinion*. London: Dent, 1940.
———. *The Works of George Santayana*. 8 vols. Edited by J. McCormick. Cambridge: Massachusetts Institute of Technology, 1986–2011.
Savage, Deborah M. *The Subjective Dimension of Human Work*. New York: Lang, 2008.
Scott, Thomas. *The Force of Truth: An Authentic Narrative*. New York: John P. Haven, 1825.
Scheler, Max. *Formalism in Ethics and Non-Formal Ethics of Values: A New Attempt toward the Foundation of an Ethical Personalism*. Translated by S. Frings. Evanston, IL: Northwestern University Press, 1973.
———. *On the Eternal in Man*. New Brunswick, NJ: Transaction, 2009.
———. *Person and Self-Value: Three Essays*. The Hague: Nijhoff, 1987.
Schofield, Philip. *Bentham*. New York: Continuum, 2009.
Schiller, Ferdinand C. S. *Studies in Humanism*. London: Macmillan, 1907.
Schilpp, Paul A. *The Philosophy of Sarvepalli Radhakrishnan*. New York: Tudor, 1952.
Schultz B, "Henry Sidgwick." https://plato.stanford.edu/entries/sidgwick/.
Scruton, Roger. *A Short History of Modern Philosophy: From Descartes to Wittgenstein*. London: Routledge, 1981.
Seeley, John R. *Ecce Homo: A Survey of the Life and Work of Jesus Christ*. Boston: Roberts Brothers, 1866.
Selby, Robin C. *The Principle of Reserve in the Writings of John Henry Newman*. Oxford: Oxford University Press, 1975.
Sellars Roy W. *The Next Step in Religion*. New York: Macmillan, 1918.
———. *Religion Coming of Age*. London: Macmillan, 1928.
Seth, James. *English Philosophers and Schools of Philosophy*. London: Dent, 1912.
Shand, John, ed. *Central Works of Philosophy*. 5 vols. New York: Continuum, 2005.

Shanley, Brian J. ed. *One Hundred Years of Philosophy*. Washington, DC: Catholic University of America Press, 2001.
Shea, Charles Michael. "Newman, Perrone, and Mohler on Dogma and History." *Newman Studies Journal* 7 (2010) 45–55.
Sheen, Fulton J. *Philosophy of Religion: The Impact of Modern Knowledge on Religion*. New York: Appleton, 1948.
Sidgwick, Henry. *Lectures on the Ethics of T. H. Green, Mr Herbert Spencer, and J. Martineau: The Methods of Ethics*. London: Macmillan, 1874.
———. *Lectures on the Philosophy of Kant*. London: Macmillan, 1905.
———. *Miscellaneous Essays and Addresses*. London: Macmillan, 1904.
———. *Philosophy, Its Scope and Relations*. London: Macmillan, 1902.
Simcox, Edith J. *Natural Law: An Essay in Ethics*. London: Trubner, 1878.
Sinnott-Armstrong, Walter. "Consequentialism." https://plato.stanford.edu/entries/consequentialism/.
Skilbeck, Malcolm. *John Dewey*. London: Macmillan, 1970.
Skinner, Burrhus F. *Contingencies of Reinforcement: A Theoretical Analysis*. Englewood Cliffs, NJ: Prentice Hall, 1969.
Smart, R. N. *Nineteenth-Century Religious Thought in the West*. 3 vols. Cambridge: Cambridge University Press, 1988.
Smart, Roderick N. *The Religious Experience of Mankind*. Englewood Cliffs, NJ: Prentice Hall, 1996.
Smith, Christian. *The Bible Made Impossible: Why Biblicism Is Not a Truly Evangelical Reading of Scripture*. Grand Rapids: Brazos, 2011.
Sorley, William R. *A History of British Philosophy to 1900*. Cambridge: Cambridge University Press, 1965.
———. *A History of English Philosophy*. Cambridge: Cambridge University Press, 1920.
Sosa, Ernest. "The Foundations of Foundationalism." In *Knowledge in Perspective: Selected Essays in Epistemology*, edited by E. Sosa, 149–64. Cambridge: Cambridge University Press, 1991.
Sparr, Arnold. *To Promote, Defend, and Redeem*. Westport, CT: Greenwood, 1990.
Spencer Herbert. *First Principles*. London: Williams and Norgate, 1870.
Spiegelberg, Herbert, ed. *The Phenomenological Movement: A Historical Introduction*. The Hague: Nijhoff, 1982.
Stephen, James F. *Essays by a Barrister*. London: Smith, Elder, 1862.
Stephen, Leslie. *An Agnostic's Apology*. London: Smith, 1903.
———. *The English Utilitarians*. London: Duckworth, 1900.
———. *The History of English Thought in the Eighteenth Century*. New York: Harcourt, 1963.
———. "Dr. Newman's Theory of Belief." *Fortnightly Review* 22 (1877) 680–810.
Strange, Roderick. *Newman and the Gospel of Christ*. Oxford: Oxford University Press, 1980.
Stroll, Avrum. *Twentieth-Century Analytic Philosophy*. New York: Columbia University Press, 2000.
Svaglic, Martin J. "The Structure of Newman's Apologia." *Modern Language Association* 66 (1951) 138–48.
Swinburne, Richard. "Problems of the Philosophy of Religion." In *OCP*, 763–65.
———. *Revelation from Metaphor to Analogy*. Oxford: Oxford University Press, 2007.

Swindal, James, Harry Gensler, eds. *The Sheed and Ward Anthology of Catholic Philosophy*. Lanham, MD: Rowman and Littlefield, 2005.
Tallmon, James M. "Newman's Contribution to Conceptualizing Rhetorical Reason." *Rhetoric Society Quarterly* 25 (1995) 197–213.
Taylor, Isaac. *Elements of Thought or Concise Explanations of the Terms Employed in the Several Branches of Intellectual Philosophy*. London: Holdsworth, 1833.
Thiel, John E. *Nonfoundationalism*. Minneapolis, MN: Fortress, 1994.
———. *Senses of Tradition*. Oxford: Oxford University Press, 2000.
Thomas, Stephen. *Newman and Heresy: The Anglican Years*. Cambridge: Cambridge University Press, 2003.
Tongiorgi, Salvatoris. *Institutiones Philosophicae*. Bruxellis: Excudebat, 1868.
Toohey, James. "Newman on the Criterion of Certitude." *Irish Theological Quarterly* 5 (1910) 444–53.
Torrance, Thomas F. *Reality and Scientific Knowledge*. Edinburgh: Scottish Academic, 1985.
Tristram, Henry. "Cardinal Newman's Theses de Fide and his Proposed Introduction to the French Translation of the University Sermons." *Gregorianum* (1937) 219–60.
Troyer, John, ed. *The Classical Utilitarians: Bentham and Mill*. Indianapolis, IN: Hackett, 2003.
Trueblood, David E. *The Logic of Belief: An Introduction to the Philosophy of Religion*. New York: Harper, 1942.
Tulloch, John. "Dr Newman's Grammar of Assent." *Edinburgh Review* 132 (1870) 382–414.
Turner, Frank. *John Henry Newman: The Challenge to Evangelical Religion*. New Haven, CT: Yale University Press, 2002.
———. "Newman." In *The Blackwell Companion to Nineteenth-Century Theology*, edited by D. Ferguson, 119–38. Oxford: Blackwell, 2010.
———. "The Newman of the Apologia and the Newman of History." In *Apologia Pro Vita Sua & Six Sermons*, edited by F. Turner, 1–123. New Haven, CT: Yale University Press, 2008.
———. Review of *The Cambridge Companion to John Henry Newman*, by Ian Ker. *Journal of Ecclesiastical History* 61 (2010) 422–23.
Turner, William. *History of Philosophy*. New York: Ginn, 1903.
Turing, Alan. "Computing Machinery and Intelligence." *Mind* 59 (1950) 433–60.
Ullathorne, William B. *The Immaculate Conception of the Mother of God: An Exposition*. London: Richardson and Son, 1855.
Unknown author. "An Essay on the Development of Christian Doctrine." *English Church Review* 18 (1845) 386–433.
Unknown author. "Dr Newman's Apologia Pro Vita Sua." *Christian Observer* 64 (1864) 661–685.
Unknown author. "Dr Newman." *British and Foreign Evangelical Review* 13 (1864) 771–803.
Unknown author. "Dr Newman's Grammar of Assent." *The Christian Observer* 70 (1870) 727–39.
Unknown author. "Newman on the Development of Christian Doctrine." *The Dublin University Magazine* 27 (1846) 105–15.
Unknown Aauthor. "Mr Newman's Theory of Development." *New Quarterly Review; or, Home, Foreign and Colonial Journal* 7 (1846) 301–39.

Unknown author. "Oxford Popery." *The Eclectic Review* 16 (1836) 45–47.
Unknown author. "Oxford Theology." *The Oracle of Reason, Or, Philosophy Vindicated*, 1 (1843) 157–59.
Unknown author. "Review of Publications on the Oxford Tracts." *The Christian Observer* 42 (1842) 93–123.
Unknown author. "Some Aspects of Newman's Influence." *Ecclectic Magazine of Foreign Literature, Science and Art* 52 (1890) 707.
Upton, Charles B. *Lectures on the Bases of Religious Belief*. London: Williams, 1894.
van Inwagen, Peter. *Ontology, Identity, and Modality: Essays in Metaphysics*. Cambridge: Cambridge University Press, 2001.
van Leeuwen, Henry G. *The Problem of Certainty in English Thought 1630–1690*. The Hague: Nijhoff, 1970.
van Riet, George. *Thomistic Epistemology: Studies Concerning the Problem of Cognition in the Contemporary Thomistic School*. 2 vols. Translated by G. Franks. London: Herder, 1965.
Vargish, Thomas. *Newman: The Contemplation of Mind*. Oxford: Clarendon, 1970.
Ventresca, Robert A. "'A Plague of Perverse Opinions' Leo XIII's *Aeterni Patris* and the Catholic Encounter with Modernity." *Logos: A Journal of Catholic Thought and Culture* 12.1 (2009) 143–67.
Verbeke, Gérard. "Aristotelian Roots of Newman's Illative Sense." In *Newman and Gladstone: Centennial Essays*, edited by J. Bastable, 177–96. Dublin: Veritas, 1978.
Véron, François. *The Rule of Catholic Faith: Or, The Principles and Doctrines of the Catholic Faith*. Translated by J. Waterworth. Birmingham, UK: R. P. Stone, 1833.
———. *La Victorieuse Methode pour Combattre tous les Ministres L Par la Seule Bible*. Paris: J. Corrozet, 1621.
Vidu, Adonis. Review of *Crossing the Threshold of Divine Revelation*, by William J. Abraham. *The Heythrop Journal* 50 (2009) 134–35.
Vincelette, Alan. *Recent Catholic Philosophy: The Nineteenth Century*. Milwaukee, WI: Marquette University Press, 2009.
Wainwright, Geoffrey. *The Ecumenical Moment: Crisis and Opportunity for the Church*. Grand Rapids: Eerdmans, 1983.
Wainwright, William. *Reason and the Heart: A Prolegomenon to a Critique of Passional Reason*. Ithaca, NY: Cornell University Press, 1995.
———. *Religion and Morality*. Burlington, VT: Ashgate, 2005.
Walgrave, Jan H. *Newman the Theologian*. London: Chapman, 1960.
———. "Religious Experience through Conscience." *Louvain Studies* 4 (1972) 105–19.
Ward, William G. "Certitude in Religious Assent." *Dublin Review* 16 (1871) 253–74.
———. "Explicit and Implicit Thought." *Dublin Review* 13 (1869) 421–42.
———. *On Nature and Grace: Philosophical Introduction*. London: G. Barclay, 1859.
———. *The Relation of Intellectual Power to Man's True Perfection*. London: Burns and Lambert, 1862.
Ward, Wilfred P. *The Life of John Henry, Cardinal Newman, Based on His Private Journals and Correspondence*. 2 vols. London: Longmans Green, 1921.
Watts, Isaac. *The Improvement of the Mind*. London: Edward, 1821.
Weaver, Mary, ed. *Letters from a "Modernist": The Letters of George Tyrrell to Wilfrid Ward 1893–1908*. Shepherdstown, VA: Patmos, 1981.
Webster, John, "Canon and Criterion: Some Reflections on a Recent Proposal." *Scottish Journal of Theology* 54 (2001) 221–37.

Weiss, Paul, ed. *Philosophy in Process,* 11 vols. Carbondale, IL: Southern Illinois University Press, 1955–87.

Whately, Richard. *Elements of Logic.* London: B. Fellowes, 1834.

———. *Essays on Some of the Dangers to Christian Faith: Which May Arise from the Teaching and Conduct of Its Professors.* London: B. Fellowes, 1847.

White, Alan. *Misleading Cases.* Oxford: Clarendon, 1991.

Whitehead, Alfred North. *Adventures of Ideas.* Cambridge: Cambridge University Press, 1935.

———. *Science and the Modern World.* New York: Macmillan, 1925.

Wiles, Maurice. *The Making of Christian Doctrine.* Cambridge: Cambridge University Press, 1967.

Wilhelmsen, Frederick D. *Man's Knowledge of Reality: An Introduction to Thomistic Epistemology.* Englewood Cliffs, NJ: Prentice Hall, 1958.

Willam, Franz M. *Aristotelische Erkenntnislehre bei Whately und Newman.* Freiburg: Herder, 1960.

Williams, Bernard. *Moral Luck: Philosophical Papers 1973–1980.* Cambridge: Cambridge University Press, 1981.

Williams, Donald C. *Principles of Empirical Realism: Philosophical Essays.* Springfield, IL: Charles, 1966.

Williams, Thomas D. "Personalism." http://plato.stanford.edu/entries/personalism.

Wittgenstein, Ludwig J. *On Certainty.* Translated by D. Paul and G. E. M. Anscombe. Oxford: Blackwell, 1975.

———. *Philosophical Investigations.* Translated by G. E. M. Anscombe. Oxford: Blackwell, 2001.

Wojtyla, Karol J. *Valutazioni Sulla Possibilitá Di Costruire L'ética Cristiana Sulle Basi Del Sistema Di Max Scheler.* Translated by S. Bucciarelli. Rome: Logos, 1980.

Wollheim, Richard A. *F. H. Bradley.* London: Penguin, 1969.

Wolterstorff, Nicholas. *Thomas Reid and the Story of Epistemology.* Cambridge: Cambridge University Press, 2001.

Wright, Chauncey. "The Genesis of Species." *North American Review* 113 (1871) 63–103.

Yearley, Lee. *The Ideas of Newman: Christianity and Human Religiosity.* University Park, PA: Pennsylvania State University Press, 1978.

Zeno, Capuchin. "An Introduction to Newman's Grammar of Assent." *The Irish Ecclesiastical Record* 103 (1965) 389–406.

———. *John Henry Newman: Our Way to Certitude.* Leiden: Brill, 1957.

Zygmunt, Joseph F. "Movements and Motives: Some Unresolved Issues in the Psychology of Social Movements." *Human Relations* 3 (1972) 449–67.

www.ingramcontent.com/pod-product-compliance
Lightning Source LLC
Chambersburg PA
CBHW070241230426

43664CB00014B/2380